The Adobe® Photoshop® Lightroom® 2 Book

The Complete Guide for Photographers

Martin Evening

ADOBE
PRESS

Adobe

The Adobe® Photoshop® Lightroom® 2 Book
The Complete Guide for Photographers

Martin Evening

This Adobe Press book is published by Peachpit.

Peachpit
1249 Eighth Street
Berkeley, CA 94710
510/524-2178
510/524-2221 (fax)

Peachpit is a division of Pearson Education.

Find us on the Web at: www.adobepress.com

To report errors, please send a note to: errata@peachpit.com

Project Editor: Rebecca Gulick
Production Editor: Hilal Sala
Copy Editor: Liz Welch
Cover Design: Charlene Charles-Will
Compositor: Martin Evening
Indexer: James Minkin

ISBN-13: 978-0-321-55561-8
ISBN-10:   0-321-55561-9

9 8 7 6 5 4 3 2 1

Printed and bound in the United States of America

Dedicated in memory of Bruce Fraser.

Foreword

All through the early stages of Lightroom, the development team often felt that it was reinventing the wheel. Even some long-time Photoshop evangelists within the company were against Lightroom, asking "Why would Adobe build this product?" But the vision for this radical new product not only included the idea that we could help photographers make better pictures. We also had the crazy idea that working on your photographs could and should be a pleasurable experience. Even fun. We wanted to build an entirely new environment for digital photography.

It's no mystery that in just the past couple of years, the entire photographic world seems to have reinvented and reinvigorated itself. And it's no mystery why. Digital has made photography fun again! Digital captures from today's higher-end digital SLR cameras easily rival the sharpness, detail, and enlargability of most medium-format film exposures. And we now have the freedom to shoot to our heart's content, without having to worry about the prohibitive cost of film.

Of course, there is a bit of a hang-over the morning after, once you start trying to sort and process all your work from the night before. But Martin is here to help you through that. By far, the most important thing is how interesting photography has become again. Photo magazines and Web sites abound. Schools are enrolling more photo students than every before. And an entirely new world of tools for digital photography is emerging.

For me personally, a specific example comes to mind of how Lightroom makes things easier. I have a Kodachrome transparency that I shot in Japan way back in 1985. It's one of my all-time favorite photographs, but the image itself is not quite perfect. I had a high-resolution drum-scan made of this picture, and started reworking it in the computer back when Photoshop was in its infancy. But even bringing all of my digital skills to bear on this particular photo, I was never really satisfied with the result. Because I felt so sure that there was a great, unfinished gem in there somewhere, I kept coming back to this photo over the years, trying new things. Even though I knew just about every trick in the Photoshop book, I was just not able to easily make it look or print the way I envisioned it. So this particular photo has languished in my archive as one of those filed under "almost great."

Recently I needed to do some Lightroom 2 test printing of RGB files, so I brought a copy of this old Kodachrome scan into my Lightroom catalog. Starting at the top of the Basic panel in Develop, I made a quick adjustment to the White Balance. A small tweak to the Temperature slider did the trick. Because the white point and black point had more or less been chiseled into stone during the scanning process, I left the Exposure and Blacks controls alone. A quick check of Vibrance vs. Saturation revealed the same answer I get 90% of the time: Vibrance provided a more natural look, and a small boost improved the photo quite a bit. Next, it was down to the Tone Curve. As with so many other photographs, bringing up the Darks and crushing down the Shadows made an easy but dramatic improvement. And finally, coming from film, this scan was already loaded with plenty of midtone contrast, so there was no need to fiddle with the Clarity slider.

What did I accomplish in this very quick runthrough of some of Lightroom's most basic correction tools? Tapping the L key twice to turn the lights out, and then using the backslash key, I was able to quickly see *before* and *after* views of my correction.

Hey, wait a minute. That looks better! Much better, in fact. Better than I had ever been able to make it look over the course of so many years. I decided to make a quick inkjet print just to see if I was imagining things. A few minutes later, I'm holding the best print of my favorite photograph that I've ever produced. As it turns out, having the right controls, in the right order, in the right context, makes all the difference in the world.

So now, for me, working in Lightroom is making photography a lot more interesting. Photography is fun again! Learning to use Lightroom to process and correct my pictures has become a process of learning how to trust what my eyes are telling me. And that is very much what photography is all about.

OK, so that's processing. But processing is only half the battle. Now how about workflow? Well, that part is still very much evolving. While Lightroom provides you with a strong set of the basics (integrated library and processing workflow, smart collections, keywords, compare modes, etc., etc.), what you do with them is still very much up to you. Building an efficient workflow is not easy. I admit it. But once you have a glimpse into how much time and effort can be saved, you'll never look back. Martin Evening is one of a handful of photographers who knows the roadmap and has the extraordinary gift of being able to teach it. Turn the page, and you'll be well on your way, not only to making better pictures, but also toward building an efficient digital workflow.

George Jardine
Pro Photography Evangelist
Adobe Systems Inc.

Introduction

Work on the Adobe Photoshop Lightroom program began toward the end of 2003 when a small group of Adobe people, headed by Mark Hamburg, met up at photographer Jeff Schewe's studio in Chicago to discuss a new approach to raw image management and editing that would be built to meet the specific needs of all those photographers who were "going digital" and who needed a better way to work with their growing libraries of photographic captures. It was shortly after this that I was invited to join the early alpha test program and help thrash out what Lightroom (or Shadowland as it was known then and Photoshop Lightroom as it's called now) should be. As we all discussed our various digital photography workflows, it became increasingly obvious why there needed to be a better way of managing and processing our photographs. Lightroom underwent some pretty major changes in those early stages, with the team trying out different workflow ideas, not to mention numerous interface changes.

Back in the early days of Lightroom's development, I remember taking a car journey from a conference in Laguna Beach back to Los Angeles with my friend and fellow author, Bruce Fraser. During the trip we talked among other things about Shadowland, and Bruce was quite enthusiastic about it, saying then, "I think Adobe would probably like us both to write a book each about the new program." Some of you reading this will be aware that, sadly, Bruce passed away in December 2006. He had been too ill to continue working for much of that year, and the last thing on his mind was writing more books. Even so, he was still keenly involved in helping guide the Shadowland development process, and at one critical point teamed up with Jeff Schewe to support Mark Hamburg at a point where Lightroom's future was looking uncertain. Bruce was dearly loved and respected by all: the many readers of his books, my editor Pamela Pfiffner (who was previously married to Bruce), and of course his family, friends, and widow Angela. We all loved him dearly. This is why I have dedicated this book to a man I admired greatly and from whom I learned so much.

This version 2 book now represents the culmination of four years' effort in which I have worked actively with the team who created Lightroom. I have called this "the complete guide" to Photoshop Lightroom, because I think you will find that just about every detail of the program is covered. I have to confess that when I first started on this project I never imagined this second edition of the book would end up being over 600 pages in length, and I really had no idea then just how much extra work would go into making Lightroom as complete as it is today. There were even times when I had my doubts, but it is a program I now enjoy working with on a daily basis.

How to Use This Book

Lightroom is principally aimed at anyone who takes photographs with a digital SLR camera. When I set out to write the book, I had very much in mind both amateur photographers as well as professional users. I have taken the trouble to explain fundamental aspects of digital imaging such as white balance and exposure in simple, easy-to-understand terms, so that no one reading this book should ever feel too left out. This book is intended to be the ultimate reference guide to Lightroom and help you get the maximum benefit out of the program.

So many changes have taken place since Lightroom 1.0 was released that not only has this new version of the book ended up being 56% bigger, but I have also rewritten almost everything that was in the original edition. Because there have been lots of rather subtle changes in the Lightroom 2 behavior, I advise readers to treat this as a brand-new book. I therefore suggest that you approach the book by reading it in chapter order, starting with the introduction to Lightroom in Chapter 1, in which I have used a professional shoot that was carried out specifially for the book. This shows just one of the ways you can integrate Lightroom into a photography workflow. The catalog features of Lightroom are equally as important as the Develop module controls. I recognize that all photographers, from beginners to pros, have differing requirements when it comes to organizing their image libraries, so I have devoted over 170 pages of in-depth advice to working with the Library module, including how to make use of keywords and metadata to manage your photos better.

Overall, I am very excited about Lightroom, and I hope the book provides inspiration and insights into how you can get the most out of Lightroom. As it says in Rule 5 of the Lightroom Five Rules Help dialog: Enjoy!

Martin Evening, June 2008.

Acknowledgments

I would like to thank my editor, Pamela Pfiffner, for prompting me to get started on this project and for her advice and help during the planning stage of this book. For this edition, Rebecca Gulick has project managed the book and done an excellent job of making sure everything went smoothly. And I would also like to thank Hilal Sala and Charlene Will from Peachpit for their work on the book production.

Lightroom is really the brainchild of Mark Hamburg, and my involvement with Lightroom began several years before the first announcement of the program, when Mark and the other lead engineers invited me to provide feedback on some of the ideas they were working on. In that time I have been helped a lot by the engineers and other members of the team to gather the background technical knowledge required to write this book. In particular, I would like to thank Thomas Knoll, Michael Jonsson, Zalman Stern (who worked on the Camera Raw engineering), Troy Gaul, Melissa Gaul, Tim Gogolin, Seetha Narayanan, Eric Scouten, Kevin Tieskoetter, Andrew Rahn, Phil Clevenger (who designed the Lightroom interface), and Andrei Herasimchuck (who helped guide Lightroom through the early stages). I would also like to thank product manager Tom Hogarty and product evangelist George Jardine for the huge amount of support and help they have given me. Thanks also go to Frederick Johnson, Addy Roff, and Mala Sharma on the Photoshop and Lightroom marketing teams. I would especially like to thank Ian Lyons, who tech-edited the book. Thank you, Ian, for helping me get the technical points clarified and for providing some additional insights.

I also self-commissioned a photographic shoot to help illustrate the book for which I would like to thank the models: Yuliya and Kelly from Zone and Lucy at Bookings Agency, Camilla Pascucci for make-up, Terry Calvert for hair, Harriet Cotterill for the clothes styling, Stuart Weston for the use of his studio, and Harry Dutton for assisting me, plus a big thank-you to Jeff Schewe and George Jardine for documenting the shoot with stills and video.

It has been an interesting experience to see a new program emerge from scratch and has been a pleasure to share the development process in the company of a great group of alpha testers and fellow authors who were willing to share their knowledge about the program with one another. From this group I would most like to pay tribute to John Beardsworth, Richard Earney, Katrin Eismann, George DeWolfe, Bruce Fraser, Peter Krogh, Karl Lang, Sean McCormack, Michael Reichmann, Seth Resnick, Andrew Rodney, Jeff Schewe, Daniel Sroka, David Schloss, and Michael Tapes, who have all made valuable contributions to Lightroom's continued development.

A book like this would be rather boring to read through without having some decent photographs to illustrate it with. To supplement my own photography I would therefore like to thank Greg Gorman, George Jardine, and Jeff Schewe for letting me use their photographs, which are all individually credited throughout this book. And lastly, I would like to thank my wife, Camilla, for yet again being so understanding and patient while I was glued to the computer!

Contents

1 Introducing Adobe Photoshop Lightroom ... 1

What is Adobe Photoshop Lightroom? 2
    Keeping things simple 2
    Modular design 2
    Lightroom performance 4
        Adobe Camera Raw processing 4
        Color controls 5
    The Lightroom workflow 6
        Managing the image library 6
        Integrating Lightroom with Photoshop 8
What you'll need 9
Installing Lightroom 10
    Lightroom preferences 11
    Customizing the Identity Plate and appearance 14
    Help menu 17
Introducing the Lightroom interface 18
A quickstart guide to Lightroom 22
    Importing the photos into Lightroom 23
    Viewing photos in the Library module 24
    Simplifying the interface 26
    Zooming in 28
    Working in the Develop module 29
    Synchronizing Develop settings 30
    Reviewing and rating the photos 31
    Making contact sheet prints 32
    Reviewing the final shortlist in Survey mode 33
    Dimming the lights 34
    Saving the shortlisted photos as a collection 35
    Retouching a photograph in Lightroom 36
    Editing a copy in Photoshop 37
    Creating a Web photo gallery 38
    Making a final print 39
    Exporting the edited photos 40
Working through the book 41

2 Importing photos 43

Importing images from a card 44

Importing images from a folder 48

Importing photos by copy................................ 50

Organizing files imported by copy....................... 51

Renaming options at import time.................. 52

Renaming catalog images later 53

Converting to DNG 54

Updating DNG files.. 54

Adding metadata information at import................. 55

Importing existing photos from folders 56

Importing images via drag and drop 57

Bridge as a front end to Lightroom 58

Adding a watched folder in Bridge 60

Importing folders into Lightroom via Bridge 61

Importing photos directly from the camera.............. 62

Connecting the camera to the computer 62

Camera capture software......................... 63

Speedier tethered shooting 67

How imported photos are organized 68

Image management by metadata 68

3 Navigating the Library module 71

The Library Module panels............................... 72

Navigator panel... 74

The Catalog panel 74

The Library module toolbar............................. 74

Folders panel... 75

Filter bar.. 75

Exploring the Library module.............................. 76

Grid View options... 76

Library Grid navigation................................... 78

Working in Loupe view..................................... 79

Working with photos in both Grid and Loupe views.. 80

Loupe view options 82

Loupe view navigation. 83
About the Lightroom previews 84
Establishing the default Develop settings 84
Preview size and quality 85
Loupe zoom views 88
Loupe view shortcuts 88
Working in Survey view 88
Compare view display options. 91
Compare view mode in action step by step 92
Navigating photos via the Filmstrip. 94
Working with a dual-monitor setup 96
How to get the most out of working with two
displays. 98
Refining image selections. 100
Rating images using picks and rejects 100
Working with color labels 104
Lightroom and Bridge labels 105
Other labeling methods 105
Three ways to filter the catalog 107
Filtering photos via the Filmstrip 108
Filtering flagged photos 109
Filtering options 109
Creating refined filter selections via the
Filmstrip 109
Color label filtering 110
Virtual copy and master copy filters 112
Subfolder filtering 113
Grouping photos into stacks 114
Image selection options 116
Removing and deleting photos 117

4 Managing photos in the Library module . 119

Working with metadata 120
The different types of metadata. 121
A quick image search using metadata 122
Metadata panel 126
Metadata panel view modes. 126

General and EXIF metadata items 128
   File Name.. 128
   Sidecar Files...................................... 128
   Copy Name 128
   Metadata Status................................... 130
   Cropped photos 131
   Date representation................................ 131
   Capture time editing.............................. 132
   Camera model and serial number................. 133
   Artist EXIF metadata 133
Custom information metadata.......................... 134
   Metadata presets.................................. 135
   Editing and deleting metadata presets 136
   IPTC metadata.................................... 136
   An efficient way to add metadata 139
Metadata editing and target photos 140
   Mail and Web links............................... 142
   Copyright status.................................. 143
Keywording and Keyword List panels 144
   Three ways to add new keywords 144
   Applying and managing existing keywords 146
   Autocomplete options............................ 146
   Removing keywords 148
   Keyword hierarchy................................ 148
   Importing and exporting keyword hierarchies ... 149
   Implied keywords 150
   Keyword sets 151
   Creating your own custom keyword sets 152
   Suggested keywords 153
The Painter tool....................................... 154
Photo filtering and searches 157
Filter bar... 157
   The Filter bar layout 158
Text filter searches 158
   Search rules...................................... 159
   Combined search rules............................ 160
   Fine-tuned text searches 160

Attribute filter searches 161

Metadata filter searches.............................. 161

    Metadata filter categories........................ 162

Custom filter settings.................................. 165

    Empty field searches 165

    No content searches.............................. 166

    Advanced searches............................... 168

Quick Collections...................................... 170

Collections.. 172

    Collections sets 174

    Smart Collections................................. 174

Saving and reading metadata.......................... 175

    Saving metadata to the file 176

    Tracking metadata changes 177

    XMP read/write options.......................... 179

    Where is the truth? 183

Synchronizing IPTC metadata settings.................. 183

    Synchronizing folders 184

Sorting images 186

    Sort functions.................................... 187

    The sort by label text solution.................... 189

Extra tips for advanced users 190

    Audio file playback............................... 190

    GPS metadata and linking to Google Earth............. 191

    How to embed GPS metadata in a photo.............. 194

5 Working with catalogs 199

About Lightroom catalogs................................. 200

    Creating and opening catalogs 201

        Creating a new catalog............................. 202

        Opening an existing catalog........................ 202

    Exporting catalogs.................................... 203

        Exporting with negatives.......................... 203

        Exporting without negatives 204

        Including available previews....................... 204

    Importing catalogs.................................... 205

Limitations when excluding negatives 206
Export and import summary 207
Copying a catalog to another computer 207
A catalog export and import in action 208
How to merge two catalogs into one 212
General Catalog Settings 218
The catalog/folders relationship 219
Finding the link from the catalog to a folder 220
Adding new folders 222
Lightroom folders and system folders 223

6 Develop module image editing 225

Image editing in Lightroom 226
Smarter image processing 226
Camera Raw compatibility 227
Smarter retouching 227
Steps for getting accurate color 228
Calibrating the display 228
Choosing a display 228
Calibrating and profiling the display 229
White point and gamma 229
Macintosh 1.8 gamma 230
Matching white balances 230
Steps to successful calibration and profiling 230
Quick Develop panel 234
Quick Develop controls 234
Color controls 234
Tone controls 235
A typical Quick Develop workflow 237
Quick Develop cropping 240
Synchronizing Develop settings 241
Raw or JPEG? 242
The Develop module interface 244
Develop module cropping 246
Rotating the crop 246
Crop aspect ratios 246
Repositioning a crop 250

Crop guide overlays. 251

Crop guide orientation 253

Cancelling a crop. 253

Tool Overlay menu. 254

 The Tool Overlay options 254

Histogram panel 255

Basic panel controls. 256

Basic image adjustment procedure 258

White Balance tool 259

 White Balance corrections 261

 Creative white balance adjustments 263

Basic adjustments and the Histogram panel 264

 Auto Tone setting 265

Vibrance and Saturation. 271

Clarity slider 274

 Levels decompression 275

 Negative Clarity adjustments 276

Correcting an overexposed image 278

Correcting an underexposed image 280

Match Total Exposures. 282

Tone Curve controls. 284

The Tone Curve zones 286

Combining Basic and Tone Curve adjustments. 288

 Tone Range split point adjustments. 294

HSL / Color / Grayscale panel 296

 Selective color darkening 298

Detail panel: Chromatic aberration. 300

 Chromatic aberration adjustments. 300

 Defringe controls. 302

 All Edges corrections 303

Vignettes panel 306

 Post-crop vignettes. 308

Camera Calibration panel 310

 Creating a custom calibration via Photoshop. 310

 Creative use of Camera Calibration panel 312

Assessing your images. 314

 Comparing before and after versions 314

 Managing the before and after previews 316

Image retouching tools 320

   Spot Removal tool 320

      Clone or Heal 322

      Spot size 322

      Click and drag 322

      Click only 322

      Editing the spot circles 323

      Hiding the spot circles 323

      Undoing/deleting spot circles 323

      Heal mode synchronization 323

   Synchronized spotting 324

      Auto Sync spotting 325

      Red Eye Correction tool 326

      Adjusting the cursor size 326

   Localized adjustments 330

      Initial Adjustment brush options 331

      Editing the Adjustment brush strokes 332

      Saving effect settings 332

      Automasking 334

      Previewing the brush stroke areas 336

      Beauty retouching with negative clarity 336

      Hand-coloring in Color mode 338

      Sharpening and blurring 340

   Graduated Filter tool 342

   History panel 345

   Snapshots panel 346

      Synchronizing snapshots 348

Easing the workflow 350

   Making virtual copies 350

   Synchronizing Develop settings 352

   Lightroom and Camera Raw 354

      Viewing Lightroom edits in Camera Raw 354

      Viewing Camera Raw edits in Lightroom 354

      Keeping Lightroom edits in sync 355

      Synchronizing Lightroom with Camera Raw 356

   Copying and pasting Develop settings 358

Copying and pasting settings in the Library
module 358
Applying a previous Develop setting 359
Saving Develop settings as presets. 360
Auto Tone preset adjustments 361
The art of creating Develop presets. 361
Understanding how presets work 363
How to prevent preset contamination 364
Reset settings. 367
How to set default camera Develop settings 368

7 The art of black and white 371

Black and white conversions 372
Black and white Develop controls 372
Black and white conversion options 374
How not to convert 374
Grayscale adjustments 375
Temperature slider conversions 376
Auto grayscale plus white balance adjustments 378
Manual grayscale adjustments 382
Grayscale slider tip 383
Black and white infrared effect 384
Fine-tuning black and white images 388
Split Toning panel. 388
Split toning a color image 390
HSL panel: desaturated color adjustments 392
The HSL grayscale method 393

8 Sharpening and noise reduction 397

Capture sharpen for a sharp start 398
Output sharpening 399
Default Detail panel settings 399
Sharpen preset settings. 399
Sharpen – Portraits 400
Sharpen – Landscapes. 401
Sample sharpening image. 402

Evaluate at a 1:1 view 403

Luminance targeted sharpening 403

The sharpening effect sliders 403

Amount slider 404

Radius slider 406

The suppression controls 408

Detail slider 408

Interpreting the grayscale sharpening preview .. 411

Masking slider 411

Applying manual sharpening adjustments 414

Noise reduction 416

Noise reduction tips 417

9 The Photoshop connection 419

Opening images in Photoshop 420

The Edit in Photoshop options 420

The Edit in External Editor options 422

How to use the external editing options 424

Photoshop as a sandwich filler for Lightroom 426

Extended editing in Photoshop 430

Opening photos as Smart Objects in Photoshop .. 432

Exporting from Lightroom 434

Export presets 434

Export Location 434

Exporting to the same folder 436

File Naming and File Settings 438

Saving non-raw files as DNG 438

Image Settings 439

Image sizing 440

When to interpolate? 441

Output sharpening 442

Metadata 443

Post-processing 443

Adding export actions in Lightroom 444

Export plug-ins 448

Exporting catalog images to a CD or DVD 449

10 Printing 451

Preparing for print 452
  The Print module 452
  Image Settings panel 454
  Layout panel in Contact Sheet / Grid mode 457
  Layout panel and Guides panel options 458
    Page grid and cells 458
  Multiple cell printing 460
  Layout Engine panel 462
    Image Settings panel 462
    Rulers, Grid & Guides panel 462
    Cells panel 462
    Overlays panel 465
  Overlays panel 466
    How to add a photographic border to a print . . . 468
    Page Options 470
    Photo Info 471
  Page Setup 472
    Print resolution 473
  Print Job panel 474
    Print job color management 474
    The Lightroom printing procedure 474
    Managed by printer print settings (Mac) 475
    Managed by printer print settings (PC) 476
    Print 478
    Printing modes 479
    Print sharpening 479
  16-bit output 480
  Print to JPEG File 480
  Custom profile printing 481
    Managed by Lightroom print settings (Mac) 482
    Managed by Lightroom print settings (PC) 483
    Rendering intent 484
  Saving a custom template 485

11 Presenting your work 487

The Slideshow module 488

   The Slide Editor view in the Content area 490

   Layout panel 491

   Options panel 492

   Overlays panel 494

      Creating a custom Identity Plate 495

      Adding custom text overlays 496

      Working with the anchor points 498

   Backdrop panel 500

   How to create a novelty slideshow template 502

   Titles panel 506

   Playback panel 507

   Preview and Play 508

      Navigating slideshow photos 509

   Slideshows and selections 509

   Template Browser panel 510

   Exporting a slideshow 510

The Web module 512

   Engine panel 514

      The Lightroom HTML and Flash galleries 514

      HTML gallery 515

      Flash gallery 516

      AutoViewer gallery 517

      PostcardViewer gallery 518

      SimpleViewer gallery 519

      Third-party gallery styles 519

   Site Info panel 521

   Color Palette panel 522

      Choosing a color theme 522

   Appearance panel 524

      Appearance settings for the HTML gallery 524

      Appearance panel settings for the Flash gallery .. 525

      Appearance panel settings for the Airtight
galleries 528

      Identity Plate 528

Image Info panel.. 529

    Adding titles and captions......................... 529

    Customizing the title and caption information .. 530

Output Settings panel...................................... 534

Previewing Web galleries.................................. 535

Exporting a Web gallery.................................... 536

Uploading a Web gallery................................... 537

Template Browser panel.................................. 541

Appendix A
Lightroom Preferences 543

General preferences.. 544

  Catalog selection.. 544

  Completion sounds and prompts 545

Presets preferences... 545

    Default Develop settings 545

    Camera-linked settings............................ 546

    Location section 546

    Lightroom defaults section 546

Import preferences.. 548

  DNG options 549

    DNG image conversion options 550

External Editing preferences............................... 551

File Handling preferences.................................. 553

Interface preferences....................................... 554

  Panel end marks 554

    Custom panel end marks 554

  Panel font size 555

  Lights Out 556

  Background 556

  Filmstrip preference options 556

  Interface tweaks 557

Appendix B
Lightroom settings ... **559**

Lightroom settings and templates ... 560

The Lightroom preference file ... 560

Accessing saved template settings ... 561

The Lightroom catalog folder ... 562

The catalog database file ... 562

Journal file ... 564

Lightroom previews data ... 565

Thumbnail processing routines ... 566

Customizing the Lightroom contents ... 568

The Lightroom RGB space ... 570

RGB previews ... 572

Tone curve response ... 572

Balancing the tone curve ... 574

Lightroom vs. Photoshop curves ... 575

About the curve comparison creation method ... 577

Comparison results ... 579

Conclusions ... 580

The ideal computer setup for Lightroom ... 581

RAM memory ... 581

Graphics card ... 582

Hard drives ... 582

Drive configurations ... 583

Striped RAID ... 583

Mirrored RAID ... 584

A mirror of stripes ... 584

Just a bunch of disks ... 585

Backup strategies ... 586

Backup software ... 587

Index ... **588**

1 Introducing Adobe Photoshop Lightroom

An introduction to the main features in Lightroom, showing an example of a typical studio shoot workflow

Welcome to Adobe Photoshop Lightroom, an image processing and image asset management program that is designed to meet the needs of digital photographers everywhere. This book will help explain all the main tools that are in Lightroom and provide inspiration and advice on how to get the most out of the program. It also offers tips on how to set up your computer and how to get the best results from your digital camera files.

Lightroom was designed from the ground up to provide today's digital photographers with the tools they most need. This is reflected in the way Lightroom separates the various tasks into individual modules, is able to process large numbers of images at once, and lets you archive and retrieve images quickly. But before I get into too much detail, let me begin by explaining a little about the basic concept of Lightroom. Then I'll move on to an overview of all the main features and how you might go about using them in a typical digital photography workflow.

What is Adobe Photoshop Lightroom?

Lightroom is essentially a high-quality image processor and image database management system rolled into one, with a modern interface and fast image processing capabilities. The guiding light behind Lightroom's development is its chief architect Mark Hamburg, who up until recently had been the chief scientist working on Adobe Photoshop. For the past few years Mark and the rest of the team at Adobe have been looking closely at how photographers work digitally and the problems they face when processing and managing large numbers of digital images. Lightroom is the result of this research. Lightroom is not so much a single, monolithic application, but instead should be viewed more as a suite of application modules that combine to provide an ideal workflow for digital photographers.

Keeping things simple

One of the early goals of the Lightroom project was to remove complexity and right from the start, the founding principle of Lightroom was to provide "unreasonable simplicity." Lightroom's tools are therefore designed to streamline the image management and editing process, and to make the user experience as smooth and simple as possible. The program aims to provide photographers with the tools they most need and eliminate the call for complicated workarounds. You will find that for the most part, Lightroom has managed to do this. It does not have complex preference dialogs nor does it demand that you do anything special to optimize the program settings before you get started. For example, there are no color management settings dialogs to configure, since the color management in Lightroom is carried out automatically without requiring too much user input. On the whole, Adobe has been successful in this regard, but as the program has evolved, these principles have sometimes been compromised with the introduction of more and more options and new features.

Modular design

Lightroom was created from scratch, which has allowed the engineers to build upon their experience and knowledge of how Photoshop works to produce a brand-new program that is purpose-built for modern-day image processing requirements. The Lightroom program

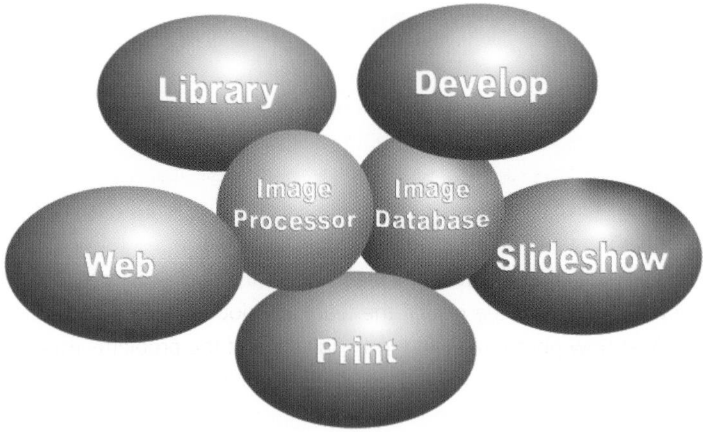

Figure 1.1 *Lightroom is engineered using a modular architecture system. At the heart of Lightroom are its image processor and image database. Lightroom is designed so that all individual modules are able to tap into these two core components of the application. This is what gives Lightroom its speed and adaptability.*

is composed of individual, self-contained modules built around a core that contains an advanced image processing engine and image database engine (**Figure 1.1**). Each module can be thought of as offering a unique set of functions, and in Lightroom 2 you will see five separate modules: Library, Develop, Slideshow, Print, and Web. This modular approach will make it easier in the future to add new features and maintain them. For example, if at some point it is decided that Lightroom needs a high dynamic range image editing module, a new self-contained module might be added. From an engineering point of view this enables Lightroom to run more efficiently because each module can have direct access to the central engines at the core of the program. And if there are flaws or bugs in any particular module, these will only show up in the functionality of that module: they will not compromise or affect the performance of any of the other modules.

One of the reasons Adobe Photoshop rose to such prominence as an image editing application was because of the way Adobe openly encouraged third-party companies to create their own filter plug-ins for Photoshop. Lightroom continues that tradition. The potential is there for third parties to create plug-ins and we have already seen the arrival of third-party Export plug-ins. It is too soon to tell if this will result in lots more third-party products for Lightroom, but rest assured that as new modules are added, Lightroom will never risk becoming bloated, because it will be quite easy to turn off or remove the modules you don't need.

NOTE

A number of filter-like features are available in Photoshop, such as Liquify and Vanishing Point, that have to be implemented via a separate modal dialog. The downside of this approach is that modal plug-ins do not have access to the central Photoshop image engine to carry out the image processing work. They are like applications that have to work within the Photoshop application, and this explains why most modal plug-ins act quite sluggish compared to when you are working directly in Photoshop. Lightroom's modular architecture means that as new features are added they will all have equal access to the image processing and image database engines in Lightroom.

NOTE

You can use the following Mac shortcuts when switching between individual modules (PC users should use Ctrl Alt plus the number):

⌘ Alt –1 to select Library
⌘ Alt –2 to select Develop
⌘ Alt –3 to select Slideshow
⌘ Alt –4 to select Print
⌘ Alt –5 to select Web
⌘ Alt ↑ to go back to the previous module

In addition, G selects the Library module in Grid mode, E selects the Library module in Loupe mode, and D selects the Develop module.

NOTE

There is certainly no shortage of "experts" who love to argue that the raw processor program they use produces superior results compared to everything else. I won't argue or deny the quality and potential of other raw processing programs, such as Capture One from Phase One and the proprietary software that is bundled with certain digital cameras. Who am I to try to dissuade people of their heartfelt opinions if they are satisfied with the results they are getting? But Adobe Camera Raw does have some unique features not found in other raw converter programs. More important, the Camera Raw image processing as implemented in Lightroom benefits from a more streamlined workflow.

Lightroom performance

As long as the computer you are using exceeds the minimum requirements provided on page 9, you will have all that's needed to get started with the program, although Lightroom's performance will be relative to the size of your image captures. The basic specifications may be fine for 5–6 megapixel camera captures, but if you are shooting with an 11–22 megapixel camera, you will definitely want to use a modern, dual-core processor computer with a minimum of 1.5 GB of RAM in order to get the best performance from the program. With the right computer configuration you can quickly navigate a collection of images, zoom in and out, and apply image adjustments with ease. Image library searches are fast and the Lightroom interface is designed to make it easy to update the metadata and narrow down your search selections within the Content area. Wherever possible, Lightroom utilizes the cached image data used to generate the previews. As a result you will find it takes no time at all to generate a slideshow or a Web photo gallery. And when you are in the Print module, it will only take a few seconds to generate the file to print out a set of contact sheets in Draft mode. This is because Lightroom is able to print directly from the high-quality image previews instead of having to rerender each image from the master file.

Adobe Camera Raw processing

If you are accustomed to using the Adobe Camera Raw plug-in via the Adobe Bridge/Photoshop dialog, some of the controls in Lightroom's Develop module will already be familiar. Lightroom shares the same Adobe Camera Raw (ACR) processing engine that is used in Photoshop and Bridge. The Adobe Camera Raw processing engine was originally developed by Thomas Knoll, who with his brother John Knoll created the original Photoshop program. It has since evolved to become one of the best raw processing tools on the market, supporting more than 175 different proprietary raw file formats, including most notably the full Canon range of digital SLRs. And Thomas has now been joined by Zalman Stern and Michael Jonsson (formerly of Pixmantec) who have both made a significant contribution with their work on Camera Raw. Michael, incidentally, was also the main engineer who worked on the Capture One raw processing application, before going on to create the highly successful Raw Shooter program. Evidence of his contribution can be seen in Lightroom's raw editing features such as the Vibrance and Fill Light sliders.

Color controls

The Develop module's image adjustment controls are easy to access, and pressing D always takes you directly to the Develop module. Lightroom is mainly intended for working with raw images, but the image adjustment controls in the Develop module can also be applied to TIFF, PSD, or JPEG images that are in RGB, Grayscale, or Lab mode (but note that Lightroom image adjustments are always carried out in RGB). The Basic and Tone Curve panels provide intuitive controls with which you can easily adjust the white balance and tones in any photograph. And the Grayscale Mixer offers an adaptable approach to black-and-white conversions whereby you can adjust the balance of color information that is used to create a monochrome version of a color original. As you dig deeper you will discover that the split tone controls work nicely on color images as well as black-and-white converted pictures, and with a little experimentation you can easily produce quite dramatic cross-processed type effects. The Develop module also provides a greater range of controls over the colors and tones in your photographs. For example, when you adjust the luminance of a color in the HSL / Color / Grayscale panel, the sliders behave exactly the way you would expect them to, so you can easily darken colors selectively. Or if you want to darken the color of a sky, you simply adjust the Blue and Aqua Luminance sliders.

It is worth pointing out that all the Develop adjustments in Lightroom are nondestructive and are recorded as edit instructions that are stored with the image. That means a single raw master file can be edited in many ways and printed at different sizes without having to make lots of different pixel image versions from the original. Any image edits and ratings you make in Lightroom will also be recognized in current versions of Bridge and Photoshop. The same is true of labels and metadata. Any metadata information that is added to an image via another program that can be recognized by Lightroom will be preserved and updated in Lightroom. For example, if you add keywords and assign a colored label to an image in Bridge, these changes will be transferred to Lightroom and updated in the Lightroom library—although this does raise the question of which setting is correct when a single image has been modified in two separate programs. In this situation, Lightroom informs you of any conflicts and lets you decide (see the accompanying Note on updating settings in Lightroom).

NOTE

An Adobe Camera Raw adjustment made in one Adobe program will always preview identically in any other Adobe program. If an image is altered outside Lightroom, a warning exclamation mark will alert you and let you decide whether to stick with the current image setting or update the new one that was applied outside Lightroom.

NOTE

Some photographers probably feel comfortable using a folder management stysytem for organizing their photos. But metadata management is now becoming increasingly popular. For example, there are now smarter ways to search a computer archive, such as the Spotlight feature on Mac OS X, which bypasses the need to navigate by folder when you are searching for a specific file. Similarly, Windows Vista encourages you to search the contents of your hard drives using a text search to discover files that have matching text data.

The Lightroom workflow

The modules and controls are all presented in a logical order, from the import stage where you bring photos into the Library module, process them in the Develop module, and finally export files for output or output them via Slideshow, Print, or Web.

Managing the image library

Lightroom has been designed to offer a flexible workflow for all types of photographers that meets their different requirements. When you work with Lightroom, you begin by explicitly choosing the images you would like to add to the Lightroom library. From this point on, the way Lightroom manages those images is actually not that much different than working with any other type of browser program. Most browser programs are like glorified versions of the Mac Finder or Windows Explorer and mainly useful for inspecting the contents on a computer and allowing you to see everything that is on a drive or in a specific folder. The main difference with Lightroom is that you control which images are imported into the Lightroom catalog. Images can be imported from a camera card, directly from the camera (via an Auto Import folder), or by copying them from an existing folder. Or, you can tell Lightroom to add photos to the catalog by importing them from the current folder location. After images have been imported into the Lightroom catalog, anything you do in Lightroom (such as changes to a folder or filename, file deletions, or moving of files) will all be mirrored at the system level. When deleting, you have the option to remove the file from the catalog only or move the file to the trash for permanent deletion. Working with the Folders panel in Lightroom is therefore not dissimilar from working with a hierarchical folder list tree view in a browser program. But in Lightroom the list tree in the Folders panel shows only those photos that you have requested to be in the catalog and nothing else.

Of course, a hierarchical folder management is fine if you know in which folders your images are stored. But when you start working with many thousands of pictures, you will soon find this is no longer such a practical solution. Lightroom can store all your images in a neat hierarchy of folders, but its real power as an image asset manager comes when you use the Filter and Browse features to search for images in a catalog. Once you get into the habit of entering descriptive keyword information each time you import a batch of images, this will soon enable you to search your archive more easily and more quickly when browsing for specific photos.

Where does Photoshop fit in?

For many years now, Photoshop has pretty much dominated the pixel image editing market, and has constantly adapted to meet the varying demands of lots of different types of Photoshop customers, from graphic designers to illustrators to special effects artists working in the motion picture industry. Although Photoshop is a very powerful image editing program with a wide range of tools to suit everyone's requirements, it has also become increasingly more complex. When the two Knoll brothers, Thomas and John, first created Photoshop, they could hardly have predicted then what Photoshop users in the future would be doing with their program, much less predict the technological demands that digital capture would make. Photoshop started out as a program for editing single images in real time, and the legacy of this basic Photoshop architecture has led to various compromises being made as the number of features in Photoshop have expanded.

Many Photoshop authors love to write about what they describe as "simple Photoshop techniques," but then proceed to take up eight pages with step-by-step instructions. (Before anyone gets too upset, I confess that I have been just as guilty as anyone else when it comes to writing about Photoshop!) And then there are all those bits of contradictory advice, such as "don't use Convert to Grayscale to convert a color image to black and white," or "don't use the Brightness and Contrast dialog to adjust the brightness and contrast." But sometimes it is almost impossible to avoid going into such detail because to write any less would only cause more confusion. Plus, some features, such as the Brightness and Contrast command, have been in Photoshop for so long that it would be unwise to remove them now. Lightroom is unencumbered by such legacy issues. You don't have to follow complex workarounds to achieve optimum results, and the Develop module controls all do exactly what you expect them to.

Because Lightroom was built from scratch, its engineers designed a program that not only addresses current demands but anticipates future needs. Take image adjustments, for example. Whenever you apply consecutive image adjustments in Photoshop, you progressively degrade the image. Lightroom, on the other hand, allows you to make as many adjustments and changes as you like, but only applies them as a single adjustment at the point where you choose Edit in Photoshop or export the image as a fixed-pixel image.

NOTE

Once you start bringing images into Lightroom, you won't necessarily find yourself locked into working exclusively in Lightroom the way you are with some other programs. Lightroom is flexible enough to allow you to work simultaneously with Bridge or other image browser programs.

The Adobe Camera Raw plug-in used by both Bridge and Photoshop does provide the same level of flexibility, but only up until the point where you render a raw file as a pixel image to be edited in Photoshop. You can create slideshows, generate Web galleries, or make print outputs without at any stage having to convert the original photos into fixed-pixel images. In Lightroom, the photos in the catalog are like your digital negatives. Whether they are raw files, PSDs, TIFFs, or JPEGs, the photos in the catalog are always preserved in their original state throughout the entire Lightroom workflow.

Integrating Lightroom with Photoshop

At this stage it is too soon to judge if Lightroom could ever become a complete replacement for Photoshop. I somehow doubt it, because Photoshop will always be a specialist tool for retouching single images, making photo composites, and other essential production tasks such as CMYK color conversions, although this may all change in the future. However, Lightroom can currently be used to perform many of the jobs that up until now would have been carried out in Bridge and Photoshop. Lightroom is an ideal front-end application for importing new images and building a searchable database of images on your computer. Once your photos are in Lightroom you have all the controls you need to carry out image edit selections, grouping and renaming of photos, plus the ability to make basic and advanced Develop adjustments.

When you're ready to take your photos into Photoshop you can use the Photo ⇨ Edit in Adobe Photoshop command, or use the File ⇨ Export command to process selected images and have these automatically added to the catalog in the same folder as the master files, or if you prefer, to a separate new folder location. Personally, I prefer to keep the archives of the raw files on one drive and the Photoshop-edited derivative files on a separate drive and back up each one up separately.

Although you can use the Photoshop Print dialog to output your photos as prints, the Print module in Lightroom is perfect for all types of print jobs from draft to fine art printing, especially with the dedicated output print sharpener built into the print processing.

What you'll need

Lightroom is designed specifically for photographers working with digital photos, so above all you will need a camera, of course! Lightroom can process JPEG, TIFF, or raw images, but if your camera is capable of capturing raw images, I advise you to shoot in raw mode whenever possible. Lightroom currently supports more than 175 different raw camera formats.

You will require a computer that meets the minimal specifications listed at the bottom of this page. Although it is possible to run Lightroom on a three-year-old laptop computer with just 1 GB of RAM memory, you will notice a substantial improvement in performance with a more up-to-date computer. Lightroom will certainly benefit from having as much RAM as possible, and it is recommended that you have, if possible, at least 1.5 GB of RAM installed on your computer. Although you don't need much hard disk space on your computer to install and run Lightroom, you will need to give serious consideration to how you will store all your image archive files. Some people can easily shoot 10 GB worth of images (or more) in a single day. And if you export some of those files as rendered TIFFs or PSDs, you can see how your storage requirements might grow considerably in a short amount of time. For more information on computer systems and backup strategies, see Appendix B.

TIP

To see if the raw files from your camera are supported in Lightroom, go to the Adobe Photoshop Web site at www. adobe.com/products/ photoshop/cameraraw.html.

Those cameras that are capable of capturing raw images using the Digital Negative (DNG) format can also be supported by Lightroom. Because DNG is a self-contained raw format, it is the ideal format to use when exporting images with the raw data preserved within the file.

Mac

G4, G5, or Intel Macintosh processor running at 1 GHz or higher

Mac OS X 10.4.3 or later or Mac OS X 10.5

1 GB of RAM (minimum recommendation)

1 GB or more of hard disk space

Color monitor display with 1024 x 768 resolution or greater

NOTE

As discussed on the following page, Lightroom also offers 64-bit compatibility for Mac Intel computers and Windows computers running the 64-bit version of Vista.

PC

Intel Pentium 4 (or compatible) processor

Windows XP Professional or Home Edition with Service Pack 2 (SP2)

Windows Vista Home Premium, Business, Ultimate, or Enterprise

1 GB of RAM (minimum recommendation)

1 GB or more of hard disk space

Color monitor display with 1024 x 768 resolution or greater

NOTE

Lightroom's performance will be relative to the size of your master image files. The minimum specifications outlined here may suffice if you are only editing raw or JPEG files from a 5 or 6 megapixel camera. If you want to process files larger than this, you almost certainly need a faster computer with a lot more RAM.

Lightroom 2 is now enabled for 64-bit processing in both the Mac (Intel) and Windows (Vista 64 bit) versions of the software. Intel Mac users will need to follow the instructions in **Figure 1.4** to enable the program in 64-bit mode, while Windows Vista users will need to download or install the 64-bit version of the program.

Lightroom will also be able to go beyond the 4 GB RAM limit that was imposed on 32-bit operating systems (assuming you have more than 4 GB of RAM installed on your computer). If your computer is capable of running in 64-bit and you have more than 4 GB of RAM installed, then you should see an 8–12% boost in performance speed.

Installing Lightroom

The Lightroom installation process is quick and easy. All you need to do is to download the program or load the installation DVD and launch the installer. **Figure 1.2** shows the Mac OS installation dialog and **Figure 1.3** shows the PC version installer. Simply click the Continue or Next button and follow the on-screen instructions. All you have to do is confirm which drive you want to install Lightroom to and that's it. If you have an earlier version of Lightroom on your computer, the Lightroom installer will automatically overwrite the older program. The first time you launch Lightroom you will need to read and agree to the terms and conditions of supply, and if installing for the first time, enter a program serial number. If you are installing Lightroom 2 and updating an existing Lightroom catalog, you may be asked at this stage if you would like Lightroom to run a verification process to test the integrity of the current catalog.

Figure 1.2   *The Lightroom installation dialog on the Mac.*

Figure 1.4   *To enable Lightroom in 64-bit mode for an Intel Macintosh computer, locate the application, go to the Finder, and choose File ⇨ File Info. Uncheck the box that says "Open in 32-bit mode" and relaunch Lightroom.*

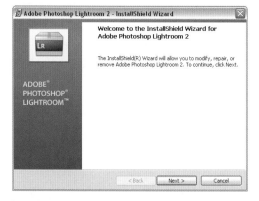

Figure 1.3   *The Lightroom installation dialog on the PC.*

Lightroom preferences

The default Library location for your Lightroom catalog is the *username*/Pictures folder (Mac) and the *username*\My Documents\My Pictures folder (PC). If you want to create a new catalog in a different location, you can do so by restarting Lightroom with the Alt key (Mac) or the Ctrl key (PC) held down during startup. This displays the Select Catalog dialog shown in **Figure 1.5** where you can click the Create New Catalog button to select a location to store a new Lightroom catalog. To start with, you will probably want to work with just one Lightroom catalog, which, if you run out of space on your main hard drive, can always be moved to a new disk location at a later date. After you have successfully launched the program, go to the Lightroom menu (Mac) or the Edit menu (PC) and choose Preferences. This opens the dialog shown in **Figure 1.6** followed by the other preference sections shown in **Figures 1.7** to **1.10**.

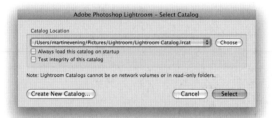

Figure 1.5 *Holding down the Alt key (Mac) or the Ctrl key (PC) during startup will allow you to select the catalog you wish to use, or create a new catalog.*

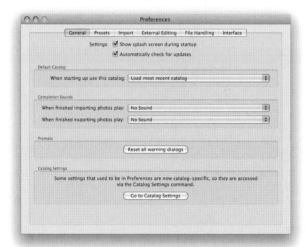

Figure 1.6 *In the General Preferences, the Default Catalog section lets you choose which catalog to use when you launch Lightroom. The default setting uses "Load most recent catalog," or you can choose "Prompt me when starting Lightroom." If you have already created other catalogs, you can select them here from the drop-down menu.*

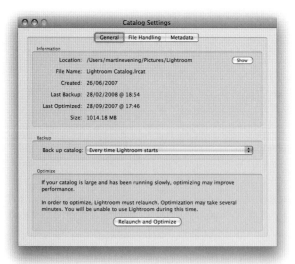

Figure 1.7 *You can then click Go to Catalog Settings in Figure 1.6 to open the Catalog Settings dialog. This will allow you to set the Catalog backup policy, the Catalog previews sizes, and Metadata handling settings. You can read more about configuring the Catalog settings later in chapters 3 and 5.*

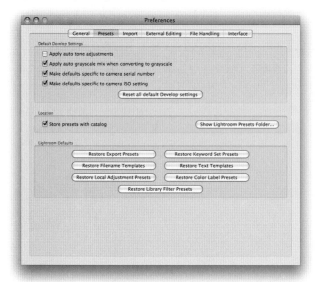

Figure 1.8 *Back to the General Preferences dialog again and here you can see the Presets section. If you mostly take photographs of mixed subjects, especially where you have no control over the lighting, then you might like to check the "Apply auto tone adjustments" option. Otherwise leave it unchecked. But I would suggest checking the "Apply auto grayscale when converting to grayscale" option. We'll be looking at the camera default settings later, but for now leave these unchecked. However, you might like to check the "Store presets with Catalog" option. This allows you to store custom preset settings as part of the catalog. This means when you export a catalog (see Chapter 5), you can include all custom presets with the catalog.*

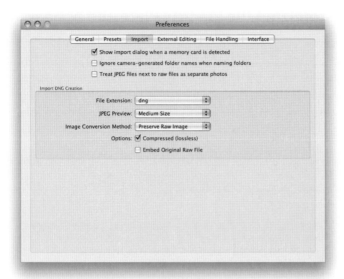

Figure 1.9 *If you want the Lightroom Import Photos dialog to default to appearing whenever you insert a camera card, make sure that "Show import dialog when a memory card is detected" is checked In the Import section. Below that are the DNG settings for when you choose to import and convert to DNG directly (the DNG options are discussed more fully in Appendix A).*

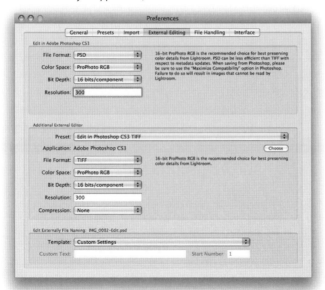

Figure 1.10 *In the Lightroom External Editors preferences you can customize the pixel image editing settings for Photoshop plus an additional external editor. These are the file format, color space, and bit depth settings that are used whenever you ask Lightroom to create an Edit copy of a catalog image to open in an external pixel editing program. There is an example of how to edit a Lightroom catalog image in an external program coming up a little later in this chapter.*

NOTE

The File Format options include Photoshop's native PSD file format or TIFF. The Color Space can be ProPhoto RGB (which is fairly close to the chromaticities of the native Lightroom workspace), or Adobe RGB (which many photographers like using in Photoshop), or sRGB (which is ideal for Web-based output only). The Bit Depth can be 16 bits, which preserves the most amount of Levels information, but doubles the output file size; or 8 bits, which is a more standard bit depth, but won't necessarily preserve all the Levels information that is obtainable from your master library images.

Customizing the Identity Plate and appearance

There are several ways that you can customize the appearance of the
Lightroom program. To start with we will look at the Identity Plate
options where you can replace the standard Lightroom logo with one
of your own custom designs. You can also edit the font and colors for
the top panel module selector as well as edit the background color/
pattern for the main Content area.

1. The top panel in the Lightroom interface contains the Lightroom
   Identity Plate and module selectors. If you go to the Lightroom
   menu and select Identity Plate Editor, you will see the dialog shown
   here. This allows you to enable the Identity Plate, which then
   appears in the top-left section of the Lightroom interface, replacing
   the normal Adobe Photoshop Lightroom logo. The standard,
   Styled text Identity Plate displays the name that is registered as
   the computer administrator using the default Zapfino font. But
   you can change the font type and font size and use any font
   that is available for use on your computer. In the example shown
   here I edited the text to show the full name for my company and
   changed the font to Helvetica.

2. After you have configured a custom Identity Plate, go to the
   Identity Plate pull-down menu and choose Save As to save this
   setting as a new custom template design.

3. If you select the "Use a graphical Identity Plate" option, you can add an image logo by copying and pasting or dragging a PDF, JPEG, GIF, PNG, TIFF, or PSD image into the Identity Plate area. The logo image you place here cannot be more than 60 pixels tall, but can contain transparent pixels. A graphical Identity Plate can be added to Slideshow and Web module templates, but be warned that a 60-pixel tall logo will be far too small for most print layout template designs that use Identity Plates. You can also customize the appearance of the module selector by choosing a new replacement font in any size you like. And if you click the little color swatch icons (circled), you can change the font colors for the active and non-active modules.

NOTE

PSD files can only be added via the Identity Plate Editor using the Mac OS version of Lightroom.

TIP

Graphical Identity Plates can be more than 60 pixels tall. For print work you will probably want to create Identity Plate graphics that are bigger than 60 pixels.

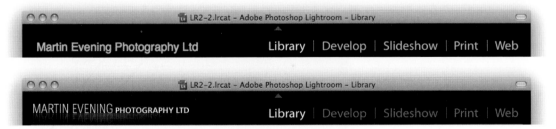

4. Now let's see how the top panel looks after customizing the Identity Plate using the Styled text and Graphical Identity Plate options. The top view shows a customized styled text Identity Plate and the bottom view shows a customized graphical Identity Plate.

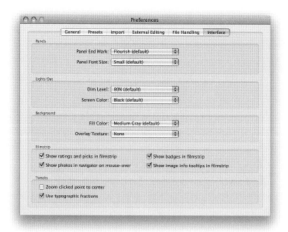

5. In the Lightroom Interface preferences you can customize the appearance of the interface when using the Lights Out and Lights Dim mode (which is discussed later in Step 12 on page 34). You can also customize the background appearance when viewing a photo in Loupe view.

6. In this example, the Background Fill Color is set to Medium Gray with the Overlay Texture set to Pinstripes.

Help menu

Figure 1.11 shows the Help menu, as found in the Library module. If you select Library Help, you can access the off-line Lightroom 2 User guide where you can browse the help guide options for the current module (**Figure 1.12**). Select Help Resources Online and this takes you to the Adobe Lightroom Resources page, where if you click on the Live Docs link, you open the Lightroom community help pages (**Figure 1.13**).

Figure 1.11   *The Help menu is common to all Lightroom modules. This screen shot shows the Library module Help menu, but the other modules look similar except they will have help items and help shortcut relevant to that particular module.*

Figure 1.12   *The Lightroom off-line Help guide. This guide is installed with the program and will display the contents in a Web browser format.*

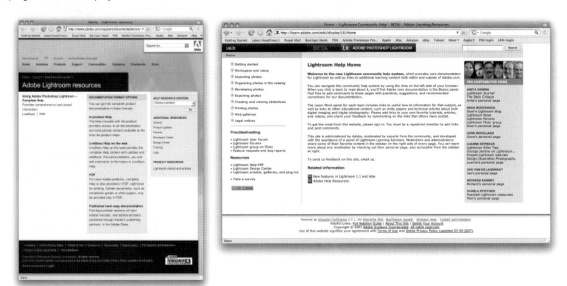

Figure 1.13   *The Adobe Lightroom Resources and Lightroom Community help pages.*

Introducing the Lightroom interface

Lightroom menu bar

As with any application, the main menu commands are located in the Lightroom menu bar at the top of the screen (Mac), or at the top of the document window (PC). If you are in absolute full-screen mode, the menu bar will be hidden, but it can be revealed by simply rolling the mouse to the top of the screen.

Top panel

The top panel section contains the Identity Plate, which normally shows the Lightroom logo. But you can customize this via the Lightroom ⇨ Identity Plate Setup menu. For example, you can replace this with your own name or add a company logo graphic. On the right you have the module selector menu for selecting the Lightroom modules. The Library module is where you preview and manage your catalog collections. Develop is for processing images. Slideshow enables you to output image collections as onscreen presentations. The Print module is for outputting images to print. And the Web module allows you to generate Web sites and upload them automatically to a specified FTP server. You can use the **F5** key to toggle showing and hiding the Top panel.

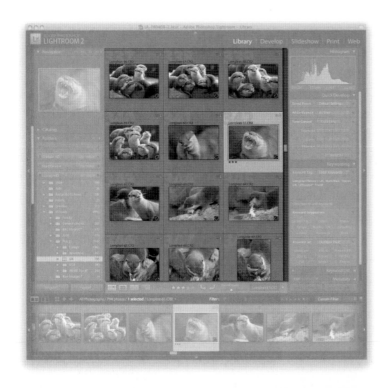

Content area

The Content area is the central section of the interface where you can view the photos you are working on. In the Library module Grid mode (shown here), you see the images displayed as thumbnails in a grid cell layout. In the Library module in Loupe mode and the Develop module, the photos are displayed at a fit-to-view or 1:1 scale size. In the other modules, Print, Slideshow, and Web, you can see previews of how the images or screen pages will look before you output them from Lightroom.

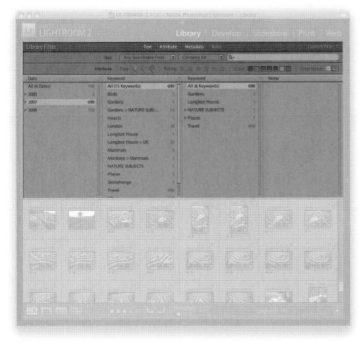

Filter bar

This is new to Lightroom 2 and appears at the top of the Content area when you are in the Library module in Grid view. It replaces the Find panel, which is where you would have gone previously to carry out a find search by name and/or time period. This section now allows you to carry out more detailed searches by using the customizable panels in the Browse section to search for photos using additional search criteria, such as by a specific Date, Camera type, or Lens type. You can use the ⎩\⎭ key to toggle showing and hiding the top panel in the Content area and use the ⎩⇧Shift⎭ key to display more than one item at a time.

Toolbar

The Toolbar appears in all of the Lightroom modules at the bottom of the Content area. The Toolbar options will vary depending on which module you are in and can be customized when you are in the Library or Develop module. You can use the T key to toggle showing and hiding the Toolbar.

Left panel

In the Library module, the left panel is mainly used for selecting the source photos via the Catalog, Folders, or Collections panel. In the Develop module it is used for the Presets, Snapshots, and History panels and in the remaining modules it is mainly used for accessing preset settings and collections. For example, if you are working in the Develop module, you can save custom Develop settings as presets, where they can be readily applied to other images. The individual panels can be expanded or collapsed by clicking on the panel bar header. Alt –clicking a panel bar toggles expanding to show the contents of that panel only or expanding to show all panels. You can use the Tab key to toggle showing and hiding both the left and right panels.

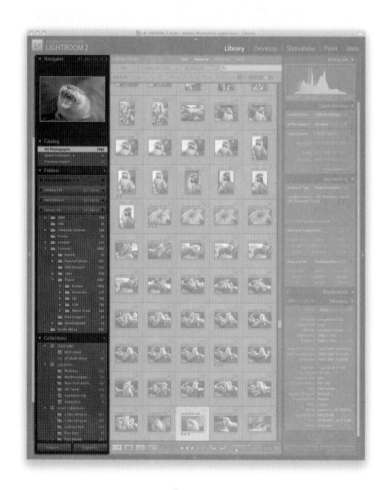

Right panel

The right panel mostly contains the controls for adjusting an image, the information about an image, or image layout settings. In the Library module you can apply Quick Develop settings and synchronize them across multiple images. The Develop module lets you make more advanced image adjustments, whereas in the Slideshow and Print modules the right panel features all the controls that govern layout and output. As with the Left panel, the individual panels can be expanded or collapsed by clicking on the panel bar header. Alt–clicking a panel bar toggles expanding to show the contents of that panel only or expanding to show all panels. But you can also use the ⌘ key (Mac) or Ctrl key (PC) in combination with a keypad number (0, 1, 2, 3, etc.) to toggle opening and closing the individual panels in the order they are listed from the top down. You can use the Tab key to toggle showing and hiding both the left and right panels.

Filmstrip

The Filmstrip is located at the bottom of the screen and contains thumbnails of all the images currently displayed in the Library, highlighting any that are selected. The Filmstrip thumbnails can be accessed via all the other modules and this allows you access to individual images or subselections of images without having to switch back to the Library module.

A quickstart guide to Lightroom

Let's start with a quick overview of how to use Lightroom. I thought that the best way to do this would be to carry out a shoot specifically for the Adobe Photoshop Lightroom 2 book (**Figure 1.14**). The idea here was to provide an example of a complete workflow from start to finish, showing how Lightroom can be used to process and manage photos that were taken on a typical studio fashion shoot. Of course there are lots of ways that you can integrate Lightroom into a photography workflow, but rather than try to introduce every feature in the program, I thought it better to show you the way one person uses Lightroom in a studio setting. Hopefully the workflow that is described over the following pages will provide a clear insight into what Lightroom does, how it can be used to help speed up the way you work, and how best to integrate Lightroom with Photoshop.

Figure 1.14   *Here is a picture of me photographing the model, Dunja, for the first shot in a series of beauty photographs.*

Importing the photos into Lightroom

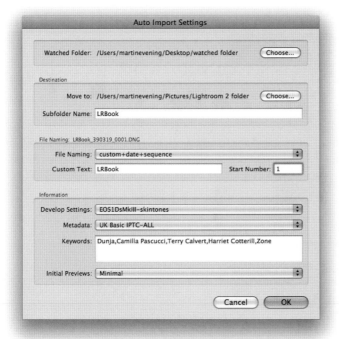

NOTE

Notice that Lightroom requires you to enter a destination subfolder name. By using meaningful names for your imported shoots, this can help you keep track of where your image files are stored. The same is true if you add keywords and other metadata at this stage. This information will further help with the management of your Lightroom catalog.

NOTE

Tethered shooting mode is where the camera is connected directly to the computer and you use software such as the camera manufacturer software to import the photos to a watched folder. From there, Lightroom can automatically import these photos into the catalog.

1. There are several ways that you can import your photos into Lightroom. The standard way is to insert the camera card, which will display the Import Photos dialog, where you can configure the import settings. Because this was a studio shoot, I chose to shoot in tethered shooting mode (which is described more fully in Chapter 2). With a tethered setup, photos can be imported directly from the camera to the computer using the camera-supplied software and from there, the photos can be automatically imported into Lightroom. At the beginning of a shoot I'll go to the File menu and choose Auto Import ⇨ Auto Import Settings. In the Auto Import dialog shown here I made sure that the Watched Folder location matched the folder where the photos were downloaded to by the camera software. The File Naming, Start Number, and Metadata sections should only need to be configured once at the beginning of the day. The only settings that need adjusting on a shot-by-shot basis are the Develop settings (which may need to be customized for each new shot) and the Keywords, which again, might need altering for each new model that is photographed. Once the shoot settings had been configured I clicked OK and was able to start taking photographs (**Figure 1.15**).

Figure 1.15 *Whether you prefer to work in tethered mode or by importing directly from the camera card, once the Import settings have been configured at the beginning of the day, you can carry on shooting and let Lightroom rename and batch process the photos for you.*

Viewing photos in the Library module

The activity viewer indicates Lightroom is busy importing images and/or building a preview cache.

The imported files will show here using the subfolder name assigned in the Import Photos dialog.

The Library view is currently in Grid (G) mode.

Figure 1.16 *The status indicator shows the progress of background processes such as importing images or rendering previews.*

2. The imported images started to appear in the Library module, which is shown here in Grid view. The activity viewer in the top-left corner indicates that Lightroom is actively carrying out background processes such as importing photos or building previews. If more than one operation is taking place at a time, you will see the grouped status indicator. If you click the small arrow to the right, you can toggle the status indicator between each task that is in progress and the grouped indicator (**Figure 1.16**). The imported images will appear in the grid in order of preference (such as sort by filename or capture time in ascending or descending order), and you can make selections of images by using either the grid or the Filmstrip at the bottom. At this stage you can rearrange the order of the photos in the grid by dragging and dropping the images (note that the order sequence you apply here will be carried through to all the other modules).

This image is currently displayed using the Fit to view Loupe mode. A single click will magnify the image to a 1:1 or custom zoom view. Click to return to the previous view.

The Library view is currently in Loupe (E) mode.

The scroll bar

3. We'll now switch to viewing photos in the Loupe view, where you can preview the photos on the screen one at a time. You can go to the Loupe view from the grid by clicking the Loupe view button, by pressing the E key, or just double-clicking an image to switch to Loupe view. The arrow keys on the keyboard let you quickly shuttle through all of the images in the current image selection. To scroll through a selection without scrolling the images, just drag the scroll bar in the Filmstrip at the bottom of the screen. The base magnification can be set to either Fit or Fill the width of the Content area, while the magnified Loupe view can be set from a 1:4 to an 11:1 zoomed pixels view (yes, Lightroom goes to 11!). The Loupe view is ideal for checking photos for detail and focus and rating your photos. Also shown here is the Quick Develop panel, which can be used for making rough Develop adjustments without having to switch to the Develop module.

TIP

You can open and close the Lightroom panels by clicking anywhere on the panel tab. If you Alt -click a panel tab, you can switch to a solo mode of operation, where clicking an individual tab will open that panel only and close all the others. Alt -click a panel again to restore the normal panel behavior.

Simplifying the interface

Clicking this arrow collapses the top panel (this also applies to the Filmstrip below).

Mouse drag the panel edge to resize the panel width.

Roll the mouse over to the side of the display to temporarily reveal the hidden side panel.

As well as dragging the sidebar to scroll the panels, you can mouse down and drag anywhere in the panel area.

4. Now let's look at ways to make Lightroom's interface simpler to work with, learn how to hide interface components, and place more emphasis on the images. Start by pressing the Tab key. This will temporarily hide the two side panels and provide more space for the photo to be displayed in the Loupe view. However, you can still access the side panels by rolling the mouse cursor over to the edges of the screen. Do this and the panels are revealed one at a time. You will notice how the panels temporarily overlay the image below, but you can still access the panel controls as usual. If you click the little arrow on the side of the screen in the middle, you can lock these panels independently. When you do this the image will center-adjust to reveal the entire image area again. Press Tab and the two side panels will be revealed once again. The Panel rollover behavior described here can be modified via the contextual menu (see side panel).

5. So far, we have been working with the Lightroom interface in the Document Window mode. If you press the F key, the interface switches to full-screen mode and expands to fill the whole screen. Press F a second time, and the interface switches to absolute full-screen mode (shown above) where the system menu bar disappears and Lightroom overrides any operating system rollover behaviors. For example, on the Mac, the absolute full-screen mode overrides the Dock as you roll the mouse cursor to the bottom or side of the screen. But you can still access the system menu bar by rolling the mouse cursor to the top of the screen. Press the F5 key to toggle between hiding and showing the Lightroom menu bar. Press the F6 key to hide and show the Filmstrip at the bottom. In addition, you can use ⇧Shift Tab to hide and show everything!

TIP

If you ever get stuck in a situation where you need to reset the interface layout, press ⇧Shift Tab a couple of times to restore everything back to the default layout.

Zooming in

You can select an area to zoom to by clicking anywhere in the Navigator preview.

To scroll the image, drag the zoom rectangle in the Navigator.

You can also use the Zoom slider to set the Zoom view.

TIP

You can use ⌘ + (Mac), Ctrl + (PC) to zoom in and ⌘ − (Mac), Ctrl − (PC) to zoom out. This will magnify the photo from Fit to view, to Fill view, to 1:4 and a 1:1 magnification. You can also use ⌘ Alt + (Mac), Ctrl Alt + (PC) to zoom in using gradual increments up to 11:1 and use ⌘ Alt − (Mac), Ctrl Alt − (PC) to zoom out again using gradual zoom increments.

6. Let's stay in the full-screen Loupe mode with the side panels hidden and roll the mouse over to the left of the screen to reveal the left panel, which can be locked into position (see Step 4). Click anywhere in the picture, and the image zooms smoothly to a 1:1 or custom magnified pixels view. Click the image again, and it returns to fit the normal screen view. Whether you are in Grid or Loupe view, if you press Z, the image will instantly display at the 1:1 (or custom) magnified view mode. Press Z again and the image reverts to the Library Grid view. The Navigator panel can also be used to zoom and scroll the image. Click inside the image preview to select an area to zoom to and then drag the small rectangle to scroll the photo. You can also use the Spacebar to toggle between the standard and magnified Loupe viewing modes.

Working in the Develop module

The basic Develop controls are a great place to start adjusting the tones and colors in an image.

Click the switch icon to toggle turning panel adjustments on or off.

7. If we go to the Develop module we can now start adjusting individual images for color, tonal range, image cropping, and sharpness. If you are accustomed to working with the Adobe Camera Raw plug-in in Bridge and Photoshop, you will probably already be familiar with the Basic controls. There is a lot you can do to correct an image by using just these Basic panel adjustments as well as the other controls, such as Tone Curve, HSL / Color / Grayscale, Split Toning, Detail, and Camera Calibration panel controls. Plus in Lightroom 2 we now have a Vignettes panel for applying post-crop vignettes, not to mention the new localized adjustment tools. On a busy photo shoot I typically use the Basic panel controls to fine-tune the white point and adjust the tone controls such as Exposure and Blacks. If I already have a Color Calibration preset for the camera, I'll apply this as well and lastly, I'll enlarge the photo to a 1:1 view, go to the Detail panel, and adjust the noise and sharpening sliders for the currently selected image. **Figure 1.17** shows how to save Develop settings.

Figure 1.17 *You can save your favorite Develop settings such as camera-specific Develop settings as a preset.*

Synchronizing Develop settings

Use the Filmstrip to select the photos you want to synchronize in Develop.

Click Sync to synchronize the settings to those of the selected target image.

Figure 1.18 *Develop settings such as the Spot Removal, Crop, and Straighten settings can be selectively synchronized across other images.*

8. Once you have adjusted the Develop settings to get one photo to look the way you like, you might want to synchronize those settings with other photographs that belong to the same shoot sequence. To do this, select the photos you want to synchronize via the Filmstrip (or briefly pop back to the Library grid view, if you find this easier). Make sure that the image you want to synchronize from is the "most selected" image, and click the Sync button to synchronize all the other selected photos with this image (**Figure 1.18**). Note that Lightroom offers unlimited undo options, so you can always choose Edit ⇨ Undo or ⌘Z (Mac), Ctrl Z (PC) any time you need to revert to a previous step. If you want to redo a step, use ⌘ ⇧Shift Z (Mac) Ctrl ⇧Shift Z (PC). The History panel offers even more flexible control, allowing you to preview and revert to any of the history steps associated with the image (these will always remain stored with the photo). Selected history states can also be saved as snapshots via the Snapshots panel.

Reviewing and rating the photos

9. So far the first set of photos have been added to the catalog using the Auto Import settings that were applied at the Import stage. These were used to determine which folder the photos would be copied to, to rename the files, and to add essential metadata plus relevant keywords. In the Develop module I made a few image adjustments and synchronized the settings across all of the photos. We are now ready to start reviewing the pictures and mark which ones are the favorites. You can do this in the Develop or Library module, but the Library module is faster for this kind of editing. By now Lightroom should have processed the photos to create standard previews, but if not, you can go to the Library menu and choose "Render Standard-sized previews." You can then rate the best images using the flag system (press P to mark a photo as a flag pick), or use the numbered rating system. In this example I pressed 1 to mark photos with a 1-star rating, 2 to mark those that deserved a 2-star rating, and so on. In the above screen shot, all the 1-star and higher images are currently selected.

TIP

Use ⌘ D (Mac) or Ctrl D (PC) to deselect a Library selection of images, and use ⌘ ⇧ Shift D (Mac) or Ctrl ⇧ Shift D (PC) to select the most selected (or active) photo only.

Making contact sheet prints

Use Draft mode for fast print outputs.

The Print settings are used to set and save the print driver settings.

The Print One button (bypassing the system dialog)

Click here to configure the Page Setup settings.

The Print button (via system dialog)

Figure 1.19 *Some clients prefer to have contact sheets of the 1-star rating and higher images. One reason for this is because they can edit the photos anywhere without the need for a computer, plus they can write notes on the contact sheet prints.*

10. I am often required to provide clients with contact sheets from a day's shoot (**Figure 1.19**). This is where the Draft Mode Printing option in the Print module comes in use. In the example shown here, I kept the same selection of images active and selected a modified contact sheet print template from the Template Browser panel. Lightroom displays a preview of the contact sheet that contains the currently selected images. The Info overlay indicates that you are looking at page 11 out of 15 printable contact sheet pages. For speedy printing, the Draft Mode Printing option is checked in the Print Job panel. This grays out all the other options, meaning that you must turn on the printer's color management option when you configure the Print Settings, and are using a correctly matched media/paper type setting. I'll be discussing the Page Setup and Print Settings options in Chapter 10.

Reviewing the final shortlist in Survey mode

11. Contact sheets aren't absolutely necessary, but as you can see in **Figure 1.20**, it does make it easier for clients to spread the contact sheets out on a table and compare all the shots. If there is time to go through the pictures on the screen, you can always do so using Loupe view. Whichever method you use, the goal will be to narrow down the selection so that you end up with a shortlist of favorite images from which you may wish to select just one or two final candidate images. For this, it can be useful to switch to the Survey view in the Library module (press Ⓝ). The main advantage of the Survey view is that you can more easily compare shortlisted selections with the individual images displayed as big as possible on the screen, because in Survey view the selected images will automatically resize to fit within the Content area. If you want to inspect a particular image close-up, double-click to open it in Loupe view and double-click or press Ⓝ to return to the Survey view mode again. When you are in Survey view, you can ⌘–click (Mac) or Ctrl–click (PC) on an image to remove it from the current selection.

Figure 1.20 *Here is a shot of me sorting through a set of contact sheet prints before giving them to the client.*

Dimming the lights

The default Lights Dim and Lights Out modes use varying opacities of black. If you go to the Lightroom Interface preferences (see page 16), you can set the Lights Out screen color to other shades of gray and adjust the dim level opacity. This is useful if you prefer to view your images isolated against a light neutral gray instead of solid black.

12. Sometimes it can help to work in Lightroom with the program interface hidden. To this end Lightroom has a Lights Dim and a Lights Out mode. These two viewing modes allow you to dim or hide the interface so you can focus more on what is going on in the photographs, yet still have easy access to the interface when you need it. To see how these work, press the ⌊L⌋ key once. This switches Lightroom to Lights Dim mode (you could choose Window ➪ Lights Out ➪ Lights Dim, but pressing the ⌊L⌋ key is easier to remember). The Lights Dim mode just darkens the interface so you can still see (and access) all the Lightroom controls and menu items. Press ⌊L⌋ a second time to take you to the Lights Out mode, and then press ⌊L⌋ again to take you back to the default viewing mode. Note that if you roll the mouse to the top of the screen, you will always be able to view the menu bar at normal brightness.

Saving the shortlisted photos as a collection

This Catalog panel shows the number of images that have been grouped as a Quick Collection.

The Quick Collection images have been saved as a new collection in the Collections panel.

13. Ratings or flags are preserved with the photos so that you can at any time make a filtered rating selection like the one shown here, or show a shortlisted selection of, say, the highest-rated images. However, you can only do this to reveal the filtered photos in one folder at a time or when filtering a particular keyword selection. To save groups of images from different filter search results, you need to use collections. You can use collections to save groups of images that have portfolio potential or group photos from two or more shoots. In the example shown here I selected some of the highest-rated photos and pressed the B key to add these to the Quick Collection section of the Catalog panel. Quick Collections are useful for creating temporary image groupings. If you want to make a collection more permanent, you can click the plus button in the Collections panel to add a new collection to the list. In Lightroom 2, collections can be used to store module-specific attributes. Plus you can set up Smart Collections to automatically add photos to a collection based on set criteria.

NOTE

You can use the Filter bar at the top of the Content area to filter photos by ratings higher than, lower than, or by a specific rating only. You can also filter photos by flagging or color labels, and the text search field can be used to carry out text-based searches.

Retouching a photograph in Lightroom

NOTE

The new localized adjustments will also let you apply other types of adjustments to a photo such as darken, boost the saturation, add clarity, or colorize portions of a photo. There is a linear gradient tool mode as well.

14. Once you have decided which photos have made the final shortlist, the next stage is to take them through to the photo finishing stage before making a final print output. The Develop tools in Lightroom have come a long way from the early days of Adobe Camera Raw for Photoshop. In this latest version of Lightroom we now have tools to make localized image adjustments in addition to the clone and healing brush tools that were introduced in version 1. In this particular example I made a few fine-tuning adjustments to the Basic panel settings and adjusted the Tone Curve to get the optimum tone contrast. I then used the new brush retouching tool to apply a lightening exposure adjustment to the hair. This was done to help make the hair look more shiny. In the screen shot shown here you can see how I was able to fade the brush adjustment to get the lightness on the hair just right. Finally, I selected the Remove Spots tool to retouch out a couple of sensor dust spots on the edge of the frame.

Editing a copy in Photoshop

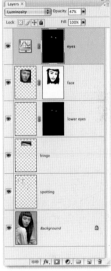

15. For lots of photos Lightroom may have all the retouching tools that you need. But for beauty images such as this it will always be necessary to use Photoshop to carry out the detailed retouching. In the example shown here, I went to the Photo menu and chose Edit in Applications, where I configured Photoshop as the external editing program (⌘ Alt E [Mac] Ctrl Alt E [PC]). Because I was opening a raw master image, there was just the one option available: Edit a Copy with Lightroom Adjustments. This opens a copy of the master raw image in Photoshop and adds it to the same catalog folder location as the master. I then used my Photoshop skills to tidy up some of the loose hairs and smooth out the skin tones. When I was done editing, I saved the image, which then appeared updated in the Lightroom catalog.

NOTE

Edit a Copy with Lightroom Adjustments is the only option available the first time you open a raw master image. But once you have opened a photo this way and saved it out of Photoshop, the next time you open the Photoshop edited image via Lightroom, remember to choose the Edit Original option, which will reopen the Photoshop-edited image rather than create a new copy.

Creating a Web photo gallery

Figure 1.21 *The Configure FTP File Transfer dialog.*

16. The Web module can generate Web photo galleries using HTML or Flash gallery styles. This screen shot shows a preview of the final shortlist of shots, displayed using an Airtight PostcardViewer gallery style. The Web module options allow you full control to modify and create your own Web photo galleries. The preview displayed in the Content area actually shows you a Web browser view of a fully coded Web site. When you are happy with the way the site looks, you can click the Upload button to specify where Lightroom should upload the complete site files and folders. You only need to configure the FTP settings for your server once, and then add the settings as an FTP preset (**Figure 1.21**). After you have configured your server settings and saved them as a preset, it becomes an easy process to upload new Web photo galleries to a saved favorite server location. Web galleries offer a great way to share photos with friends, create portfolio presentations, or as shown here provide clients with an overview of work in progress on a job.

Making a final print

17. To make a high-quality print output, try selecting one of the default single-page templates and customize the settings to suit the paper size you will be using. Depending on how you want the image to appear on the page, you might want to click the Page Setup button to configure the printer for landscape or portrait printing. In the Print Job panel, you will now want to disable Draft Mode Printing and select a profile that matches the printer and print media from the Color Management section. If you don't see the profile you are looking for listed here, select Other to browse the profiles folder. In the screen shot shown here I selected a known profile for the printer/paper combination I was about to print to, selected the Relative Colorimetric Rendering intent, and set the Print Sharpening to Medium and for Glossy media. The Print Settings needed to be configured for the correct media paper setting with the printer color management turned off. All I had to do then was click the Print One button to bypass the system Print dialog to make a print.

TIP

As you create custom print settings, they can be saved with as user print templates. To update an existing template, hold down the Ctrl key (Mac only), or hold down the right mouse button (both Mac and PC), select a print preset, and choose "Update with current settings" from the contextual menu. This saves the page setup and print settings to the print template preset. This can really make printing a lot more foolproof. After you have saved all your print settings to a template, there is no need to reconfigure them when you select that template again.

Exporting the edited photos

18. The Export command can be used whenever you wish to apply the Lightroom settings to an image and export that photograph (or collection of images) as a JPEG, PSD, TIFF, or DNG file. To export from Lightroom, make a selection of images either in the Library Grid or in the Filmstrip and then choose File ⇒ Export (or click the Export button). This will open the Export dialog, where you can choose which folder the images should be exported to, how you might want to rename them, and the file format you want the files to be in. In this example, I selected the For E-mail preset, which can be used to prepare low-res versions of the master photos using the sRGB color space at a size appropriate for sending by email.

Working through the book

This more or less concludes the introduction to working with Lightroom. In the remainder of the book you will explore each aspect of the program in greater depth. Lightroom has been designed almost exclusively for digital photographers. This makes my task slightly easier, because being a photographer myself I have a clearer idea of what other photographers will find important and useful to know. To this end I have structured the book to match a typical workflow, starting with the import and export of images to and from Lightroom. At the beginning of this chapter I described how the philosophy behind Lightroom was to offer "unreasonable simplicity." If Adobe has been successful in this mission, you should find that much of the Lightroom program is fairly self-explanatory. For example, if you go to the Help menu, you will see a Shortcuts item for whichever module you happen to be using at the time. **Figure 1.22** shows the shortcuts for the Library module. In keeping with the spirit of Lightroom, I have tried as much as possible to avoid discussing the technical workings of the program and have focused on discussing what Lightroom does best: managing, editing, and printing photographs. And if you really want to know more about how Lightroom works, I have reserved a technical section at the back of the book in the appendices to elaborate on features like the Lightroom native RGB space. I have also included several pages devoted to side topics that relate to working in Lightroom, and you will also find lots of quick tips in the page margins of this book.

TIP

To find out all the latest news about Adobe Photoshop Lightroom, go to the Lightroom News Web site at http://lightroom-news.com.

Library Shortcuts

View Shortcuts

Esc	Return to previous view
Return	Enter Loupe or 1:1 view
E	Enter Loupe view
C	Enter Compare mode
G	Enter Grid Mode
Command + Return	Enter Impromptu Slideshow mode
F	Cycle to next Screen Mode
Command + Option + F	Return to Normal Screen Mode
L	Cycle through Lights Out modes
J	Cycle Grid Views

Rating Shortcuts

1-5	Set ratings
Shift + 1-5	Set ratings and move to next photo
6-9	Set color labels
Shift + 6-9	Set color labels and move to next photo
0	Reset ratings to none
[	Decrease the rating
]	Increase the rating

Flagging Shortcuts

`	Toggle Flagged Status
Command + Up Arrow	Increase Flag Status
Command + Down Arrow	Decrease Flag Status

Photo Shortcuts

Command + Shift + I	Import photos
Command + Shift + E	Export photos
Command + [	Rotate left
Command +]	Rotate right
Command + E	Edit in Photoshop
Command + -	Zoom out
Command + =	Zoom in
Z	Zoom to 100%
Command + G	Stack photos
Command + Shift + G	Unstack photos
Command + R	Reveal in Finder
Delete	Remove from Library
Command + Shift + C	Copy Develop Settings
Command + Shift + V	Paste Develop Settings
Command + Left Arrow	Previous selected photo
Command + Right Arrow	Next selected photo

Quick Collection Shortcuts

B	Add to Quick Collection
Command + B	Show the Quick Collection
Command+Shift+B	Clear Quick Collection

Panel Shortcuts

Tab	Show/Hide the side panels
Shift + Tab	Hide/Show all the panels
T	Hide/Show the toolbar
Command + F	Activate the search field
Command + Option + Up Arrow	Return to the previous module

Figure 1.22 *It is always worth selecting the Shortcuts item in the Help menu—⌘ / (Mac) or Ctrl / (PC)—to find out more about the shortcuts for each module.*

Photograph: © Matt Wreford 2006
Nikon D70 | 28 mm | 400 ISO | f9 @ 1/60th

2 | Importing photos

A guide to the various ways you can bring your photos into Lightroom

Lightroom is essentially a catalog management program and raw image processor combined into one. To use Lightroom to manage your photos, you must first import them into the Lightroom catalog.

It is important, therefore, to appreciate how a program like Lightroom differs from browser programs such as Adobe Bridge, which you can point at any folder to inspect the contents. The browser approach is really suited for those times when you want the freedom to search everything on your computer. The downside of this is that you first have to know where to look to find what you are searching for. You will also be shown all the files contained in any folder, which can make image browsing quite tricky when you have to sort through all the non-image files as well. Lightroom is different. For a start, Lightroom is only interested in showing image files. And because Lightroom requires you to explicitly import photos into the catalog, you are making a conscious choice as to which photos you want to see added to the catalog.

This chapter guides you through the first stage in the Lightroom workflow: I show you how to import photos from a card, how to use the drag-and-drop method, how to import photos from their current location without having to copy the originals, and, lastly, I show you how to import photos directly from the camera.

Importing images from a card

We'll start with the most common method of file import: how to automatically import, rename, and manage your image captures each time a camera card is inserted into a card reader.

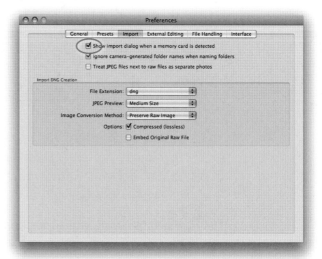

1. Before importing any photos, go to the Lightroom menu and choose Preferences. In the Import section check the "Show Import dialog when a memory card is detected" option. This lets you decide how Lightroom responds when a memory card is detected. When checked, Lightroom will automatically show the Import Photos dialog every time you connect a memory card.

EOS_DIGITAL

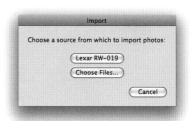

2. To start importing photos, insert a memory card into the computer so that it mounts on the Desktop. If the Show Import dialog option is unchecked, you will have to import the photos manually by choosing File ⇨ Import Photos from Device, or click the Import button in the Library module. This will open the dialog shown here, where you should click the button for the card device.

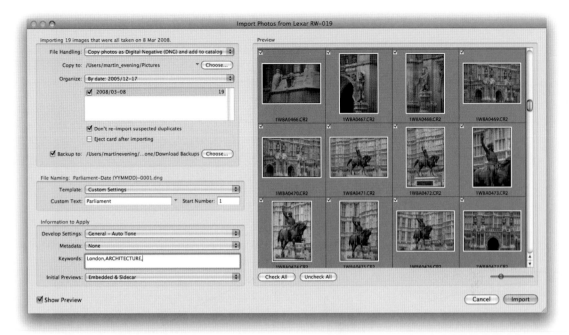

3. If the Lightroom Preferences are configured as shown in Step 1, Lightroom automatically opens the Import Photos dialog every time a card is inserted. When you check the Show Preview box, the Import Photos dialog shows thumbnail previews of all the images you are about to import and allows you to choose in advance which images to import. If you're importing from a camera card, the quickest option is to select "Copy photos to a new location and add to catalog." Alternatively, you can select the "Copy Photos as Digital Negative (DNG) and add to catalog" option. The latter makes a duplicate copy of all the images on the memory card, converts to DNG, and saves them to the folder designated in the Importing section. Check "Eject card after importing" if you want the card to be ejected at the end of the import. I won't go into detail about how to configure all the Import Photos options just yet, but I'll just mention now that it is a good idea to add metadata information that would be useful to apply in bulk, such as keywords that relate to the subject matter and a Develop setting that you want to apply to the photos as they are brought into Lightroom. Plus you can apply a custom file renaming scheme (**Figure 2.1**). New to Lightroom 2 is the ability to choose Embedded and Sidecar previews for the initial preview generation.

Figure 2.1 *You can create your own custom renaming schemes and save them as a custom template for use in the File Naming section.*

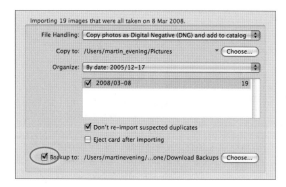

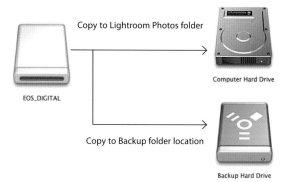

Copy to Lightroom Photos folder

EOS_DIGITAL

Computer Hard Drive

Copy to Backup folder location

Backup Hard Drive

Figure 2.2 *If you have a large number of images to import, the date calculation dialog may appear, indicating that Lightroom is reading in the capture date metadata of all the files that are available to be imported.*

4. You can also specify a secondary folder to copy the images to. Check the "Backup to" check box and then click the Choose button to specify a backup folder. This option should be mandatory whenever you are importing valuable images and want to ensure you have a backup of all your imports. After you have renamed and edited the master selection of images and have backed up these images in their modified state, you no longer need to keep the initial backup copy files. But nonetheless, it is a wise precaution at this stage to temporarily keep more than one copy of each master file stored in the system.

5. After you have configured the Import Options and clicked the Import button, Lightroom imports the files from the card to the Lightroom library. As the images are imported, the thumbnails start to appear one by one in the library Content area. If you used the "Organize by date" option and there are a lot of files to import, you may see the dialog shown in **Figure 2.2**. Meanwhile, the status indicator in the top-left corner will show the import progress. Oftentimes, there may be at least two processes taking place at once: the file import and the preview rendering. The progress bars give you a visual indication of how the import process is progressing. And if more than one operation is taking place at a time, you will see the grouped status indicator (above left). If you click the small arrow to the right, you can toggle the status indicator between each of the tasks in progress, plus the grouped indicator.

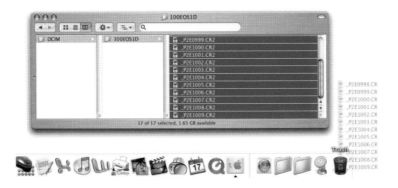

NOTE

When you choose Copy Photos as DNG and then import, the DNG converter should report a problem whenever it is unable to convert any supported raw file that has a raw file extension (including the Canon .tif extension). However, this does not guarantee that all file corruptions will be reported. Only those that the Lightroom/Adobe Camera Raw processor is able to detect will be reported.

NOTE

The backup copy images will remain in their raw format (i.e., CR2, NEF), even though the images being imported into the catalog may be converted to DNG. It's also the case that the backup files will not have any metatdata assigned to them.

6. Normally, you should not encounter any problems when importing files from a camera card. But if you choose the Copy Photos as DNG option, you will be alerted to any corruptions in the files as they are imported. After you have successfully imported all the images to the computer and backup drive (if applicable), you can safely eject the camera card and prepare it for reuse. However, at this stage I usually prefer to completely delete all the files on the card before removing it from the computer. The reason I suggest doing this is because when you reinsert the card in the camera, you won't be distracted by indications that there are still images left on the card, which might cause you to wonder whether you have removed all the images from the card (it can get confusing on a busy shoot). I would also advise you to always reformat the card (in the camera) before you start capturing more images. This is a good housekeeping practice that will help reduce the risk of file corruption as new capture files are written to the card.

Importing images from a folder

Lightroom can also import images from an existing folder on the computer. You have the option to either copy the images to the catalog (as shown in the previous example) or create a link that references the files in their current location. When importing images from a folder, it is usually more common to import them by referencing the files in their current location ("Add photos to catalog without moving").

1. If you want to manually import images from an existing folder, you can do so by clicking the Import button. If a camera card disk happens to be mounted on the computer, you will see a choice of import source options (as shown above). Or simply use the keyboard shortcut ⌘⇧Shift I (Mac) or Ctrl ⇧Shift I (PC) to bypass this dialog completely.

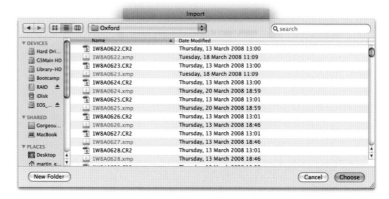

2. If a card is connected to the computer and you click the named camera card button, Lightroom takes you directly to the Import Photos dialog shown in Step 3 on page 45. But if you click the Choose Files button, a navigation menu opens from which you can choose the folder of images to import from. If there is no camera card mounted on the computer, you will just see a normal file navigation dialog at this step.

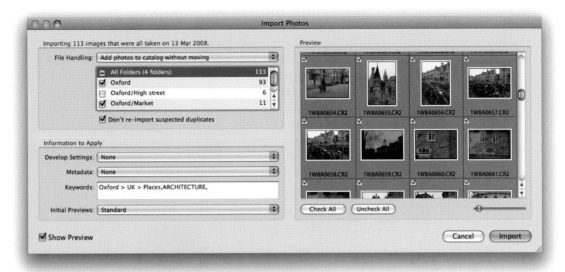

3. When you import images from a folder, the Import Photos dialog will look a little different. The folder I am about to import from happens to contain several subfolders of images, and in the example shown here I have highlighted just two of them.

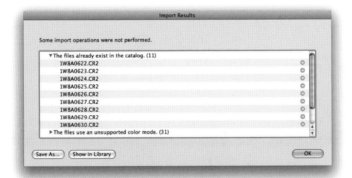

Figure 2.3 *To ensure that your layered Photoshop format (PSD) files are recognized in Lightroom, make sure that all PSD files saved out of Photoshop have the Maximum Compatibility option switched on in the Photoshop General preferences. If you are unable to import PSD files into Lightroom, try switching this option on in Photoshop and resave the PSDs, overwriting the originals.*

4. If you choose to manually import images (either by reference or by copying) from an existing folder on your computer, these may sometimes contain files that Lightroom cannot process or are already in the Lightroom catalog. If this is the case you will encounter a warning dialog like the one shown here. Lightroom is able to import all the supported raw file formats plus RGB, Lab, and grayscale images saved using the TIFF, JPEG, or PSD file formats. Non-raw images can be in 16-bits or 8-bits per channel mode, but PSD files must be saved from Photoshop with the Maximum Compatibility option switched on (**Figure 2.3**). If there are no compatibility problems, all files will successfully import.

Importing photos by copy

Let's look more carefully at the two ways in which images can be imported: by copying from a device or folder, or by referencing the source files. **Figure 2.4** shows the Import Photos dialog when importing images from a camera card. There are two file handling options: The "Copy photos to a new location and add to catalog" option makes a duplicate copy of all the images on the memory card and stores them in the designated Copy To folder and subfolder. The "Copy Photos as Digital Negative (DNG) and add to catalog" option copies the files from the card and at the same time converts them to the DNG file format. This option offers more peace of mind, because the DNG file format is widely regarded as a more versatile and therefore more appropriate file format for the long-term archival storage of raw camera files. The DNG conversion process also conveniently flags any files that happen to be corrupted as they are imported. On page 46 I showed you how the camera files were copied to the designated Lightroom Photos folder and backed up to a secondary hard drive. The "Backup to" option is therefore extremely useful, because you never know when a hard disk failure might occur. If you copy the original camera files to two separate hard drives at the import stage, the chances of losing all your camera files due to disk failure or human error will be greatly diminished.

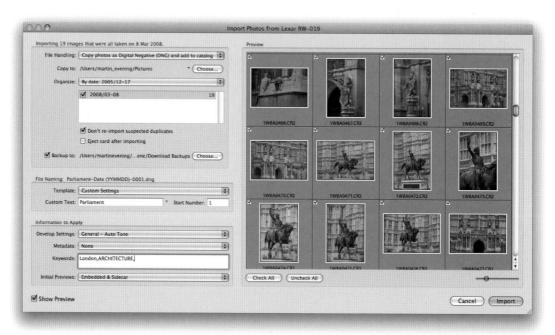

Figure 2.4 *The Import Photos dialog when importing images from a camera card.*

Organizing files imported by copy

If you import files by copy, you need to decide how they should be organized as they are added to the catalog. Very often I prefer to import all the files from a card and group them using the "Into one folder" method of organization (**Figure 2.5**). By checking the "Put in subfolder" option, you can create a unique folder (or match an existing) folder destination.

TIP

Which is the best folder organization method? If you are less than rigorous in applying keyword metadata to every image you import, then maybe it is better to import and organize your photos into named folders. You can still apply keyword metadata and have the option to search by keywords or effectively browse by folder name. But the problem with folder-based organization is how do you categorize something like a wedding? Do you organize the folder by Event > Name of couple, by Place > Location, or do you use a folder marked Family photos? If you are using keyword metadata extensively to catalog all your images, it really should not matter which folder your photos live in because you can search for everything by metadata. Therefore, organizing imports by date perhaps offers a more consistent approach to folder organization for those who regularly apply keywords to all their photos.

Figure 2.5 *If you select the "Into one folder" Organize option, all the images from the import source will be amalgamated into a single destination folder.*

Alternatively, you can select one of the "By date" segmenting options (**Figure 2.6**). If the photos you are about to import were shot over two or more days, Lightroom displays the files by segmenting them into their separate shoot dates (**Figure 2.7**). This allows you to import files by select dates only and apply the folder naming structure shown in the Organize menu list (Figure 2.6).

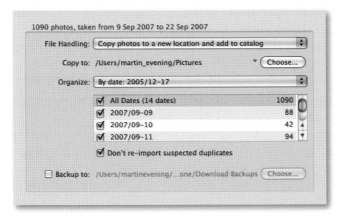

Figure 2.6 *The Import Photos Organize menu offers you a choice of ways to organize the imported images within the destination folder. You can segment the imports into one folder as shown in Figure 2.5, or use one of the date segment options shown here.*

Figure 2.7 *If you select one of the segment by date options, Lightroom will organize the imported files by date, using one of the options listed in Figure 2.6.*

Renaming options at import time

If you want to manage and track your image files successfully, it is important to rename them, and ideally this should be done at the import stage (although you can always select Library ➪ Rename Photos to do it later). The File Naming section has a pop-up menu that contains several file renaming templates that are ready for immediate use (**Figure 2.8**). For example, if you select the "Custom Name – Sequence" template, you can enter text in the Custom Text field and the imported files will be renamed using this text followed by a sequence number starting with the number entered in the Start Number box. The sample filename at the top of the File Naming section gives an advance indication of how the chosen renaming will be applied to the imported files.

If you choose the Edit option, this opens the Filename Template Editor (**Figure 2.9**). This allows you to customize and save your own File Naming template designs using tokens or data descriptors such as date. In the Figure 2.9 example, I clicked the Insert button next to the Custom Text item in the dialog to add a Custom Text token at the beginning of the File Naming template. Next, I went to the Additional section and selected a series of Date format tokens, each time clicking Insert to add one of them to the template. Then I went to the Numbering section and added a four-digit Sequence number token. This template was then saved and added to the File Naming template list.

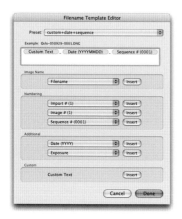

Figure 2.9 *The Filename Template Editor dialog.*

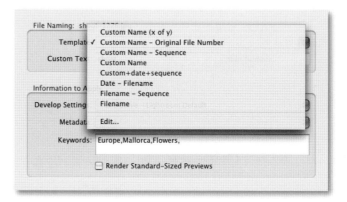

Figure 2.8 *Here is the File Naming template list, including the Custom+date+ sequence template that was created from the Filename Template settings shown in Figure 2.9. The Custom Name (x of y) template numbers the imported files using a sequence number (x) followed by a number for the total number of images in the sequence (y). The Original File Number option preserves and uses the sequence number that was added by the camera.*

Renaming catalog images later

Images can be renamed at any time after you have imported them into Lightroom. When in the Library module, you can make a selection of images via the grid or Filmstrip by selecting Library ⇨ Rename Photos (alternatively, you can use the F2 keyboard shortcut). Do this and the Rename Photos dialog shown in **Figure 2.10** appears. You can use the File Naming menu to select (or create) a custom file renaming scheme as shown in **Figure 2.11**.

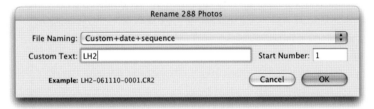

Figure 2.10 *In the Rename Photos dialog shown here, I selected a pre-created custom file renaming scheme from the File Renaming menu, entered custom text that would be utilized during the renaming, and set the Start Number to "1."*

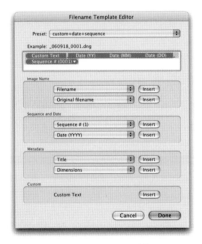

Figure 2.11 *The Filename Template Editor is used for creating custom File Naming settings.*

NOTE

The DNG (Digital Negative format) is an Adobe-devised format for archiving raw capture files.

Converting to DNG

The Convert to DNG feature is useful for converting raw files to the DNG format. While it is possible to convert other file formats such as JPEG to DNG, you only really want to use this feature for converting actual raw files to DNG, so it is best to leave the "Only convert RAW files" option selected (see **Figure 2.12**). Lightroom also lets you delete the original raw files after successfully converting them to DNG. Busy photographers will appreciate this feature because it allows you to import your raw files quickly immediately after shooting without having to convert them at the import stage. When you are busy in the studio this can easily save an hour or more of computer processing time, which is impotant when time (as we all know) is money. You can always convert the raw files to DNG at a time when it is more convenient to do so, such as after the shoot has finished.

Figure 2.12 *The Convert Photos to DNG dialog.*

Updating DNG files

The DNG file format has been around for several years now and has been widely adopted as a preferred format for archiving raw camera files. For all its benefits, one problem has been the inability to update the JPEG preview. This was not necessarily a problem if you were using DNG in Bridge or Lightroom, since the preview was referenced by the file preview cache and rebuilt when transferring a DNG file from one Lightroom/Bridge setup to another. But this approach was less convenient when working with other DNG-aware programs such as iView Media Pro. To get around this problem, go to the Meatdata menu and and choose Update DNG Previews & Metadata. This does two things: it updates the metadata the same way as the Save Metadata to Files command does. But in addition, it rebuilds the JPEG preview contained within the DNG file.

Adding metadata information at import

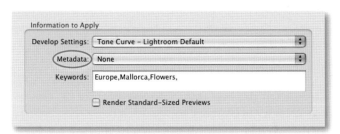

Figure 2.13 *The Information to Apply section of the Import Photos dialog.*

As you import new images by copying them to the Lightroom catalog, you can batch-add Develop settings and metadata as you do so. **Figure 2.13** shows a close-up view of the Import Photos dialog, focusing on the Develop Settings menu, which allows you to select a saved Develop setting and apply it to all the photos as they are imported. The Develop Settings menu provides access to all the settings you currently have saved in the Develop module Presets list. This is extremely useful because it means you can instruct Lightroom to apply a favorite Develop preset to new photos as they are imported.

Sensible folder naming and file naming can certainly make it easier to retrieve images later, but as your library grows you will begin to appreciate the benefit of using keywords and other metadata to help track down your images, especially when searching a large catalog collection of photographs. The Library module offers a number of ways to search for a specific image or groups of images. For example, the Metadata Browser can help you search for files using criteria such as by "Date," "Camera," or "File Type." This method of searching requires no prior input from the user of course, but in the Import Photos dialog you can go to the Metadata menu (circled in Figure 2.13) to create Metadata presets that contain regularly used International Press Telecommunications Council (IPTC) metadata information. These can be configured by choosing New from the Metadata menu and filling out the items in the New Metadata Preset dialog shown in **Figure 2.14**. Metadata presets are useful for instantly adding common information such as your contact details and image copyright status. The Keywords section can be used for adding shoot-specific metadata, such as the name of a location or a common descriptive term for all the photos you are about to import. Adding bulk metadata at the time of import can very much assist you later when conducting searches for specific images. Also, the metadata information entered at this stage will be applied to any derivative created from the master photos.

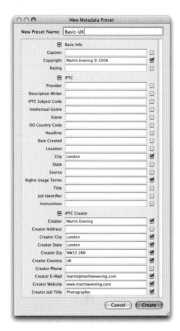

Figure 2.14 *Use the New Metadata Preset dialog to create Metadata presets that you can then use to apply to all newly imported images. The information sections shown here all conform to the standard IPTC format that is recognized throughout the industry.*

NOTE

As you type in keyword terms, Lightroom has the ability to auto-complete your entries by referring to the current Keyword Tags panel contents.

Importing existing photos from folders

If you are importing images from a preexisting folder of images, the Import Photos dialog presents you with different options. In most cases, the "Add photos to catalog without moving" option is the fastest and most practical solution (**Figure 2.15**). Although you could choose "Copy Photos to a new location and add to catalog," this is only useful if you want to import and make a backup copy of the original master files at the same time. Or you could choose the "Move Photos to a new location and add to catalog" option. This can be used if you want to move files from an intermediary location to a new location and delete the original files.

Unless you have an expensive, high-capacity RAID (Redundant Array of Independent Disks) server, it is unlikely you will have the storage capacity to keep all your catalog photos on a single drive. My work setup includes three large-volume disk drives for storing data. One is used for importing all new work images, and the other is used for storing personal and travel photographs. These are archive drives for storing the digital negative files, where the photos are imported using the copy and import option. The third drive is used for storing derivative files. These are the Photoshop-edited, layered PSD or TIFF files that have been created from the Lightroom catalog master photos. As I work on the selected images from a shoot, I find it helps to separate the derivative files in this way. What I usually do is export a selection of photos as PSDs or TIFFs to a new master folder on this other drive. This process is made easier now in Lightroom 2, because exported photos can be simultaneously added to the Lightroom catalog as part of the export process.

Figure 2.15 *Here is the Import Photos dialog for importing photos from an existing folder. Importing by reference is the best and fastest option. The other options mirror the import by copy options that are available when importing from a card.*

Importing images via drag and drop

Another way to import images into Lightroom is to simply drag and drop files from a camera card or folder into the Library module. It does not matter which folder (if any) is selected. This method of import will always open the Import Photos dialog to allow you to determine how the new images are to be imported.

TIP

Note that this method of importing works with both Mac and PC computers, but the Library module must be active.

1. To drag and drop images into the Lightroom library, locate the images you want to import and then drag them into the library grid area.

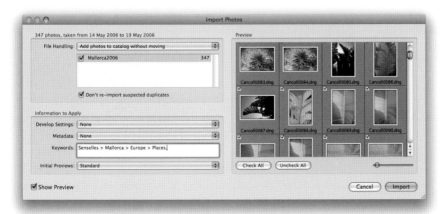

2. This action opens the Import Photos dialog and lets you decide how you want the new images to be imported.

NOTE

This particular tip works fine if
you are using Windows XP, or have
updated to Mac OS X 10.5.2 or higher.
Remember that you must navigate
to the Applications folder and add
Lightroom from there. It won't work
if you drag the program or an alias of
the program via the Finder/Explorer.

Bridge as a front end to Lightroom

Although Lightroom is advertised as being a member of the "Photoshop family," Lightroom and Photoshop do at times feel more like distant cousins rather than close relatives. People are often puzzled about the relationship between Lightroom and Adobe Bridge and why it is you can browse images easily via Bridge, but in the case of Lightroom, you have to import everything first. The following tips do assume that you already own Photoshop CS2 or later and therefore have access to Adobe Bridge, which is the browser component of the Creative Suite (Adobe Bridge comes with Photoshop whether you buy the entire Suite package or just the stand-alone program). We are not done yet with drag-and-drop methods, because in addition to the technique shown on the previous page, you can use a drag-and-drop method to manage imports via Adobe Bridge. Over the next few pages I want to show you how you can improve the flow between working in Bridge and working in Lightroom.

1. Wouldn't it be good if you could have a hot button in Bridge that took you directly to Lightroom? Well, you can. All you need to do is navigate to the Applications folder (Mac) or Programs folder (PC) and add the Lightroom program as a favorite in Bridge. Just drag the application icon to the Favorites panel so that it is added to the list of Favorites.

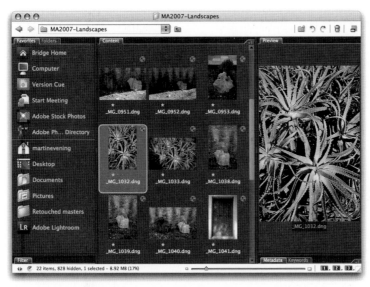

2. Once you have added Lightroom as a favorite to the Favorites panel, you can simply click on the Lightroom favorite to jump straight over to Lightroom from Bridge.

3. And then when you are in Lightroom you can use the ⌘–H (Mac) or Alt–Tab (PC) keyboard shortcut to hide the Lightroom window and return to the last used program, which in this case will be Bridge.

Adding a watched folder in Bridge

1. Following on from the last example, you can add an auto-import folder as a Bridge favorite. In Lightroom, choose File ➪ Auto ➪ Enable Auto Import and follow this by opening the Auto Import settings dialog and choose a "watched folder." Then go to Bridge and add this folder as a new Bridge Favorite.

2. You can now drag and drop images from Bridge into the designated auto-import folder. These will then be automatically imported into Lightroom and appear in the Auto Import destination folder.

Importing folders into Lightroom via Bridge

TIP

This particular tip can be really useful if you are just starting out in Lightroom and beginning to add photos to the Lightroom library. You can use Bridge as a preview browser to inspect folders before proceeding to import them. This can easily save you lots of time since you won't have to go through the Import Photos dialog to preview the images before importing. Bridge can offer you a much faster route for browsing the photos beforehand.

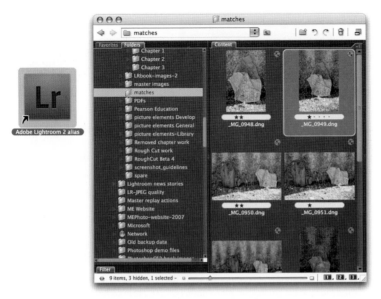

1. Unfortunately, you can't drag and drop folders from Bridge onto the Lightroom program in Favorites and have them import. But if you keep an alias/shortcut of Lightroom on the Desktop, you can drag and drop folders from the Folders panel to the alias/shortcut.

2. In this example I dragged the folder shown in Step 1 to the Adobe Lightroom alias icon, which launched the Lightroom Import Photos dialog shown here. This workflow technique will let you use Bridge to browse your computer hard disks to inspect image folders in detail before choosing which image folders to import.

Importing photos directly from the camera

Figure 2.16 *This shows the computer setup that I normally use when shooting in tethered mode in the studio using the Canon EOS 1Ds Mk III camera.*

NOTE

The Canon EOS Utility described on these pages is software that comes with the Canon EOS cameras and can also be downloaded free of charge from the Canon cameras Web site: www.canon.com (look for the download library section on the site).

At the time of this writing, there is no official support for tethered shooting in Lightroom (**Figure 2.16**). But if you can connect your camera directly to the computer and import photos to a folder, you can configure Lightroom to work in tethered mode. Photographs can be quickly brought into Lightroom, bypassing the need to import from a camera card. However, to do this Lightroom needs to rely on the use of camera manufacturer-supplied software that can communicate with the camera and download captured files to a specified folder location. Once such software is running, you can configure Lightroom to automatically import the photos directly into the catalog.

Connecting the camera to the computer

To shoot in tethered mode you need the ability to connect your camera to the computer. Ideally, you want the fastest connection possible. Most existing professional digital SLRs offer a FireWire (IEEE 1394) connection (although many cameras are now moving toward USB 2.0), which in practice allows you to shoot and download at about the same speed as you can with a fast camera memory card and in some cases quicker. The only downside is that you must have your camera connected to the computer via a FireWire or USB 2.0 cable, and this can restrict the amount of freedom you have to move about without pulling the cable out, or worse still, pulling a laptop computer off the table! Another option is to shoot wirelessly. At the time of this writing, wireless units are available for some digital SLR cameras that will allow you to transmit images directly from the camera to a base station linked to the computer. Wireless shooting offers you the freedom, up to a certain distance, to move about without the restrictions of a tethered cable. But the current data transmission speeds with some cameras are a lot slower than those you can expect from a FireWire or USB 2.0 connection. Rapid shooting via a wireless connection can work well if you are shooting in JPEG mode, but not if you intend on shooting raw files only. But of course, that may change in the future.

Camera capture software

Lightroom is able to appropriate the tethered shooting component of the camera communication software, and from there directly take over the image processing and image management. Here's how it works: The camera communication software can be configured to download the files to a specific folder location. When the files appear in this "watched" folder, Lightroom can be configured to immediately copy the files into the Lightroom library. And because the files are simultaneously deleted from the watched folder, you effectively bypass the camera software and the images appear directly in Lightroom.

It is possible to use Lightroom in conjunction with the various Canon capture software programs designed for the Canon EOS range of cameras, and over the next few pages I have outlined the steps needed to set up a Canon EOS 1Ds Mark III to automatically import files directly into Lightroom via the Canon EOS Utility program. Nikon users will find that Nikon Capture includes a Camera Control component that works the same way as the Canon software and establishes a watched folder to download the images to. The latest version of Nikon Capture supports all the D Series cameras as well as the Nikon Coolpix 8700. Alternatively, you might want to consider buying Bibble Pro software from Bibble Labs (www.bibblelabs.com). Bibble Pro (version 4.9 at this writing) enables tethered shooting with a wide variety of digital cameras, and again allows you to establish a watched folder for the downloaded images. Unfortunately, I have not yet been able to test these other programs. Whichever program you use, you should be able to adapt the following steps to automatically import tether-captured images into Lightroom.

NOTE

On Nikon equipment, you can shoot wirelessly via PTP/IP or FTP. It appears so far that PTP/IP is better and should rival FireWire, since PTP/IP is able to transfer files much faster due to the compression built into the transmission.

NOTE

Here is an interesting technology to look for in the future: Eye-Fi is about to introduce a product called Eye-Film, which is a media card incorporating 802.11b/g Wi-Fi and 1 GB of Flash storage. Eye-Film will come in the form of an SD card (a Compact Flash Type-II adapter will allow digital SLR users to put these in cameras without an SD slot). When you start shooting, the card transfers photos from within your camera to any computer with Wi-Fi support. With Eye-Film, the originals remain on the card and are transmitted to the computer. So far only JPEG files can be transmitted in this way. For more information, go to www.eye.fi.

1. To initiate a tethered shoot session you need to have the camera tethered to the computer and switched on. Next, launch the camera-supplied software, which in the example shown here is the Canon EOS Utility program. Here you can see the welcome screen, and I began by clicking the Preferences button so that I could configure the EOS Utility settings to get everything ready for tethered shooting.

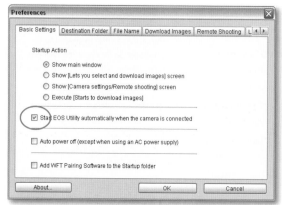

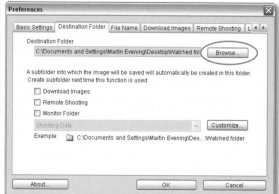

2. The preferences will vary with different tethered software programs. In this example I chose to make EOS Utility the default program that launched whenever the camera was connected to the computer. In the Destination Folder section I clicked the Browse button to select a destination folder for the downloaded images to go to. This was a new empty folder that I had added to the Desktop that was simply called "Watched Folder." I clicked the OK button to close the Preferences dialog window and this took me back to the EOS Utility welcome screen.

TIP

If you do a lot of tethered shooting
you may find the cable connector on
the camera body wears out over time.
This was particularly a problem with
the EOS 1Ds Mk I and Mk II cameras
that used a heavy FireWire cable.
One solution is a little plug adaptor
that I was able to purchase from a
company in the UK called Fixation:
www.fixationuk.com. You may be able
to obtain these elsewhere, but you'll
have to do your own search. You can
see a photo of one in **Figure 2.17**.
It is a small adaptor that you can
glue to the end of a cable, which fits
snugly into the connector socket
compartment of the supported
camera body.

3. In the welcome screen window I clicked the Camera settings/
Remote shooting button, which launched the EOS Capture
window shown here. This lets you control the camera remotely.
You can use this window to adjust the main camera settings such
as the lens aperture, shutter speed, and ISO setting. Notice at
the top of the window is the watched folder name you set in the
preferences. Click the folder icon next to it to open the Destination
Folder preferences shown in Step 2. You can click the large camera
control button in the EOS Capture window to take photographs
remotely. Or, you can use the camera body shutter release as you
would do normally.

Figure 2.17 *The adaptor shown in
this photograph can be glued to the
end of a tethered shoot cable and help
prevent it from dropping out from the
camera body.*

4. You now need to go to Lightroom to complete the tethered
link setup between Lightroom and the camera software. In the
Lightroom File menu select Auto Import ⇨ Auto Import Settings.

TIP

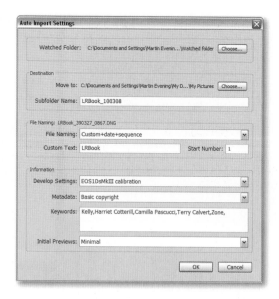

It should be possible to configure the Auto Import settings once at the beginning of a shoot and have everything you photograph subsequently be handled completely automatically. But of course, things can never be guaranteed to run so smoothly! Keep in mind that if you update the Develop settings used in the Auto Import, you need to reselect them again before you continue shooting. With some tethered software programs, having a camera tethered to the computer can quickly drain the battery. If you find this to be the case, switch the camera off between shots. Another alternative is to use a DC power supply to power the camera while working in the studio.

5. The Auto Import Settings dialog can be used to configure the import settings for the automatically imported files. These will be applied to all the images that are about to be captured and for the duration of the shoot. Click the Choose button and select the same watched folder as you selected in Step 2. Then go to the Destination section, choose a destination folder location, and enter a Subfolder Name for the current shoot. In this example I selected the same custom File Naming template as I used in Figure 2.1 and entered a short shoot description in the Custom Text field. I also selected a custom Metadata template and custom Develop Settings template. I then added some custom Keywords to apply as the files were imported.

6. After you have done that, go to the Auto Import menu again and highlight the Enable Auto Import menu item to switch it on.

The Sort order and ascending/descending order options

TIP

When you shoot using the tethered mode, it is useful to see new images appear at the top of the Content area as they are imported. To enable this feature, choose View ➪ Sort ➪ Descending. You may want to switch the sort order back to Ascending for normal editing. If the Ascending/Descending toggle action appears to be broken, it may be because you have a Custom sort order selected. Make sure the Sort order option is set to Import Order or Capture Time.

7. We are now ready to shoot tethered. Here is how it works: as you start shooting, the EOS Utility imports the camera files directly to the watched folder you selected in Step 2. From there, Lightroom recognizes that a new image has been added to the watched folder and automatically imports these captures to the new Lightroom catalog folder that was specified in Step 5, using the preconfigured Auto Import settings. Basically, once you have configured a tethered shoot setup at the beginning of a shoot, you can leave all the settings as they are and continue taking pictures all day, apart from the times where you might need to edit the Keywords for a particular shot or apply a different default develop setting.

Speedier tethered shooting

You will notice that although I am normally a Macintosh user, I choose to run Lightroom via the Windows XP operating system when shooting tethered. This is because the Canon software happens to work about 4–5 times faster in Windows than it does on the Mac. This situation may change with further program or operating system updates, but it is worth keeping an open mind and exploring different combinations of software and operating systems when trying to find the ideal combination for your camera tethered shoot setup (see side panel).

NOTE

After purchasing a new EOS 1Ds Mk III and Intel iMac computer, I did a lot of testing to find out what would give me the greatest speed advantage when shooting tethered. In the tests I conducted, I discovered that the Canon Utility software is capable of downloading the Mk III files at a data transfer rate of approximately 12 MB per second via the USB 2 interface, running on Windows XP. You have to add to this the time it takes for the photos to appear in Lightroom (roughly a further second per image). Even so, this is certainly quicker than downloading from a fast camera card and is one more reason why shooting tethered can prove to be the speediest shooting option. Other tethered shooting setups definitely have slower data transfer rates of just a few MBs per second. It is therefore always worth investigating different options to find which tethered workflow will allow you to work best with Lightroom.

TIP

If you need to reconcile changes made to the folder contents at the system level, you can go to the Library module Library menu and choose "Synchronize folder." This will force Lightroom to scan the system folder to see if the contents match the associated Lightroom catalog folder and let you update the Lightroom catalog, synching deletions and importing any photos that are missing in the current catalog. See **Figure 2.18** for the alert that appears when you move files to a new disk location.

Figure 2.18 *If moving a folder via Lightroom means moving the files to a new disk location, Lightroom alerts you to this, meaning that the move process may take a little longer to accomplish than expected. There may be a further warning if there is not enough room on the destination drive.*

How imported photos are organized

As you import photos into the Lightroom catalog, the folders will appear listed in the Folders panel, which is in some ways like a normal list tree folder view that you would find in a file browser program. However, there are some important differences to note here. The Folders panel will only display image folders of photos that have been explicitly imported into the catalog. The folders are primarily displayed by hard drive volume and in alphabetical order, showing the root folder first (such as My Pictures). These can be expanded to reveal any subfolders in the folder hierarchy. For example, **Figure 2.19** shows a typical Folders panel view, which happens to contain four drive volumes. In the Library-HD volume there is a root-level folder called Pictures that contains several image subfolders. When you compare this with the operating system folder, you can see the exact same set of folders are listed there as well. When working with the Folders panel, you can rename folders, change the hierarchy order, move files and folders from one location to another, or delete them. Whatever you do in Lightroom will always be reflected at the system level. One benefit of this approach is that you can more easily switch between working in Lightroom and a file browser program such as Adobe Bridge. However, if you rename a folder at the system level, or move the location of a folder, the link between the system folder and the Lightroom catalog folder will become broken and the Lightroom catalog folder name will appear dimmed with a question mark. In these situations you can easily restore the link by following the instructions given in **Figure 2.20** and click on the question mark that appears in the thumbnail cell to restore the broken link. If a hard drive volume is off-line, the volume header will appear dimmed and the off-line folders will have a question mark.

Image management by metadata

Lightroom takes full advantage of the metadata already contained in the image files and the metadata that is added as you import your pictures into Lightroom. It then helps you use this information to make the searching for and grouping of images faster and easier to accomplish. In many respects, the way Lightroom manages the catalog is more like iTunes in that it uses the image file metadata for the image organization and management. This process kicks in as soon as you import new images and are offered the chance to enter a new folder name and add custom keywords. These are all vital pieces of metadata information that will help Lightroom keep track of the images in the catalog.

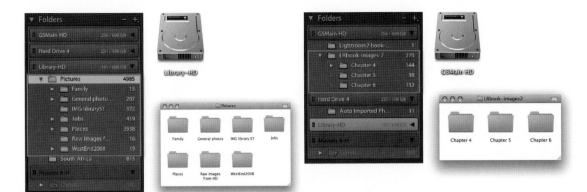

Figure 2.19 *The Folders panel displays the folders of all the photos that have been imported into Lightroom. In the example shown here, the Folders panel view of the Lightroom catalog shows that the imported photos came from two separate drives. On the left, you see how the contents of the Pictures folder on the Library HD drive are all grouped identically in the Pictures folder in the Folders panel. On the right you see how the contents of the LRbook-images2 folder on the G5Main HD drive relate to the LRbook-images2 folder in the Folders panel.*

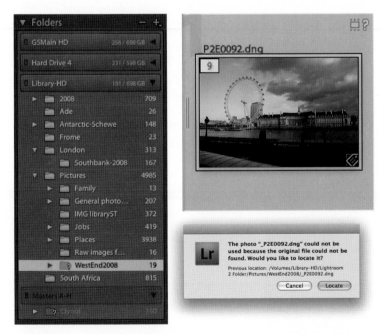

Figure 2.20 *If for some reason the link is broken between a thumbnail in a folder and its source image, the Folder listing will appear dimmed and show a question mark, while the thumbnail image will also have a question mark in the top-right corner of the cell. You can restore a link by clicking the thumbnail cell question mark, which displays the warning dialog shown here. Click the Locate button to relocate the original source photo on the computer. Correct the link for one image and you will find that all the other photos in the folder should relink.*

Photograph: Cape Point, South Africa, © Martin Evening 2005
Canon EOS 1Ds Mk I | 45 mm | 200 ISO | f6.3 @ 1/1000th

3 | Navigating the Library module

Tips for navigating the Catalog module and how to make refined selections of photos

In this chapter we are going to take a first look at the Library module and in particular, how to use the Library module controls to navigate the photos in your catalog. Lightroom uses fast image caching methods to build preview images of all your imported photos and from there you can quickly navigate and view any of the pictures in the catalog. You can select individual images, zoom in and zoom out, see multiple selections of images all at once on the screen, and compare single shots alongside others. Plus now in Lightroom 2 you can do this over two displays at once, or as a second window on your main display.

We will also look at the tools you can use to refine your image selections, through the use of flags or by rating your images with stars to mark the pictures that you like most. From there you can use the filtering tools in the Library module to make selections of specific photos or create shortlists of your favorites. You can then decide which photos you wish to keep in the Lightroom catalog and how you should handle those images that have been left unmarked or marked as rejects.

The Library Module panels

When the Library module is selected, the contents of the catalog are displayed in the Content area in a Grid view, which gives you a multiple-image view using a grid cell layout; Loupe view, which shows a magnified, single-image view; Compare view, which lets you compare two photos side by side; or Survey view, where all the photos in a current selection are displayed in the Content area. The Library module controls are split between the left and right panels (**Figure 3.1**). The Catalog panel provides you with a fast way to view the contents of the entire library, a Quick Collection of images, or the Previous Import of recently acquired images. The Folders panel lists all the folders in the catalog in volume and alphabetical order and only displays the folders of those photos that have been explicitly imported or referenced to Lightroom. You can use the Folders panel to select specific image folders, but as you will see, there are also several other ways you can search and locate photos in the catalog. The Collections panel allows you to select a group of photos from the catalog and save them as a named collection. However, an individual image can exist in any number of collections. New to Lightroom 2 is the ability to create "Smart Collections" that automatically create collections based on customized settings. You can also make Quick Collections by pressing the B key to mark favorite images. These can then be viewed by selecting Quick Collection in the Library panel. The new Filter bar (located at the top of the Content area) combines the previous Find panel and Filmstrip filters and provides a one-stop location for making refined photo selections based on text searches, ratings, and/or metadata. For example, you can filter the catalog based on a keyword search combined with a ratings filter, followed by a metadata filter based on which camera the photograph was taken with. Quick Develop offers basic Develop module controls, which allow you to make basic Develop adjustments without having to pop over to the Develop module. The Keywording panel is where you go to enter or edit new keyword metadata, plus you can select keyword sets including the new "Suggested Keywords" set, which offers adaptable keyword suggestions based on your current photo selection. Keywords can be applied to images by dragging and dropping keywords onto selections in the Content area or dragging images onto keywords, or by making a selection and adding keywords via the Keywording panel on the right. Other metadata information, such as the camera's EXIF data, can be viewed via the Metadata panel, which offers several data list view options. You can use this panel to add custom IPTC data such as the title, caption, and copyright tag.

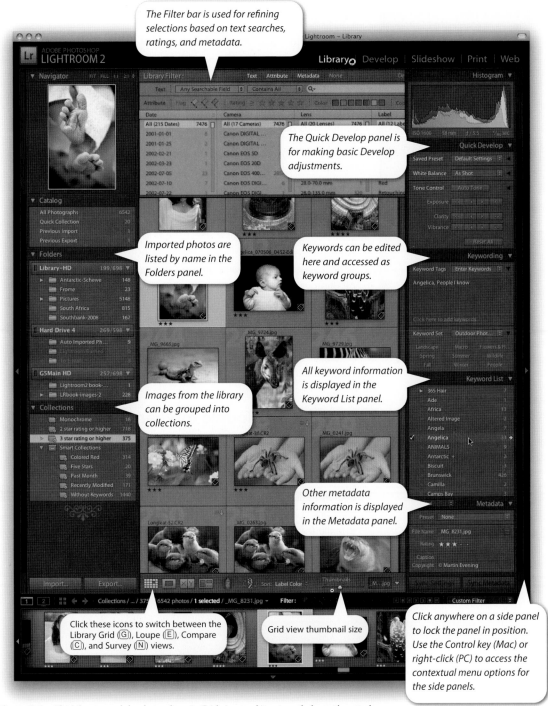

The Filter bar is used for refining selections based on text searches, ratings, and metadata.

The Quick Develop panel is for making basic Develop adjustments.

Imported photos are listed by name in the Folders panel.

Keywords can be edited here and accessed as keyword groups.

All keyword information is displayed in the Keyword List panel.

Images from the library can be grouped into collections.

Other metadata information is displayed in the Metadata panel.

Click these icons to switch between the Library Grid (G), Loupe (E), Compare (C), and Survey (N) views.

Grid view thumbnail size

Click anywhere on a side panel to lock the panel in position. Use the Control key (Mac) or right-click (PC) to access the contextual menu options for the side panels.

Figure 3.1 *The Library module, shown here in Grid view and its expanded panel controls.*

Figure 3.2 *The Navigator panel.*

Figure 3.3 *In the Library panel you can select All Photographs, a current Quick Collection, or just the most recently imported images from the Previous Import. All Photographs shows two numbers: the number of visible images followed by the total number of images in the library. Some of the items that appear in the Catalog panel are temporary collections and can be removed via a right-click.*

TIP

Remember to select All Photographs in the Catalog panel if you want to deselect all folders in the Folders panel and add a new, root-level folder.

Navigator panel

The Navigator panel (**Figure 3.2**) displays a large preview of the currently selected image and offers a number of controls for zooming and scrolling the photo (see page 88). The Navigator panel will also update as you roll the mouse over the Folders panel or Collections panel lists. When you do this it will preview the first photo that appears in the folder, thus providing a visual reference to make it easier to locate the folder you are looking for.

The Catalog panel

The Catalog panel displays information about the catalog and allows you, for example, to quickly select the photos that were most recently imported or the current Quick Selection photos. The All Photographs option selects all the images in the catalog. Always remember to select All Photographs if you want a filter search to include all photos in the catalog. It's easy to forget this and wonder why a search turned up no results! As you work with Lightroom, other items will appear on the list such as Missing Photos. Some of these are temporary and can be removed: right-click to access the contextual menu and click "Remove Temporary collection" (**Figure 3.3**).

The Library module toolbar

The default Library module toolbar contains the Grid, Loupe, Compare, and Survey view buttons, plus the Painter, Sort control, Thumbnail size and Info window (**Figure 3.4**). But you can customize the toolbar by adding Rating, Flagging, Color labels, Rotate, Navigate and Slideshow playback controls (the Library module toolbar can be customized individually for both Grid and Loupe views). It is useful having the toolbar visible, but you can use the T keyboard shortcut to toggle showing and hiding the toolbar.

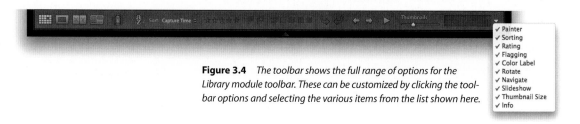

Figure 3.4 *The toolbar shows the full range of options for the Library module toolbar. These can be customized by clicking the toolbar options and selecting the various items from the list shown here.*

Folders panel

The Folders panel provides front-end management for all the folders that make up the Lightroom catalog. The one rule you have to bear in mind here is that there can only be one master version of an image in the Lightroom catalog. This means you can't make copies of the master image or assign images to more than one folder. After images have been imported into the Lightroom Catalog they can be grouped into folders any way you like (as long as they are stored on the same volume). Any changes you make to the folder structure in Lightroom are reflected at the system level, and the system files and folders will always correspond with the hierarchy of the Folders panel in Lightroom. Similarly, as you move folders around or rename them at the system level, these changes are recognized and updated in the Lightroom Folders panel. **Figure 3.5** shows how imported folders are listed alphabetically in the volumes they are stored on. As well as rearranging the hierarchy of folders, you can freely move images from one folder to another and the Volume header bars can be collapsed, making it easy to view the folders by individual volumes. See page 219 for more about the Catalog/Folders relationship.

Filter bar

The Filter bar (**Figure 3.6**) consists of a Text search by filename, caption, metadata, and so forth. The Refine section duplicates the filter controls at the bottom of the Filmstrip, while the Metadata section replaces the Metadata Browser in the left panels section and lets you filter by metadata. This offers a neater solution compared to Lightroom 1, where you had to negotiate the Keyword Tags panel, navigating through every keyword in the catalog to find the specific keywords to filter by. With this new method, the metadata search options reduce as you narrow the search criteria at each stage. On the downside, it wastes space in the Content area. But you can use the \ keyboard shortcut to toggle showing/hiding the Filter bar display.

Figure 3.5 *The Folders panel displays imported image folders by volume and in alphabetical order. The green light in the volume header indicates that a disk drive is connected and has ample spare storage space, and the numbers in the bar indicate the number of free GB of data alongside the GB capacity of a drive. If a disk drive is currently off-line, the volume name appears in black and if a folder name is dimmed, this means there are broken links to one or more of the images within that folder.*

TIP

If you hold down the Shift key as you click the Text, Refine, and Metadata options, you can add them to the Filter bar display. Shift–click again to remove each one and return to single option displays.

Figure 3.6 *The new Library module Filter bar.*

TIP

You can use a drag and drop to rearrange the image order in both the Library Grid and Filmstrip.

Exploring the Library module

Grid View options

As new photos are imported, low-resolution previews will appear in the Grid view. If you selected the Standard-Sized Previews option at the import stage, the initial rendering may take a little longer but you will see better-quality previews. If the camera used to capture the images has camera orientation embedded in the metadata, the thumbnail previews will automatically correctly rotate to portrait or landscape accordingly. Otherwise, you can use the rotate buttons to manually turn the previews or use the keyboard shortcuts (⌘⟮ rotate left and ⌘⟯ rotate right (use Ctrl⟮ and Ctrl⟯ if on a PC).

To open the Library View Options, go to the View menu, select View Options (or press ⌘J [Mac] or Ctrl J [PC]) and choose Grid View. There are two modes for the Library Grid View: Compact Cells (see **Figure 3.7**) and Expanded Cells (**Figure 3.8**). The General cell view options allow you to select items that can be common to both view modes, such as Include Quick Collection Markers and Include Pick Flags. The "Show clickable items on mouse over only" option refers to the Quick Collection markers and rotation buttons. When this is checked, clickable items will only be revealed as you roll the mouse over a grid cell. When the "Tint grid cells with color labels" option is checked, this shades the entire cell border when a color label is applied to a photo. In the Cell Icons section,

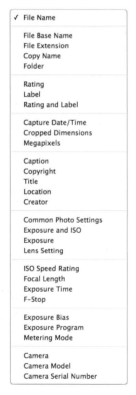

Figure 3.7 *The label options available in Compact Cell Extras in the Library View Options menu.*

Figure 3.8 *The Library View Options dialog.*

check the Flags option if you want the image's flag status to appear in the cell border. The Flag icons indicate if an image has been identified as a pick (■) or as a reject (■) (see pages 100–101 for more about working with flags). If a photo has been added to a Quick Collection, it will be identified in the Grid view with a filled circle Quick Selection Marker in the top-right corner. You can also click inside this circle to toggle between adding or removing an image from a Quick Collection. The Thumbnail Badges are the small icons you see in the bottom-right corner. Three types of icons can be displayed here. If you double-click the icon with the label tag (■), it automatically takes you to the Keywording panel in the Library module, where you can start adding or editing keywords linked to this particular image. If you double-click the rectangle icon (■), this takes you to the Develop module with the Crop overlay made active. If you double-click the plus/minus icon (■), this takes you directly to the Develop module. Let me also point out a useful shortcut here. Alt–double-clicking in a grid cell takes you directly to the Develop module, and Alt–double-clicking on a photo in the Develop module takes you directly back to the Library Grid view. Check the Unsaved Metadata option if you wish to see an alert in the top-right corner when a photo's metadata is out of sync with the main catalog (this is discussed later in Chapter 4).

Figure 3.9 shows an example of a Compact Cell view (which is the default view when you first launch Lightroom). This particular cell view has the grid cell Index Number (the large dimmed number in the cell background) displayed in the Top Label section, along with a custom item from the Figure 3.7 list. The Bottom Label section has room for the Rotation buttons plus one other custom item from the Figure 3.7 list. When Rating is selected, the image rating is displayed using stars, with five stars as the highest rated and no stars as the lowest. Although it is possible to assign ratings by clicking on the dots in the grid cell area, a more common way to assign ratings is by entering numbers or using the square bracket keys ([,]) on the keyboard.

Figure 3.10 shows an example of an Expanded Cells view. Use the Show Header with Labels check box in the Expanded Cell Extras section to turn the header display options on or off. With the Expanded Cells view there is room for two rows of information in the header, and you can use the four pull-down menus to completely customize what information is displayed here. You can also select which items to include in the footer by checking the Rating, Color Label, and Rotation options. That concludes all the customizable options for the grid cells, but note that pressing ⌘ Shift H (Mac) or Ctrl Shift H (PC) toggles showing and hiding all the items in the grid cells.

This is a "flagged pick" image.

A filled circle indicates the image has been added to a Quick Collection.

Filename

Index number

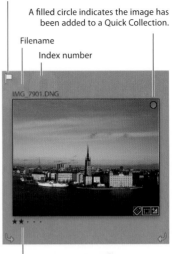

Image rating status

Figure 3.9 *Here is an enlarged view of a Library grid cell in Compact Cells mode.*

Index number   File extension

Cropped dimensions   Filename

Image rating status   Label color

Rotate thumbnail   Rotate thumbnail
counterclockwise   clockwise

Figure 3.10 *Here is an enlarged view of a Library grid cell in the Expanded Cells view.*

TIP

When making image selections via the Library Grid or Filmstrip, use the ⇧Shift key to make a contiguous selection of images, that is, a continuous selection from point A to point C. Use the ⌘ key (Mac) or Ctrl key (PC) to make a noncontiguous (nonconsecutive) selection of images. You can use the forward slash key (/) as a shortcut for deselecting the most active photo in a grid selection.

TIP

Macintosh users may experience problems navigating using the keyboard arrows. If so, go to the System Preferences, select Keyboard & Mouse, and where you see "Full Keyboard Access: In windows and dialogs, press Tab to move the keyboard focus between," check the "Text boxes and Lists only" button.

TIP

Use the + key and – key to increase or decrease the cell size by one cell per row.

Library Grid navigation

The Grid view is the main way you can browse photos in the catalog (**Figure 3.11**). You can make the thumbnail size bigger or smaller by dragging the Thumbnails slider at the bottom, and you can navigate the grid by clicking on individual grid cells or use the arrow keys on the keyboard to move from one cell to the next. As explained in Chapter 1, the Library Grid is displayed in the main Content area, and the side panels can be hidden by double-clicking a panel's inner edges or just clicking the side bar arrows, which will collapse the panels to the edge of the screen. Panels can then be revealed by rolling the mouse cursor toward either side of the screen, or locked in place by clicking the side bar arrow. An even easier way to manage the Library Grid view is to use the Tab key, which toggles displaying the Content area with both side panels in view and enlarging the Content area to fill the width of the screen completely.

Click the arrow or anywhere on the side bar to collapse or expand a side panel.

Thumbnail cell size slider

Figure 3.11 *This shows the catalog contents displayed in Grid view. Note how the Content area image selection, showing all the images in the Ade folder, is duplicated in the Filmstrip below. You can navigate the grid either by clicking on an image in the Grid or Filmstrip, or by using the highlighted arrow keys on the keyboard to move from one image to the next. The Home and End keys can be used to jump to the first or last image in the grid, and you can also scroll through the grid by using the Page Up and Page Down keys.*

Working in Loupe view

Lightroom has two Loupe viewing modes: standard Loupe view and close-up Loupe view. Standard Loupe view either fits the whole of the image within the Content area or fills the Content area with the narrowest dimension—Fit or Fill (**Figure 3.12**). Close-up Loupe view can be at 1:1 magnification or a custom view setting such as 2:1. The simplest way to get to the Loupe view is to double-click an image in the grid or Filmstrip. If you have more than one image currently selected, the image you double-click fills the screen. The selected group will still be preserved in the Filmstrip, and you then can use the left and right arrow keys only to navigate through those pictures. If you double-click the Loupe view image, you will return to the Grid view once more. In the accompanying sidebar notes I have listed some of the other keyboard shortcuts you can use for switching views.

NOTE

There are some alternative keyboard shortcuts for navigating between the Grid and Loupe views. The Ⓖ key always takes you to the Library Grid view from whichever module you are currently in. Likewise, the Ⓔ key always takes you to the Library module Loupe view. The ⌘➕ key combination takes you from Grid to Loupe view and the ⌘➖ key combination takes you from Loupe back to Grid view.

NOTE

The selected thumbnail previews are shown in the Grid and Filmstrip with a light gray surround. Within any selection there will always be a primary, or most selected image (this will be the image displayed in the Navigator). In the grid or Filmstrip, the primary selected image is the one shaded a slightly lighter gray than all the other selected thumbnail cells.

A selection is a temporary collection of images, and selections can be used in many different ways. For example, you might want to make a selection and apply a rating to all the selected images at once. Or you might want to select a group of images in order to synchronize the Develop settings. In that case you would synchronize the settings to whichever is the most selected image.

Figure 3.12   *Here is an image shown in Loupe view. An active selection is visible in the Filmstrip. You can use the left/right arrow keys to navigate such a selection.*

Working with photos in both Grid and Loupe views

1. In the Grid view mode you can make a selection of photos and the selection will be mirrored in the Filmstrip below.

2. If you use Quick Develop to make Develop adjustments, these will be applied to all the photos in the Grid and Filmstrip selection (the Quick Develop panel is ideal for such adjustments). In this step, I increased the Vibrance for all the selected photos.

3. However, if you go to the Loupe view mode and apply a Quick
    Develop adjustment (such as convert to Grayscale), it will only be
    applied to the current photo, even though the photo selection
    remains active in the Filmstrip (you can use the ⌘+left/right arrow
    keys [Mac] or Ctrl+left/right arrow keys [PC] to navigate from one
    photo to the next).

Click anywhere in this shaded area to deselect a selection of photos.

4. Back in the Grid view you can deselect a photo selection by click-
    ing anywhere in the cell border area to deselect the other photos.

Loupe view options

The Loupe View options within the Library View Options let you
customize what is displayed when you switch to the Loupe view. In
Figure 3.13, I customized the Loupe View options for Loupe Info 1
to overlay the image with the File Name, the Date Time, and Cropped
Dimensions. This appears information briefly when an image is first
displayed in the Loupe view (**Figure 3.14**).

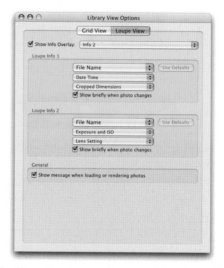

Figure 3.13   *The Library View Options dialog showing the Loupe View settings.*

Figure 3.14   *Here is how the information is displayed for Loupe Info 1 when you
view images with the Show Info Overlay option checked. If the "Show Briefly when
photo changes" option is selected, the Info display fades out after a few seconds.*

Loupe view navigation

From the standard Loupe view you can magnify the image preview in a number of ways. A further click zooms the Loupe view preview to a 1:1 magnification, centered on the mouse. Another click takes you back to the previous Loupe view. So clicking on the photo shown in Figure 3.14, near the left eye (in standard Loupe view), will make the preview zoom in to provide the close-up view shown in **Figure 3.15**.

You can now scroll the photo by click-dragging the photo and navigating in the close-up view mode. In the top-left corner of the Library module is the Navigator, which offers you an alternative way to navigate your photos. In the magnified view in Figure 3.15, the rectangle in the Navigator represents the area that is currently visible in the Content area, relative to the whole image. You can drag the rectangle to quickly scroll the image with a minimum amount of mouse movement. And lastly, you have the Zoom view slider in the toolbar. This lets you magnify the image even more from a Fit to window view, right up to 11:1 magnification.

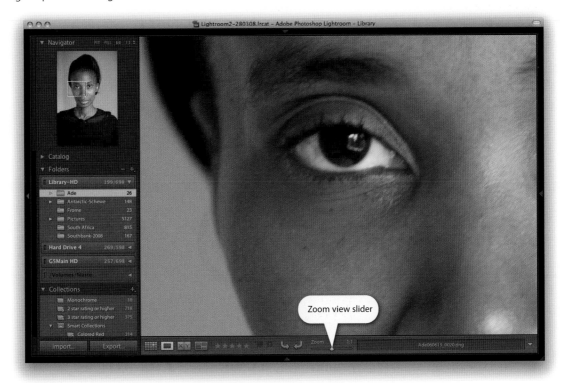

Figure 3.15   *In Loupe view, you can scroll the image by dragging the rectangle in the Navigator, which indicates the area currently being magnified. You can also use the Zoom view slider to quickly adjust the zoom level.*

Figure 3.16 *The thumbnail and standard Loupe previews will start off looking pixelated and quite possibly flat in color. These will change appearance as the Lightroom settings kick in and render a Lightroom preview version that replaces the original preview.*

The Auto Tone adjustment logic has been changed for version 2. Lightroom tends now do a better job estimating which Develop settings to apply when you select Auto Tone.

About the Lightroom previews

When you first import new photos, Lightroom will make use of whatever thumbnails are embedded in the file and use them to populate the Library grid. Lightroom then automatically builds larger, standard-sized previews of the photos which, depending on the camera default settings you are using, will usually cause the thumbnail to change appearance. In **Figure 3.16** you can see a typical example of the appearance change from the low-res, camera-embedded JPEG thumbnail to the Lightroom-generated preview.

Establishing the default Develop settings

Some people say they prefer the look of the camera-generated previews, and in some cases the camera-embedded preview may indeed look better. Often it is because they have not yet established a suitable camera default setting. In the Lightroom preferences (**Figure 3.17**) you can check the "Apply auto tone adjustments" option in the Presets section, which automatically applies Auto Tone adjustments every time you import a new set of photos. This usually produces a snappier-looking photo (like the lower preview shown in Figure 3.16). The downside is that this default setting will be applied to all newly imported photos and the Auto Tone setting does not always work so well for all types of images, particularly those shot using controlled studio lighting.

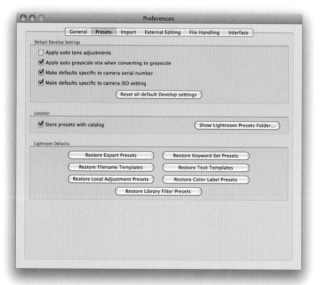

Figure 3.17 *If you open the Lightroom Preferences (⌘-⸴, [Mac], Ctrl-⸴ [PC]), you can check or uncheck the default Develop settings as described in the main text.*

If while you are working in the Develop module and create a Develop setting that you feel is suited to the processing requirements of a particular camera, you can go to the Develop menu and choose Set Default Settings. This will open the dialog shown in **Figure 3.18** where you can click the Update to Current Settings button to update the default settings for the camera model listed in the same dialog. But if at the same time you have "Make defaults specific to camera serial number" and "Make defaults specific to camera ISO setting" checked in the Lightroom Presets preferences (see Figure 3.17), clicking Update to Current Settings will make the default setting specific to the camera serial number and ISO setting. The combination of the Set Default Settings and Default Develop Settings preferences will therefore allow you to establish the default settings that are applied to all newly imported photos and how the previews look when they are first rendered by Lightroom as thumbnails and standard Loupe view previews.

Figure 3.18   *When you select the Set Default Develop settings option you can update the default Develop settings for any camera. Depending on how the Lightroom Presets preferences have been configured, this action may apply the defaults to the camera type only, a specific camera serial number, or a combination of a specific camera body and ISO setting.*

Preview size and quality

To set the Standard preview size, choose File ⇨ Catalog Settings. This will open the Catalog Settings dialog shown in **Figures 3.19** and **3.20**, where you can determine the pixel size for the Standard size previews. My advice here is to select a pixel size that is suited to the size of display you are working with. If you are using a small laptop computer, then you won't need the standard-sized previews to be any bigger than 1,024 pixels in either dimension. If you are using a large 30" screen, then it is better to select the largest preview size available. Since the preview pixel dimensions will also affect the size of the preview file cache, it makes sense to keep the cache size as small as possible. There is no point in making the standard previews unnecessarily large since this will simply consume more hard drive space than you need to. The

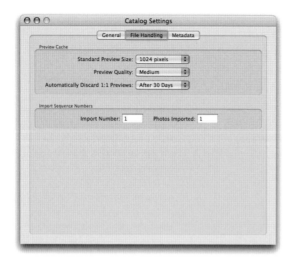

Figure 3.19 *For smaller-sized displays there will be no need to set the Standard Preview Size any larger than 1,024 pixels. Also, if hard drive space is at a premium, then set the Preview Quality to Low or Medium.*

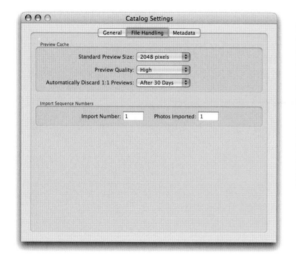

Figure 3.20 *If you are working with a large screen such as a 30" monitor, then set the Standard Preview Size to 2048. If you set the Preview Quality to High, this will ensure the best-quality previews are generated and that they are archived using the ProPhoto RGB space.*

preview quality will determine how much compression is applied to the preview files. A Low Preview Quality compresses the previews more, at the expense of image quality, while a Medium setting uses less compression and produces larger, better-quality previews. The High setting uses the least amount of compression for the best image preview quality.

Over in the Import Photos dialog (**Figure 3.21**) you will see the Initial Preview menu where you can select Minimal, which will import photos as quickly as possible without devoting resources to building previews just yet. The Embedded & Sidecar option makes use of previews embedded in the original image or sidecar file. This can help speed up the import process from a camera card, and let you see some kind of image preview right away, but the previews will only offer a rough guide to image appearance. You can force Lightroom to build Standard previews as the files are imported, or choose 1:1, which will go the whole nine yards and force a full-sized preview (this can really slow down the import times). Fortunately, Lightroom will prioritize importing the photos first before proceeding to render the finer-quality previews.

Figure 3.22 *The Discard Photos warning dialog. Note here that if you have just one photo selected, the dialog gives you the option of discarding one photo (the selected image), discard all, or cancel.*

When you point Lightroom at a particular folder, it will, as a matter of course, build 1:1, full-sized previews of all images; Lightroom will do this in the background as and when it can. But not every image will be seen to have a 1:1 preview because the process does take a while to complete. Therefore, it depends on how long you spend with a particular folder in view. However, you can force Lightroom to generate 1:1 previews by choosing Library ⇨ Previews ⇨ Render 1:1 Previews. Large previews are useful because they speed up the time it takes to review images at a 1:1 zoom view, but they can also be costly in terms of taking up room on the hard disk. So the options available here will allow you to automatically discard 1:1 Previews after a designated period of time or not at all, if you think you have the drive capacity to handle a *Catalog Previews.lrdata* file that keeps growing in size.

Figure 3.21 *A detail view of the Import Photos dialog, showing Initial Preview options.*

Generating the 1:1 previews

Standard previews are generated quickly from the master file, but crucially skip applying the sharpening and noise reduction steps. The full-sized, 1:1 previews are rendered with the sharpening and noise reduction included and therefore take longer to generate. Lightroom automatically generates 1:1 previews once all the standard-sized previews have been rendered, but will make this a low-priority task. If you need to prioritize building the full-sized previews, then go to the Library menu and choose Previews ⇨ Render 1:1 Previews. This forces Lightroom to generate 1:1 previews and regenerate the standard-sized previews at the same time.

Figure 3.23 *Here is a view of the Navigator panel, showing all the available custom Zoom view options. They can range from 1:4 (25%) to 8:1 (800%) and all the way up to 11:1. But as in the movie* This Is Spinal Tap, *I suspect the real zoom value here is in fact closer to 10:1.*

Loupe zoom views

As mentioned earlier, there are actually four different Loupe views and the Navigator panel displays a zoom view readout of each in the top-right corner. They are in order of magnification: Fit view, which magnifies the standard Loupe view to fill the available Content area both horizontally and vertically; Fill view, which magnifies the standard Loupe view to fill the width of the available Content area on-screen, cropping the top and bottom of the picture as necessary; close-up Loupe view, which offers a standard 1:1 view; and lastly, the fourth close-up view mode, which offers customizable magnification levels. You can extend the range of the close-up Loupe view by selecting a zoom view from the Navigator fly-out menu (**Figure 3.23**). It's important to understand that the Loupe zoom essentially offers two zoom modes: a standard and a close-up view. You can use the Navigator panel to set the standard view to Fit or Fill, and the close-up view to either 1:1 or one of the custom magnified views. The zoom view modes you select via the Navigator panel will establish how Lightroom behaves when you use either a single click or the Spacebar to toggle between the two zoom views.

Loupe view shortcuts

You can use the ⌘ key (Mac) or Ctrl key (PC) with the + key to zoom in progressively from the Grid view to the standard Loupe view to the magnified Loupe view. And you can use the ⌘ key (Mac) or Ctrl key (PC) with the = (minus) key to progressively zoom out again. If you use the ⌘ Alt key (Mac) or Ctrl Alt key (PC) with the + and = buttons, you can zoom in and out in gradual increments for the close-up Loupe view.

Working in Survey view

If you have multiple image selections active, you can view them all at once by clicking the Survey view button in the Library module toolbar. Alternatively, you can switch to Survey view while in any module at any time by using the N key. Whenever you are in Survey view, the Content area is used to preview the selected images as big as possible. **Figure 3.24** shows a Survey view of all the photos that have been selected via the Filmstrip. (We'll discuss the Filmstrip a bit later in this chapter.) The arrangement and size of the individual previews will dynamically adjust according to the number of photos you have selected and the amount of screen real estate that is available in the Content area.

The primary, or most selected, image is shown with a white border, and you can navigate the images displayed in the Survey view by click-selecting individual photos or using the left and right arrow keys. You can remove images from a Survey view selection by clicking on the X in the bottom-left corner, or by ⌘–clicking (Mac) or Ctrl–clicking (PC) the photos you want to deselect (either in the Content area or via the Filmstrip). The image previews will automatically resize to make full use of the screen space available.

NOTE

Removing a photo from Survey view simply removes it from the selection. It does not remove a photo from the catalog.

NOTE

The relationship between the Survey and Loupe view is the same as that between the Grid and Loupe view. If you double-click an image in a Survey view, you will be taken to the standard Loupe view. Double-clicking will take you back to the Survey view.

Figure 3.24 *Shown here is an image selection made via the Filmstrip in the Library module Survey view. To navigate through the selected images, use the left and right arrow keys only, as shown highlighted above.*

Working in Compare view

If you click the Compare view button in the toolbar, Lightroom displays the currently selected image as a Select image and the one immediately to the right in the Filmstrip as a Candidate image (**Figure 3.25**). In this setup, the Select image will remain locked and you can use the keyboard arrow keys to navigate through the remaining photos in the selection to change the Candidate image view and thereby compare different Candidate images with the current Select. A white border indicates which image is active, and you can use the Zoom view slider to adjust the Zoom setting for either photo. When the zoom lock is switched on, you can lock the level of magnification and synchronize the zoom and scrolling across both image views.

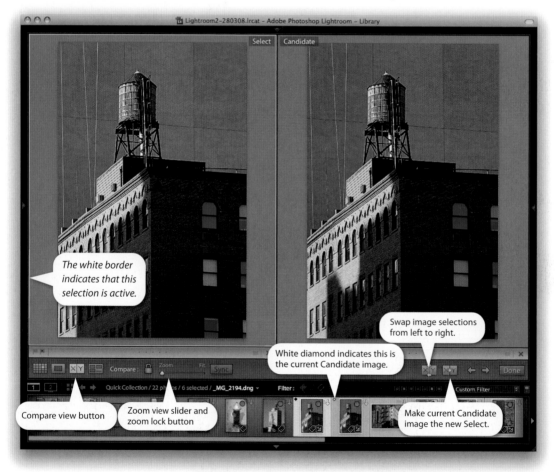

Figure 3.25   *In Compare view you can compare a Select image with various Candidates. You can use the left and right arrow keys to navigate through alternative shots in the Filmstrip.*

Compare view display options

If the Navigator panel is open, you can use it to navigate the Compare view display (**Figure 3.26**). Use a single click in the Navigator preview to zoom in to whatever the close-up view zoom level is and then click-drag the zoomed-in rectangle to analyze different areas of the two images. Of course, you still have the lock button in the toolbar to unlock the zooming and scrolling for the two images in order to navigate each one separately. To return to the normal zoomed-out view, double-click anywhere inside the Navigator preview. When you have decided which image is the favorite Select, click the Done button to display the current Select image in a standard Loupe view.

NOTE

When using the Compare view mode to compare images side by side, you can also make the info overlay visible. To enable this, go to the Library module View menu ⇨ Loupe Info ⇨ Show Info Overlay. Or use the ⌘ I (Mac), Ctrl I (PC) keyboard shortcut.

Figure 3.26 *The Compare view with the Navigator panel and Loupe Info visible.*

Compare view mode in action step by step

The following steps show an example of using the Compare view mode to edit a selection of photos made via the Filmstrip.

1. In the Filmstrip you can tell which photo is the Select and which the Candidate by the icon in the top-left corner. The Select photo is indicated with a filled diamond and the current Candidate photo is indicated by a hollow diamond.

2. Here is an example of the Compare view mode in action. In this first screen shot I have the photo highlighted with the red border as the current Select and the photo highlighted with the blue border as the current Candidate.

3. I proceeded to use the right arrow key to move forward through the selection comparing other photos with the original Select.

4. When I found a new photo that I liked more, I used the up arrow key to promote this Candidate photo to become the new Select.

Navigating photos via the Filmstrip

The Filmstrip is located at the bottom of the Lightroom window. You don't get to see the same amount of additional information in the Filmstrip as you can see in the Library Grid cells, although the Lightroom Interface preferences does have a "Show ratings and picks in filmstrip" option that allows you to make these two items appear at the bottom of the thumbnail cells in the Filmstrip (**Figure 3.27**).

The Filmstrip provides a secondary view of the library contents and is always accessible as you move between modules in Lightroom (**Figure 3.28**). The Filmstrip therefore offers a constant link between the images that are selected in the current Library view and when working in the other Lightroom modules (**Figure 3.29**). As with the Library Grid, the Filmstrip allows you to select photos to work on. Drag-and-drop editing is possible via the Filmstrip, and any drag-and-drop changes you make will also be reflected in the Library Grid. Custom sort order changes such as these are remembered whenever you save a selection of images as a collection.

The Filmstrip allows you to navigate through your photos just as you can in the Library Grid view. For example, you can press the left or right arrow key to progress through the folder thumbnails one at a time, or hold down an arrow key to quickly navigate through the thumbnails and see the Loupe preview update as you do so. Or, you can drag the Filmstrip's slider bar to scroll even more quickly.

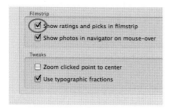

Figure 3.27 *In the Lightroom Interface preferences section is a Filmstrip section where you can choose to display ratings and picks in the Filmstrip thumbnail cells.*

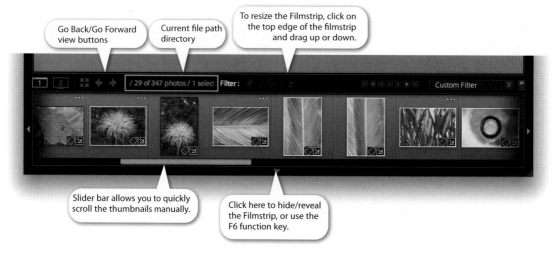

Go Back/Go Forward view buttons

Current file path directory

To resize the Filmstrip, click on the top edge of the filmstrip and drag up or down.

Slider bar allows you to quickly scroll the thumbnails manually.

Click here to hide/reveal the Filmstrip, or use the F6 function key.

Figure 3.28 *The Filmstrip sits at the bottom of the Lightroom interface screen and is present in all the Lightroom modules. The Go Back/Go Forward buttons let you skip between the current and the previous Lightroom views.*

Figure 3.29 *The Filmstrip allows you to keep a view of the currently selected catalog contents as you switch from one module to another.*

✓ Show	⌘F11
✓ Full Screen	⇧⌘F11
Show Second Monitor Preview	⌥⇧⌘F11
✓ Grid	⇧G
Loupe – Normal	⇧E
Loupe – Live	
Loupe – Locked	⇧⌘↵
Compare	⇧C
Survey	⇧N
Slideshow	⌥⇧⌘↵
✓ Show Filter View	⇧\
Zoom In	⇧⌘=
Zoom Out	⇧⌘-
Increase Thumbnail Size	⇧=
Decrease Thumbnail Size	⇧-

Figure 3.30 *The Window ⇨ Secondary Display submenu.*

NOTE

If you are in Grid view mode in the main window and select the Grid view for the secondary display, the main window will automatically switch to a Loupe view mode.

Working with a dual-monitor setup

Lightroom is normally run on a single display, but you can now take advantage of a dual-monitor setup by having a second Lightroom window on the other screen. Assuming you have two monitors, there are several ways you can do this. You can go to the Window ⇨ Secondary Display submenu shown in **Figure 3.30** and select Show. You can use the ⌘F11 (Mac), Ctrl F11 (PC) keyboard shortcut to toggle the secondary display on or off, or you can click the second monitor icon (circled in **Figure 3.31**) to open a second display window. The ⌘⇧Shift F11 (Mac), Ctrl ⇧Shift F11 (PC) shortcut toggles the secondary display appearing in Full screen or Window mode, which means that you can also use the secondary display feature on a single-monitor setup to provide you with two separate Lightroom windows.

Let's now look at how you might use the dual-monitor feature. Figure 3.31 shows the secondary monitor Grid view (⇧Shift G toggles showing/hiding the secondary Grid window). You have here the same controls as are found in the normal Grid view, including a menu list of recently visited folders, a thumbnails slider to adjust the size of the grid display, and a ⇧Shift \ keyboard shortcut to show/hide the Filter bar. **Figure 3.32** shows the secondary monitor Loupe view (⇧Shift E toggles showing/hiding the secondary Loupe window), where there are three options in the top-left corner. The Normal mode displays the

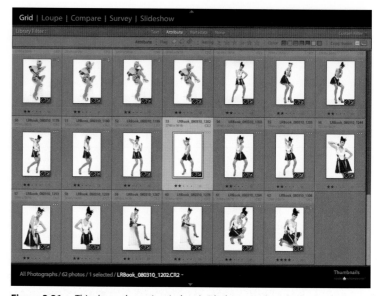

Figure 3.31 *This shows the main window (with the secondary display button circled) plus a secondary Grid view window.*

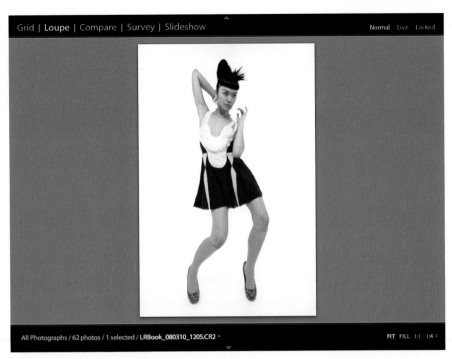

Figure 3.32 *The secondary display Grid view window.*

Figure 3.33 *The secondary display Compare view window.*

TIP

By now, you may have caught on now to the fact that all the keyboard shortcuts for secondary display are just the same as those used for the normal display, except you add a ⇧Shift key to the shortcut.

NOTE

You have the same zoom controls in the secondary Loupe view window as you do in the Navigator panel, but you can set the Loupe zoom to a different magnification setting. This means you can preview a photo in Fit to screen Loupe view on one screen while using, say, a 1:1 view on the other.

current image and updates whenever you make a new image active. The Live view updates as you roll the mouse over the photos in the main Grid view or the Filmstrip, which is handy if you want to inspect other photos up close without losing the current image selection. But it also means that if you have the secondary display set to 1:1 view, you can run the mouse over the photos in a Grid view and use the 1:1 Loupe view as a quick focus checker. You should try this out—it is like running a large magnifying glass over a set of contact sheets! The Locked view option locks the Loupe view in place and does not update until you unlock from this view mode. This offers an alternative way to compare photos side by side, which leads us to the secondary Compare view mode shown in **Figure 3.33** (⇧Shift E toggles showing/hiding the secondary Compare window). The secondary Compare view shown here works just like the main Compare view and basically extends the scope of how you can carry out Compare view editing.

How to get the most out of working with two displays

Now let's look at a few examples of how a secondary display can be useful to you when working in Lightroom. On the facing page I have suggested three ways that a secondary display can ease your workflow. **Figure 3.34** shows how you can have a selection of photos in Survey view mode on the main screen and use the Compare view on the secondary monitor. With this arrangement you can preview a Select image alongside a Candidate on the secondary screen and choose alternative candidates by clicking on the individual photos in the main screen in Survey view mode. In the **Figure 3.35** example you can see the Loupe view in use on the main screen with a Grid view on the secondary display. With this setup you can have full access to the Grid and Loupe views at once, rather than have to rely on the Filmstrip (one thing you can't have is two Grid views active at once). And lastly, you can combine any module view on the main screen with a Grid, Loupe, Compare, Survey, or Slideshow view on the secondary display. In the **Figure 3.36** example I used the main screen to display a photo in the Develop module, where I was able to use the Develop tools to edit the photograph. Meanwhile, I had the current selection of photos displayed in the Survey view mode on the secondary display. With this kind of setup you can use the secondary display to select photos from the Survey view (it doesn't have to be Survey mode; you could use Grid or Compare) and edit them directly in Develop, thereby bridging the gap between these two separate modules.

Figure 3.34 *The Survey view used with the Compare view.*

Figure 3.35 *The Loupe view used with the Grid view.*

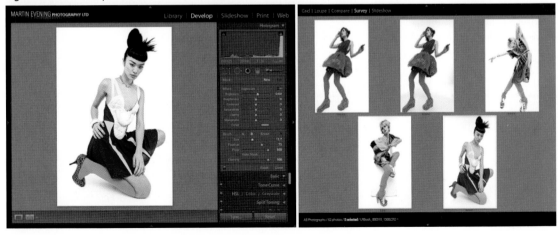

Figure 3.36 *A Develop module view used with the Survey view.*

Figure 3.37   From the Library menu,
you can choose the Refine Photos
command. This will open a dialog that
informs you that if you proceed with this
command, Lightroom will automatically
mark the unflagged photos as rejects
and mark the previously picked photos
as unflagged. The intention here is to
allow you to make successive passes at
the image selection editing stage and use
flagging (in a rather brutal way) to narrow
down your final picture choices.

Refining image selections

Rating images using picks and rejects

Your next step in managing your images is to decide which photos
you like best by assigning ratings. Image ratings are normally used to
progressively mark the pictures you like best from a shoot. In the days
of film, you would use a pen to mark the shots worth keeping with a
cross and the ones you liked best with two crosses. These same editing
principles can be applied when using the rating system in Lightroom to
edit the photos from a shoot. The flag controls on the toolbar provide
a simple method for marking favorite and rejected photographs. (See
Figure 3.37 to learn about the Refine Photos command.) You can then
use the Filters controls in the Filmstrip (**Figure 3.38**) to narrow down
the display of your flagged selections. This simple binary approach
lets you mark the pictures you like with a flag by clicking the Pick flag
button in the toolbar (or use the P keyboard shortcut). You can then
click the Filter Picks Only button in the Filmstrip to filter just the Pick
images (**Figure 3.39**). Meanwhile, you can use the Reject flag button
(or use the X keyboard shortcut) in the toolbar to mark an image as
a reject (which will also dim the thumbnail in the Grid view). Likewise,
you can use the Filter Rejects Only button to filter just the rejects
(**Figure 3.40**). This raises the question of what do you do with the
reject photos. Some people suggest the rejects should then be deleted,
but I advise against this approach since you never know when a reject
photo may come in useful. Perhaps there is an element in the shot you
may find useful later? The only photos I ever permanently delete are
those where the flash failed to fire. I keep everything else, but I tend to
filter out the rejects or unmarked photos, burn these to backup disks,
and then delete them from the computer. Lastly, you can use the U
keyboard shortcut as a kind of undo command to mark a photo as
being unflagged. You can therefore use the U keyboard shortcut as a
means to remove the pick or reject flag status from any image. Also on
the Filmstrip is a Filter Unflagged Photos Only button, which will allow
you to filter just the unflagged images.

Figure 3.38   *Here is a close-up view of the Filmstrip filters. The flag buttons are
cumulative, which means that you can click each to show or hide the flagged,
unflagged, and reject photos. In this example only the Flagged and Reject buttons are
checked, which would mean all photos are displayed except for the unflagged images.*

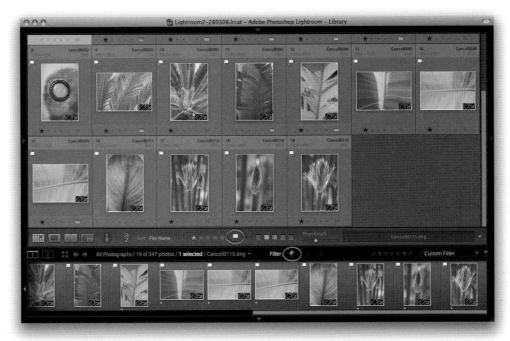

Figure 3.39 *Use the flag pick (or press P or ‵) to mark your favorite images. In the Filmstrip at the bottom, I clicked the Filter Flag Picks Only button to see my favorite picks.*

Figure 3.40 *Use the reject flag button (or press X) to mark an image as a reject. To see the reject photos only, click the reject flag icon in the Filter options.*

TIP

You can assign ratings to batches of images by making a selection in the Grid or Filmstrip and then assigning a rating either with the keyboard shortcuts or by going to the Photo menu and checking Set Rating, followed by the rating value. Another way to rate your images is to click the empty dots in the cell grid just below the thumbnail. But I don't recommend you do this because it can be a really fiddly operation, especially when using a large monitor display with a fine-pitch screen resolution. All in all, the keyboard shortcuts offer the quickest solution.

TIP

Clicking on a rating dot resets the image rating to zero. So if an image has a two-star rating and you click the second star, the rating resets to zero. You can also adjust the ratings by clicking on a star and dragging with the mouse.

Rating images using numbered star ratings

The picks and rejects method is fine for making simple picture edits, but to my mind the most effective way to rate your images is to use the keyboard numbers ⓪ through ⑤ to assign a specific numbered star rating. (In **Figure 3.41** I show how you can save custom filter presets.) Or you can use the right square bracket key 〔]〕 to increase the rating or the left square bracket key 〔[〕 to decrease the rating for an image (see **Figure 3.42**).

With the number rating system you can assign a star rating to reflect a particular photo's importance. When you are review editing a set of photos, you can use a single-star rating to make a first pass selection of "pick" images and then make further edit passes to refine the selection. For example, in **Figure 3.43** you can see how I used the Filter rating control in the toolbar to display only those images with a one-star rating or higher in the Content area. You can then carry out a second pass edit in which you mark the pictures you like most with a two-star rating. Where you have second thoughts about pictures you had rated previously, you can mark them with a zero rating.

With Lightroom you have the potential to rate your images on a scale from 0–5. I suggest you use a zero rating for images that have yet to be rated or are unsuitable for further consideration, and use a one-star rating for pictures that are not obvious rejects. During a second pass I use a two-star rating to mark the favorite images that are candidates for final selection. I may later use three stars to mark the final choice images, but I prefer not to assign higher star ratings too freely because this leaves me some extra headroom to assign higher ratings later to distinguish which shots have a higher importance. At this point in time, I have a fairly large library of images that will surely grow over the next 10–20 years. I want to be careful as to how I allocate my four- or five-star ratings. These ratings should be reserved to mark the portfolio master shots only.

Figure 3.41   *Use the Custom Filter menu to save a filter setting as a new custom preset. In the example shown here, I saved the current filter setting as a "3-star filter."*

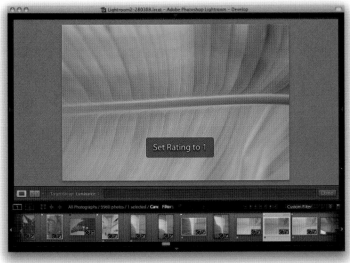

Figure 3.42 *The most convenient way to rate images is to navigate with the keyboard arrow keys and use the ⓪–⑤ keys to apply number ratings (use ⇧Shift + number to apply a rating and move to the next photo), or use the ⟦⟧ to increase the image rating or the ⟦⟧ to lower the image rating (pressing ⓪ resets a rating to zero).*

Figure 3.43 *After applying all your ratings to the images, you can use the Filter rating controls in the Filmstrip to narrow down the selection to display the rated photos only. In this example I chose to filter the photos with a one-star rating or higher.*

Figure 3.45 *If you go to the Metadata menu and choose Color Label Set ⇨ Edit, you can create and save your own custom interpretations of what the label colors mean or refer to. Start by using the Review Status set that comes with the program.*

Working with color labels

In the previous sections we learned that flags and ratings are used to mark images as rejects, keepers, or favorite shots. Color labels, on the other hand, can be used to separate images into different groupings.

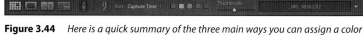

Figure 3.44 *Here is a quick summary of the three main ways you can assign a color label. You can use the Photo ⇨ Set Color Label submenu, use the keyboard numbers from 6 to 9 (there is no keyboard shortcut for a purple label), or click on a label color in the toolbar.*

In **Figure 3.44** you can see that color labels can be assigned via the Photo menu by choosing Set Color Label, followed by the label color. Color labels can also be assigned by clicking a color label button on the toolbar, or you can use keyboard numbers to quickly assign labels as follows: red (⑥), yellow (⑦), green (⑧), blue (⑨) (note that there is no keyboard shortcut available for purple). You can even type in a color label by name in the Color Label field of the Metadata panel.

Note that color labels are always specific to the color label set used. The implication here is that when you use the Color label filter buttons in the Filmstrip or Filter bar to filter according to a color label, the filter will only work with the currently active color label set. This means that if you select a new color label set (**Figure 3.45**) and apply say, a purple color label filter, this will only select the purple-labeled photos that were edited using that specific color label set. It won't select any purple-labeled photos that were edited using other color label sets (where the text description does not match). If color label filters are not working as expected, check that you have the correct color label set active.

Lightroom and Bridge labels

If you use color labels in Bridge to classify your photos, the color label settings are preserved when you import them into Lightroom or modify a Lightroom imported image via Bridge. However, this does assume that the Bridge color label setting matches that used in Lightroom. The problem here is that Lightroom and Bridge both use two different default descriptions for the color labels, and this can lead to metadata conflicts between the two programs. So while the color label "colors" may match, the text descriptions don't and this can lead to metadata confusion where neither program can read the labels fully. However, you can use the Label Color command on the Sort menu shown in **Figure 3.46** to overcome this. Lightroom 2 also features two new color label filtering options (**Figure 3.47**). You can now filter by Custom Label. This will filter out the photos with color labels like those in the previous scenario where the label color and label color text don't match. There is also a No Label filter option that allows you to quickly filter the unlabeled photos only. For more about sorting and how to deal with color label metadata conflicts, refer to page 187 in Chapter 4.

Figure 3.46   *The Sort menu in the toolbar will allow you to sort photos by the label color or by the label text description.*

Figure 3.47   *In Lightroom 2 there are now two new color label filtering options: Custom Label and No Label.*

Other labeling methods

While ratings can be used to indicate how much you like or don't like an image, color labels can provide an overlapping means for classifying images into categories that have nothing to do with how much you rate an individual image. For example, on a wedding shoot you could use red labels to classify photos of the bride and groom, yellow labels for all the family group shots, and green labels for the informal style photographs. Peter Krogh, in *The DAM Book: Digital Asset Management for Photographers* (O'Reilly), describes how he uses color labels to assign negative ratings to his images. He uses red to mark images that have yet to be rated, yellow to mark the outtakes (which he doesn't want to delete yet even though he won't use them), and the green label to mark images that definitely need to be trashed. Then he uses the blue and purple labels for making ad hoc temporary selections, such as when making a shortlist of Candidate shots to send to a client.

TIP

When a filter is in effect, you can use Library ⇨ **Enable Filter** to toggle it on and off, or use the ⌘L (Mac) or Ctrl L (PC) keyboard shortcut.

Filtering photos in the catalog

Now that you have edited your photos using a rating system of your choice, you can start using these ratings in conjunction with folder, keyword, and other selections to refine your image selections and retrieve pictures quickly.

The Lightroom image catalog can be thought of as having a pyramid-type structure in which the zero-rated images are the most numerous, fewer images have a one-star rating, and even fewer images have a five-star rating (**Figure 3.48**). Meanwhile, library image searches can be filtered by selecting folders or keywords via their respective panels, or by using the Library Filter bar to search by both, entering a specific term in the search field. Whether you filter by folder, filter by collections, or by metadata in combination with a ratings filter, you can always quickly narrow down a selection of images from any library to find the specific pictures you want.

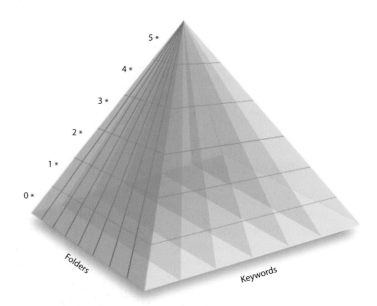

Figure 3.48 *An illustration showing the library contents classified into a pyramid shape structure.*

Three ways to filter the catalog

I will focus on metadata and metadata filtering in Chapter 4, but for now let's look at the filter options as they relate to flags, ratings, and color labels. **Figure 3.49** shows the Library module Library menu where you can filter by Flag, Rating, Color Label, or Copy Status. These options are identical to those found in the Filters section of the Filmstrip (**Figure 3.50**). For example, you could filter the photos displayed in the Content area by choosing Library ⇨ Filter by Rating ⇨ One Star and higher, to make only those photos with a one-star rating or greater visible. Or, you could simply click the one-star button in the Filmstrip (and select the equal and greater than option) to make only the one-star photos or higher visible. The other way to filter catalog photos is to use the new Filter bar, which is accessible from the top of the Content area whenever you are in the Library Grid view. In the **Figure 3.51** example, the Refine section of the Filter bar was selected and a one-star and higher filter was applied to the photos in the Grid.

NOTE

When you are working in modules other than the Library module, the Library ⇨ Filters submenu shown in Figure 3.49 will appear in the File menu instead.

Figure 3.49 *Here is a view of the Library module Library menu. In this example the Library menu is being used to select photos with a one-star rating and higher only.*

Figure 3.50 *You can also click the one-star button in the Filmstrip (with "rating is greater than or equal to" selected), to achieve the same filter result method.*

Figure 3.51 *Alternatively, you can click the one-star button in the Filter bar Refine section and select the "and higher" filter option.*

Filtering photos via the Filmstrip

Now let's look at the top panel of the Filmstrip in more detail, and in particular, consider how you can use the Filmstrip controls to filter images according to their rating, pick status, and label color (**Figure 3.52**). The Folder/Collection section displays the current folder path directory or collection name. Click anywhere here to view a list of recently visited places to select a recently visited folder or collection. The Refined Filters section can be expanded or collapsed by clicking Filter. The Filter section contains the "Filter based on flag status" selectors, which can filter by showing "all Picked images only," "all unflagged images only," or "all rejected images only" (click the flag icons again to undo these selections). To use "Filter based on rating," click on a star rating to filter the images and choose from one of the options shown in the pop-up menu (circled) to display images of the same rating or greater, same rating or lower, and those photos equal to that rating only.

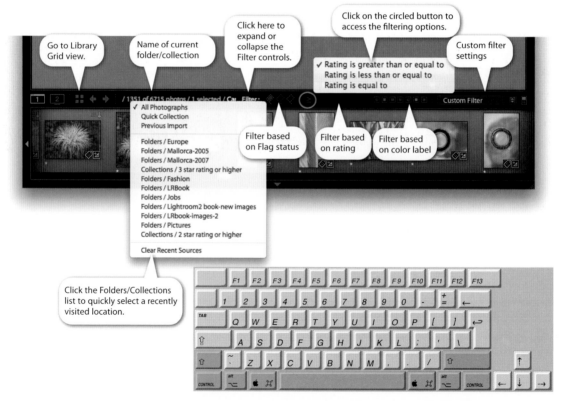

Figure 3.52 *You can toggle between hiding/showing the Filmstrip by clicking the arrow at the bottom of the interface or by using the F6 function key. Use the left/right arrow keys to navigate through the photos shown in the Filmstrip.*

Filtering flagged photos

The flag buttons in the Filmstrip can take a little getting used to. Start with all the flag buttons dimmed. Click the first pick flag (■) to filter the images to display the picks only. Click it again to turn off the filtering and reveal all the images. Click the middle flag (■) to show the unflagged images only. Click it a second time to reveal all the images. Click the third, the reject flag (■), to display the rejects only. Click again to show all images. Now try clicking both the pick flag and reject flag buttons. This reveals both picks and rejects, but not the unflagged images.

Filtering options

If you click the icon to the left of the rating symbols you can choose from one of the following options (see **Figure 3.53**) to decide what the filtering rule should be: "Rating is greater than or equal to," "Rating is less than or equal to," or "Rating is equal to."

Figure 3.53   *The Filmstrip rating menu options.*

Creating refined filter selections via the Filmstrip

You can also use the Filmstrip buttons to create image selections based on the flag and color label status. If you hold down the ⌘ key (Mac) or Ctrl key (PC) as you click any of the flag or color label buttons, instead of filtering the photos you create an image selection based on the buttons that were clicked. If you hold down the ⇧Shift key as well as the ⌘/Ctrl key as you click these Filmstrip buttons, you can add further photos to the selection. To remove photos from a selection, use ⌘ Alt (Mac), Ctrl Alt (PC) as you click on the flag or color label buttons. And lastly, if you Alt –click on a color swatch you can create an inverted color swatch selection. For example, if you Alt –click on the red color swatch, this will select all the photos except those that have the red color label applied.

TIP

If you go to the File menu the Filters ⇨ Filter by Color Label submenu includes options to filter photos by No Label, to select all those photos that have no label status. There is also an Other Label option that will allow you to filter photos that have a label status not completely recognized by Lightroom. In other words, choosing File ⇨ Filters ⇨ Filter by Color Label ⇨ Other Label will allow you to filter photos that have had their color labels edited in Bridge where the label text descriptions are not currently synchronized with those used by Lightroom (see page 105 for the reasons why Lightroom and Bridge sometimes have different ideas about what these color labels mean).

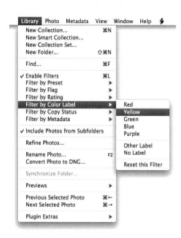

Figure 3.54 *The Library module Filter by Color Label options.*

Color label filtering

To filter photos by color label, you can go to the Filter by Color Label menu in the Library module Library menu (**Figure 3.54**), or use the color label buttons in the Filmstrip. (See **Figure 3.55** to learn how to customize the Library grid cell view.)

1. The color swatch buttons in the Filmstrip allow you to quickly make selections based on color labels. These buttons work independently: Click the red button to display all red label images. Then click the yellow button to add yellow label images; click the red button again to remove the red label images from the filter selection.

2. In this example you can see a collection of photos from a holiday trip in which a red color label was assigned to the food shots, yellow was used for the general detail shots, green for the town landscapes, and blue for the night sky pictures. At the moment no filters have been applied and all images are visible in the Library module Grid view.

3. In this next screen shot I clicked the red and green filter buttons in the Filmstrip, to filter just the red-and green-labeled photos.

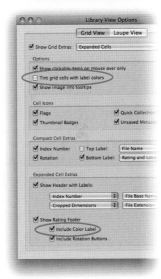

Figure 3.55 *You can customize the Library grid cell view by pressing ⌘ J (Mac), Ctrl J (PC), which will open the Library View Options. If you don't want to see the cell color tinted, then deselect the "Tint cells with label colors" option. Instead, check the Include Color Label item in the Show Rating Footer section.*

4. In the color label filter swatch section of the filmstrip it is possible to Alt –click on a color swatch to make an inverted color swatch selection. The inverted swatch selection will exclude photos that have no color label. In this example, I Alt –clicked on the Yellow swatch to display all photos except the yellow-labeled ones.

NOTE

You can find out more about working with virtual copies on page 350 in Chapter 6.

Virtual copy and master copy filters

Most of the photos in the catalog will be master copy images. These are the original source files of which there can only be one version of each in the catalog. However, you can create virtual copy versions of the masters, and this allows you to edit the virtual copy versions as if they were separate originals, but without physically copying the master.

The Virtual copy and Master copy filters can therefore be used to filter the display to show or hide virtual copy photos only, and show or hide the master copy photos only. You can go to the Library module Library menu and choose Filters ⇨ Filter by Copy Status and choose Virtual Copies, Master Photos, or All Photos (see **Figure 3.56**). But it is far simpler to use the Virtual Copy and Master Copy filter buttons. These are located in the Attribute section of the Filter bar.

Figure 3.56   *You can use File ⇨ Filters ⇨ Filter by Copy Status ⇨ Virtual Copies to filter the catalog to display the virtual copy photos only or master photos only. However, it is probably simpler to use the Filter by Virtual Copy and Filter by Master Copy buttons that are circled here.*

Subfolder filtering

The Include Photos from Subfolders filter (highlighted in Figure 3.56) lets you determine whether to include or exclude photos in subfolders. This menu item therefore allows you to include or hide photos that are contained in subfolders.

To give you an example of how this works, in the Folders panel view in **Figure 3.57**, I have selected a folder called Casting 2008 that contains 709 photos, of which 683 photos are contained in the five subfolders. This means there are 26 photos floating around in the Model castings folder that are not assigned to either of these two subfolder items. If I were to deselect Include Photos from Subitems in the Library menu, clicking on the 2008 folder will show just these 26 photos and exclude the other 683.

Figure 3.57 *This view of the catalog shows a Casting images folder titled "2008" selected with the Include Photos from Subfolders unchecked in the Library menu. We now only see the 26 photos contained in the root-level folder, instead of all 709 (which we would see in this filtered view if Include Photos from Subfolders had been checked).*

Group into Stack	⌘G
Unstack	⇧⌘G
Remove from Stack	
Split Stack	
Collapse Stack	S
Collapse All Stacks	
Expand All Stacks	
Move to Top of Stack	⇧S
Move Up in Stack	⇧[
Move Down in Stack	⇧]
Auto-Stack by Capture Time...	

Figure 3.58   *The Photo ⇨ Stacking submenu, which can also be accessed via the contextual menu (right-click anywhere in the Content area and navigate to Stacking in the menu list).*

Figure 3.59   *The Auto-Stack by Capture Time dialog.*

Grouping photos into stacks

Just as photographers used to group slides on a lightbox into piles of related photographs, Lightroom lets you group photos into stacks. You can do this manually by selecting a group of images from the Grid or Filmstrip and choosing Photo ⇨ Stacking ⇨ Group into Stack or by pressing ⌘G (Mac) or Ctrl G (PC). From there you can press S to Collapse Stack so that all the stacked images are represented by a single thumbnail cell and press S again to expand the stack. Note that the number of images in a stack is indicated in the upper-left corner of the cell. If you need to unstack the stacked images, choose Photo ⇨ Stacking ⇨ Unstack or press ⌘⇧Shift G (Mac) or Ctrl ⇧Shift G (PC).

The easiest way to access the Stacking submenu is to use the contextual menu and right-click in the Content area to quickly access all the submenu items (**Figure 3.58**). If you want to remove an image or selection of images from a stack, select the image or images first, and then use the contextual menu to choose Remove from Stack. Similarly, you can use this same menu to choose Collapse All Stacks or Expand All Stacks.

Whenever you choose Photo ⇨ Create Virtual Copy, the virtual copy (or proxy) image will automatically be grouped in a stack with the master image. (Virtual copies are also discussed later in Chapter 6.) When you choose Photo ⇨ Edit in Photoshop, there is a preference for stacking the edited copy photo with the original.

You can also choose which photo best represents the images in a stack. If you are using stacks to group a series of related photos, it may be that the first image you shot in a sequence is not necessarily the best shot to represent all the other pictures in a stacked group. You can expand the stack and select the photograph you like most in the series and use ⇧Shift [to move that image up the stacking order, or use ⇧Shift] to move an image down the stacking order. Or to make things simpler, just select the photo you want to have represent all the images in the stack and use the Move to Top of Stack command (⇧Shift S).

My favorite feature in the Stacking menu is the Auto-Stack by Capture Time item. This allows you to automatically group a whole folder of images into stacks based on the embedded capture date and time metadata (**Figure 3.59**). On the facing page, I show an example of how to use the Auto-Stack feature to automatically group a series of image captures into stacks.

1. Here is a Library view of a folder of images I wanted to group together automatically. I went to the Photo ⇨ Stacking menu and chose Auto-Stack by Capture Time. I then adjusted the Time Between Stacks slider to group all the photos that were shot within a minute of each other.

2. The photos in the Content area were now stacked, but the stacks remained expanded. To collapse a stack, click the badge icon in the top-left corner (which also indicates how many images are in the stack) and click again to expand the stack. You can also right-click and choose Collapse All Stacks from the contextual menu.

NOTE

The general idea here is that you
can use successive Add to Selection
commands to build lots of different
kinds of filter selections. For example,
you can use the Select by Color Label
menu to add yellow label images
to a red yellow photo selection. You
can also use the Select by Rating
⇨ Intersect with Selection menu to
create selections of photos that have
matching criteria only. By using this
method you can select the one-star
rated photos that have a red or yellow
label. The Edit ⇨ Select by menu
options can be used in this way to
create any number of selection rules,
which is useful when managing large
collections of photos.

Image selection options

The Edit menu contains a series of "Select by" submenu items. These
let you make filtered selections of photos from the current catalog view.

1. Go to the Edit menu and choose a "Select by" submenu item.
   In this example, I chose Edit ⇨ Select by Rating ⇨ one star.

2. I then opened the Edit menu again and chose Select by Color
   Label ⇨ Add to Selection ⇨ Green.

Removing and deleting photos

After completing an image selection edit, you then need to consider what to do with the images that don't make it past a zero rating. Should you keep them or delete them? I generally prefer not to permanently delete anything since you never know when a rejected photo might still be useful. For example, there have been times where a client has not agreed with my first-round edit choices and requested to see more shots. There have also been occasions where I have taken a photograph and not thought too much of it, only to discover later that the picture has a greater significance than I had realized at the time I took it. On client jobs I may shoot a hundred frames or more of each subject. After an initial edit I separate out the zero-rated images, export them as DNG files, archive them to disk, and then remove them from the Lightroom library, leaving only the raw files with a one-star rating or higher. For all other shoots, such as personal shots where the pictures are more varied, I only delete the obvious outtakes, such as where the flash failed to fire or a picture is badly out of focus. If you press the Delete key you will see the dialog shown in **Figure 3.60**. If you click Remove, this will simply remove the photo from the Lightroom catalog, but the original file will remain on the computer hard disk. If this is what you want to do and you wish to avoid having to go through the dialog each time, you can instead choose the Photo ⇨ Remove Photos from Catalog command, or use the [Alt][Delete] shortcut. The other option is to Delete from Disk. This will remove the photos from the catalog and then send them to the system trash/recycle bin. Although the warning message says that this process cannot be undone, it does not completely delete the file just yet. To permanently remove files from the hard disk, you need to go to the Max OS X Finder and choose Finder ⇨ Empty Trash ([⌘][⇧ Shift][Delete] Mac) or choose Empty Recycle bin (PC). You can also click Cancel to cancel the delete/remove operation.

TIP

The fact that the Delete command does not irrevocably remove files from your system provides you with a margin of safety in case you delete files accidentally. You can always rescue the deleted images from the trash and move them back into the Lightroom library again.

TIP

On page 100 we looked at working with the flag rating system and how to mark photos as picks or rejects. Once you have edited a set of photos and marked some of them as rejects using the reject flag or the [X] keyboard shortcut, you can go to the Photo menu and choose Delete Rejected Photos or use the [⌘][Delete] (Mac), [Ctrl][Delete] (PC) shortcut. With this single command you can send all your rejected photos directly to the trash, ready to be deleted.

Figure 3.60 *The dialog on the left appears whenever you use the* [Delete] *command. The default option is Remove, which simply deletes the link from the Lightroom library database. Click the Delete from Disk button if you are sure you want to remove the selected images from Lightroom permanently. If the folder you are about to delete is a top-level folder, the options are different and assume that you might want to delete the top-level (containing) folder and promote all the subfolders within to the top level.*

Photograph: Storms River, South Africa, © Martin Evening 2004
Canon EOS 1Ds Mk I | 24 mm | 200 ISO | f6.3 @ 1/640th

Managing photos in the Library module

How to use the metadata tools in Lightroom to manage your catalogs

Lightroom is designed to help you organize and catalog your images from the very first moment you import your capture files into the program. And from there on, Lightroom provides a flexible system of file management that can free you from the rigid process of having to organize your images within system folders. Although Lightroom does still use a folder system for storage, it can also manage your images globally by using metadata to filter your image selections. A good example of how such a system works is to look at the way music files are managed on an Apple iPod using the iTunes software. If you are familiar with importing music via iTunes, you know that it doesn't matter which folders the MP3 files are stored in, so long as iTunes knows exactly where to locate those files. When you select a track to play on an iPod, you search for the music by using the metadata, such as the song or album title.

Lightroom works in exactly the same way by encouraging you to use relevant naming for your folder imports and add keywords and other metadata to everything at the time of import. Through the use of careful file naming, custom metadata, and keywords, you can make image searching equally as fast and easy as locating music on your iPod.

NOTE

Metadata is usually described as data about data and is used all the time to help categorize information. For example, the cable TV system I have at home allows me to search for movies not just by using an A–Z listing but also by genre, by release date, and by director. iTunes allows you to sift through a large music collection on your iPod using metadata. Lightroom also lets you organize your image files by metadata. For example, you can sort through images in various ways: by folder name, by image rating, or by favorite collections. Lightroom helps you manage the images in the library by using the metadata in the files rather than by the folder location or filename alone.

Working with metadata

With a folder-based organizational system, your file searching success depends on your ability to memorize the folder structure of the hard drive and know where everything is stored. Anyone who is responsible for maintaining a large image archive will already be aware that this method of file management soon becomes unwieldy. What is needed is a cataloging program that can keep track of everything. Therefore, the trend these days is to use file management by metadata, where you search for a file by searching its attributes rather than trying to remember which folder you last put something in.

As your image library grows, you will come to rely on Lightroom's Filter bar and Filmstrip filters to narrow down the selections of images in Lightroom. Some examples have already been given, such as the use of the Filmstrip Filters (see page 108) to narrow down a selection to show ratings just of one star or higher, or two-star images only, and so on. We have also looked at how to use the Folders panel to manage the image library. But the real power of Lightroom is its database engine, which enables you to carry out specific searches and help find the images you are looking for more quickly.

It is in no way mandatory that you follow all of the advice offered in this chapter, as each person will have his or her own particular image management requirements. You may indeed find that you just want to use the Folders panel to catalog your library images and that is enough to satisfy your needs. But hopefully one of the key things you will learn in this chapter is that the time invested in cataloging an image collection can pay huge dividends in the time saved when tracking down those pictures later. The image management tools in Lightroom are far from being a complete asset management solution, but they do offer something for nearly everyone. Some people may find the cataloging tools in Lightroom insufficient. But even so, the data you input via Lightroom is fully accessible in other more advanced image asset management programs.

The different types of metadata

Lightroom is able to search the database quickly by using the metadata information that is linked or embedded in the images. The metadata used in Lightroom falls into several types. One type is informational metadata, such as the EXIF metadata that tells you things like which camera was used to take a photograph along with other technical information such as the lens settings and image file type. Custom metadata is used to enter information about who shot the photograph, how to contact the creator of the photograph, and the rights usages allowed. Another type of metadata is keywords information, which you can enter to categorize your images.

As explained earlier, the way Lightroom uses this metadata is fairly similar to the way a program like iTunes categorizes your music collection. For example, when you search for a music track on an MP3 player such as an iPod, instead of searching for tracks by folders, you search for them using the metadata information embedded in the individual music files. In the case of MP3 files, they mostly have the necessary metadata information already embedded when you buy the music tracks. You can also use iTunes software to automatically locate the metadata information for newly imported music CDs via an online database.

In the case of Lightroom, most of the catalog information has to be added manually by the person who took the photographs. This process requires that you spend time entering this information (although there are various tips coming up in this chapter that show you how to avoid repetitively entering this data for every single image). But the trade-off is that the time invested in cataloging your images in the early stages will reap rewards in the time saved when retrieving your files later. In most cases you only need to configure essential metadata once to create a custom metadata template, and you can then get Lightroom to apply this bulk metadata automatically to a set of imported photos. You can take metadata cataloging further and assign custom metadata information to individual images. It really all depends if this is important for the type of work you do. However, the effort spent adding metadata has to be proportional to how useful that information will be later.

There is a lot of detailed content coming up in this chapter about how to apply, edit, and use metadata such as IPTC metadata and keywords. I thought, therefore, that the best way to introduce this subject would be to first provide a quick example of how metadata can be used to carry out a search of the Lightroom catalog.

NOTE

There can only be one physical copy of each image in the catalog, and a catalog image can only ever exist in one folder (or else it's unclassified).

A quick image search using metadata

One of the key new features in Lightroom 2 is the Filter bar, which is accessible in the Content area whenever you are in the Library Grid view mode. The Filter bar combines the old Find panel and Metadata Browser features into one, along with the search functionality of the Keyword List panel. The following steps suggest just one of the ways you can use a metadata filter search to find photos quickly and gather them together into a permanent collection. We'll be looking at keywords and collections later in this chapter, but for now let's run through a typical image search procedure to demonstrate the usefulness of tagging your photos with keywords.

1. Let's begin by showing how you can search for photos quickly, without needing to refer to the folders that the images are stored in. In the example shown here, I wanted to search for photos taken in a town in Spain. Now let's say that I couldn't remember the actual name of the place I was looking for, but I did know that it was somewhere on the island of Mallorca. You need to be aware that the left panel defines the source and the Filter bar will filter whatever is selected there first. To carry out a complete catalog filter search, I first selected All Photographs in the Catalog panel and then went to the Filter bar, clicked the Text tab, set the text search criteria to Keywords, and typed *Mallorca*.

2. I have visited this island several times and taken over 1,700 photos there. To narrow the search, I clicked the Metadata tab. This revealed the Metadata search options, where I clicked the 2007 year date in the Date list.

3. I could now see a narrowed set of keywords in the Keyword list next to the date panel. As I expanded the Places keyword subfolders I came across the keyword for the town of Sineu—that's the place I was looking for! I clicked the Attribute tab and then clicked the two-star filter to narrow the selection further.

4. I hid the Filter bar (\), applied an Edit ⇨ Select All to select all of the photos, and pressed the [B] key to add the selected photos to a Quick Collection.

5. I pressed [\] again to reveal the Filter bar and did a new search. This time, I used a text search for photos with the keyword *Malta* and with a rating of two stars and higher. I then pressed [B] to add them to the current Quick Collection.

6. The Quick Collection now contained 23 selected photos and it was time to make this temporary collection more permanent. I chose Edit ⇨ Select All to select all of the photos, clicked the Add Collection button at the top of the Collections panel, selected the Create Collection option, and titled this new collection *Mediterranean towns*.

7. Here is the final stored collection, which represents the combined result of the two separate Lightroom catalog searches. This quick intro by no means covers everything about metadata searches and collections. But it does at least give you a rough idea of how and why it is useful to tag photos in the catalog and also why you don't necessarily need to be concerned with how the photos are actually stored in the system folders.

Figure 4.1 *Here is the default view of the Metadata panel information, which shows just the basic file info metadata. The action arrow buttons that appear in the Metadata panel views provide useful quick links. For example, if you click the Folder button (circled), this will take you directly to a view of the folder contents the selected photo belongs to.*

Figure 4.2 *The Metadata view options.*

Metadata panel

Let's now look at the Metadata panel. **Figure 4.1** shows the default Metadata panel view, which displays a condensed list of file and camera information. At the top is the Metadata Preset menu with the same options as those found on the File Import menu (for more about creating and applying metadata presets, see page 135). Below this are fields that show basic information about the file such as the File Name and Folder. Underneath that are the Title, Caption, Copyright, Creator, and Location fields. These are all editable, and when you click in a blank field, you can directly enter custom metadata, such as the image title and copyright information. Below this are the image Rating and Label information, followed by the basic EXIF data items. This data is informational only and shows things like the file size dimensions, the camera used to take the photograph, camera settings, lens, and so forth.

Many of the items in the Metadata panel have action arrows or other buttons to the right of each metadata list item, and these provide additional functions. For example, if you click the action button next to the Folder name (see the action button circled in Figure 4.1), this will take you directly to a Grid view of the source folder contents.

Metadata panel view modes

If the metadata panel in your version of Lightroom looks different from the one shown in Figure 4.1, this is probably because you are using one of the seven other Metadata panel layout views. Each photo can contain a huge amount of metadata information, so if you want to see everything, you can select the All view. But if you want to work with a more manageable Metadata panel view, then I suggest you click the view menu shown in **Figure 4.2**, which will let you access the alternative Metadata panel view options (**Figure 4.3** compares some of the main Metadata panel view modes). You can then select a Metadata panel view more suited to the task at hand. For example, the EXIF view mode displays all the non-editable EXIF metadata, while the IPTC view mode concentrates on displaying the IPTC custom metadata fields only. The Large Caption view mode displays a nice, large Caption metadata field, which gives you lots of room in which to write a text caption (the large caption space here does at least make the Caption field easy to target—click anywhere in the Caption field and you can start typing). While you are in data entry mode, hitting Enter or Return now allows you to add a carriage return in this field section rather than committing the text.

The Location view mode offers a metadata view that is perhaps more useful for reviewing travel photographs. And finally, the Minimal and Quick Describe view modes are suited for compact Metadata panel viewing such as when working on a small-sized screen or laptop.

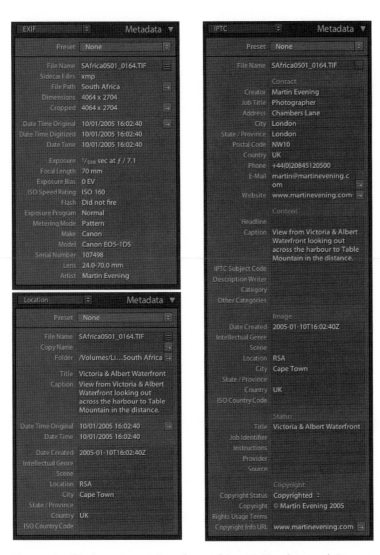

Figure 4.3 *This shows a comparison of some of the main Metadata panel view modes.*

General and EXIF metadata items

Let's now look in more detail at the items that can be displayed in
the Metadata panel. **Figure 4.4** shows a complete list of what items
you might see listed when using the All view mode. There are a lot of
metadata items that can be displayed here, and most of them are fairly
self-explanatory. So I've provided explanations for those that are not so
obvious, or that offer some interesting hidden tips and features. You
might not see everything listed here when you compare this with what
you are seeing on your computer; that's because certain items require
the metadata to be present before it will be displayed. So if you don't
have an audio sidecar file attached or GPS metadata embedded in the
file, nothing will be shown in the panel.

File Name

This displays the filename for the currently selected photo. If you need
to change the name of a file, you can't do so directly in the Content
area as you can in Bridge, so use this field to make any name changes.
If you want to carry out a batch rename action, select the photos and
click the button to the right to open the Rename Photo dialog.

Sidecar Files

The Sidecar Files item shows up whenever there is a sidecar file
associated with an image. They are always hidden from view when you
inspect images in Lightroom, and so this extra item in the Metadata
panel lets you know if an .xmp sidecar is present.

Copy Name

The Copy Name field refers to virtual copy images made in Lightroom.
Each virtual copy image can be an alternative version of the original
master (or negative as it is sometimes described in Lightroom). By
making virtual copies you can apply different crops or color treatments.
But since virtual copies all refer to the same master, they all share the
same root filename. Now, whenever you create a new virtual copy,
Lightroom will label each new virtual copy as *Copy 1*, *Copy 2*, etc.
But you'll most likely want to edit this name. To explain this further,
refer to **Figure 4.5**, in which an original DNG image has been selected
and three virtual copies are associated with the master (you can tell
they are virtual copies because they have a turned-up page icon in

— Batch rename

— Go to Master
— Show this folder in Lightroom

— Resolve metadata conflict
— Play Audio file

— Go to Crop mode in Develop module

— Filter photos in the Content area to show them with same date

— Go to Google Earth

— Launch mail program and create new email
— Go to Web site

— Go to Web site

Figure 4.4 *The Metadata panel showing the All view mode.*

Figure 4.5 *Here is a view of a master photo with three virtual copies. The copy names will be shown in the Metadata panel.*

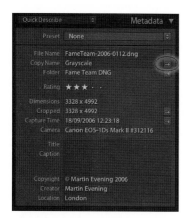

Figure 4.6 *If you are inspecting a virtual copy image, its copy name will appear in the Copy Name field. Click the action button next to it to locate the master image.*

Figure 4.7 *If a catalog photo's metadata appears to be out-of-sync, the Metadata Status item will appear in the Metadata panel and indicate it has been changed. Click the button to the right to reveal what needs to be done to get the metadata back in sync again. If there is no synchronization problem, the Metadata Status item will remain hidden.*

the bottom-left corner). In **Figure 4.6**, I renamed the Copy 2 photo (second one from the right) to Grayscale, which brings us to the Go to Master action arrow (circled). If you have a virtual copy image selected in Lightroom, you can always locate the parent master photo by clicking this button. Virtual copy images can quite often end up being separated from the master, because you may have assigned a different star rating to the virtual copy version, or they may be grouped in a collection, removed from the master, parent image. With this action button, you can quickly trace the master version photo.

Metadata Status

If there is an issue with the metadata status of a catalog image, the Metadata Status item will show up to indicate that the metadata status is in the process of being checked (you see an ellipsis [...] in the Metadata Status field), or that the metadata for the photo has been changed. This message tells you that the metadata status is out-of-date. It could mean that the metadata, such as the metadata text, keyword, rating, or Develop setting, has been changed in Lightroom and has not yet been saved to the image's XMP space. Clicking the button to the right provides a quick answer (see **Figure 4.7**), as will a quick check to see if there is a warning icon in the photo's grid cell. Or, it could mean that the metadata has been changed by an external program such as Bridge and that you need to go to the Metadata menu in the Lightroom Library module and select Read Metadata from File. The ins and outs of metadata saving, XMP spaces, and Lightroom settings form quite a complex subject. For a more detailed explanation, please refer to pages 175–182 in this chapter.

Cropped photos

If a photo has been cropped in any way, the Cropped item will appear in the Metadata panel, showing the crop dimensions in pixels. If you click the action button next to it, it will take you directly to the Crop mode in the Develop module.

Date representation

There are a few changes to the way file dates are handled and displayed in the Metadata panel compared to version 1. Date Time Original and Date Time Digitized means the date that a photo was captured or was first created, while the Date Time field indicates the time the file was last modified **Figures 4.8–4.11** explain the differences between these bits of metadata information.

Next to Date Time Original is the Go to Date action button (this only applies to digital capture images). Clicking this button will filter the catalog view to show only those photos with matching capture dates. To exit this filter view, use the ⌘L (Mac), Ctrl L (PC) shortcut, which will toggle the catalog filters on or off.

Figure 4.8   In the case of camera capture files that have not been converted to DNG, the Date Time Original, Date Time Digitized, and Date Time entries will all agree.

Figure 4.9   Where a camera capture image has been converted to DNG, the Date Time entry reflects the fact that the file was modified, resaving it in a different file format. In this case a raw file was converted to DNG a few days after the time of capture.

Figure 4.10   Similarly, if I were to create an Edit copy as a TIFF, PSD, or JPEG version of the original, the Date Time would reflect that this version of the master image was created at a later date.

Figure 4.11   And if you import a photo that was originally created as a new document in Photoshop or was originally a scanned image, only the Date Time field will be displayed showing the date that the file was first created.

Capture time editing

If you know that the camera time and date settings are incorrect, you can address this by selecting Metadata ⇨ Edit Capture Time while working in the Library module. The resulting dialog (see **Figure 4.12**) allows you to amend the Date Time Original setting for an individual image or a group selection of images. If you are editing the capture time for a selection of images, the dialog preview displays the most selected image in the sequence and notifies you that the capture times for all the images in the current selection will be adjusted relative to the date and time of this image.

The Edit Capture Time feature is useful for a couple of reasons. One is that the internal clock on your camera may be wrong. Did you forget to set the internal clock correctly when you first bought your camera? If this is the case, you can select the "Adjust to a specified date and time" option and reset the date and time accordingly. In fact, for critical, time-sensitive work (such as GPS tagging via a separate GPS device), you may want to keep a regular check on your camera's internal clock to ensure that it is accurate.

When you travel abroad, do you always remember to set the camera for the correct new time zone? If you select the "Shift by set number of hours (time zone adjust)" option, you can compensate for the time zone differences for date and time entries that would otherwise be correct (unless of course you want the dates and times of all your captures to be recorded relative to a single time zone).

If you ever need to revert to the original embedded date and time, you can select the "Change to file's creation date" option to reset everything back to the original capture date and time setting.

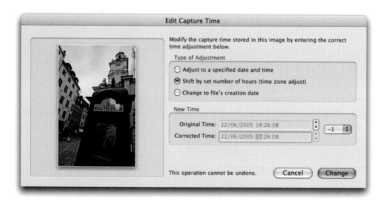

Figure 4.12   *The Edit Capture Time dialog.*

Camera model and serial number

These items instantly tell you which camera model and specific serial number were used to take a particular photograph. If you shoot using more than one digital camera body or have photos in the catalog taken by other photographers using the same camera type, this data can prove really useful, especially if you want to track down exactly which camera was used. Let's say there is a problem with one of the cameras. There may be damage to the sensor or a camera focusing problem. Using this data, you can pinpoint which specific body is responsible.

Artist EXIF metadata

The Artist name EXIF metadata will only show up if you have uploaded it as a custom user setting to your camera. I work with the Canon EOS cameras and use the EOS Utility program (see **Figure 4.13**) to access the Camera Settings. This allows me to enter my name as the camera owner. If you use a different camera system, the camera-supplied software will vary, but basically you should be able to do something similar to this by tethering the camera to the computer and using the utilities software that came with the camera to customize the camera settings as shown in Figure 4.13.

TIP

Check out the section on setting default camera-specific develop settings in Chapter 6 on pages 346–347.

TIP

Embedding your name as the owner in the camera settings seems like a pretty good idea. This ensures you get your name embedded in the capture file data even if you forget to add your name to the custom IPTC metadata. I have yet to hear of a case where a thief had been caught this way through using a stolen camera, but I am sure it will happen one day. Just remember that if you borrow someone else's camera or rent one, always check what the owner name metadata says. Once the owner metadata is embedded in the raw capture files, you won't be able to remove it so easily! If you are feeling brave, this metadata can be changed using an EXIF editor (ExifTool by Phil Harvey, http://www.sno.phy.queensu.ca/~phil/exiftool/) but this is a command line–based editor and therefore not all that easy to use.

Figure 4.13   *This shows the Canon EOS Utility program welcome screen. Click the Camera Settings/Remote Shooting option to open the Camera Capture window shown here and then click the Set-up menu button (circled) to set the owner name.*

Figure 4.14 *The Metadata panel in IPTC mode.*

Custom information metadata

So far I have mostly described the fixed, embedded camera metadata that is displayed in the Metadata panel. We are now going to look at working with custom metadata, which is data that is used to add image-specific information. This can broadly break down into information about the image such as the caption, headline, and location details of where the picture was shot. Also included is contact information about who created the photograph, such as your name, address, telephone number, email, and Web site. Finally, this information includes how the photo might be classified and what copyright licensing restrictions might be in force. As you start applying metadata to individual photos or groups of images, you gain the ability to differentiate them further and can reap the benefits of having a carefully cataloged image database. Applying such metadata now will help you in the future. Not only will it allow people to contact you more easily, it will also help when you are working in Lightroom and want to make targeted image searches.

In **Figure 4.14** you can see the Metadata panel in the IPTC view mode. You can see here that I have filled in the editable sections with examples of how you might use this panel to add descriptive information to a photo in the Lightroom catalog. You could, for example, select all the photos in a particular folder from the same shoot and start typing in custom information to categorize them. Most of the items in this panel, such as Creator, Job Title, and Address, are all pretty self-explanatory, and this is data you would want to apply to nearly every photo. However, the Headline and Caption fields can be used to add image-specific information. The Headline field might be used to describe a photo shoot, such as *Xmas catalog shoot 2007*, or *White on white fashion shoot*, while the Caption field can be used to provide a brief description of a scene, such as *Crowds lining the streets at local festival parade*. These custom bits of information are essential when submitting images to a picture library, and are particularly useful when you take into account that the value of an individual image can be increased as more information about the photograph is added. But even with a small-scale setup, you may find it rewarding to methodically catalog your photographs with basic metadata information in the Contact and other IPTC sections.

Metadata presets

You certainly don't want to spend too much of your time repetitively entering the same metadata. This is where the metadata presets come in handy, because you can use them to apply the metadata information that you need to input on a regular basis. To create a new metadata preset, click the Presets menu shown in **Figure 4.15** and select "Edit Presets," which will open the dialog shown in **Figure 4.16**. The fields in this dialog will be populated with any IPTC metadata already entered in the currently selected photo. So if you have already entered some custom metadata, this will appear ready to use as a new preset. Click the Done button at the bottom to open the Save Changes dialog where you can select Save As to save these settings as a new metadata preset.

Figure 4.15   *To select, add, or edit a metadata preset, go to the Preset menu near the top of the Metadata panel and click the menu list.*

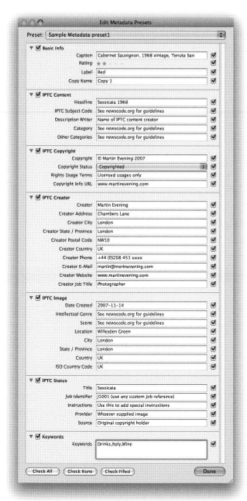

Figure 4.16   *Edit Metadata Presets dialog.*

Metadata presets provide a useful way to batch-apply informational metadata either at the import stage or later via the Metadata panel. You might therefore find it useful to create several metadata templates for the different types of shoots you normally do. Let's say you are a sports photographer and are often required to photograph the home football team whenever the team plays a game at the local stadium. You could save yourself a lot of time by creating a template with the name of the football team plus location information and apply this template every time you photograph a home game.

Editing and deleting metadata presets

If you want to edit an existing preset, first choose the preset you want to edit and then select Edit Presets. Apply the edit changes you want to make and click the Done button. This will open the Save Changes dialog again where you will have to select Save As and choose a new name for the preset (it must be a new name—you can't overwrite an existing preset). To remove a metadata preset, go to the Username/Library/Application Support/Adobe/Lightroom/Metadata Presets folder (Mac) or Local disk (C:\Username\Application Data\Adobe\Lightroom\Metadata Presets folder (PC) and delete the preset. Lightroom metadata templates will appear listed with the .lrtemplate suffix.

IPTC metadata

The editable items you see listed in Figure 4.15 and Figure 4.16 conform with the latest International Press Telecommunications Council (IPTC) standard file information specifications, used worldwide by the stock library and publishing industries. The items listed in the Metadata Preset dialog are not as comprehensive as those found in Photoshop, Bridge, or iView Media Pro, but they do conform to this IPTC metadata standard. Therefore, the metadata information you input via Lightroom will be recognizable when you export a file and use any of these other programs. Conversely, Lightroom is only able to display the metadata information it knows about. It won't be able to display all the data that might have been embedded via Bridge or iView. Should this be a cause for concern? For those who regard this as a shortcoming of Lightroom, it may well prove to be a deal breaker. But for others, the metadata options that are available should be ample. **Figure 4.17** provides some suggestions on how to complete the Basic and IPTC fields. It is not mandatory that all the listed fields be completed; just fill in as many as you find useful. The IPTC Creator section normally contains your contact details, and this information along with IPTC Creator details such as the Rights Usage Terms, will most likely remain the same until you move or change your email address. It is a good idea to begin by creating a metadata template that lists your copyright information and completes all the IPTC Creator sections. Save this template as a basic metadata preset and apply it to each set of new images that you import into the library. This way, you can ensure that after every new import, all the images carry complete copyright and contact information.

TIP

For help in understanding how to complete some of the advanced IPTC fields (such as IPTC Subject Code), try visiting the newscodes.org Web site.

TIP

When entering date information in the Metadata panel IPTC section, always enter the date in the following format: YYYY/MM/DD. The date field will then complete the date information as shown in Figure 4.17.

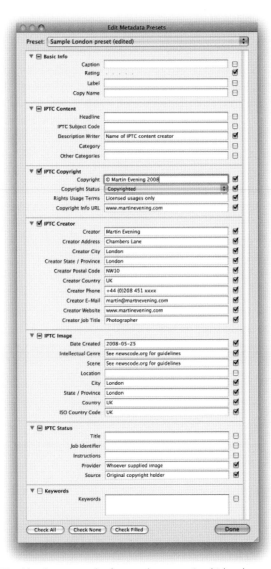

Figure 4.17   *Here is an example of a metadata preset in which only some of the fields have been filled in and the corresponding check boxes selected.*

The IPTC Image section allows you to enter information that is specific to the image, such as who provided the photograph. But note the distinction between this and the Description Writer field, which refers to the person who entered the metadata information: this might be a picture library editor, your assistant, or a work colleague. The remaining fields can be used to describe when and where the photograph was shot, job reference (such as a client art order), and so on.

In Figure 4.17 you will notice that I did not enter data into all the fields listed there and for those that were empty, I deliberately left the check boxes deselected. This is because a selected check box is saying "Change this metadata." When you create a metadata preset you will often want to devise a preset that is general enough to cover specific types of shoots but without including terms that will make a preset too specific. If you create a metadata preset to apply metadata to specific IPTC fields, you may not want to overwrite any other fields that contain existing, important metadata. Going back to the Figure 4.17 example you will notice that I only checked the boxes that contained new preset metadata. Let's say I had an image that had a caption, label, and rating information already added. If I applied the metadata preset shown in Figure 4.17 with all the boxes checked, this would overwrite these existing metadata settings with zero values, thereby erasing the caption, label, and rating. So when you create new presets it is always worth checking to make sure that you select only those items that you intend to change; otherwise your metadata presets can soon start messing up the photos in a catalog rather than enhance them. Of course, you can always edit an existing preset and deliberately set the preset to erase older metadata if you think that would be useful. But the overall message here is to configure these presets carefully and always test them out to make sure that they are doing exactly what you expect them to do.

An efficient way to add metadata

One of the things that has always bugged me about Bridge is the way the metadata entry is engineered. Even in Bridge CS3, if you select an image, make the Description field active, and enter new text, you have to press Enter to commit, select the next image, then re-target the Description field all over again to enter more text for the next photo.

Here is how it works in Lightroom. In **Figure 4.18** you can see a Library Grid view of images taken at a model casting. I tend to shoot model castings with the camera tethered to the computer and update the Title field with the model's name and model agency as I go along. In the screen shot shown here you can see that the Title field is currently active and I have typed in the model's details. Instead of hitting Enter to commit this data entry, you can use ⌘ (Mac), Ctrl (PC) plus a right or left arrow to progress to the next or previous image. This step will commit the text entry and progress to the next photo. It also keeps the metadata field active so that you are now ready to carry on typing in the information for the next photo.

Figure 4.18 *Here is an example of how to update the metadata for a series of photos without losing the focus on the field that's being edited in the Metadata panel.*

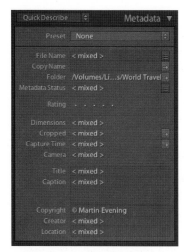

Figure 4.19 *This shows how the metadata information displayed in Lightroom will look when more than one photo is selected and the photos all have different metadata information.*

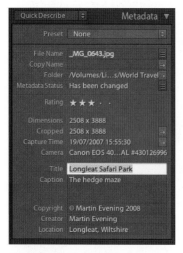

Figure 4.20 *If Show Metadata for Target Photo Only is selected, the Metadata panel displays the information for the most selected (target) photo.*

Metadata editing and target photos

If you have a group of images selected and go to the Metadata panel, the metadata information will display <mixed> values whenever the file attributes are varied. Only those values that remain constant (such as the copyright) will display the information that is common to all the selected photos (see the example in **Figure 4.19**). When you are in this "default" mode of operation, you can edit individual fields in the Metadata panel to update the metadata you wish to be common to all the selected files. So for example, if you want to apply the same title to all the selected images, you can edit the Title field and this will update all the selected images so that they share the same data.

However, if Show Metadata for Target Photo Only is selected in the Metadata menu, the Metadata panel display will look like the version shown in **Figure 4.20**, where it will now be possible to read the metadata information for the most selected or target photo only, even though you may have more than one photo selected in Lightroom.

To show you how this feature might be used, in the **Figure 4.21** example I have selected all of the photos from a folder in the catalog. The Metadata panel displays the information for the photo that is the most highlighted (the target photo). By using the ⌘ + arrow keys (Mac) or Ctrl + arrow keys (PC), you can navigate from one photo to the next without deselecting the active photo selection and read the metadata information for each individual image as you do so.

With the Show Metadata for Target Photo Only mode, the one thing you do need to be aware of is that you are now only able to edit the metadata on a per-image basis. This is a good thing because it means that you can keep an image selection active and edit the metadata of individual images. But a lot of people will be accustomed to making image selections and then using the Metadata panel to edit settings globally across the selection. So just be aware that although this menu item can prove useful (for the reasons I have just described), you probably won't want to have it enabled all of the time, as it can lead to some confusion.

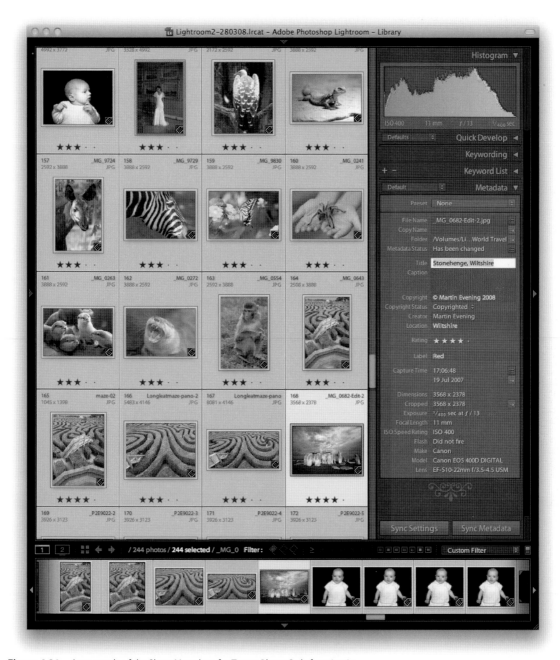

Figure 4.21 *An example of the Show Metadata for Target Photo Only function in use. Note that although all the photos have been selected and the titles are different, we can now read the information for the most selected photo.*

Mail and Web links

The E-Mail field now has an action button next to it. Another Lightroom user can send an email to the creator by simply clicking the action button. Lightroom then creates a new mail message using the default email program on the computer. If the mail program is not currently running, Lightroom will launch it automatically. Similarly, if you click the action button next to the Website field this will launch the default Web browser program and take you directly to the creator's Web site link.

1. In this view of the Metadata panel you can see the action buttons next to the E-Mail and Website items.

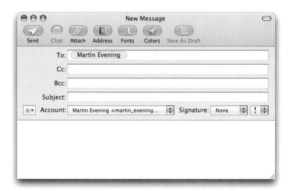

2. When you click the E-Mail action button, this automatically launches your default email client program and prepares a new email message, ready to be sent, using the email address entered in the Metadata panel's E-Mail section.

Copyright status

The Copyright section also has an action arrow next to the Copyright Info URL, which when clicked will take you directly to the Web site link. Above that there is also a Copyright Status field (see **Figure 4.22**), where you can set the copyright status as being Unknown, Copyrighted, or Public Domain. You can edit the copyright status via the Metadata panel, or you can go to the Metadata panel Presets menu, choose Edit Presets, and create a new custom metadata preset via the Metadata Presets dialog (as shown in **Figure 4.23**).

I should write a word or two here about what the term "copyrighted" means. Strictly speaking a copyrighted image is one that has been registered with the U.S. Library of Congress, and this is a term that applies to the United States only. So if you say an image has been copyrighted, it has an explicit meaning in the United States that does not translate to mean the exact same thing to those photographers who operate outside of the country where U.S. copyright laws do not apply. If you operate in the United States and use this field to mark an image as being copyrighted, then you should be aware of the precise meaning of the term and get these images registered. If you choose to use the Copyright field only to indicate this is your copyright, this statement should be clearly understood in nearly all countries and is all that you need to enforce your ownership rights.

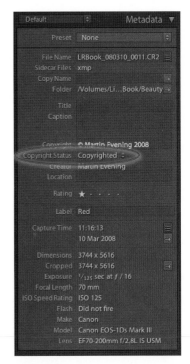

Figure 4.22 *You can set the Copyright status by clicking the menu highlighted here in the Metadata panel.*

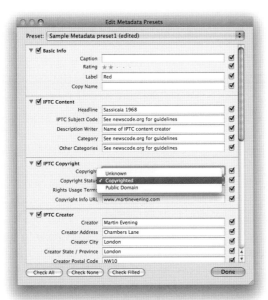

Figure 4.23 *The Edit Metadata Presets dialog, showing the Copyright status options.*

Figure 4.24 *In this example, the Seascapes keyword is a subset of Nature Subjects and the Bygdøy peninsula keyword is a subset of Places > Europe > Norway.*

Keywording and Keyword List panels

The most effective way to categorize your images is to label them with keyword information so you can use the Filter bar to search for pictures, either by typing in a specific text term to search for (such as a keyword), or by carrying out a general, filtered metadata search.

You can add keyword metadata via the Import Photos dialog as you import your images, or you can add and edit the keywords later via the Keywording panel. **Figure 4.24** shows how I have sorted the keywords in the Keyword List panel into a hierarchy, which makes it easier for me to locate specific photographs. Notice how some of the keywords have been sorted into categories such as *Nature subjects* and *Places*. In the *Places* keyword category is a keyword subcategory called *Europe* and within that *Norway*, and then a sub-keyword: *Bygdøy peninsula*. You will find that it pays to establish a proper keyword hierarchy that suits the content of your library. Because you can assign multiple keywords to associate different criteria with a particular photo, you can then search for your images in lots of various ways. Note that the photo illustrated here also contains the keyword *Seascapes*. So you could categorize this image via using both *Nature subjects > Seascapes* and *Places > Norway > Bygdøy peninsula*.

You can also filter by keyword using the Keyword List panel. Just click the arrow next to the keyword count number.

Three ways to add new keywords

To start using keyword metadata, you can add new keywords as you import images into the catalog (**Figure 4.25**) or add and edit keywords via the Keywording panel (**Figure 4.26**). You can also add keywords to the Keyword List panel in anticipation of the keywords needed (**Figure 4.27**). Then select an image you want to update, select a keyword, and click in the box to the left (**Figure 4.28**). Whichever method you use, once a keyword has been added, it will then always be listed in the Keyword List panel. Once the keywords are there, you can arrange them into a suitable hierarchy. After a keyword has been logged into the system, Lightroom then autocompletes keywords for you as you start typing in the first few letters for a new keyword entry. Apart from making it quicker to enter new data, this helps you avoid duplicating keyword entries through careless spelling or typos. Lightroom also autoassigns the correct hierarchy. For example, the next time I add the keyword *Seascapes*, the *Seascapes* keyword will automatically be assigned under the *Nature subjects* category in the Keyword List panel.

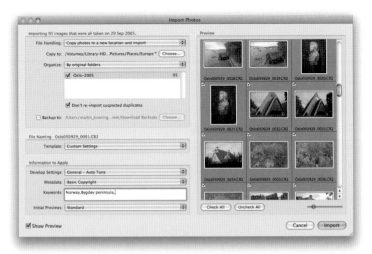

Figure 4.25   *You can add keywords at the time of import. In this example, I entered the relevant keywords into the Keywords field. Lightroom will offer to autocomplete a keyword if it recognizes that it might belong to the Lightroom keyword database.*

Figure 4.28   *When you roll the mouse over a keyword in the Keyword List panel, a check box appears to the left of the keyword. If you click in this box, you can add a tick mark, which means the keyword is added to the currently selected image or images. If you click the arrow to the right of the keyword count number, Lightroom filters the catalog to show all photos that share the same keyword.*

Figure 4.26   *Alternatively, you can go directly to the Keywording panel and type in the keyword or keywords you wish to assign to a selected photo (in the box where it says "Click here to add keywords"). Here, I typed in "Bygdøy peninsula > Norway > Europe > Places" to add the keyword "Bygdøy peninsula" with the desired hierarchy.*

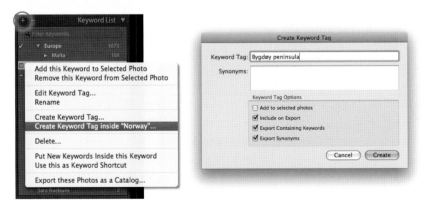

Figure 4.27   *You can also add keywords in advance. In this example, I right-clicked on the Norway keyword and chose Create Keyword Tag inside "Norway." This opened the Create Keyword Tag dialog. I then added "Bygdøy peninsula" as a child of Norway.*

Figure 4.29 *Keywords associated with a single image or group of images are listed in the Library module Keywording panel. In the example shown here, I highlighted all the images from the New York folder shown in Figures 4.30 and 4.31. The keywords marked with an asterisk indicate that these keywords apply to a sub-selection of images only.*

TIP

Most of the time, autocompletion can be a useful thing to have active. However, there are times when it can become a pain. For example, when I do a model casting and enter the names of models in the Caption field of the Metadata panel in the Library module, I don't find autocompletion particularly helpful. Some model names can be subtly different, and often I find it easier to switch this off rather than fight with the suggestions that Lightroom is making on my behalf.

TIP

When you double-click on a keyword category or individual keyword, or single-click on the number to the right of a keyword, Lightroom displays those keyword images in the Content area. In this respect, the Keyword List panel behaves like a metadata filter tool.

Applying and managing existing keywords

The Keywording panel is located directly above the Keyword List panel and provides an overview of all the keywords associated with a specific image or collection of images. When you click an image, you will see any keywords present listed in this panel, separated by a comma (there should be no spaces). As with the Import Photos dialog, you can add a new keyword by typing it into the Keywords field in the Keywording panel, and Lightroom will attempt to autocomplete the entries as you type. If you have multiple images selected, the Keywording panel displays all the keywords that are active in the image selection. Those keywords that are common to all images in the selection are displayed as normal, but those keywords that apply only to a sub-selection of the images will be marked with an asterisk (**Figure 4.29**). If you have a multiple selection of images and want to unify a particular keyword across all of the images in that selection, simply highlight the asterisk and press the Delete key. This will ensure that all the selected images are now assigned with the keyword. If you want to change a particular keyword, you can always highlight it and type in a new word or press Delete to remove it from the selection.

You can apply keywords to photos in the catalog in a couple of ways. **Figure 4.30** shows how you can apply a keyword to a selection of images by dragging a keyword to the image selection. The good thing about this method is that it is easy to hit the target as you drag and drop the keyword. The other option is to make a selection first in the Content area and then drag the selection to the keyword. In **Figure 4.31** I selected the same group of images and dragged the selection to the keyword *New York*.

Autocomplete options

As you enter metadata for keywords and other editable metadata fields, it can save time to have the "Offer suggestions from recently entered values" option checked in the Metadata Catalog settings (see Figure 4.68 on page 176), where you can also click the Clear All Suggestion Lists button to reset the memory and clear all memorized words. If you type in a keyword where there are two or more possible sources, Lightroom will offer these as choices such as *Salisbury > Wiltshire > UK*, or *Salisbury > Maryland > USA* (assuming both are logged as keywords). See page 150 for more about the way Lightroom handles identical keywords such as these.

Figure 4.30 *You can apply keywords to an image or selection of images by highlighting the images you want to apply the keyword to and then dragging a keyword from the Keyword List panel to the image selection.*

Figure 4.31 *You can also apply keywords to an image or selection of images by highlighting them in the Content area and dragging the selection to the relevant keyword in the Keyword List panel.*

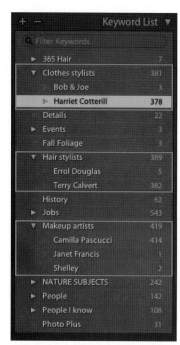

Figure 4.32 *Keywords can be used to categorize the images in ways that are meaningful to your business. In the Keywords panel view shown here, you can see how I am able to select images based on the personnel who worked with me on commercial jobs.*

TIP

We'll be looking at how to filter photos shortly, but there is also a Filter Keywords section at the top of the Keyword List panel (see Figure 4.32) where you can type in a keyword to check if a keyword exists and therefore narrow the number of keyword items that appear in the Keyword List panel. For example, if I typed in "Camilla," it would narrow down the Keyword list to show "Camilla" in Makeup artists as well as "Camilla" in People I know.

Removing keywords

It is easy enough to remove keywords. You can go to the Keyword List panel, select the keyword or keywords you want to delete, and click the minus button at the top of the panel. This will delete the keyword from the Keyword List hierarchy list and also remove it from any photos that had that keyword assigned to them. Of course, if you do remove a keyword via the Keywords panel you will only be deleting it from the Lightroom database. If you think that the keyword had already been saved to the file's XMP space, you will need to force-save the metadata change (the keyword deletion) back to the file's XMP space by choosing Metadata ⇨ Save Metadata to Files. By the same token, if keywords are removed using an external program, the keywords will not appear removed when you view the photo in Lightroom.

As photos are removed from the catalog, keywords that were formerly associated with those pictures will consequently become unused. You can remove them by selecting and deleting as I have just described, or clear them from the Keyword List panel by going to the Metadata menu and choosing Purge Unused Keywords. Just so that you don't remove these keywords accidentally, a warning dialog appears asking you to confirm this action.

Keyword hierarchy

It is important to plan not only your keyword list but also the hierarchy of keywords using a controlled vocabulary of keyword categories. The keyword list can be edited in the Keyword List panel by dragging and dropping the keywords in whichever way suits your needs best. It is possible to have several tiers of subcategories. For example, you could organize place name keywords in the following order: *Places > Country > State > City*. When you are working in the Keywording panel, you can enter new keywords and assign a hierarchy by including a > character after the keyword, followed by the category. So if you wanted to add a new keyword called *Elephants* as a subcategory of *Animals* and *Nature subjects*, you would type *Elephants > Animals > Nature subjects*. When you press (←Enter), you will see the Elephants keyword appear as a new subset keyword in the Keyword List panel and be listed in the Keyword List section of the Keywording panel.

How you categorize library images is entirely up to you, but if you submit work to an external photo library, you will most likely be given guidelines on the acceptable keywords and categories to use when annotating photographs for submission. These guidelines are normally supplied privately to photographers who work directly with the picture agencies. But there are online resources that you can refer to that describe how to use what is known as a "controlled vocabulary," which ensures that the keyword terms used to describe the images conform to prescribed sets of words universally used by others working in the same branch of the industry. When you get into complex keywording (and I do know photographers who assign images with 50 keywords or more), it is important to be methodical and precise about which terms are used and the hierarchy they belong to.

Keyword categories can also be used to catalog images in ways that are helpful to your business. For commercial shoots, I find it is useful to keep a record of who worked on which shot. Some catalog programs let you set up a custom database template with user-defined fields. In Lightroom you can set up keyword categories for the various types of personnel and add the names of individuals as a subset, or child, of the parent keyword category. **Figure 4.32** shows how I created keyword categories for *Clothes stylists*, *Hairdressers,* and *Makeup artists*. Inside these categories I created subcategories of keywords listing the people I work with regularly. Once I have established such a keyword hierarchy, all I have to do is start typing in someone's name. If Lightroom recognizes this as a possible match to an existing keyword in the Lightroom keyword database, Lightroom autocompletes the keyword metadata entry in addition to correctly placing the keyword within the established hierarchy. This type of organization is also useful for separating library images by job/client names. When the keyword names are in place, you should find it fairly easy to keep your catalog of images updated.

Importing and exporting keyword hierarchies

You can create your own keyword hierarchy from scratch or import one that has already been created. All the keywords that are currently utilized in Lightroom can be exported by selecting Metadata ⇨ Export Keywords. A keywords export is saved as a text file using a tab-delimited format. Similarly, you can choose Metadata ⇨ Import Keywords to import keywords into Lightroom from a tab-delimited keyword file (**Figure 4.33**).

Figure 4.33   *Here is an example of a keyword list to which I added an imported "D-65" keyword list, created by Seth Resnick for attendees of his D-65 workshops.*

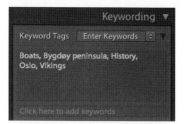

Figure 4.34 *When Enter Keywords is selected in the Keywording panel, you can edit the keywords directly, but the implicit keywords will be hidden from view.*

Figure 4.35 *When Keywords & Containing Keywords or Will Export is selected in the Keywording panel, the implicit keywords will be made visible so that you can see a flattened view of all the keywords applied to a photo, but you won't be able to edit them.*

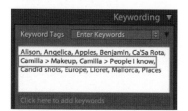

Figure 4.36 *In Enter Keywords mode, you won't always see the keyword hierarchy (as used when typing in a new keyword) unless there are identical keywords but with different parents.*

A tab-delimited file is a plain text file with a tab between each indented level in the text. Tab-delimited files are one way to import and place data that is arranged in a hierarchical format. In the tip to the left you will see a link to David Riecks' ControlledVocabulary.com Web site, from which you can purchase a ready-made vocabulary that is compatible with Lightroom. To install this, download the file, launch Lightroom, and choose Import keywords from the Metadata menu. That's it—these keywords will be added to the Keyword List panel. Similarly, you can export a keyword hierarchy for sharing on other computer systems or catalogs by selecting "Export keywords."

Implied keywords

The Keywording panel lists keywords that have been applied explicitly to images in the Keyword List section. But as I mentioned, some of the keywords that you enter will already have implicit keywords associated with them. So if in the future, I apply the keyword *Bygdøy peninsula*, it automatically includes the implicit keywords: *Places* and *Europe*. So I don't have to type in *Bygdøy peninsula > Oslo > Europe > Places* if there is already a keyword with such a hierarchy in the database. It should only be necessary to type in the first few letters such as *Byg...* and Lightroom will autocomplete the rest. If the Keyword List menu is set to display Enter Keywords (**Figure 4.34**), you can edit the keywords in this mode but the implicit keywords will be hidden (although they will nonetheless remain effective when conducting searches). If you select Keywords & Parents or Will Export (**Figure 4.35**), you will see a flattened list of keywords that includes the implicit keywords, but you won't be able to edit them in the Keywording panel when using these modes.

When you enter a new keyword, you use the > key to signify that this keyword is a child of the following keyword (such as *Chicago > Illinois > USA > Places*). This establishes the hierarchy, and as I explained, when you use the Enter Keywords mode, all you will see is the first keyword; the parent keywords will be hidden. However, if you apply a keyword that is identical to another keyword where both have different parents, you will then see the > hierarchy appear in the Keywords dialog. To give you an example of why this is the case, take a look at **Figure 4.36**, in which you see the Keyword *Camilla* repeated twice. This is because my wife Camilla is both a makeup artist as well as being "someone I know." I can add the keyword *Camilla* in two separate contexts. Lightroom is able to differentiate between the Camilla I know and the Camilla I work with.

Keyword sets

The Keywording panel can also be used to display sets of keywords. Having commonly used keywords quickly accessible in this way can easily save you a lot of time when keywording certain types of photo projects. It offers a quick method for adding commonly used keywords to images in the Content area. Select an image or a group of images and click a keyword to apply it to the selection. To access a keyword set list, click the disclosure triangle (circled in **Figure 4.37**) to reveal the Set section of the Keywording panel. This will normally display Recent Keywords, which can be useful for most keywording jobs. Or, you can select one of the supplied Keyword Set presets such as Outdoor Photography, Portrait Photography, or Wedding Photography. In Figure 4.37 you can see an example of one such Keyword preset and instructions for previewing the keyboard number shortcuts for each keyword in the set. For example, if want to assign a *Flowers & Plants* keyword, I would hold down Alt to preview the number shortcuts in the Keywording panel and note that I need to use the Alt–9 shortcut to apply this particular keyword (see also **Figure 4.38**).

Figure 4.37 *The Keywording panel shown here displays the custom keyword set created on this page. Hold down the* Alt *key to preview the keyboard shortcut numbers and use the* Alt *key plus number shown in the panel list preview to quickly assign a keyword.*

Figure 4.38 *Here is an example of the Outdoor Photography keyword set in use. With this loaded you have a set of nine keywords at your disposal with which to annotate a set of photos.*

Creating your own custom keyword sets

If you have lot of photos to edit from a specific trip, or there are certain types of events that you photograph regularly, you will most likely find it useful to create your own keyword sets for these types of shoots. To do so, follow these instructions:

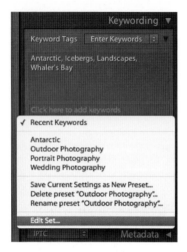

1. To create a custom keyword set, go to the Keyword Set section of the Keywording panel and click "Edit set." This will open the dialog shown here (using the current keyword set list) where you can edit which keywords you would use for quick access when keyword-editing a particular project. In this example, I created a keyword set that I could use when editing photographs taken in Antarctica.

2. After creating a new custom keyword set, go to the Metadata menu and check out the Keyword Set submenu to see the short-cuts listed for applying keywords (these shortcuts are toggled). The Keywording panel shown here now also displays this new custom keyword set. Hold down the Alt key to preview the keyboard shortcuts and use the Alt key plus a number to quickly assign any of these keywords.

Suggested keywords

Here is a brand-new Lightroom 2 feature. If you select Suggested
Keywords from the Keyword Set menu, Lightroom will adapt the list
of keywords that are available for use based upon the keywords that
are already in that image plus those photos that are close neighbors
in terms of capture time. The logic system that's used here works
really well when trying to guess what other keywords you might like
to add to a particular photograph. In **Figure 4.39**, the selected image
had the keywords *New York* and *USA*. Lightroom was able to suggest
adding the other keywords shown in the Keyword set list such as *Times
Square*, *Central Park*, *Manhattan*, and *Architecture*. This is because all
the other photos that had *New York* and *USA* as keywords *also* had
one more of these keywords assigned. The list of suggested keywords
was also prioritized based on the keywords found in photos taken
shortly before or after the current photograph.

TIP

The more keywords you have in the
source photo or neighboring photos,
the more accurate the suggested
keywords will be. The diversity of your
keywording will also count too. If all
the keywords in a set of images are
nearly identical, there is not much
Lightroom can do when it comes to
suggesting alternative keywords.

Figure 4.39 *Here is an example of Suggested Keywords in use. One photograph is
selected here and the Keyword set list adapts to display a list of keywords based on
an analysis of the keywords assigned to similarly keyworded photos taken around the
same time.*

TIP

In Keywords mode you can enter more than one single keyword into the painter field. You will also notice in the Keyword List panel that the keywords entered will appear with a plus sign next to them (see the Keyword List panel view in Step 3 on the facing page).

Keywords

Labels

Flags/Picks

Ratings

Metadata

Develop settings

Rotation

Figure 4.40 *The Painter tool cursor icon will change appearance depending on the mode you are using to reflect the type of setting that is being applied.*

The Painter tool

The Painter tool is located in the Library module toolbar where it can be activated by clicking on the tool to float it from the docked position (see **Figure 4.40** for the cursor styles). You can also access the Painter tool by going to the Metadata menu and choosing Enable Painting, or use the ⌘ Alt K (Mac) or Ctrl Alt K (PC) shortcut. You can then select which type of settings you want to apply with the Painter tool (see **Figure 4.41**).

The Painter tool is ideal for whenever you want to repeatedly apply a keyword or combination of keywords to photos in the Library module Grid view. You can do this by clicking on single photos that you wish to edit (or click and drag over several photos). But that's not all; you can also use the Painter tool to paint using labels, flags, ratings, metadata, or Develop settings. As you can see, there are lots of potential uses for this tool: not just applying keywords, but other tasks such as painting with a saved Develop setting. Although the Painter tool is very versatile, you do have to use it carefully. Some Painter tool actions (such as applying labels or ratings) have a toggle action whereby clicking or dragging a second time causes the cursor to switch to an eraser cursor (✐), which will undo a setting. Also keep in mind that you have to be careful to target the thumbnail and not just the cell area. For jobs where you are constantly applying the same instruction, like "rotate this photo 90°," or "apply this set combination of keywords," the Painter tool does have its uses, but often it can be much easier to just select the photos first and then apply a setting to all the photos in one shot.

Figure 4.41 *With some of the Painter tool options such as Rotation you will have menu options to choose from.*

1. To work with the Painter tool, go to the Library module toolbar and click the tool icon to activate it (or use the ⌘ Alt K [Mac], Ctrl Alt K [PC] shortcut). The Painter tool spray can will undock itself from the toolbar and replace the normal pointer cursor as you move it within the Grid view area.

2. You can enter the keyword or keywords you wish to apply in the empty field in the toolbar, and as you enter each keyword, Lightroom will autocomplete the text by referencing previous or recently used keywords in the database. Alternatively, you can choose Metadata ⇨ Set Keyword Shortcut, or press ⌘ Shift K (Mac) or Ctrl Shift K (PC) to open the Set Keyword Shortcut dialog and enter the keywords there.

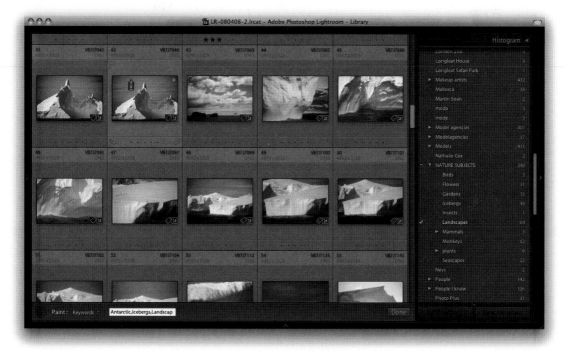

3. The Painter tool is now ready for use. Basically, you just click or drag with the Painter tool anywhere in the Grid view. In this example I used the Painter tool to "paint" the keywords entered in Step 2. When you have finished using the Painter tool and want to switch out of "paint" mode, click in the empty area of the toolbar where the Painter tool normally lives, or use the ⌘ Alt K (Mac), Ctrl Alt K (PC) shortcut.

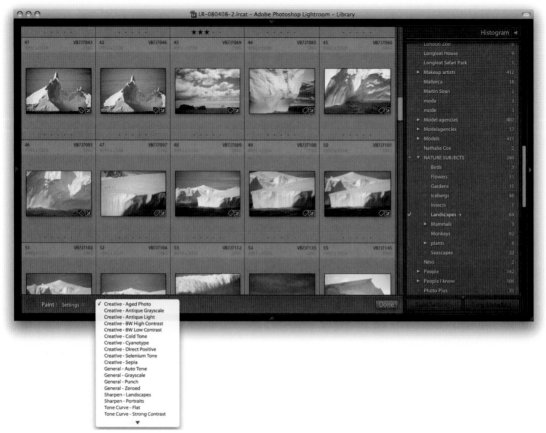

4. As was pointed out in the main text, you can use the Painter tool to apply other things than just keywords. In this example the Painter tool is currently in Settings mode. When this mode is selected, you will see a menu list of saved Develop presets. If you select Rotation, the menu will change to allow you to select a specific rotation or to flip an image. If Metadata is selected, the menu list will let you choose from pre-saved metadata templates. And likewise, if Rating, Pick, or Label is selected, you are also offered a choice of settings in this section.

Photo filtering and searches

So far we have looked at how to manage images using folders to group the images in the catalog. We then looked at how to rate images and separate the keepers from the rejects, and lastly how to add metadata information, including keywords to describe the image content, thus adding context, meaning, and ultimately more value to the pictures in the catalog. Now let's look at how to use the Library module tools to conduct image searches to find specific photos.

Filter bar

One of the key new features in Lightroom 2 is the Filter bar (see **Figure 4.42**), which can be accessed in the Content area whenever you are in the Library Grid view mode. The Filter bar replaces the Find panel and Metadata Browser in Lightroom 1 and combines the best features of these two panels with the search functionality of the old Keywording Tags panel. The Filter bar is now the main place to go for making refined filter selections of photos in the catalog (although you can still use the Filmstrip controls for filtering by rating and labels). The Filter bar has therefore rationalized the filter controls that were previously in Lightroom, in order to make the filtering process more centralized and flexible.

TIP

The most important tip of all here is to remember that the \ key will toggle the Filter bar visibility on or off. Another important tip is to use ⌘L (Mac) or Ctrl L (PC) to toggle the catalog filters on or off. Quite often you will find yourself trying to work out where all your photos have disappeared to, and this is all because you forgot there was a filter active!

NOTE

Basically we have a new and more streamlined approach to the Library module panels layout. The left panels contain the catalog source controls such as Folders and Collections, and the right panels contain the catalog edit controls, such as the Quick Develop and Keywording panels.

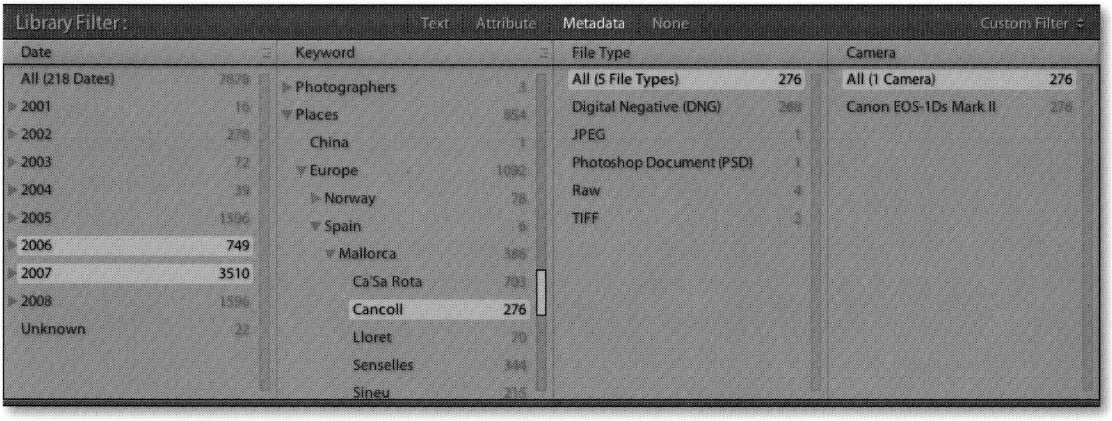

Figure 4.42   *The Filter bar lets you filter the photos shown in the catalog using Text, Attributes (like those in the Filmstrip), and Metadata.*

The Filter bar layout

There are three components to the Filter bar: Text, Attribute, and Metadata. These can be used to make a filter search of the entire catalog, or a subset of catalog images. This is an important point to remember, because if you want to conduct a search of the entire catalog, you must remember to go to the Catalog panel and select All Photographs first. This will allow you to carry out a global search. For speedier, targeted searches, make a sub-selection of photos first before using the Filter bar. It is so easy forget this important rule; there are many times where I will go to the Filter bar with the intention of carrying out a global search yet forget that I have a sub-selection of photos active! So if a Filter bar search doesn't seem to be working properly, check that you have All Photographs selected. If you wish to undo a Filter bar search or toggle a Filter bar search on or off, use the Enable Filters shortcut: ⌘ L (Mac) or Ctrl L (PC).

Text filter searches

If you click the Text tab in the Filter bar and then click in the search field, you can type in a text term that will filter the photos in the current catalog selection for any terms that match (**Figure 4.43**). The search target can be limited to the following: Filename, Copy Name, Title, Caption, Keywords, searchable IPTC data, searchable EXIF data, Metadata, or Any Searchable Field (should you wish to search all types of text data). A Filename search is fairly obvious. I often search specifically by Filename using a Contains rule and type what I am looking for in the search field. I use this filter method when clients make their final image selections and send me a list of filenames. All I need to do is make a general selection of the client images and type in the last four digits. This is usually enough to quickly locate the images I am after. I discussed Copy Name more fully in the Metadata panel section earlier. Basically you can use this to search the copy names that have been used for all your virtual copy images. All the other types of searches will enable you to narrow the range of a text search to concentrate on the selected metadata type such as Caption only or Keywords only. If you are unsure of where to search precisely, then the easiest option is to choose Any Searchable Field, but doing so might mean you end up with too many matches to choose from. Therefore, narrowing down the search range can make things easier here. For example, in **Figure 4.44** a general search for "ann" could yield any number of matches, probably too many to be really useful. By limiting the search to Metadata only, I was able to restrict the number of filter results.

Figure 4.43 *Filter bar text searches can be carried out by searching Any Searchable Field (as shown here) or by searching specific library criteria only, such as keywords, filenames, or captions.*

Search rules

You can limit a filter search further via the Rule menu in the Text filter section (Figure 4.44). You can choose rules such as Contains (where there is a partial match), Contains All (for an exact match), Doesn't Contain (to exclude files that match the text entered below), Starts With (obviously anything that begins with the phrase entered) and Ends With (for anything that ends with the phrase entered). This further search refinement can again make all the difference in ensuring that you have full control over the filtering process and don't end up with too many matches.

TIP

Note that you can choose Library ⇒ Find or press ⌘F (Mac) or Ctrl F (PC) to go directly to the Search field in the Filter bar.

Click the X icon to clear the current search term.

Figure 4.44 *Here is an example of the Filter bar being used to search for a term that contains the letter sequence "ann." You can select the search criteria containing those letters in any part, matching exactly, not containing those letters, or starting with or ending with those letters.*

Figure 4.45 *The combined Search Target and Search Rule menu.*

Combined search rules

If you click the search field icon circled in **Figure 4.45**, this opens a combined menu for all the Search Target and Search Rules options. You can navigate this single menu to choose the desired settings. Note that if you click the X icon on the right, you can use this to clear a current text filter term and undo the current text filter.

Fine-tuned text searches

You could apply the "Start with" rule when searching, but it is handy to know that you can conduct a search for anything that begins with a specific search term by typing + at the beginning. If I type *+cape* in the search field, this will display photos with any keywords that begin with *cape,* such as *Cape Point* or *Cape Town,* and exclude keywords like *Landscape* that don't begin with *cape* (**Figure 4.46**). Inverse searches can be made by typing an exclamation mark before the search term. If I want to search for keyworded photos that were shot on location but not include Jobs, Europe, or USA, I can type *Places !Europe !USA !Jobs* in the Find panel search field.

To further illustrate the points made here, you can use a search term like *+cape* to search for all terms that start with the word *cape* and combine this with *!USA* to also exclude any USA locations that start with the word *cape*. So you could end up with search results that include *Cape Point*, but exclude *Cape Canaveral*, Florida.

Figure 4.46 *Examples of refined text searches using a + or ! in the search field.*

Attribute filter searches

The Attribute filter tools are something that I touched on earlier in the previous chapter when discussing the Filmstrip filter controls. The Filter bar offers the exact same set of tools, except they can be accessed directly in the Filter bar alongside the other filter items (**Figure 4.47**). It is therefore simply a case of it being easier to integrate a refine filter search based on criteria such as the flag status, the star rating, color label, or whether you wish to filter the master images or copy images only. Everything is the same here; you can click the buttons to apply a filter and click the star rating options to specify whether to filter for photos with a star rating that is the same and higher, the same and lower, or the same rating only.

Figure 4.47   *The Attribute section of the Filter bar showing the rating options menu.*

Metadata filter searches

The Metadata section replaces the former Metadata Browser panel and, as I mentioned earlier, integrates the filter functionality of the Keyword List panel (formerly known as the Keyword Tags panel). It used to be the case that you would have to navigate the (potentially complex) hierarchy structure of the Keyword Tags panel to locate a keyword you were looking to filter by, and then go to the Metadata Browser panel to select additional criteria to search with. It was doable providing you didn't have too many keywords and you knew how and where all the keywords were listed. The Metadata filter section (**Figure 4.48**) provides customizable columns that you can adapt in an almost infinite number of ways to carry out a filter search.

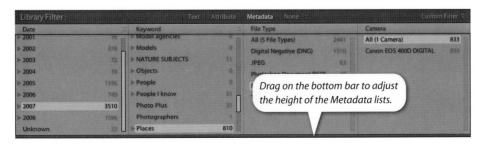

Drag on the bottom bar to adjust the height of the Metadata lists.

Figure 4.48   *The Metadata section of the Filter bar.*

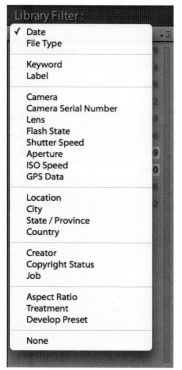

Figure 4.49 *This shows the expanded list of options for a Filter bar Metadata search.*

Metadata filter options

The Metadata section can be adjusted in height by dragging the bar at the bottom up or down. When the metadata panels are expanded in height, they can consume a lot of valuable space in the Grid view Content area, which is a problem if all you are interested in doing is applying a filter using one panel only. This is another reason why it is important to remember the \ keyboard shortcut, which will toggle hiding and showing the Filter bar. It is unfortunate that the screen animation for this is rather slow compared to the speed with which the side panels and toolbar appear and disappear from the screen, but you can at least conveniently move the Filter bar out the way when it is not needed.

The individual panels can be customized by clicking on the panel name and selecting from one of the many other search criteria that are available (**Figure 4.49**). Because you are able to customize the layout of the panels, this provides lots of opportunities for you to filter the catalog photos in different ways. Basically, you can use the ⇧Shift or the ⌘ key (Mac), Ctrl key (PC) to select more than one search term in a single panel. And because you can customize each panel by metadata filter type, you can have more than one panel used to filter by, say, Keyword (or whatever else it is you may wish to duplicate). The default view gives you four panels to work with, but you can customize the layout by clicking the + icon at the top right in each panel (**Figure 4.50**) to remove or add extra columns (up to eight in total).

Metadata filter categories

The Date categories allow you to progressively filter by date. You can follow the example shown in **Figure 4.51** and use a Date list to search first by year date, then expand the year folders to search by month and then by date.

Figure 4.50 *Adding or removing a column in the Filter bar Metadata section.*

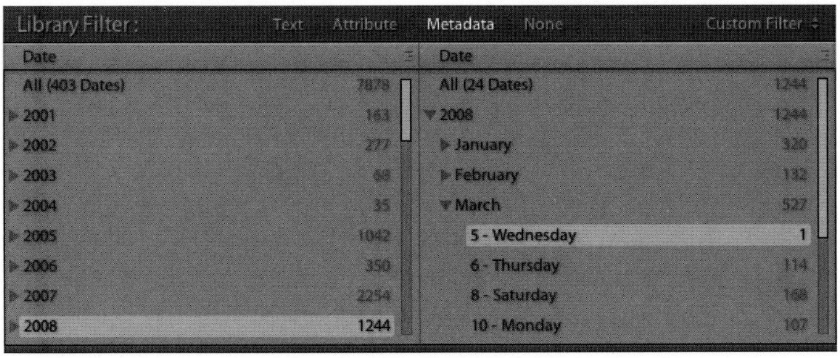

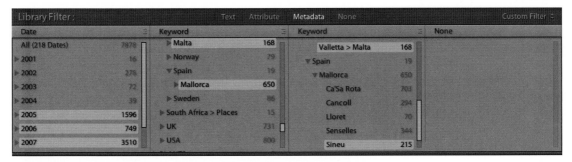

Figure 4.51 *This shows a metadata Date filter being used to filter photos by year. In the second column I show how you can expand the folder dates to filter by month or by individual dates.*

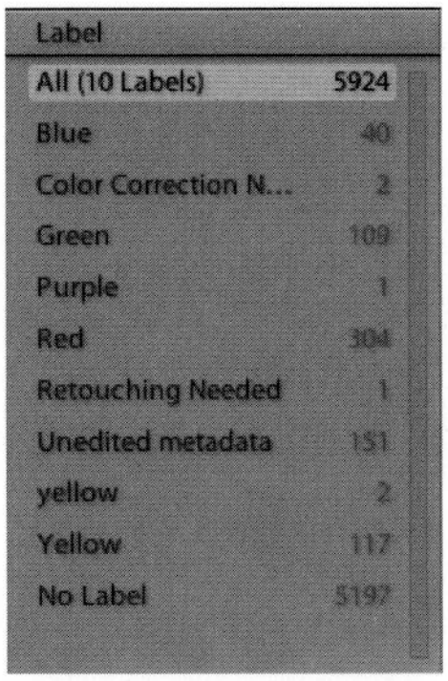

Figure 4.52 *The Color Label category allows you to filter labels by swatch color as well as by the color label text description.*

The File Type section can be used to separate images by file format to make it easy for you to quickly filter out images, such as the PSD masters or the raw DNG images. The Keyword category is one that you will probably want to use all the time when searching the catalog.

The Label category (**Figure 4.52**) is almost the same thing as clicking on a color label swatch in the Filters section of the Filmstrip. The main difference is that the Label filter used here allows you to distinguish between the color of a label and any text associated with that label. To understand what I mean by this, please refer to the section on sorting Color labels coming up on page 187.

Figure 4.53 shows an example of a Filter bar search that achieves the same filter result as the two-step approach described at the beginning of this chapter. The Filter bar search applied here was based on a one-star filter for photographs taken from 2005 to 2007, using the keywords *Mallorca* or *Malta*, and a further keyword filter for photos with the keywords *Sineu* and *Valletta*.

TIP

Selecting multiple items within a single panel will add photos to a filter selection. Adding metadata items from other panels will "intersect" with the photo filter selection to narrow the search further.

NOTE

In Figure 4.53, I used the Shift key to make contiguous selections of Metadata items and the ⌘ key (Mac), Ctrl key (PC) to add discontiguous items to a filter list.

Figure 4.53 *By repeating the keyword across two or more panels, you have more flexible options when filtering by keyword to carry out OR and AND type searches .*

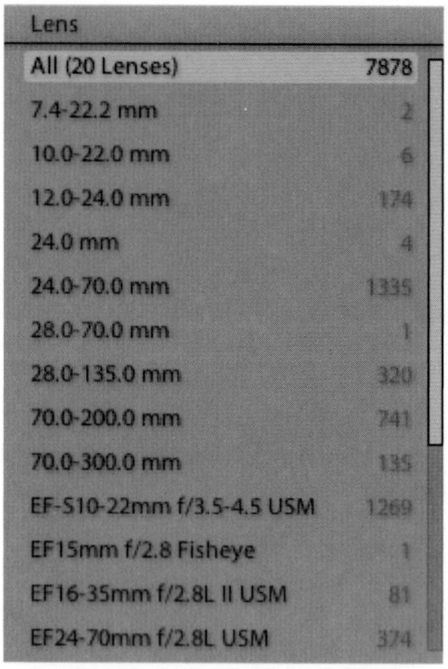

Lens	
All (20 Lenses)	7878
7.4-22.2 mm	2
10.0-22.0 mm	6
12.0-24.0 mm	174
24.0 mm	4
24.0-70.0 mm	1335
28.0-70.0 mm	1
28.0-135.0 mm	320
70.0-200.0 mm	741
70.0-300.0 mm	135
EF-S10-22mm f/3.5-4.5 USM	1269
EF15mm f/2.8 Fisheye	1
EF16-35mm f/2.8L II USM	81
EF24-70mm f/2.8L USM	374

Figure 4.54   *The Lens filter category.*

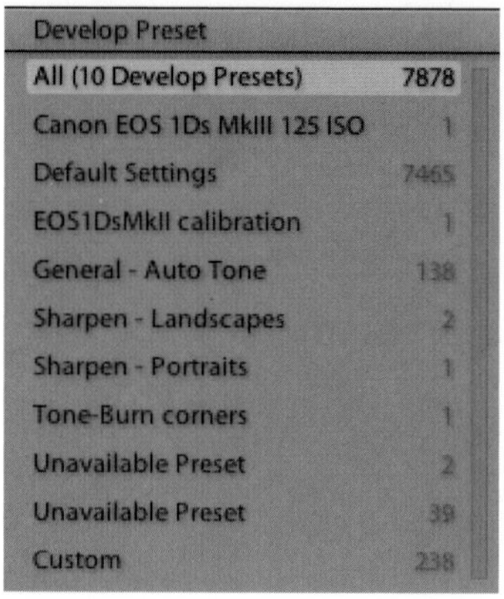

Develop Preset	
All (10 Develop Presets)	7878
Canon EOS 1Ds MkIII 125 ISO	1
Default Settings	7465
EOS1DsMkII calibration	1
General - Auto Tone	138
Sharpen - Landscapes	2
Sharpen - Portraits	1
Tone-Burn corners	1
Unavailable Preset	2
Unavailable Preset	39
Custom	238

Figure 4.55   *The Develop Preset filter category.*

The Camera section lists photographs by both camera model and serial number. Suppose, for example, you suspected that a fault was developing with one of your camera bodies. Inspecting the images by camera type can let you filter out the images that were shot using that specific camera. The Lens section (**Figure 4.54**) is great for filtering the library by lens type, which can be really handy when you are searching for, say, shots that were taken with an ultra-wide angle lens. The Shutter Speed section allows you to filter photos according to the shutter speed the photos were shot at. Likewise, the Aperture section lists every aperture setting that has been used, which might be useful for shortlisting pictures shot at the widest lens aperture and therefore with the shallowest depth of focus. With ISO Speed Rating you can quickly filter the high ISO speed shots from all the rest. The last few sections require that you have entered custom metadata in the catalog photos. The Location and Creator categories can be useful if you are in the habit of editing the associated IPTC fields via the Metadata panel. If so, you can quickly select and filter the catalog photos by any of the IPTC metadata items you see here. Location, City, State/Province, and Country all refer to the Location IPTC metadata used to describe where a photo was shot (you may use keywords to do this as well, but only the IPTC data is referenced here). The Creator section lists the photographs by the creator of the photograph. With some camera systems you can configure the camera settings so that the creator name is always embedded at the capture stage for each and every shot. The Copyright Status and Job reference are also more examples of IPTC metadata that has to be entered by the user.

The Aspect Ratio category lets you filter according to whether the photos are landscape, portrait, or square. Treatment refers to whether the photos are in color or have received a grayscale conversion treatment via Lightroom. By this I mean a proper grayscale treatment, where the photo has been treated using the Grayscale panel controls, rather than a photo that has been desaturated to look like a grayscale conversion. And lastly, the Develop Preset category (**Figure 4.55**) lists all the Develop module presets that have been applied to the images in the catalog, including those that have just had the default settings applied. This is a useful filter for tracking down photos that have had a particular type of treatment, such as a favorite grayscale conversion or split toning technique. Are you looking for inspiration? You could select All Photographs to view the entire catalog and use this filter category to check out how the various Develop presets looked when applied to various images. You could then copy a Develop setting or apply the original preset to another image.

Custom filter settings

We touched on working with the Custom filters in the previous chapter, where I showed how you can save custom filter settings via the Filmstrip. Such custom Filter settings are also accessible via the Filter bar. You can also save more detailed filter settings that make use of Metadata filter terms, which in turn can be accessed via the Filmstrip. In **Figure 4.56**, I created a filter search for photos that matched the keyword *Jobs* (to select all client job photos), where the File type was a PSD file (which is what I generally use when editing retouched master images), that had a star rating of two stars or higher. I then clicked the Custom Filters menu to save this as a new preset setting, named it *Client select masters*, and clicked Create. I was then able to use this custom filter whenever I needed to access a shortlist of all my client retouched master images.

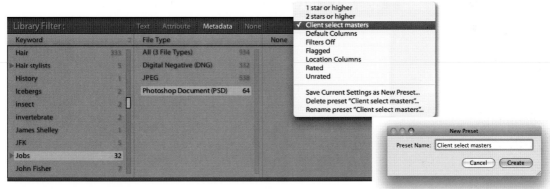

Figure 4.56   *This shows the Custom Filters menu options, where you can save a Filter bar setting as a new preset.*

Empty field searches

Let's go back now to the Text filter section of the Filter bar, where in the Search target section you can choose to search by caption. In the accompanying Rules section you find rules such as Is Empty and Isn't Empty, and for keyword searches, Are Empty and Aren't Empty. The purpose of these rules is to let you search for photos where no caption or keywords have been added, or alternatively select only those photos that do have captions titles or keywords (note that when either of these rules is selected, the field search is overridden and the search field box dimmed). Let's now look at how and why you would want to use an "empty field" search.

TIP

Color labels are specific to the color label set used. See page 104 in Chapter 3 for information on working with different color label sets.

No content searches

The idea of using Lightroom to search for nothing may sound strange, but trust me, there is method in such madness. The Is Empty and Are Empty rules can be used to easily filter out photos that have yet to be edited. This offers a quick way to filter the pictures that still need keywording or caption editing.

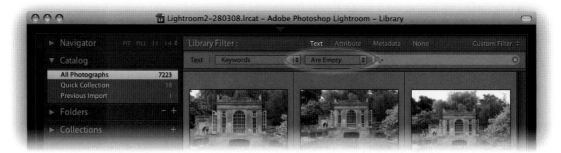

NOTE

To summarize, the point of this exercise is to show how you can use an Is Empty search as a general housekeeping tool for quickly isolating photos that haven't been tagged fully yet with keywords or other metadata.

1. The Is Empty and Are Empty rules can be applied to keyword or caption searches only. For this example I made a selection of All Photographs and made a Keywords, Are Empty Filter bar text search. This action filtered all the photos in the library that had yet to have keywords added.

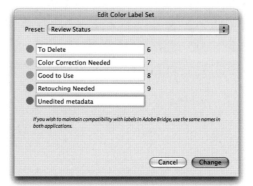

2. Now, you can (if you like) apply a color label that can act as a semipermanent marker for all the photos in the catalog that have empty keyword metadata. To show you what I mean, I chose Edit from the Metadata ⇨ Color Label Set menu, selected the Review Status preset, and changed the purple label so that instead of saying "To Print" it said "Unedited metadata." I don't really need a label to say "print these pictures" and I suppose this makes a better use of this lesser-used label. I then saved this as a new color label set.

3. With this new label set active, I applied a purple color (Unedited metadata) label to the selected, empty keyword images.

4. I only suggest the use of color labels as a helpful reminder. Here I am showing the photos that were selected at Step 1 (without the color label) and with the "Keywords are empty" filter in force. I could now add keyword metadata, and as I did so, the photos automatically removed themselves from the filtered selection.

TIP

Just to remind you once more: After a Filter search has been made, you can use ⌘L (Mac) or Ctrl L (PC) to toggle switching the image filter on or off.

Advanced searches

Let's finish this section with a complete example of a complex search where several different types of search criteria are combined together to create a precise, targeted selection of the catalog. All the tools you need are located in the Filter bar, and the following step-by-step example will hopefully provide guidance and inspiration to help you get the most out of Lightroom's search abilities (I have enlarged the Filter bar in these screen shots so that you can see the settings more clearly).

1. I first selected All Photographs in the Catalog panel, then went to the Filter bar, checked the Text tab, and chose to search by keywords only using the Contain rule. I then typed in the name of one of my clients, *Antoni*, to initiate a catalog search for photos that were keyworded with the word *Antoni*. As I began typing in the first few letters, the search started narrowing down the selection of images in the grid to show all the photos where the keywords metadata contained this same sequence of letters. As you can see, the Filter bar search filtered the photos in the grid to show over 1,500 photos that had been shot for this client. This included everything: the raw files as well as the PSD masters. The next task was to whittle this selection down to something more specific.

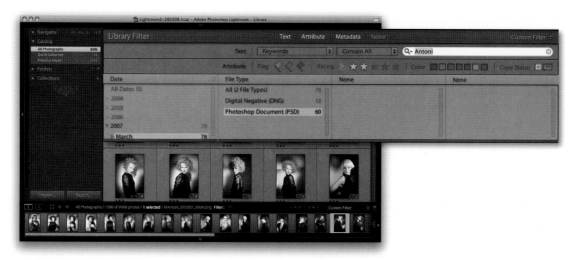

2. I clicked the Attribute tab and applied a two-star filter to show only the two-star or higher images. I also clicked the Metadata tab to reveal the Metadata filter options and used a Date panel to search for photos that had been shot in 2007 only. And lastly, I used a File Type panel to search for the Photoshop Document (PSD) File Types. This resulted in a filter selection that showed only the PSD file format photos that had been shot during 2007 that had been rated with two or more stars.

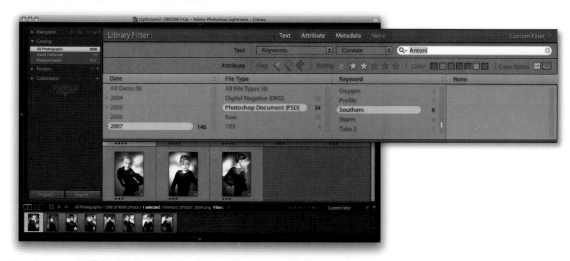

3. Even so, I still had 34 images to choose from. I used a Keyword panel to select *Southern*, which is an awards entry category keyword. This now filtered the catalog to show photos taken for the specified client that had been shot during 2007 that had a rating of two stars or more, that were PSD files only, and that also had the keyword *Southern > Awards categories > Jobs*.

Figure 4.57 *To view a Quick Collection, click the Quick Collection item in the Photo Catalog panel.*

Figure 4.58 *Press ⌘ Alt B (Mac) or Ctrl Alt B (PC) to save a Quick Collection as a permanent collection to add to the Collections panel.*

Quick Collections

When it comes to combining search results, it is good to familiarize yourself with the Collections features in Lightroom. A selection only offers a temporary way of linking images together in a group, and as soon as you deselect a selection or select a different folder in the library, the selection vanishes. Of course, you can still choose Edit ⇨ Undo, or use the keyboard shortcut ⌘ Z (Mac) or Ctrl Z (PC) to recover a selection, but the main point is that selections offer only a temporary means of grouping images together. If you want to make a picture selection more lasting, you can convert a selection to a Quick Collection by choosing Photo ⇨ Add to Quick Collection or by pressing the B key. Any images that have been added to a Quick Collection will be marked with a filled circle in the top-right corner in both the Library Grid and Filmstrip views. Note that you can have only one Quick Collection at a time but that you can make further selections and keep adding fresh images to the Quick Collection. The other advantage is that a Quick Collection is always remembered even after you quit Lightroom—no saving or naming necessary—and the images remain grouped until you decide to remove them from the Quick Collection.

Quick Collections can be accessed by clicking the Quick Collection item in the Catalog panel (**Figure 4.57**). You can also choose File ⇨ Show Quick Collection or press ⌘ B (Mac) or Ctrl B (PC) to display the Quick Collection images only and choose File ⇨ Return to Previous Content (press ⌘ B or Ctrl B again) to return to the previous Library module view.

With Quick Collections you can make selections of photos from separate sources and group them in what is effectively a temporary collection. Quick Collections remain "sticky" for however long you find it useful to keep images grouped this way. If you want to save a Quick Collection as a permanent collection, you can do so by using ⌘ Alt B (Mac) or Ctrl Alt B (PC). This will open the Save Quick Collection dialog (**Figure 4.58**) and let you save as a normal Library Collection. Once you have done this, it is usually good housekeeping practice to clear the Quick Collection, which you can do by selecting File ⇨ Clear Quick Collection or pressing ⌘ ⇧Shift B (Mac) or Ctrl ⇧Shift B (PC). See **Figure 4.59** for an example.

Figure 4.59 *One of the advantages of Quick Collections is that you can group images from different source locations (i.e., different folders) and then select the Quick Collection to view all the selected images at once. In the example shown here, I have highlighted the source folder locations in the Folders panel for the photos that make up this current Quick Collection.*

Figure 4.60 *This shows the Collections panel, now common to the Library, Slideshow, Print, and Web modules with the different kinds of Collections icons that can be nested in Collections sets.*

Collections

A Quick Collection can be converted into a collection, or you can convert any selection directly into a collection via the Collections panel. Whereas a catalog image can only be assigned to one folder at a time, you can use collections to create multiple instances of the master files. Collections are therefore useful for grouping images together from different folders in ways that are useful or meaningful (**Figure 4.60**). For example, **Figure 4.61** shows a Library collection I made from filtering *UK* and *Travel* photos. As you conduct various catalog searches you can save the results as general collections (▢). However, since the Collections panel is now accessible in the Slideshow, Print, and Web modules, you can also save module-linked collections. Figure 4.60 shows examples of the different collection types, which are distinguished by the Collection icon appearance: Slideshow (▣), Print (▤), and Web (▦). The way this works is that you can create a module-specific collection while working in any of the above modules, and have the collection be associated with the module where it was created. **Figure 4.62** shows the Create Collection dialog, and **Figure 4.63** shows

Figure 4.61 *To create the collection shown here, I filtered the photos in the Library module to show photos that matched the keywords UK and Travel. I then clicked the Add Collection plus icon and chose Create Collection, which opened the dialog shown here, where I made this new collection a child of the Locations Collection set.*

a Slideshow collection being created within the Slideshow module, which then appears in all the other module Collections panels with the Slideshow collection icon (▣). When you click on a module-specific collection, this selects the collection photos from the catalog (regardless of what filters are applied, what collection type it is, or which module you are in). But if you double-click on a module-specific collection, it selects the photos from the catalog *and* takes you directly to the module the collection was created in. To give you an example of how you would use this, I double-clicked on the *Stockholm trip* collection to select the *Stockholm trip* collection photos and go directly to the Slideshow module. Once there, a single-click on any of the other listed collections allows me to access other collections directly within the Slideshow module. To help organize your collections, you can choose Create Collection Set. This adds a new collection folder (▣) allowing you to create folder groups for your collections (as shown in Figure 4.60). **Figure 4.64** explains renaming a collection.

Figure 4.62 *The Create Collection dialog is different for the Library and Print modules, in that you can choose "Include selected photos" (the Slideshow and Web modules only allow you to include all photos from the Filmstrip).*

  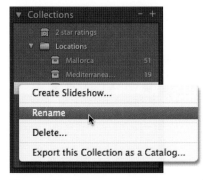

Figure 4.63 *You can create a Slideshow collection by clicking the + button and choosing the Create Slideshow option. You can then enter a name and set location and choose to include photos from the Filmstrip. You can also add more new photos by dragging them from the Filmstrip to the collection in the module Collections panel.*

NOTE

The module-based collections also preserve any Slideshow, Print, or Web module settings that are associated with the collection.

Figure 4.64 *To rename a collection, use a right mouse-click to access the contextual menu and choose Rename. This opens the Rename dialog shown here.*

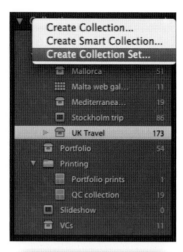

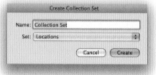

Figure 4.65 *Click the + button in the Collections panel to choose Create Collection Set and create a new collection set in the Collections panel.*

Collections sets

Collections can also be placed into collection sets. These are container folders for managing hierarchies of collections. To add a new collection set, click the + button in the Collections panel header (**Figure 4.65**), or right-click anywhere in the Collections panel to access the contextual menu. Choose Create Collection Set, name the set, and drag and drop to manage the collections as you wish.

Smart Collections

Smart Collections can be used to establish rules for how photos should be grouped as a collection, and Lightroom will automatically update the photos that should be included in that collection. To do this, you need to again click the + button or use the contextual menu to select Create Smart Collection. This will open the Edit Smart Collection dialog shown in **Figure 4.66**, where you can set up a series of rules to determine which photos will go into a particular Smart Collection. In this example, I used a Keywords filter to select photos with the keyword *Jobs*, a Filename filter to select photos with the *.psd* extension (Photoshop file format images), and lastly a Capture date filter to select images that were captured throughout the year 2008. You will note in the Match section that "all" was used. This means that photos would have to match the combined rules before being added. An "any" match can be used where you want to select photos that match multiple terms, but not exclusively so. You could create a Smart Collection with an "any" match to group photos that had both red labels and yellow labels taken in the date range of 2007–2008.

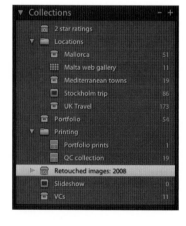

Figure 4.66 *The Edit Smart Collection dialog and to the left, the Smart Collection, as it appears in the Collections panel.*

Saving and reading metadata

Another pain point for newcomers to Lightroom has been the question of the best way to save images. In our very first computer lesson we all learned how important it is to always save your work before you close down a program. Some Lightroom users have been confused by the fact that there is no "save" menu item and left wondering if they would lose all their work after they quit Lightroom. Of course you realize soon after using the program that all work is saved automatically. Even if Lightroom suffers a crash or there is a power failure, you should never lose any of your data.

It is important to remember that as you carry out any kind of work in Lightroom—whether you are adjusting the Develop settings, applying a color label or star rating, or editing keywords or other metadata—these edits are initially all stored in a central Lightroom catalog on your hard disk. For simplicity's sake we can summarize these by grouping them under the term "metadata edits." Whenever you alter a photo in Lightroom, you are not recording anything in the actual image file. Lightroom is built around the principle that the imported images are the master negatives: Lightroom records the changes made as metadata information and these edit changes are initially stored at a central location in the Lightroom catalog. This is why Lightroom is so much faster at searching images compared to a browser program like Bridge. You can add, search, and read metadata information much more quickly, because the metadata information is stored in an easy-to-access database. However, it is possible to have the metadata information stored in both the database and the individual picture files. In the case of JPEG, TIFF, PSD, or DNG images, there is a dedicated XMP space within the file's header that can be used to store the metadata. While with proprietary raw files, it has to be stored separately in what is known as an XMP sidecar file.

If you work on an image in the Lightroom catalog using another program such as Photoshop or Bridge and you make any changes to the metadata, these edit changes will always be made to the file itself. When such an image is opened up via Lightroom again we can find ourselves having to decide whether the "truth is in the database" (the Lightroom catalog database) or the "truth is in the file."

TIP

Saving metadata to the file can be seen as a good thing to do because it adds an extra level of security and allows the metadata entered via Lightroom to be shared when viewed in other programs. But this security does come at a cost. The good thing about having all the metadata information stored in a single database file is that it is lightweight. When it comes to backing up data to another hard drive, the backup process can take just a minute or so, even for a large catalog, to copy from one drive to another. When you export the metadata to the files, this means that once a file has been modified, the whole file has to be backed up. This means that all DNG, TIFF, PSD, and JPEG files will have to be copied as complete files during the backup process and what would otherwise take a minute starts taking hours to process. Interestingly, you could argue that there is an advantage here if raw files are not converted to DNG since backing up the .xmp sidecar files is a lot quicker than backing up the DNGs where the XMP metadata is embedded.

Figure 4.67 *If Lightroom detects that the catalog database file has become corrupted, there is an option to Repair Catalog. But click the See Adobe Technote button first, to read more about such file corruptions before you do so.*

Saving metadata to the file

For all the time that you are working in Lightroom it should not really matter if the metadata information is stored only in the central database. Of course it feels kind of risky to trust everything to a single database file, but that is why there is a built-in database backup feature in Lightroom as well as a diagnostics and a self-repair function (see **Figure 4.67**) to help keep your database file protected. Plus I highly recommend that you back up your data regularly anyway. Despite all that, it is still important to save the metadata edits to the files so that the "truth is in both the database and the file." By doing this you can maintain better compatibility between the work you do in Lightroom and the work you do using external programs.

So what is the best way to save metadata to the files? If you go to the File menu and choose Catalog Settings, you will see the dialog shown in **Figure 4.68**, where there is an option called "Automatically write changes into XMP." In the previous version of this book I recommended you keep this option switched off because it could slow down the Lightroom program. However, since the version 1.3 update, it has been OK to leave this switched on because Lightroom will now only automatically write to the files' XMP space when it is convenient to do so, without affecting the program's performance. Checking this option will ensure that all the files in the Lightroom catalog will eventually get updated. However, if you want to be sure that a file's XMP space gets updated right away or you have "Automatically write changes into XMP" switched off, then you can use the Metadata ➪ Save Metadata

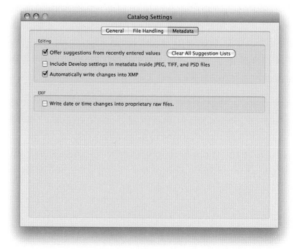

Figure 4.68 *The Metadata Catalog Settings.*

to Files command (or Photo ⇨ Save Metadata to Files, if working in the Develop module). This forces an immediate export of the metadata information from the Lightroom internal catalog to the image file's XMP space. In practice I'd recommended using the ⌘S (Mac), Ctrl S (PC) shortcut anyway every time you wish to export and update the metadata to a photo or a group of selected photos.

Tracking metadata changes

In order to keep track of which files have been updated and which have not, Lightroom does offer some visual clues. If you go to the View menu and open the View Options dialog, there is a check box in the Cell Icons section called Unsaved Metadata. When this is checked you may see a "calculating metadata" icon (≡↓) in the top-right corner of the grid cells as Lightroom scans the photos in the catalog, checking to see if the metadata is in need of an update. You will also see this when Lightroom is in the process of saving or reading metadata from a file. If the metadata in the catalog and the file are in sync, the icon will disappear. If there is a "metadata status conflict" you will see either a down arrow (**Figure 4.69**) or an up arrow (**Figure 4.70**). The down arrow indicates that the metadata information embedded in the photo's XMP space is now out of date compared to the current Lightroom catalog file and that now would be a good time to choose Metadata ⇨ Save Metadata to File (⌘S [Mac], Ctrl S [PC]). **Figure 4.71** shows the Library View Options dialog with the Unsaved Metadata option circled.

Figure 4.69 *When the Unsaved metadata icon is enabled in the Library View grid options, the icon in the top-right corner will indicate the metadata status has changed. A down arrow indicates that Lightroom settings need to be saved to the file.*

Figure 4.70 *An up arrow indicates that settings have been edited externally and that the file metadata settings may possibly need to be read in order to update the Lightroom catalog.*

Figure 4.71 *The Library View Options.*

Figure 4.72 *The Metadata Status item in the Metadata panel will also alert you if the file metadata is out of sync.*

In the Metadata panel (**Figure 4.72**) is an item called Metadata Status, which will say "Has been changed" if anything has been done to edit the photo metadata settings since the last time the metadata was saved to the file. This is basically telling you the same thing as the metadata status icon that appears in the Library grid cells.

Choosing Save Metadata to File will make the metadata status icon in the Library grid cells disappear, but if you are uncertain what to do you can click the icon in the grid to open the dialog shown in **Figure 4.73**. This dialog asks if you want to save the changes to disk (better described as "do you wish to confirm saving the metadata changes to the photo's XMP space?").

Figure 4.73 *This dialog will appear to confirm if you wish to save changes to disk.*

The up arrow shown in Figure 4.70 indicates that the metadata information embedded in the image file's XMP space is out of sync and more recent than the current Lightroom catalog file. This will most likely occur when you have edited a Lightroom catalog file in Camera Raw and the externally edited image has a more recently modified XMP than the Lightroom catalog. To resolve this choose Metadata ⇨ Read Metadata from file.

Figure 4.74 *If there is a metadata status conflict where the settings have been modified both in Lightroom and another external program, you will see the warning icon shown here.*

The other possibility is that a Lightroom catalog photo may have been modified in Lightroom (without saving the metadata to the file) and also been edited by an external program, resulting in two possible "truths" for the file. Is the truth now in the Lightroom catalog, or is the truth in the externally edited file XMP metadata? If you see the icon shown in **Figure 4.74**, click to open the dialog in **Figure 4.75** where you can either choose Import Settings from Disk if you think the external settings are right, or choose Overwrite Settings if you think the Lightroom catalog settings are the most up to date.

Figure 4.75 *This Metadata status conflict dialog.*

XMP read/write options

Let's now take a closer look at what this XMP settings business is all about. The XMP space is the hidden space in a document such as a JPEG, TIFF, PSD, or DNG file that is used to write the metadata settings to. In the case of proprietary raw files it would be unsafe for Lightroom to write to the internal file header, so .xmp sidecar files are used instead to store the XMP metadata. The XMP metadata includes everything that is applied in Lightroom, such as the IPTC information, keywords, file ratings, flags, and color labels, as well as the Develop settings that are applied via Quick Develop or the Develop module.

In the Metadata section of the Catalog Settings (Figure 4.68), the "Include Develop settings in metadata inside JPEG, TIFF and PSD files" option lets Lightroom distinguish between writing the Develop settings metadata to the XMP space for all files including JPEGs, TIFFs, and PSDs, or to raw and DNG files only. This is a preference that predetermines what gets written to the XMP space when you make an explicit command to save the file metadata out to a file. The ability to save Develop settings with the file can be a mixed blessing. If you are sharing images that are exported from Lightroom as individual images (or as an exported catalog) with another Lightroom user, you will most definitely want to share the Develop settings for all the images that are in the catalog. But if you are sharing files from Lightroom with Bridge CS3 or later, this can lead to some unexpected file behavior when you open non-raw files via Bridge. Basically what will happen is that raw and DNG images that have had their Develop settings modified via Lightroom will open via Camera Raw in Bridge exactly as you expect to see them, since Bridge is able to read the settings that were created in Lightroom. However, where you have non-raw files such as JPEGs, TIFFs, or PSDs that have been edited using the Develop settings in Lightroom, and the Develop settings have been written to the file's XMP space, Bridge may now consider such files to be like raw files and open them up via Camera Raw rather than open them directly in Photoshop. That's what I mean by mixed blessings. If you want Lightroom to retain the ability to modify the XMP space of non-raw files for data such as file ratings, keywords, and labels but exclude storing the Develop settings, you should uncheck the "Include Develop settings in metadata inside JPEG, TIFF and PSD files" option. Do this and the Lightroom Develop settings for non-raw files will only get written to the catalog and they won't get exported to the files when you choose Save Metadata. But raw and DNG files will be handled as expected. On the plus side, you will never be faced with the confusion of seeing your non-raw images such as JPEGs unexpectedly default to open via Camera Raw when you try to open them up in Photoshop CS3 or later. The downside is that if you modify a non-raw image in Lightroom using Develop, these changes will only be seen in Lightroom and not by Bridge. For these reasons, my advice is to turn off "Include Develop settings in metadata inside JPEG, TIFF and PSD files." To help explain the settings and how they affect image files after being modified in Lightroom, I have summarized how these options affect the way different file formats will be handled. Please note that these steps do assume that you are using Photoshop CS3 with Bridge CS3 (or later) and have updated Camera Raw to version 4.1 or later.

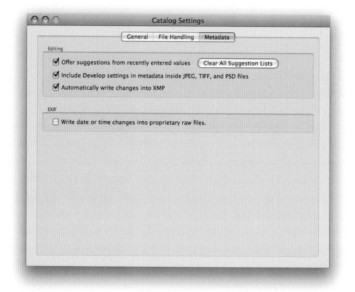

1. If a photo in Lightroom is modified using the settings shown here with "Automatically write changes into XMP" and "Include Develop settings in metadata inside JPEG, TIFF and PSD files" switched on, then all the adjustments that are made to the image will automatically be saved to the Lightroom catalog and also saved to the original image file. In the case of proprietary raw files, the XMP metadata will be written to an XMP sidecar file and when opened via Bridge, will (as you would expect) open via the Camera Raw dialog with the same Develop settings that were applied in Lightroom. In the case of DNG files, the XMP metadata will be written internally to the file and these too will open in Camera Raw. In the case of JPEG, TIFF, and PSD files, because you are including the Lightroom Develop settings in the export to the XMP space, they will default to opening in Bridge via the Adobe Camera Raw dialog.

Where is the truth?

The main point to learn here is that the most up-to-date or "truthful" settings can reside in the Lightroom catalog or in the files themselves. If you only work in Lightroom, the answer is simple: The truth will always be in the catalog. But if you adopt a more complicated workflow where the files' Develop settings and other metadata can be edited externally, the truth will sometimes be in the file. To summarize, the "Automatically write changes to XMP," "Save Metadata to Files," and "Read Metadata to Files" options allow you to precisely control how the metadata is updated between the Lightroom catalog and the image files.

Synchronizing IPTC metadata settings

You will often want to apply or synchronize metadata settings from one photo to other photos in the catalog. To do this, make a selection of images and click the Sync Metadata button, which opens the Synchronize Metadata dialog (**Figure 4.76**). The check box options in this dialog can help you select which items you want to synchronize. You can then click the Synchronize button to synchronize the metadata information in the most selected image with all the others in the selection. You can also select an image and press ⌘ Alt ⇧ Shift C (Mac) or Ctrl Alt ⇧ Shift C (PC) to use the "Copy Metadata settings" command and then use ⌘ Alt ⇧ Shift V (Mac) or Ctrl Alt ⇧ Shift V (PC) to paste those settings to another selected image or group of images.

NOTE

At this point in time it is not yet possible to synchronize the keywords metadata using the Sync metadata button.

NOTE

Figure 4.76 shows how you can also synchronize the keywords in an image when you choose to synchronize the metadata.

Figure 4.76 *If you make a selection of images and click the Sync Metadata button, the Synchronize Metadata dialog opens. Here you can check the individual IPTC items that you wish to synchronize with other photos in a selection.*

Synchronizing folders

Some folder synchronization will happen automatically in Lightroom. For example, if you import a folder of images and later change the name of that folder at the system level, the name change will be updated in the Lightroom Folders panel. Likewise, if you edit a folder name in Lightroom, the system folder name should update too.

When it comes to synchronizing the folder contents, this will require an explicit Lightroom command to check and compare the folder contents in Lightroom with the items in the system folder it refers to. What often happens is that you may import a folder at the start of a project and as you continue working with that folder between Lightroom and Bridge (or in the Finder/Explorer), new subfolders get added, files may get moved into these subfolders, and some photos may get deleted and new ones added. All this can lead to a situation where the Folder view in Lightroom is no longer an accurate representation of what is in the real system folder.

The Synchronize Folder command is located in the Library menu and can be used to interrogate the system folder that the Lightroom folder refers to. **Figure 4.77** shows the Synchronize Folder dialog, which as you can see, provides initial information about what differences there are between the two, such as whether there are any new photos to import, whether any photos in the Lightroom catalog are missing their master images, and whether any metadata updates have been applied externally that need to be read to update the Lightroom database.

Figure 4.77 *The Synchronize Folder dialog.*

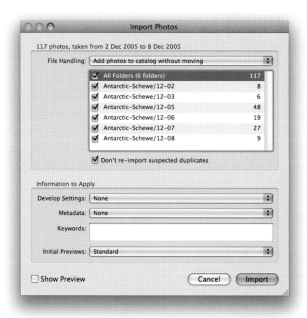

Figure 4.78   *The Import Photos dialog.*

If you check the Import New Photos option in the Synchronize Folder dialog, you can choose to simply import and update the catalog. The default settings for Synchronize Folder will automatically import the files to the same folder they are in currently without showing the Import dialog and without modifying the filename, Develop settings, metadata, or keywords. However, you can also choose "Show import dialog before importing," which will open the Import Photos dialog shown in **Figure 4.78**. The main reason for choosing to show the Import Photos dialog when synchronizing a folder is so that you can adjust any of these settings as you carry out an import and update the Lightroom catalog. Note that if you have removed any photos from the folder at the system level, Synchronize Folder will also remove these files from the catalog, thereby keeping the Lightroom catalog completely updated for new additions as well as any photos that are no longer located in the original system folder.

"Scan for Metadata updates" works identically to the "Read metadata from files" option in the Library module Metadata menu (see page 178). For example, if you edit the metadata in any of the catalog images in an external program such as Bridge or another program where the metadata edits you make are saved back to the file's XMP header space (or saved to an XMP sidecar file), you can use Synchronize Folder to sync any metadata changes to the Lightroom catalog.

Figure 4.79 *The Library module toolbar sort order buttons.*

Sorting images

You have the option of sorting images in Lightroom by Capture Time, Added Order, Edit Time, Edit Count (for sorting Edit versions of master images in the order they were created), Rating, Pick, Label Text, Label Color, File Name, File Extension, File Type, or Aspect Ratio. You can set the sort order by selecting the View menu and highlighting an item in the Sort submenu. An easier method is to click the Sort menu in the toolbar. Next to the Sort menu is the Sort Direction button, which allows you to quickly toggle between ordering the images in ascending or descending sort order (**Figure 4.79**). For example, if you come back from a shoot with several cards full of images, there is a high probability that the order in which you import the photos may not match the order in which they were shot. If the files are renamed at the time of import, you may want to correct this later by re-sorting the capture files by Capture Time and then reapplying a batch rename by selecting Library ⇨ Rename Photos. The descending sort order can be particularly useful when you are shooting in tethered mode and you want the most recent images to always appear at the top of the image selection in the content area. **Figure 4.80** shows the Sort menu.

Figure 4.80 *The image sort order is by default set to photo Capture Time. This is probably the most useful sort order setting. In the View menu you can choose to sort the images by Import Order or by image Rating.*

Sort functions

If you are viewing a folder, a filtered folder view, or a collection, you can manually sort the image order by dragging and dropping photos either in the Grid view or via the Filmstrip. Sorting the photos manually will default the sort order menu to a User Order sort setting, and the User Order sort will remain in force after you exit a particular Folder or Collection view. But as soon as you switch to any other sort order menu option, such as Capture Time, the previous User Order sorting will be lost.

The Sort menu also resolves some of the possible contradictions in the way color labels are identified in Bridge and Lightroom. Instead of having a single sort option of sorting by color labels, there are two options: Sort by Label Color and sort by Label Text. And the reason for this is as follows:

NOTE

You can only drag and drop photos in the Grid or Filmstrip view when a single folder view or a collection is selected. You cannot drag and drop grouped folders or filter selections that span more than one folder.

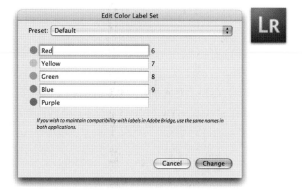

1. In Lightroom, the default color label set uses the following text descriptions alongside each label: Red, Yellow, Green, Blue, Purple (to access the dialog shown here, go to the Library module Metadata menu ⇨ Color Label Set ⇨ Edit). OK, this is not a particularly imaginative approach, but the label text that is used here neatly matches the label text descriptions that were used in Bridge CS2 (as included with the CS2 Creative Suite). Note that the Lightroom dialog shown here says, "If you wish to maintain compatibility with labels in Adobe Bridge, use the same names in both applications." So far, so good. If you follow this advice, Lightroom can be compatible with the CS2 version of Bridge because both programs use identical color label text descriptions.

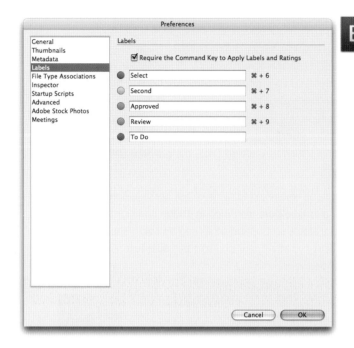

2. However, in Bridge CS3, as included with the CS3 Creative Suite, the text naming was changed to a new default setting. Shown here is how the default label text appears in the Bridge CS3 program's Labels preferences. If you install Bridge CS3 and use the default settings in this and Lightroom, the label text descriptions will differ. This has led to problems such as white labels appearing in Bridge CS3 where Bridge CS3 is unable to read Lightroom's color label metadata correctly. In these specific instances, Bridge CS3 can "see" that a color label has been applied, but it does not know how to interpret the metadata correctly. Bridge CS3 can read the color label text descriptions and display them in the Bridge Metadata File Properties section, but it does not read and apply the label color part.

3. Lightroom faces a similar problem in knowing how to manage mismatched color labels where the label color and label description text differ. But at least in Lightroom, you can use the Custom Label filter (highlighted here in the Filter bar) to filter photos that have a color label but the text descriptions don't match the current color label set.

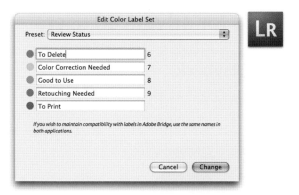

4. If you were to choose a color label set in Lightroom such as the Review Status set shown here, the problem will persist between Lightroom and Bridge CS3 because the descriptive terms used in both programs will be different. Furthermore, Bridge updates have not necessarily managed to resolve this conflict and the message remains the same. If you want to be absolutely consistent between applications when applying color labels, then make sure the label text used in both programs matches.

The sort by label text solution

If you edit a photo's color label setting in Bridge and then use the Lightroom Library module Metadata ⇨ Read Metadata from File command, a similar conflict will occur. But instead of showing a white label, Lightroom will not display any color labels in the Grid or Filmstrip views. However, if you go to the Metadata panel (**Figure 4.81**), you will notice that the Metadata panel displays the color label text data rather than the actual color of the label. This means that although in Lightroom you won't necessarily be able to see the color labels that were applied in Bridge, you still have a means to filter and sort them using the color label text metadata (or the Custom Label option referred to in Step 3). Therefore, the Sort by Label Color option allows you to sort photos by color labels that have been applied in Lightroom, and the Sort by Label Text option allows you to sort photos that have had text labels applied in Lightroom. In addition, you can sort photos where the labels have been applied via Bridge (because Lightroom is only able to read the label text part correctly).

On the subject of label colors and label color text, you might want to return to page 104 in Chapter 3, which discusses working with specific color label sets. It is important to note that the Color Label filters will only select the color label photos that were edited with a particular set.

Figure 4.81 *The Metadata panel will display the color label information using the color label text data.*

Extra tips for advanced users

In a moment, we'll be looking at how
to embed and use GPS metadata in
Lightroom, where you can use the
GPS metadata to track back to exactly
where a photo was taken. But audio
note making can also offer a way to
conveniently record the name of a
site you have just photographed or
record other useful information such
as the date an important building
was constructed or other information
that you might want to write up as a
caption later.

Audio file playback

It was thanks to Ian Lyons that I discovered this little gem. Lightroom
will recognize and play back any audio sidecar file that is associated
with a photo. The following steps show you how this would work using
a Canon EOS 1Ds MkII camera.

1. If your camera has the facility to record audio notes, you can do so
as you review the pictures that have just been shot. The method
will vary from camera to camera, but with this camera you press
the record button and speak into the microphone on the back.

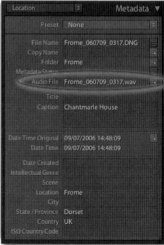

2. After importing the files to Lightroom, if there are audio sidecars
present, they will appear as a metadata item just below Metadata
Status. All you have to do is click the action button next to the
Audio filename to play back the audio annotation.

GPS metadata and linking to Google Earth

If you have GPS metadata embedded in an image file, Lightroom will let you link directly to Google Maps and locate exactly where that photograph had been taken. But in order to pull off this trick you will need to find a way to embed GPS metadata in your image capture files. This is not as difficult as you might imagine, since there are now several GPS devices capable of capturing the GPS coordinates at the time of capture and then synchronizing the GPS data with your capture images via post-processing software. For example, according to John Nack's blog, Jobo AG™ has announced photoGPS, a $149 device that sits in the hot shoe (i.e., the mounting point for a flash) of a digital SLR. Post-processing software synchronizes data captured by the device with the corresponding images. In the following steps, I have used a set of images with embedded GPS metadata, kindly provided by Ian Lyons to demonstrate how Lightroom can use such metadata to link to Google Maps. By the way, you can see more of Ian's photographs taken around the Falklands and Antarctica on his Computer Darkroom Web site.

NOTE

John Nack is product manager for Photoshop and Bridge and writes a blog titled "John Nack on Adobe" (blogs.adobe.com/jnack). It is full of lots of interesting background information on what is going on at Adobe, as well as offering off-topic posts such as links to interesting photography Web sites.

1. Here is a Library view of Ian's photographs showing a selection of images shot around the Falklands and South Georgia islands.

2. In this Loupe view mode I have focused on one of the photographs. You can see that if I roll the mouse over the arrow alongside the GPS metadata item, a tooltip dialog displays Map Location.

3. Click the arrow next to the GPS metadata and (providing you have a live Internet connection) this will take you directly to Google Maps, pinpointing exactly where the photograph was taken. If Google Maps will allow you to, you will often be able to zoom in further, to get a closer look at the location where the photograph was taken.

4. If you happen to have the Google Earth program installed on your computer, you can also copy and paste the GPS coordinates and use the more extensive navigation tools to explore the scene where the photograph was taken. In this example I tilted the view to a ground-level view of the site where Ian took his photograph.

TIP

Recording GPS metadata is not as straightforward as it sounds, or at least not at the time of this writing. First, the camera time setting must be accurate and match the computer system clock time setting. If they don't agree, the GPS points can end up being inaccurate.

The Sony device mentioned here has a rather low sensitivity cell and can therefore fail to work when cloud cover is heavy or you are inside a building. Devices like this can also consume a lot of battery power. I find that the batteries can die quite quickly, so it may be a good idea to consider using rechargeable batteries and always carry a spare when out on location.

Figure 4.82 *The Sony™ GPSCS1KA is a small, lightweight device that can be used to record GPS coordinates that can be read by appropriate software. It's easily carried around in a camera bag or attached to a strap.*

How to embed GPS metadata in a photo

OK, now that I have shown you how GPS metadata can be useful, let's see how you can capture and embed GPS metadata in a series of photos. Lightroom does not have any mechanism that will allow you to import or edit GPS metadata. In fact, it will only display the GPS field in the EXIF Metadata panel if GPS metadata is actually present in the catalog image files. The following steps show how I was able to import the GPX data from a Sony GPSCS1KA unit (see **Figure 4.82**) and merge the data with the camera captured images. This tiny Sony™ device can record the GPS coordinates of wherever the unit is, once every 15 seconds and save the GPS time-stamped waypoints as part of a log. When you get back to the computer you need to launch the LoadMytracks™ program described here to read and convert the log file and then launch the GPSPhotoLinker™ program to merge the GPS data with the camera files before importing them into Lightroom. Now you don't have to carry out the GPS data merge at this point. If you are in a hurry, you can import the photos first and locate the GPX log file and the photos folder later. But in my experience it seemed to work well to carry out the GPS data merge first and import the files from the card after.

1. I connected the Sony™ GPS device via the USB cable that came with the unit. If you open up the device folders and take a look inside, you can see the GPX data log file. This can be deleted manually later once all the log data has been successfully copied.

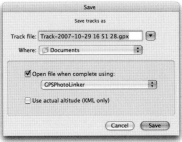

2. I used a freeware program called LoadMyTracks to read the log file from the Sony™ GPS device and save it as a GPX data file. You will want to go to the top menu to choose the device model type that matches the connected device (in this case, NMEA was the correct one to select). I wanted to export the data in a GPX format and when I clicked the Acquire button, this opened the Save dialog shown here, where I chose a folder location to save the GPX file to. You will note in the Save dialog that there is an option to automatically open the GPSPhotoLinker software after the GPX export had been successful.

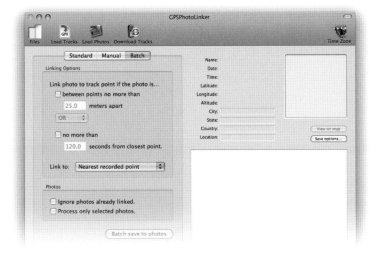

3. So providing you have GPSPhotoLinker already installed, this will launch the program. In the top bar you can see the main buttons. You have Files, which will let you inspect which GPX logs have been added so far. The Load Tracks button lets you add new GPX logs, and the Load Photos button lets you load photos that you want to add data to. We'll be looking at these features in the next few steps.

4. I began by clicking the Load Tracks button and navigated to the GPX file that I had just saved out of LoadMyTracks.

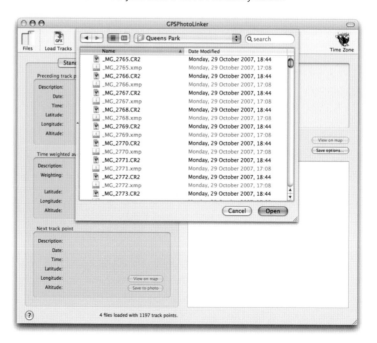

5. I then clicked the Load Photos button to locate the capture files that were shot at the same time that the GPS data was recorded.

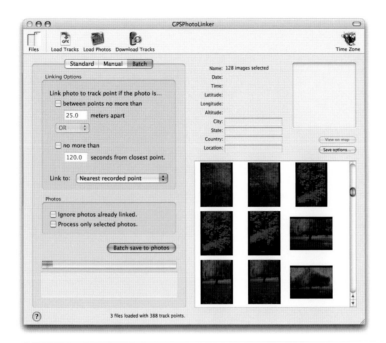

Figure 4.83 *If you click the Save Options button in GPS PhotoLinker, you can choose among these additional options when saving.*

6. Having loaded the GPX log and the photos I was ready to click the Batch mode tab button to combine the GPX data with the relevant photos. There are some Linking options to consider here that will determine how the GPS waypoints are to be interpreted. Here I kept things simple and instructed GPSPhotoLinker to link to the nearest recorded point. All I had to do then was to click "Batch save to photos" and GPXPhotoLinker wrote the GPS metadata to the correct EXIF metadata field. Ian Lyons points out that it is best not to save or overwrite the City, State, and Country data. This is because if the shots have been taken in remote areas, most software will tend to hunt down the nearest biggest city (which could be many miles away). **Figure 4.83** shows the dialog that opens when you click Save Options.

5 | **Working with catalogs**

*An explanation of the relationship between
the Lightroom catalog and the way images are
stored on the computer*

What sets Lightroom apart from other image converters is its ability to manage the descriptive content of the image library. There is much to be said for keeping your images in a well-organized catalog system where they can be retrieved easily at a later date.

The Lightroom catalog (which was referred to as the Lightroom Library in version 1 of the program) plays a central role in everything that you do in Lightroom. As you import your photos into Lightroom, the catalog keeps track of where your photos are kept, as well as what information is associated with or stored in the photos themselves.

This chapter explains how your images are physically stored and referenced as well as how to share and manage catalogs created in Lightroom.

TIP

If the current catalog refuses to open and a catalog repair doesn't work, then you do have the option to replace the current catalog with the most recent one from the catalog Backups folder.

About Lightroom catalogs

Since the very early days of managing documents on a computer, it has been common practice to organize files by placing them in separate system folders. This worked well enough when photographers were scanning in just a few images at a time and slowly building an image archive. But these days, photographers are typically capturing hundreds of new images every day. A folder system of management can work well enough for the person who is organizing the hierarchy of folders, but therein lies the weakness of such a system. As an image collection grows in size, you have to be extremely careful about how you plan your organization so you know where all your files are when you need them. Suppose you were to fall ill and a coworker needed to locate a specific image. How easy would it be for him or her to find that image on your computer? In such situations, a cataloging system is required that can manage your images and keep track of where they are all stored. Several programs are available that can do this, including Microsoft Expression Media (formerly know as iView Media Pro). Lightroom does not have the full functionality of Expression Media, but it does offer a reliable method of cataloging your images from the moment they are brought into Lightroom.

Catalog is the term now used to describe what used to be referred to as the Lightroom image Library (the file that contains all the information used to manage the images that are displayed in Lightroom). This change in terminology from Library to Catalog now provides a clearer distinction between it and the Library module.

When you first installed Lightroom, a new catalog was created and this will have been located in the username/Pictures folder (Mac OS X) or the My Documents\My Pictures folder (PC). This folder contains the following: a Lightroom Library.lrcat catalog file (the master catalog file that contains all the catalog database metadata) and a Lightroom Catalog Previews.lrdata file that contains the thumbnail previews. These two files store all the critical data that relates to the current Lightroom catalog. The most important of these is the Library.lrcat catalog file, which is why part of the catalog backup procedure is to create duplicate backup versions of the main catalog file and save these to the Backups folder (**Figure 5.1**).

Figure 5.1 *The Lightroom folder contains the .lrcat Catalog file. Also in here is a Backups folder that contains dated backups of the master Catalog file.*

Creating and opening catalogs

When you first install Lightroom, a default catalog is already created for you. If you are happy working with a single catalog, then there is no need to concern yourself with creating extra new catalogs and you can skip the next 16 pages. But let's start by looking at some of the reasons why you might want to work with more than one catalog and see if the following discussions are appropriate for your workflow.

If there is more than one person working with Lightroom on a single computer, each user might want to keep their own separate catalog. Let's say you and another family member share the same computer and are using Lightroom to archive and manage your own digital photos. In this case you will definitely find it useful to each keep a separate Lightroom catalog of your work—it's a bit like working with separate user accounts on a computer. You may even wish to split personal work from professional work by keeping each in a separate catalog. Personally, I find it more convenient to keep everything in one catalog and it really doesn't bother me if personal and client photos are all stored in the same catalog, as the search functions in Lightroom make it very easy to filter and search for the photos I am looking for. But it is certainly the case that a professional photographer will be running Lightroom on more than one computer and forced to keep a separate catalog on each. Over the next few pages I will show you how to export selected contents from one catalog and import them into another, as well as how to export a complete catalog as a lightweight version of the original, so that you can keep a copy of the master catalog on a laptop without having to copy over all the original master files.

NOTE

There has been a tendency for some writers to apply a Bridge style methodology to working with Lightroom catalogs. Occasionally you come across the suggestion that you should consider having one catalog for personal photographs, another for studio work, another for for weddings, and so on. While this approach may seem to make sense because you are segregating your catalogs neatly, it is really unnecessary. This is because it is much simpler to segregate your images when everything is contained in a single catalog.

TIP

To open an existing catalog, you can also double-click the cataog.lrcat file itself.

Creating a new catalog

To create a new catalog, choose New Catalog from the File menu to open the Create Folder with New Catalog dialog shown in **Figure 5.2**. What you need to do here is to choose a disk drive location and type in the name you wish to give the new catalog. This creates a new folder with the new catalog inside it. Initially, all you create here is a new .lrcat file. A temporary .lock file will appear alongside the .lrcat file whenever the catalog is in use. This temporary "lock" file prevents other Lightroom users from accessing the same catalog file over a computer network.

Figure 5.2   *When you create a new catalog, you will be asked to create a new folder and name the catalog .*

Opening an existing catalog

To open an existing catalog, choose Open Catalog from the File menu. Alternatively, select Open Recent and select a recently opened catalog from the fly-out menu (**Figure 5.3**). Note that whenever you create a new catalog to load an existing catalog, you must restart Lightroom in order to launch the program using the new catalog. This is because you can only open a single catalog at a time, and you can't have several catalogs open at once.

Figure 5.3   *The File ⇨ Open Recent submenu.*

Exporting catalogs

Most people are going to be fine using just one catalog for all their images. If you can avoid having to use more than one catalog on your main computer, then I recommend you do so, since the goal of good catalog management is to maintain a database of all your photos in one location. But let's say you are sharing a computer running Lightroom with other people; individual users can maintain their own separate catalog to reference and manage the images they are interested in working with.

It is more likely that photographers will want to use this feature to export images from one copy of Lightroom and then import the catalog to another computer running Lightroom. To do this, you would make a selection of photographs via the Library module or the Filmstrip and choose Export as Catalog, which will open the dialog shown in **Figure 5.4,** where you can choose a location to save the catalog to. A catalog export will, at a minimum, always export the ratings and other metadata information. But if you want to export more than just this basic information, then check the "Export negative files" and "Include available previews" options. Note that you can only use the Export as Catalog feature to create new, separate catalogs. You can't export and add to an existing catalog.

Exporting with negatives

If you export a catalog with the "Export negative files" option checked, this exports a copy of the current catalog contents that includes all the master photos, that is, the raw files, JPEGs, TIFFs, or PSD image files that are in the catalog. In other words, Lightroom exports all of the catalog information along with the original master files.

Figure 5.4 *The Export as Catalog dialog appears whenever you choose to export photos as a catalog. This includes the option to export the selected photographs only, or all the photos in the current Library module/Filmstrip view.*

Figure 5.5 *A Catalog export in progress.*

You can copy single folders or an entire catalog from one computer to another. Of course, if you are exporting the master "negatives" as you do so, the export process can slow down quite a bit and you'll see a progress bar indicator in the top panel of the Library window (**Figure 5.5**). I should also point out here that you need to have at least 200 MB of free disk space on your computer, which Lightroom will use as a temporary file storage directory when creating a new exported catalog.

Exporting without negatives

If you deselect the "Export negative files" option, you can export a catalog from your main computer that doesn't use too much disk space and is lightweight enough to run from a laptop. The advantage of this approach is that you can export a large catalog relatively quickly and use it to apply ratings and add keywords. The downside is that there are limitations as to what you can do in Lightroom when working with a catalog that is missing the master negatives. For example, you won't be able to make any adjustments in the Develop module or Library module Quick Develop panel.

Including available previews

If "Include available previews" is checked, Lightroom includes all the Library Grid thumbnails, standard resolution Loupe views (in whatever form they are rendered) and 1:1 rendered views (if available) as part of the export. If you refer to the appendices, you can read in detail about how Lightroom goes through several stages of preview rendering. At a minimum, Lightroom will have thumbnail and standard-sized previews of each photo in the catalog. How detailed the previews are depends on whether Lightroom has had a chance to render them fully. You should always see good-quality thumbnails, but if Lightroom has not had a chance to render proper standard-sized previews (at the pixel size you have set in the preferences), then the standard-sized/full-screen Loupe view previews will sometimes look pixelated because they are nothing more than enlarged thumbnail previews.

The "Include available previews" option is more critical if you are exporting a catalog without including the master negatives. This is because once a catalog has been exported without the original negatives you won't be able to re-render the previews. Selecting "Include available previews" includes the previews in whatever state they are in. So you may therefore want to consider going to the Library menu in the Library module and choosing "Render Standard-Sized Previews" before exporting a catalog. And if you need to include full-resolution previews, then you might want to choose the "Render 1:1" Previews routine instead.

But there are some good reasons for not including previews. If you need to export a catalog that contains just the metadata edits so that you can sync these up with a master catalog, then deselecting "Include available previews" saves carrying out this unnecessary step and therefore makes the export process faster.

If you check both the "Export negative files" and "Include available previews" options, you will end up with an exported catalog that looks like the folder shown in **Figure 5.6**, where the catalog folder contains an .lrcat catalog file, a Previews.lrdata file that contains the thumbnails and preview image data, along with a subfolder containing the master negatives.

Figure 5.6   *This shows a folder view of an exported catalog along with the Images folder and previews file.*

Importing catalogs

Now let's imagine you have transferred the exported catalog to another computer. You can then choose Import from Catalog from the menu, select the exported .lrcat file, and open it. This will open the Open Catalog relaunch dialog shown in **Figure 5.7**. This is because Lightroom must relaunch before loading a new catalog.

If the catalog you are about to import excludes negative files, it will open up directly. Otherwise, you'll see the Import from Catalog dialog shown in **Figure 5.8** on the next page, where you you can choose to import the images by referencing them in their present location, or by copying them to a new location and adding them to a current Lightroom catalog. Where image files already exist in the current catalog, you have the option to decide what gets preserved and what gets replaced during the import process.

Figure 5.7   *The Open Catalog relaunch dialog.*

For example, in Figure 5.8, there were 16 photos that already existed in the catalog, so in instances like this, you have to decide what to do. You can choose to replace nothing, replace the metadata and Develop settings only, or replace everything, including the negative files.

Figure 5.8   *Import from Catalog dialog.*

Figure 5.9   *If the imported catalog excludes the master negatives, the folder names will be dimmed in the Folders panel, because the source folders are effectively off-line.*

Limitations when excluding negatives

As was pointed out in the previous example, you will encounter certain limitations when working with a catalog that has been exported without including the negatives. While you can edit most of the informational metadata, export out the edited catalog, and reimport the information back into the main computer, that is about all you can really do. The Folders panel will display the catalog folders with the folder names dimmed because the links to the master folders will be considered off-line (see **Figure 5.9**). The Develop module will be accessible but inoperative: you can see which Develop settings have been used but that is all. However, you can use the Slideshow module to run slideshows (providing the pre-rendered previews are good enough) and you can use the Web module to generate Web galleries. But, the Web module will constantly remind you that the "best-available previews" are being used in place of the original masters. To be honest, this isn't always likely to be a problem. With the Print module you have the ability to make Draft mode prints. But again, the print quality will be dependent on the quality of the pre-rendered previews.

Export and import summary

You use the File ⇨ Open Catalog. command to load individual catalogs, but Lightroom can only run one catalog at a time. There is nothing to stop you from utilizing multiple catalogs, but a single catalog is probably all that you really need, even if you have a very large collection of photographs to manage. A catalog export is always a one-way process. You can only create new catalogs and you can't get a catalog export to add to an existing catalog.

The File ⇨ Import from Catalog command is the mechanism used to import catalog information from a catalog and add it to an existing catalog. Depending on the catalog you are importing from, you can either import the complete catalog contents (images and metadata), or choose to simply update the metadata information (without importing any photos). There is an example coming up on pages 208–211 that shows how to export a catalog from a main computer, import this catalog to a laptop, make some metadata edits to the catalog, and then reimport the revised catalog back to the original computer again.

NOTE

The Adobe Photoshop Lightroom end-user agreement permits you to install Lightroom on a main computer and a secondary computer such as a laptop. This is because it is recognized that a lot of Adobe product customers regularly work on more than one computer. Another useful thing to know is that you can use a single Lightroom license to run a Mac and Windows version of the program. You don't need to buy a separate license.

Copying a catalog to another computer

If you are running Lightroom on more than one computer, there are bound to be times when you might wish to access the same photos across both machines. As I explained earlier, Lightroom works by explicitly importing master photos into the catalog and from there keeps a record of where each file is and stores the information about the photos, such as the Develop settings and metadata within a central database, referred to here as the catalog. Once upon a time you would have had to think in terms of creating duplicates of all your image files if you wanted to work with them on two or more computers stored in different locations. But cataloging programs like Lightroom don't need to access the original images in order for you to search for photos, make editing decisions such as image ratings, edit the metadata, or create slideshows. Lightroom makes use of the previews to do all this, and therefore the master photos (or negatives as they are referred to here) don't always have to be present.

A catalog export and import in action

TIP

If you only need to export a sub-selection of images, make a selection of the photos you want to export from Lightroom and make sure you remember to check the "Export selected photos only" option.

1. Over the next few steps I am going to show you how to use the Catalog export and import feature to copy a Lightroom catalog from a main computer over to a laptop computer. Here is the computer that holds the master catalog collection of photos, where all the master images are stored on an internal drive.

2. My objective here was to export the entire Lightroom catalog to a removable hard drive so that I could then access it via a secondary computer. To do this, I made sure All Photographs was selected in the Catalog panel, and chose Export as Catalog from the File menu. I wanted to export the complete catalog so I deselected "Export Selected photos only." Because I wanted to export a lightweight version of the complete catalog, I deselected the "Export negative files" option. But I did keep the "Include available previews" option checked, because I wanted to preserve these previews wherever possible.

3. After I had exported the master catalog, I disconnected the removable drive from the iMac computer and reconnected it to the laptop. On the laptop computer I opened Lightroom, chose File ⇨ Open Catalog, used the navigation dialog shown here to locate the exported catalog file on the removable hard drive, and clicked Open. This opened the warning dialog shown here, where I had to click the Relaunch button to restart Lightroom with Lightroom running from the new catalog.

4. After the new catalog had opened, I was able to access the exported iMac catalog via the laptop. Now in this instance, I was accessing the catalog from the removable drive. But I could have just as easily copied the catalog to the laptop drive and opened the catalog from there.

5. If you export a catalog without including the negatives (the master photos), there is only so much that you can do with it. I listed earlier what you can and can't do, but basically you will still be able to navigate the catalog and edit the metadata. In this example, I edited various folders in the catalog, adding color labels, applying star ratings, as well as editing the keywords and other editable metadata.

6. After I had finished editing the catalog on the laptop, I was able to export the edits that had been applied on the laptop by creating a new export catalog. To do this, I chose File ⇨ Export as Catalog. I deselected "Export selected photos only" because I wanted to export all the images. Since I only wanted to export things like the ratings, color label, and keyword metadata edits, I didn't need to check the "Include available previews" option. And because I was about to export back to the main library, there was no need for me to include the previews again either.

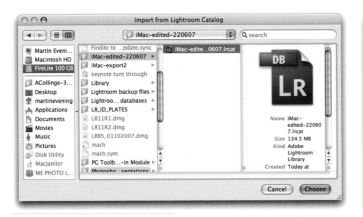

7. At this point I needed to either quit Lightroom or switch catalogs so that I could disconnect the removable hard drive from the laptop and reconnect it to the iMac computer again. On the iMac I opened Lightroom with it running the original master catalog and chose File ⇨ Import from Catalog. I selected the laptop exported catalog and clicked Choose. It was important here that in the Import from Catalog dialog I chose to replace the catalog contents using "Metadata and develop settings only."

8. Finally, here is the master catalog on the main computer after merging all the metadata edits from the laptop exported catalog. As you can see, the color labels and ratings had been updated.

NOTE

The merge catalog steps shown here will let you synchronize metadata settings such as IPTC metadata, keywords, image ratings, and Develop settings from one catalog to another and back again. However, you can't use this method to share other Lightroom settings such as Develop or Print module settings.

How to merge two catalogs into one

For a lot of Lightroom users, one catalog is all you really need. For example, I have one main catalog that I use for storing everything that I import into the computer: work and personal projects alike. If I wanted to, I could split off the work and personal photos into separate catalogs, but what works for me is to keep all the current photo files from the last 2–3 years on my main computer, stored on internal, hard drives. The files I store here are backed up to two large external disks that can easily be stored away from the computer for safe keeping. At the same time, I have a large collection of other hard drives that are used to store an archive of everything that was shot prior to 2–3 years ago, plus I use this setup to archive a lot of the raw files from shoots where I am unlikely to have to access the original raw files in a hurry.

There is no point cluttering up the main catalog with all the image files that are mainly kept off-line, and at the same time I don't like having all those additional hard drives powered up constantly so that once or twice a year I can access the files on them. Furthermore, there are an awful lot of duplicate version files in this archive from pre-Lightroom days, when I tended to generate new version copies from a single master. The solution I have adopted has been to keep separate catalogs for these two setups, which helps keep the main catalog looking tidier.

But what if I wanted to work with the contents from both catalogs at once? There are times where it is not convenient to have to keep switching from one catalog to the other and I need to see everything that is on all disks. I might also want to reconcile the keywords between the two catalogs and I can do this kind of tidying up if I work on a merged "uber" catalog. The next example uses the catalogs shown in **Figure 5.10**.

Figure 5.10   *In the following steps I'll be showing you how I created a master, merged catalog that could be used to interchange updates with two subcatalogs: my main computer database catalog and an archive catalog of off-line photos.*

Lightroom Catalog.lrcat

TIP

Depending on the size of your catalogs, the Import from Catalog step can take a long time to complete. If all you want to do is update the metadata in the master catalog for a specific folder, make a few rating edits, or add some new keywords, then it will be quicker to save the metadata changes to the files directly. Leave out the Import: Don't import new photos step (see Step 10) and relaunch Lightroom using the original subcatalog. Then all you have to do is locate the folder or collection containing the files you had modified and choose Metadata ➩ Read metadata from file.

1. My main photo catalog is held on internal drives that are backed up to the two external drives shown here. As you can see, there are over 40,000 photos in this catalog. They comprise mostly photos that have been taken recently over the last few years and are ones I need to access regularly.

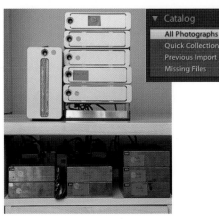

Archive catalog.lrcat

2. I also have a secondary Archive catalog used to manage the image files stored on a separate tier of disks that are kept off-line and only switched on when older data is needed.

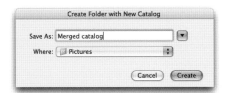

3. Let's now look at how to merge the two above catalogs into one single catalog. To do this, go to the File menu in Lightroom and choose New Catalog. This opens the Create Folder with New Catalog dialog shown here, where I named the new catalog *Merged catalog*.

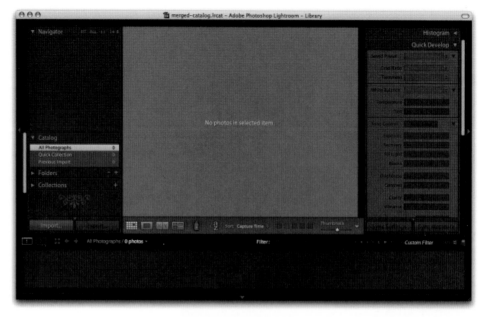

4. When you click the Create button in the previous dialog, this requires Lightroom to close down the current catalog and relaunch, opening with the newly created catalog, which to begin with contains no photos.

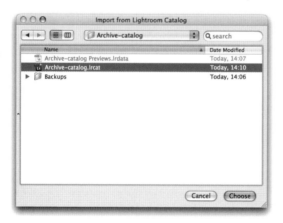

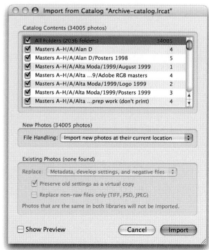

5. We are now ready to merge the first catalog. Go to the File menu again and choose Import from Catalog. Use the first dialog shown here to select the catalog to import from (in this case, the Archive catalog) and in the second dialog, under File Handling choose "Import new photos at their current location."

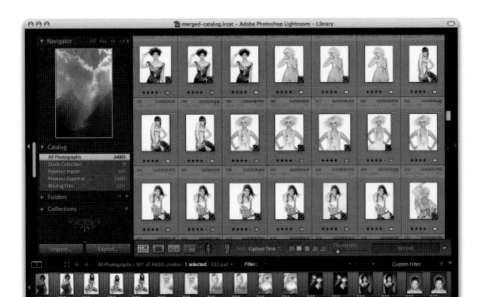

6. Here is how the Merged catalog looked after importing from the Archive catalog. At this stage it is basically a mirror of the catalog that was just imported.

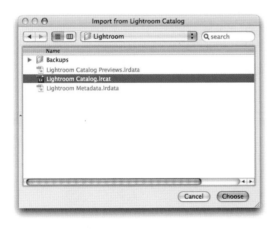
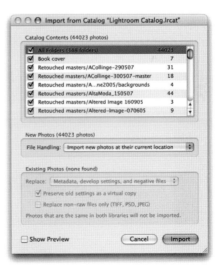

7. Now let's choose a second catalog to merge with the first. Here I repeated the same steps as shown in Step 5. I chose File ⇨ Import from Catalog, selected the main Lightroom catalog, and in the Import from Catalog dialog, I again chose "Import new photos at their current location" in the File Handling section.

Merged catalog.lrcat

8. Here is how things looked after both catalogs had been imported into the one Merged catalog. I can now do things like edit the keywords for the combined catalogs, make changes to the ratings and labels, and also edit Develop settings (providing the photos are accessible online).

Lightroom Catalog.lrcat

9. Back in the original Lightroom catalog, here is how a particular folder looked before it had been imported to the Merged catalog.

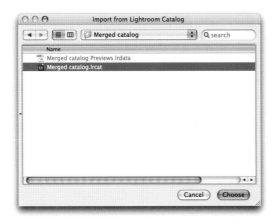

Merged catalog.lrcat

10. With the original Lightroom Catalog open, I chose Import from Catalog from the File menu. Here, I selected the Merged catalog as the source and most important of all, in the File Handling section I chose "Don't import new photos." In the Replace section I chose "Metadata and develop settings only." These settings will ensure that you don't import all the photos from the other catalog and that only the metadata edits get imported back to the original catalog.

Lightroom Catalog.lrcat

11. And here is how the same Lightroom catalog folder looked after the recently edited changes made in the Merged catalog had been updated back to the main catalog.

TIP

There is a prominent link button in the Lightroom General Preferences that says "Go to Catalog Settings." Or you can use the ⌘ Alt , (Mac), Ctrl Alt , (PC) keyboard shortcut to open the Catalog Settings dialog.

NOTE

One of the most common problems aired on the Lightroom forums is "Why is Lightroom running so slowly?" There can be many reasons for this. It can sometimes be due to the fact that people have had high expectations of how many images they can manage on a computer system that isn't powerful enough or does not have enough RAM to allow them to work efficiently. The best solution to this problem is to click the Relaunch and Optimize button, as this can often lead to an improvement in Lightroom's performance.

General Catalog Settings

Toward the bottom of the File menu we have the Catalog Settings item. This is a three-part preference dialog that contains several items previously located in the Lightroom 1 main preferences. This change was brought about with the 1.1 update and initially caused some confusion because of the way certain preference items had been moved to this submenu item. But it is one of those changes that once you have learned where the new settings are, you will soon become accustomed to the new layout. **Figure 5.11** shows the General Catalog Settings dialog. The Information section provides some basic information about the current catalog file. If you click the Show button, this reveals the location of the current catalog in the Finder/Explorer.

The "Back up catalog" section lets you decide when you want to be prompted to back up the Lightroom catalog. Personally, I wish there was an option to back up the catalog after you quit Lightroom, but never mind, maybe next time around… As before, when you want to back up the catalog you have the option to run an integrity test on the current catalog. And at the bottom there is the Relaunch and Optimize button. The Relaunch and Optimize option can be useful if you are trying to manage a large catalog of images and have seen a noticeable slowdown in performance.

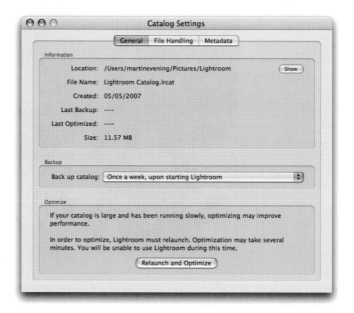

Figure 5.11   *The General Catalog Settings.*

The catalog/folders relationship

One way to appreciate how files are organized in the Lightroom catalog and their relationship to the system folders is to look at the ways you can interact between the Lightroom catalog and the system folder structure.

People often ask how using a Lightroom catalog is different from using the finder or a browser program to locate images. I point out that with a system folder setup, you usually need to know exactly where everything is kept in order to successfully retrieve something. A well-organized photographer might keep his or her photos archived on disks by date, by alphabetical order, or a combination of both. In order to retrieve photos from such a system you need to have personal knowledge of how the photos are stored: which folders are on which drives and how the subfolders are organized. Of course, if you have already added metadata to your images in the form of IPTC metadata or keywords, you can use the search command in a program like Bridge to help find the photos you are looking for. But the bottom line is that such searches will be easier if you use a dedicated cataloging program like Lightroom to manage the metadata contained in the image database.

Folder organization is also limiting because you are tied to viewing your photos in strictly segmented groups. What I mean by this is that you can use a browser to view a folder that contains photos that were shot for a particular client on a particular day, but it is less easy to view all the photos that were ever shot for that client, or all the photos that were shot during a particular month. Browsers can be made to do this, but Lightroom is designed to do it a lot faster than any browser. When you get used to being freed from the constraints of a browser navigation system for carrying out multilevel searches, the underlying folder structure becomes less relevant. If you can search quickly and easily by metadata and create and save collections, does it really matter if you know which folder the images came from? Well, yes and no. In the future we may see our computer systems place less importance on the folder structure and encourage us to use metadata to group and organize all our files. We are seeing that happen already. But when it comes to organizing and maintaining legacy folders that contain precious data, it is hardly surprising that photographers wish to know how to manage and access everything using tried and trusted methods. This is why it is useful to appreciate the inter-relationship between the catalog and the system folders they refer to. Over the next few pages, I'll be showing you how to keep both in check.

Finding the link from the catalog to a folder

1. As I mentioned on the previous page, with Lightroom you are free to organize and sort your photos in ways that are not directly dependent on knowing the underlying folder structure. For example, here I am looking at a collection of photos with a common New York Architecture theme where the photos have all originated from different folders. If I click the Folder Action button in the Metadata panel, this will take me to the Folder view in Lightroom for the most selected photo.

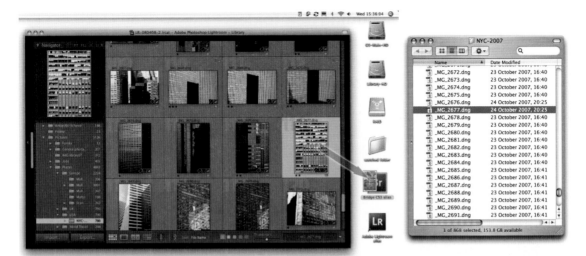

2. If you want to see where the photo actually lives at the operating
system level, you can choose Photo ⇨ Show in Finder (Mac), Show
in Explorer (PC), or use ⌘R (Mac), Ctrl R (PC), to reveal the image
file in a new Finder/Explorer window. But there is another way, one
that allows you to link back to Bridge. You can drag and drop a
photo from the content area to a Bridge program alias/shortcut.

3. When you do this, it will open the folder the photo belongs to in a
new Bridge window and the selected photo will be highlighted.

Adding new folders

Here are the steps required to create new folders within the Lightroom Folders panel. I also show you how to move selections or whole folders of images from one folder to another.

1. To create a new folder, click the plus icon in the Folders panel header (circled). This opens the Create Folder dialog. In this example, I made a sub-selection of images from a folder named November-2006 and created a new folder called Oslo-2006 as a child of the same November-2006 parent folder.

2. I then selected the remaining photos and repeated the same step as before, except this time I created a new folder called Stockholm-2006 as a child of the November-2006 parent folder.

Lightroom folders and system folders

If you rename a Lightroom folder, the corresponding system folder will be renamed as well. If you rename a folder in Lightroom or move the folder location in the drive directory, such changes are mirrored at the system level too. However, Lightroom is unable to automatically detect new images that are added to a system-level folder unless that image has been explicitly imported into Lightroom first.

NOTE

For a more detailed explanation of how the Lightroom catalog works, refer to the appendices.

1. Here is a view of the Folders panel in Lightroom and the associated system folders, where the Oslo-2006 and Stockholm-2006 folders are both stored in the November-2006 folder. I used the contextual menu to choose Shown in Finder/Explorer.

TIP

If you right-click on a photo in the Library grid, you can access the contextual menu, which will allow you to choose Show in Finder.

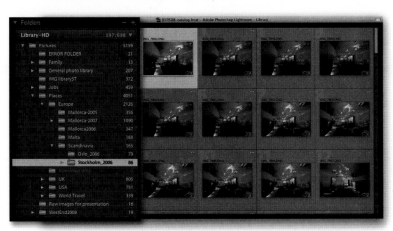

2. I then created a new folder called Scandinavia, as a child of Europe > Places. In the Folders panel in Lightroom I moved the Oslo-2006 and Stockholm-2006 folders into the Scandinavia folder. The folder directory change is also mirrored at the system level.

Photograph: New York City, NY © Martin Evening 2007
Canon EOS 400D | 33 mm | 400 ISO | f11 @ 1/320th

Develop module image editing

A definitive guide to working with the image processing controls in the Develop module

One of the most powerful features in Lightroom is the image processing engine and the way the image adjustment processing is deferred until the time you actually export an image. This method of image processing actually began in the early days of computer imaging, when deferred processing was adopted by programs such as Live Picture and xRes as a means to speed up the image editing. Computers were a lot slower back then, yet it was possible to manipulate large image files in real time on relatively slow computers (with as little as 24 MB of RAM memory) and defer the image rendering process to the end of a photo edit session.

Of course, these days, you can edit very large images in no time at all in Photoshop and with few limitations. But one of the key advantages of Lightroom is that you can apply a crop, spot the image to remove marks, adjust the color, do some more retouching, readjust the crop again, and so on without ever touching the pixels in the original photograph. In a conventional pixel-editing workflow, the pixels are always modified in a consecutive sequence of steps. When you work in Lightroom, no restrictions are placed on the order in which you do things and the edit changes you make in the Develop module are only applied when you export a photo as a rendered file, such as a TIFF or JPEG image.

NOTE

A master file in Lightroom is truly treated as a digital negative. Any operations you carry out in Lightroom to alter the image, including the retouching, are all stored as saved instructions. The other benefit of this approach is that the image pixels are eventually rendered in a single processing step.

Image editing in Lightroom

Smarter image processing

The Lightroom image processing engine is notable for a number of reasons. Adobe has made Lightroom simpler to use than Photoshop, and in my opinion, has done so without compromising the quality of color processing in any way. Lightroom uses a single RGB workspace to carry out all its image calculations, and the space used is similar to the ProPhoto RGB space that was originally specified by Kodak. It uses the same coordinates as ProPhoto RGB, but has a gamma of 1.0 instead of 1.8. By using a 1.0 gamma, the Lightroom RGB workspace is able to match the native 1.0 gamma of raw camera files, and its wide gamut can therefore contain all the colors that any of today's digital cameras are capable of capturing. For these reasons, the Lightroom RGB workspace is ideally tailored to the task of handling the color processed data from the raw camera files. Concerns about banding in wide gamut color spaces have perhaps been a little overrated, since it is really quite difficult to pull apart an image in ProPhoto RGB to the point where you see gaps appearing between the levels. Suffice it to say, the Lightroom RGB space uses a native bit depth of 16-bits per channel, which means that Lightroom is able to process up to 32,000 levels of tonal information per color channel. Since a typical digital camera is capable of capturing up to 4,000 levels per color channel, it is probably true to say that the Lightroom RGB workspace can safely handle all of the tone and color information from any modern digital camera. Admittedly, there is no support for CMYK color in Lightroom and so for prepress work you always need to use Photoshop to handle the CMYK conversions. But the good news is that there are no color management settings, color space issues, or profile warnings to worry about.

Lightroom does not use layers, but it does recognize and import layered images (providing the backward compatibility option was switched on when saving the file from Photoshop). If you need to do any kind of layering work, it is quite easy to choose the Edit in External Editor command, carry on processing the image in another program, and save the results back to Lightroom in the form of an edited copy version of the original master image.

A digital image is made up of nothing more than a series of numbers, and during the image editing process those numbers are changed to new numbers. The Lightroom image processing engine ultimately reduces all of its pixel calculations into a single calculation by the most direct route possible to produce a mathematically purer, processed result, in which any image degradation is minimized. Another advantage of the Lightroom image processing engine is that you have full access to all of the image controls when working with JPEG, TIFF, and PSD images as you have when working with raw camera files. You can use all of the image controls available in the Lightroom Develop module such as the White Balance, Exposure, and Tone Curve controls to process any imported image.

Camera Raw compatibility

With Lightroom 1 and the later 1.x versions, the Develop controls in Lightroom matched those used in Adobe Camera Raw for Photoshop CS3. The Develop settings that were applied to images in either of these two programs were fully recognized and compatible with each other. This new version of Lightroom has a number of new Develop features such as localized editing tools and post-crop vignettes that adapt to the way the image is cropped and a revised autotone logic. At the time of this writing, it is known there will be a new release of Camera Raw 4.5 for Photoshop CS3 that can read all the adjustments made in Lightroom 2 and render them in Photoshop, but you won't be able to edit any of the settings that would effectively be "new" to Photoshop CS3. However, it is probably safe to assume that the new features in Lightroom 2 will eventually be part of a later Photoshop CS4 release.

Smarter retouching

The really unique thing about the Develop module tools is that you can apply them non-destructively to any image. You can therefore carry out basic spotting work on an image in Lightroom using the Spot Removal tool in Clone mode or Healing mode, and the retouching work will be saved and stored as editing instructions. This also applies to localized adjustments made with the brush, Graduated Filter, or spot removal tools. Apart from the fact that all retouching work can be undone easily, you have complete freedom to make Develop adjustments in any order you like. It does not matter if you perform the spotting before or after you adjust the colors and tones, because Lightroom records these actions as editing instructions rather than editing the original pixels.

Steps for getting accurate color

NOTE

You don't need to be concerned with RGB workspaces or profiles when working in Lightroom. Raw files don't have profiles, and the color management of these files is handled by the internal raw processing engine plus any calibration adjustments that might be applied. In the case of pixel images imported into Lightroom, the profile recognition is handled automatically.

The image file you are working on in Lightroom can be any color space and will be color managed accordingly, provided the image has an embedded profile. If the image you are working on has no embedded profile, the situation is the same as with any other software program, and a guess has to be made as to what the colors in the file actually mean. Whenever Lightroom encounters a file with a missing profile, it will assume the image to be in an sRGB color space. There are no warning indications in Lightroom other than the appearance of the image itself. So if the colors of a particular image you see in Lightroom don't match your usual expectations, it could be due to an image file having a missing image profile. To prevent this from occurring in the first place, I suggest that you check your Photoshop Color Settings and ensure that you have the color management switched on so that Photoshop will always embed a profile in the files that are saved out of it. The easiest way to do this is to choose a General Purpose color setting, or better still, one of the Prepress color settings in the Color Settings dialog.

Calibrating the display

The color management system in Lightroom requires no configuration, as Lightroom automatically manages the colors without you having to worry about profile mismatches, which color space the image is in, or what the default workspace is. There may be problems with missing profiles, but this only applies to imported files where a conscious decision has been made to not color manage an image. Apart from these rare instances, you can rely on Lightroom to manage the colors perfectly from import through to export and print. However, you do need to give important consideration to the monitor display and ensure that it is properly calibrated and profiled before you can rely on it to judge colors, because you want the monitor to show as accurately as possible what you are likely to see in print. Calibrating and profiling the display is essential, and it does not have to be complicated or expensive. So if you want to get the colors right and want to avoid disappointments, you should regard the following pages as essential reading.

Choosing a display

The choice of display boils down to Cathode Ray Tube (CRT) or Liquid Crystal Display (LCD). The better CRT displays have mostly been discontinued and are hard to come by now, although there are a few good-quality CRT displays such as the Sony Artisan that you may find in use. But apart from that your choices these days are restricted to LCD displays, and the quality can vary greatly. There are different classes of LCD displays starting with budget-priced screens (such as those used on laptop computers), to large-screen professional LCD displays offering a high degree of color accuracy and wide color gamuts, such as the Eizo ColorEdge CG301W and the NEC LCD3090. Both these displays are easy to calibrate and profile, plus the large 30-inch screen size means they are comfortable to work with. As with all things in life, you get what you pay for. Since the monitor is what you will spend all your time looking at when making critical image adjustments, it is pointless to cut corners when choosing a display, just as it is pointless to scrimp on buying anything but the best-quality lenses for your camera.

Calibrating and profiling the display

The only truly effective way to calibrate and profile a display is to use a colorimeter or spectrophotometer, and it is possible to buy a good colorimeter along with the necessary software package for under $250. When you consider how much you might be prepared to spend on camera lenses, it really is not worth spending any less than $1,000 on the combination of a good-quality display plus calibration package. It is possible to spend a lot more on a professional calibration kit that also allows you to measure color samples and build print profiles. But if all you want to do is to calibrate and profile the display, such devices don't offer any significant advantages over what a basic colorimeter device can do, although some software packages can help you build better profiles using the same basic hardware profiling kit.

There are two stages to a profiling process. The first step is to calibrate the display to optimize the screen brightness and contrast, plus set the desired white point and gamma (**Figure 6.1**). The second involves measuring various color patches on the screen, where the measurements made from these patches provide the source data to build a profile. On a CRT display there may be buttons or dials that allow you to adjust the brightness and contrast of the monitor and possibly some color controls for setting different white points and fine-tuning the color output. These settings can be adjusted during the calibration process to optimize the performance and neutralize the display before making the profile measurements. Most LCD displays have only a brightness control that adjusts the luminance of the backlight on the screen. So when running through the preliminary calibration steps, there is nothing you can adjust, other than the brightness, and you simply skip the steps where you are unable to make any adjustments to the display.

White point and gamma

Apart from asking you to adjust the hardware settings, the calibration software will ask you to choose white point and gamma settings before you proceed building the profile. If you are using a CRT display, I recommend you always choose a white point of 6500 K. If you are using an LCD display, it is not possible to manually adjust the white point the way you can on a CRT. Although you can set a specific white point for an LCD display, doing so will often compromise the display's performance, so it is usually best to select the native white point for an LCD screen. Whether you are using a Mac or PC computer, the gamma should ideally be set to 2.2, since the 1.8 gamma Macintosh option is only really there for quaint historical reasons.

TIP

The performance of your monitor display will fluctuate over time, and therefore it is advisable to update the monitor profile from time to time. CRT monitors should be reprofiled once a week. LCD displays fluctuate a lot less, so you probably only need to re-profile just once every four weeks.

Figure 6.1   *I prefer to use the X-Rite Eye-One Photo to calibrate the display I use at work.*

Macintosh 1.8 gamma

The Macintosh 1.8 gamma dates back to the very early days of Macintosh computers, long before color displays and ICC color management was universally adopted. Back then, it was found that the best way to get an image viewed on a Macintosh screen to match the output of an Apple black-and-white laser printer was to adjust the gamma of the monitor to 1.8. These days, Adobe programs like Photoshop and Lightroom always compensate for whatever monitor gamma is used by the system to ensure that all images are displayed at the correct brightness regardless of the gamma that was selected when calibrating the display. Setting the gamma to 1.8 instead of 2.2 lightens the interface but has absolutely no impact on the lightness of the images displayed in Lightroom. These will be perceived as being displayed at the same brightness regardless of the monitor gamma. If you are mainly using your computer for image editing work, it is best to use a gamma setting of 2.2, because it means that the image tones you preview in Lightroom are rendered on the screen with a more even distribution.

Matching white balances

People often assume that your goal should be to match the white balance between different displays and viewing light sources. For side-by-side comparison this can help, but what people tend to forget is that our eyes are constantly compensating and can accommodate changes in white balance from one light source to another. You can edit an image on a display using a white point of 7000 K and check the results with a viewing box that has a white balance of 5500 K (as long as the two are a reasonable distance apart). In these situations your eyes will adjust to analyze the colors relative to what they perceive to be the whitest white.

Steps to successful calibration and profiling

For accurate calibration you first need to decide whether you want to buy a basic device for calibrating the monitor display only or a more advanced device that allows you to create your own custom print profiles. I use the X-Rite Eye-One Photo; the following steps show you how the Eye-One Match 3.6.2 software guides you through the calibration and profiling process with either the Eye-One Photo or the more affordable Eye-One Display2 calibrator. Prior to doing a calibration, make sure the calibrator head and white tile are clean before making any measurements. Also, ensure that the screen surface is clean and free of dust. The following steps walk you through the process.

1. This first screen asks you to identify the type of display you want to calibrate and profile. The decision made here affects the recommended settings shown in the next dialog.

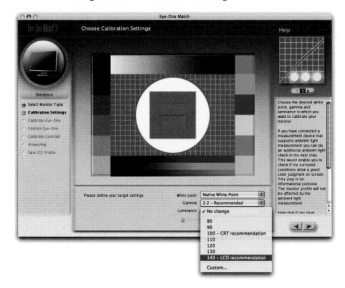

2. In the previous dialog I identified the monitor as an LCD type display and the settings shown here are those recommended for a desktop LCD display. Since you cannot physically adjust the white point of an LCD display, it is best to select the Native White Point option. Although the software recommends that a luminance of 140 candelas m^2 is ideal for calibrating and building profiles with a desktop LCD display, this is not an absolute figure. Ideally, you should use a luminance between 110 and 140 for a desktop LCD display and a luminance of around 85–100 for a CRT-type display.

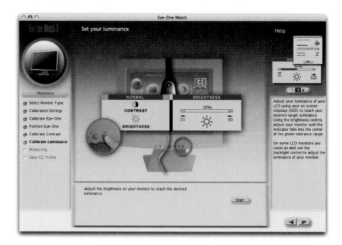

3. Now you are ready to place the calibrator on the screen and start the calibration process. To measure a CRT monitor, a suction cup-type device attaches the calibrator to the screen. To measure an LCD display, you must use a counterweight attachment to carefully hang the calibration device over the screen. The Eye-One Match software autodetects the location of the calibrator so it knows which section of the screen the calibrator should take its measurements from.

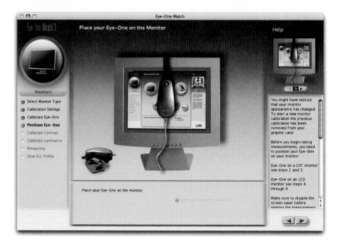

4. If you have a CRT monitor, you should be able to adjust the contrast, in which case you should set this to maximum. Next you need to adjust the brightness controls on the screen so that the measured brightness matches the desired setting. If you have a CRT display with adjustable color controls, there will be a step that allows you to manually adjust the color guns on your monitor to produce a neutral gray display.

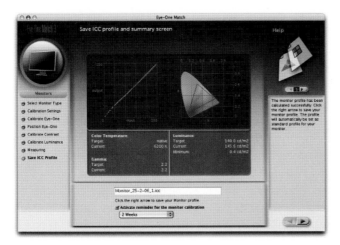

5. If you are calibrating an LCD display, then simply skip this, and proceed to the next step in which a series of color patches flash on the screen. The calibration device measures these patches and uses them to build the monitor profile. The profile measurement process takes a few minutes to complete, so you need to make sure that your screen saver doesn't kick in while the calibration is underway! For example, the settings on an LCD laptop in battery-power mode may automatically dim the display halfway through the profiling process and adversely affect the results of the profile measurement. One way to ensure this does not happen is to keep the mouse cursor moving every 30 seconds or so (outside of the area being measured of course) until the process is complete. At this stage you can click to save the monitor profile that has been generated, and it will automatically be configured as the new monitor display profile.

Figure 6.2 *The Quick Develop buttons are laid out with arrows indicating how you can increase or decrease an adjustment. To restore an adjustment to its default setting, click on the name of the adjustment. The Auto Tone button applies an automatic adjustment to the Exposure, Recovery, Blacks, Brightness, and Contrast, whereas the Reset button resets everything back to the Lightroom defaults.*

Quick Develop panel

Before I tackle all the main controls in the Develop module, I thought it would be best to kick off with an introduction to the Quick Develop panel in the Library module (**Figure 6.2**). It provides all the essential image adjustment controls that are found in the Develop module such as the White Balance, Exposure, Recovery, Fill Light, Blacks, Brightness, Contrast, and Vibrance, but without requiring you to leave the Library module. One of the main differences with Quick Develop is that Quick Develop adjustments are always applied relative to the current Develop settings. For example, if I select a number of images that already have different Exposure settings, I can use the Exposure buttons in Quick Develop to make those photos relatively lighter or darker (as opposed to synchronizing all the photos with the same Exposure value).

The other main advantage is that you can apply Quick Develop adjustments to multiple images that have been selected in the Grid view or Filmstrip. Using Quick Develop is the same as working in Develop, except you don't have quite the same degree of control as you do in the Develop module and the previews are not quite as accurate. Quick Develop is therefore ideal for a first pass edit, where you want to do most of your work in the Library module without having to switch back and forth to the Develop module to apply image adjustments.

Quick Develop controls

To use Quick Develop, go to the Library module and choose a photo, or make a selection of several photos. You are now ready to use the Quick Develop panel controls. One way you can do this is to click on the Saved Preset list shown in **Figure 6.3** and choose a default setting or a previously saved preset as your starting point. The Quick Develop buttons let you increase or decrease the tone adjustments by clicking the arrow buttons. The single-chevron icons increase or decrease a setting by small amounts and the double-chevron icons by larger amounts.

Color controls

The Treatment section lets you decide whether to process an image in Color or as Grayscale (the term "grayscale" could be considered a little misleading, because images in Lightroom are not actually converted into Grayscale mode). It could also be argued that you now need two mouse clicks rather than one to switch from color to grayscale.

But to be honest, I think it is better to memorize the V shortcut as a means for toggling between color and grayscale mode and rely on the Treatment menu as more an indicator of which mode a photo is in.

Next, we come to the White Balance options, which include the Temp and Tint controls. If you are shooting with a camera set to Auto White Balance mode, or you were using a white balance that was correct for the lighting conditions at the time of shooting, you will probably want to leave this set to As Shot. But otherwise, you can click the White Balance menu (also shown in Figure 6.3) and choose one of the preset settings listed there, or select the Auto setting and Lightroom will try to calculate an optimized White Balance setting for you (or use the ⌘ Shift U [Mac], Ctrl Shift U [PC] shortcut). An image will become incrementally cooler as you click the arrow buttons to the left and warmer as you click the arrow buttons to the right. The single-arrow buttons produce small shifts in color, and clicking the double-arrow buttons produces more pronounced color shifts.

Tone controls

In the Tone Control section we have an Auto Tone button (⌘ U [Mac], Ctrl U [PC]) that applies an automatic correction to the following Develop module settings: Exposure, Recovery, Blacks, Brightness, and Contrast. This action is undoable by clicking the Reset All button at the bottom of the panel (or you can use the ⌘ Shift R [Mac], Ctrl Shift R [PC] shortcut). An Auto adjustment can sometimes make an instant improvement. Or it will not do much because the tone adjustments were correct anyway. It is ridiculous to expect an automatic function such as this to perform flawlessly every time, but for the most part, I find that Auto Tone works well for the majority of times that I use it, especially since the Auto Tone logic has been improved for Lightroom 2. Even if Auto Tone does not produce perfect results, what it does produce can often be a useful starting point for making further Quick Develop edits.

For the following tone and color controls I advise you to start by adjusting the Exposure amount first, because the Exposure is critical for determining the clipping point for the highlights. Exposure adjustments affect the highlight clipping point and the overall brightness, and each click of an Exposure single-arrow button is equivalent to a 0.33-unit shift in the Develop module, whereas each click of a double-arrow button is equivalent to a 1.0-unit shift. Once you have set the Exposure you can if necessary adjust the Recovery, which can counteract the effect of an Exposure adjustment to preserve critical highlight detail.

Figure 6.3 The Quick Develop panel showing the Preset and White Balance menu lists. The preset list will display all default and all saved develop settings. See "Saving Develop Settings as Presets" on page 360.)

TIP

Clicking the arrow buttons in the Quick Develop panel will simultaneously update the settings in the Basic panel of the Develop module.

Figure 6.4 *The Quick Develop panel view with the* Alt *key held down, making the Saturation and Slider controls visible.*

NOTE

Note the phrase "Reset All will reset the photo settings to the default import settings." This action may reset the Develop settings to a zeroed or default state, but if you applied say, an Auto Tone on import, it will reset the settings to the Auto Tone and not a zeroed setting.

A single-arrow click is equivalent to a 5-unit shift in the Develop module, and a double-arrow click is equivalent to a 20-unit shift. Fill Light is a shadow lightening adjustment that lets you brighten the shadows more should you need to do so. A single-arrow click is equivalent to a 5-unit shift in the Develop module, and a double-arrow click is equivalent to a 15-unit shift. The Blacks controls the shadow clipping. With the Blacks button, a single-arrow click makes 1-unit shifts and double-arrow clicks 5 units. Brightness and Contrast are fairly self-explanatory but are applied *after* Exposure, Recovery, Fill Light, and Blacks, which is one reason why I suggest you apply the Exposure adjustment *before* you adjust Brightness. A single-arrow click on the Brightness and Contrast buttons is equivalent to a 5-unit shift in the Develop module, and a double-arrow click is equivalent to a 20-unit shift.

The Clarity adjustment adds localized contrast to an image. Adding clarity can make a picture look "clearer" rather than "sharper," because it is increasing the midtone contrast to make the midtone areas stand out more. Most photos can benefit from a small clarity adjustment. The Vibrance adjustment is similar to the Saturation control in the Develop module, but it works by applying a nonlinear adjustment that brightens the duller colors without oversaturating the already saturated colors. With both Clarity and Vibrance a single-arrow click is equivalent to a 5-unit shift in the Develop module, and a double-arrow click is equivalent to a 20-unit shift.

If you hold down the Alt key (see **Figure 6.4**) the Clarity adjustment switches to show Sharpening. In Alt key mode the Sharpening controls in Quick Develop are equivalent to adjusting the Sharpening Amount slider in the Develop module Detail panel. Although you don't have access to the other three sharpening sliders, you can still make an initial sharpening adjustment before fine-tuning the other settings later. If you hold down the Alt key the Vibrance adjustment will switch to show Saturation for standard, linear saturation adjustments. With both Sharpening and Saturation a single-arrow click is equivalent to a 5-unit shift in the Develop module, and a double-arrow click is equivalent to a 20-unit shift.

The Reset All button (⌘ Shift R [Mac], Ctrl Shift R [PC]) will reset all the Develop settings that have been applied to a photo (not just those that have been applied via Quick Develop) to their default import settings, so use this button with caution.

A typical Quick Develop workflow

The following steps provide a brief overview of how you can use the Quick Develop controls to edit multiple photographs in the Library module.

1. These daylight photographs were shot with a digital camera in raw mode and imported using the Default tone and color and As Shot White Balance setting. For this first step I made a selection of all the photos that I wished to adjust.

2. I first wanted to cool the colors in the selected photos, so I clicked the double-chevron button (circled here) to make all the pictures bluer in color.

3. I now wanted to apply some tonal edits. I clicked the Auto Tone button followed by the Exposure, Brightness, Contrast, and Vibrance buttons circled here. This combination of adjustments did a lot to improve the appearance of all the selected photos.

4. However, when looking as the group of images I noticed that there were two pictures in the middle of the selection that needed to be made lighter than the rest. There was no need to deselect the selection of photos. I double-clicked on the photo to work in Loupe view, where the Quick Develop controls can be applied one image at a time. In this example I added more Exposure, more Brightness, and more Vibrance.

5. This took care of that one middle photo. I clicked on the cell border of the photo to deselect all the photos in the selection and used a Shift–click to reselect this recently edited image and the photo next to it. I then clicked the Sync Settings button at the bottom.

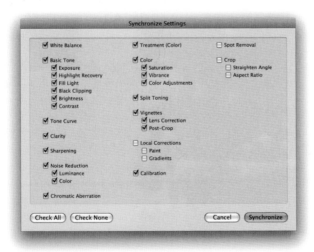

6. This opened the Synchronize Settings dialog, where I clicked the Check All button to select all settings. I then clicked the Synchronize button to synchronize the settings across the two selected photos in Step 5.

Quick Develop cropping

The Crop Ratio menu options (**Figure 6.5**) can be used to apply a preset crop ratio that evenly trims the photos at either side. Image cropping is something that you usually want to apply carefully to photographs individually, but I would say that having a quick way to change the aspect ratio of a bunch of pictures might be more useful for someone like a school photographer who wants to quickly prepare a set of portraits to a new fixed aspect ratio setting. You can also create your own Custom Aspect Ratio crop settings for use in the Quick Develop panel (**Figure 6.6**). In **Figure 6.7** I selected the *8.5 x 11* proportional crop and applied it to the selected photograph.

Figure 6.5 *The Quick Develop crop menu options contain a list of presets. You can add to this list by clicking Enter Custom to add up to nine new custom crop proportions to the list.*

Figure 6.6 *The Enter Custom Aspect Ratio dialog.*

Figure 6.7 *Shown here is a photograph to which I applied a 8.5 x 11 proportional crop to a landscape image that originally had a normal 2:3 aspect ratio.*

Synchronizing Develop settings

The Sync Settings button at the bottom of the right panel lets you synchronize all the Develop image settings, not just those that have been applied via the Quick Develop panel (**Figure 6.8**). If you have a group of images selected and want the settings to match the most selected image, just click the Sync Settings button, which calls up the Synchronize Settings dialog (**Figure 6.9**). By the way, the most selected image will be the image that is currently the most highlighted in the grid and also is the one displayed in the Navigator. Notice that the Synchronize Settings dialog contains several selectable options for all the different Develop settings. If you have just imported a collection of images and this is the first time you are editing the pictures, select Check All so that all the image setting attributes will be synchronized. This is best in the early stages of a Library photo edit, because you won't disrupt any preconfigured settings in all the other images.

The Check All option is therefore quicker to use in those situations where not much has been done to any of the pictures yet. If you are synchronizing photographs and it is likely that some of the images may have been individually adjusted, you probably won't want to override these settings when you carry out a synchronization. In these instances, it is better to make a careful selection of only the settings attributes you want to see synchronized and leave all the other settings as they are. When you are done, click the Synchronize button at the bottom to synchronize the image settings so that they will all match the most selected image.

Figure 6.8 *The Sync Settings button can be used to synchronize all Develop module settings, not just those that have been applied via the Quick Develop panel.*

TIP

Notice that the Local corrections, Spot Removal, and Crop settings are deselected by default. This is because you may not always want to synchronize these specific settings. For example, synchronizing the Spot Removal settings can be beneficial if you are synching a selection of matching shots in which you want to remove sensor dust marks that always appear in the same spot and the individual pictures don't vary too much. But if all the pictures are shots of different subjects, sharing the Spot Removal settings would just create a big mess (as well as overwriting spotting work you had done already).

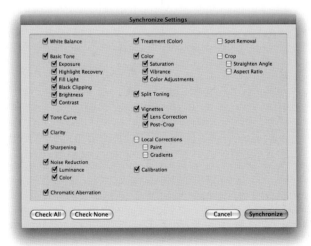

Figure 6.9 *When you click the Synchronize button in the Quick Develop panel, the Synchronize Settings dialog opens.*

Raw or JPEG?

At first glance, Lightroom appears to handle the processing of raw capture images and non-raw images as if they were the same. The fact that you now have more controls at your disposal to edit the color and tone in a JPEG capture is in one way a good thing, but it would be dangerous to conclude from this that JPEG is now equal to the quality of a raw capture. Here is a brief summary of the differences between shooting in raw and JPEG mode.

A typical good-quality digital camera is capable of capturing up to 4,096 levels of information per color channel. This does not mean that every image capture contains 4,096 levels in every channel. For example, an underexposed digital photograph will have far fewer levels than this. But even though you may capture fewer than 4,096 levels per channel, that's still plenty of levels to work with in Lightroom. A raw capture file contains the direct raw data as captured by the sensor, without any pre-image processing applied to it. The only factor that limits the potential of a raw capture file is the camera exposure and camera ISO setting. This is the major advantage of raw: when you shoot using raw mode, apart from the exposure and ISO setting, nothing else about the image processing will have been decided yet. A raw camera capture file is really like a digital negative that has yet to be processed, and as such is a master file with the potential to be edited in many different ways. Some photographers have found their initial encounters with raw images to be off-putting because some raw capture images appear dull and lifeless at first. But this in a way is a good thing because you want there to be room to expand the tones and add contrast as you see fit. The controls in Lightroom's Develop module can work wonders on any photograph, but they work best when they are used to edit raw images.

The alternative option is to shoot using JPEG mode where the camera automatically applies the image processing. This can include things like setting the white balance, adjusting shadow and highlight clipping, applying a tone curve, removing noise, sharpening the image, and converting the raw data to an 8-bit RGB output space. The JPEG capture mode will also compresses the color data (while trying to preserve the luminance) to produce a compact JPEG capture file. All the image processing is managed by an onboard image processor inside the camera. The user has limited control over the JPEG processing beyond setting the White Balance settings, sharpness, noise handling, and RGB output space before the pictures are shot.

1. If you shoot a scene such as this using JPEG mode, the clipping gamut warning seen in the clouds indicates that there is nothing that can be done to reveal more information highlights. The tonal range in this JPEG image has already been fixed.

2. If the same image is captured in raw mode, a negative Exposure combined with a positive Recovery adjustment quickly reveals the highlight detail that the JPEG capture version was unable to preserve. When you process a raw file, you potentially have more tone information to play with and therefore more flexibility when making tone and color adjustments in the Develop module.

The Develop module interface

The Develop module provides all the controls photographers need for making adjustments and corrections to their images (**Figure 6.10**). The main controls are located in the right panel section. At the top are the Histogram panel and Develop tools panel, and below that the Basic panel, which is an essential starting point for all image adjustments. This is followed by a Tone Curve panel, which provides you with a more advanced degree of control over the image tones, allowing you to further fine-tune the Tone settings that have been set in the Basic panel. In the example shown here, the Tone Curve controls have been adjusted to apply the optimum contrast and brightness in both the sky and the rock (note the unusual tone curve shape). The Tone Curve has a target adjustment tool, which when you click to activate, allows you to move the cursor over the image, click on an area of interest, and drag with the mouse to lighten or darken those tones rather than having to drag the sliders. Similar target mode controls are available when making HSL and Grayscale panel adjustments. Below that is the HSL / Color / Grayscale panel. The HSL section provides similar controls to the Hue/Saturation adjustment in Photoshop, as these sliders allow you to adjust separately the hue, saturation, and luminance components of an image. The Color section is similar to HSL, but with simpler controls (and no Target mode option). Clicking the Grayscale section ([V]) converts an image to black and white and lets you make custom monochrome conversions, creatively blending the RGB color channels to produce different types of monochrome output. The Split Toning controls can be used to colorize the shadows and highlights separately (the Split Toning controls work quite nicely on color images as well). The Detail panel lets you add sharpness to imported images. It also has controls for suppressing the color noise and luminance noise in an image and can correct for the chromatic aberration responsible for color fringing. The Vignettes panel includes Lens correction controls for global vignette control as well as post crop vignette sliders for applying vignette effects to cropped images. The Camera Calibration panel allows advanced users to apply custom camera calibration settings that can compensate for variations in the color response of an individual camera sensor. All the Develop settings can be saved as custom presets. The left panel contains a selection of default presets to get you started, but it is easy to create your own presets using all or partial combinations of the Develop module settings. Notice that as you roll over the list in the Presets panel you see an instant preview in the Navigator preview, without having to click to apply an effect to the main image.

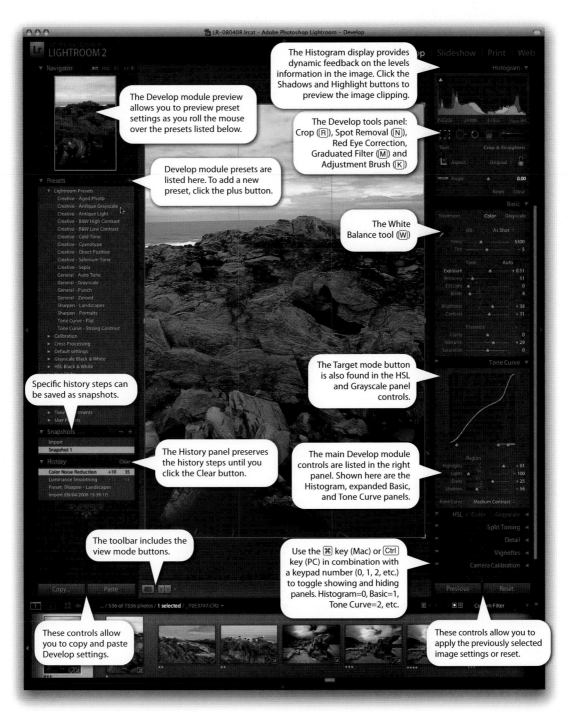

The Histogram display provides dynamic feedback on the levels information in the image. Click the Shadows and Highlight buttons to preview the image clipping.

The Develop module preview allows you to preview preset settings as you roll the mouse over the presets listed below.

The Develop tools panel: Crop (R), Spot Removal (N), Red Eye Correction, Graduated Filter (M) and Adjustment Brush (K)

Develop module presets are listed here. To add a new preset, click the plus button.

The White Balance tool (W)

Specific history steps can be saved as snapshots.

The Target mode button is also found in the HSL and Grayscale panel controls.

The History panel preserves the history steps until you click the Clear button.

The main Develop module controls are listed in the right panel. Shown here are the Histogram, expanded Basic, and Tone Curve panels.

The toolbar includes the view mode buttons.

Use the ⌘ key (Mac) or Ctrl key (PC) in combination with a keypad number (0, 1, 2, etc.) to toggle showing and hiding panels. Histogram=0, Basic=1, Tone Curve=2, etc.

These controls allow you to copy and paste Develop settings.

These controls allow you to apply the previously selected image settings or reset.

Figure 6.10 *The Develop module interface.*

NOTE

Dragging a handle moves the crop bounding box relative to its center. Dragging the cursor outside of the bounding box rotates the crop. Dragging the cursor inside the crop bounding box scrolls the image relative to the crop.

TIP

Whenever you drag one of the crop handles to make a nonrotational crop, a dividing third grid overlays the image. These thin grid lines can be useful as an aid to composition. There are lots of theories about how to create a perfect composition in a painting or photograph. One of the classic methods is to imagine the image divided into thirds and aim to arrange the picture elements within this 3 x 3 structure. The photograph in Figure 6.12 has been cropped using the dividing third guides, although you can also choose other custom overlay grids, as discussed on pages 251–254.

TIP

You can toggle the Constrain Aspect Ratio lock by pressing A.

Develop module cropping

Wherever you are in Lightroom, you can press R to switch directly to the Crop Overlay mode in the Develop module. If you are already in the Develop module, you can also click the Crop Overlay mode button in the Tools panel to activate cropping. **Figure 6.11** shows a close-up view of the Crop tool panel controls. Once you are in Crop Overlay mode, a crop bounding box appears, initially selecting all of the image. As you drag the crop handles, the image and crop edges will move relative to the center of the crop (**Figure 6.12**) and the areas outside the crop bounding box will appear shaded. Dragging the cursor inside the crop bounding box scrolls the image relative to the crop, allowing you to easily reposition the photograph relative to the crop bounding box. If you hold down the Alt key, the crop bounding box can be made to resize relative to the crop box center. To reset the Crop Overlay, click the Reset button or press ⌘ Shift R (Mac) or Ctrl Shift R (PC). Click Close to apply a crop and exit the Tools panel.

Rotating the crop

To rotate and crop an image at the same time, move the cursor outside the crop bounding box and click and drag. Alternatively, you can use the Straighten slider in the Tools panel, or the Straighten tool, to straighten the photograph. In either case the image will rotate relative to the crop bounding box (which will always remain level). You can also click the Crop Frame tool in the Tools panel (Figure 6.11) to activate it: place the Crop Frame cursor over the photograph, then click and drag to make a freeform crop (as you would with the Crop tool in Photoshop). When you have finished defining the crop, the Crop Frame tool returns to its docked position in the Tools panel.

Crop aspect ratios

When the Constrain Aspect Ratio button is checked, the current crop aspect ratio will be preserved as you apply a crop. If no crop setting has been applied yet, the aspect ratio is locked to the current image proportions. So if you check this box and drag any of the handles, such as the corner or side handles, the crop area will match the exact proportions of the current image. If you go to the Crop Presets list, you can then select one of the aspect ratio presets in the list or choose Enter Custom, which opens the Enter Custom Aspect dialog shown in Figure 6.12. Here you can enter settings for a new custom aspect ratio setting. Click OK to add this setting to the Crop presets list.

Crop Overlay mode button (R)

Crop Frame tool

Straighten tool

Clear Crop settings and reset

Crop tool Presets list

Constrain Aspect Ratio lock (A)

Straighten slider control

Close tool panel

Figure 6.11 *This shows a close-up view of the Crop tool panel controls.*

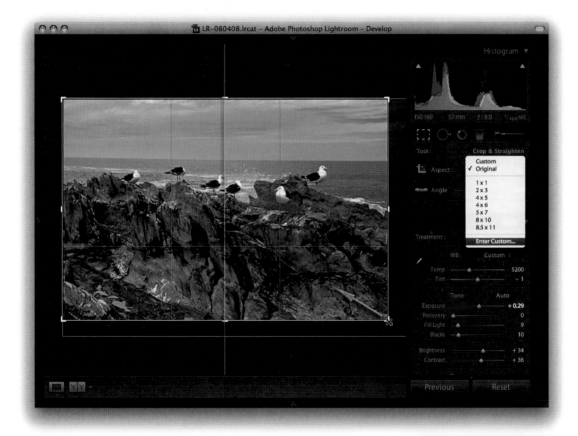

Figure 6.12 *In Lightroom, the cropped area will always be centered in the work area, and the image will move relative to the crop area. In the above example, as I drag the right side handle inward, the image shifts out the way to accommodate the change made to the crop area. You can select crop presets from the list shown here, or click Custom and create your own custom aspect ratio presets.*

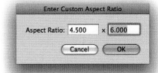

1. If you click the Crop Frame tool to select it, you can simply drag to apply a freeform crop to a photograph. Release the mouse and the Crop Frame tool returns to its usual location in the Tools panel.

2. In this next step, I clicked the Crop Lock button to unlock the fixed crop aspect ratio. This allowed me to then click a corner or side handle of the crop bounding box and drag to reposition the crop relative to the photograph.

3. I then clicked to select the Straighten tool and dragged it across the image to define a straighten angle (you can also adjust the straighten angle by using the Straighten slider in the Tools panel).

4. You can also straighten a photograph by clicking anywhere outside the crop bounding box and dragging. As you do, a fine grid appears and you can use the gridlines to help align the rotation to elements in the picture.

Repositioning a crop

The Crop tool in Lightroom always restricts the cropping to within the boundary of the document. Unlike in Photoshop, you cannot drag the Crop tool outside the image document area to increase the canvas area. You can only crop an image within the confines of the photograph. So however you drag or rotate the crop, you will always be applying the crop to the inside of the picture. When you click inside the crop bounding box, the cursor changes to show the Hand tool, which allows you to scroll the image relative to the crop. As you drag with the mouse, the crop box remains static and the image moves behind the crop (**Figure 6.13**).

Figure 6.13 *When the Crop Lock button is checked again, the crop bounding box is locked to the current aspect ratio. When you drag any of the bounding box handles, the current aspect ratio is the one that is applied. As you click on the photograph inside the crop bounding box area, you can reposition the image relative to the crop.*

Crop guide overlays

In the View ⇨ Crop Guide Overlay menu (**Figure 6.14**) you have six different Crop Guide overlays to choose from. These range from the simple Grid crop guide overlay shown in **Figure 6.15**, to other more exotic overlay designs. For example, I have included on the following pages the Diagonal crop guide overlay (**Figure 6.16**) and the Triangle crop guide overlay (**Figure 6.17**). So why should you want to use different crop guides? Cropping is partly about trimming away parts of the picture that are distracting and aligning straight edges, but it is also about creating a nice-looking, well-balanced visual composition with the picture contents. The Thirds overlay provides a standard reference that you may already be used to seeing in certain camera viewfinder screens, while the Golden Ratio and Golden Spiral crop overlays offer new ways to preview a photo as you compose a crop.

Figure 6.14 *The Crop Guide Overlay menu options.*

Note that regardless of which crop guide you choose, the Grid overlay design is the one that always appears whenever you rotate the crop by dragging with the cursor outside the crop bounding box. The Grid overlay is useful in these instances since it can help you align the horizontal or vertical lines when straightening a photograph.

Figure 6.15 *The Grid crop guide overlay.*

Figure 6.16 *The Diagonal crop guide overlay.*

Figure 6.17 *The Triangle crop guide overlay.*

Crop guide orientation

It is also worth pointing out that the $\boxed{O}$ keyboard shortcut can be used to cycle quickly through the crop guide overlays. You can use $\boxed{\text{⇧Shift}}\boxed{O}$ to cycle through the crop guide orientation for the Triangle (two overlay modes) and Golden Spiral crop overlays (eight overlay modes). In **Figure 6.18** I have shown the Golden Spiral with an inverted overlay.

Figure 6.18 *You can use the* $\boxed{\text{⇧Shift}}\boxed{O}$ *shortcut to switch the orientation of the Triangle and Golden Spiral crop guide overlays.*

Cancelling a crop

You can also use the $\boxed{\text{Esc}}$ key to revert to a previously applied setting made during a crop session. Let's say that the picture shown in Figure 6.18 had been cropped slightly on the left. If you were to alter the crop by adjusting the crop ratio or crop angle and then hit the $\boxed{\text{Esc}}$ key, you would always be taken back to the original crop setting. If, on the other hand, you adjusted the crop, exited the crop mode for this photo, started editing photos in another folder, and returned later to this picture, the new crop setting would become the one that Lightroom reverts back to when you readjust a crop and then hit $\boxed{\text{Esc}}$.

Figure 6.19 *The Tool Overlay menu options.*

Tool Overlay menu

The Tool Overlay menu controls the behavior of not just the Crop Guide overlays, but the Spot Removal, Red Eye, and Adjustment brushes as well. I'll be covering the use of these particular tools toward the end of the chapter. But for now let's look at how the Tool Overlay menu options affect working with the above tools.

The Tool Overlay options

The Tool Overlay options are accessed via the View menu (**Figure 6.19**). The tool overlays refer specifically to the crop guides that appear inside a cropped area when using the Crop tool, the Red Eye Correction and Spot Removal circles, and the Adjustment brush pin markers. If you select the Always Show menu option, the tool overlays will remain visible at all times. If you want to hide the tool overlays, select Never Show from the menu. When this menu option is selected the overlays remain hidden, even when you hover over the image. But as soon as you start working with a tool, the tool overlay behavior automatically switches to the Auto Show mode; and if you look at the Tool Overlay menu, you will see this option is the one highlighted.

The Auto Show mode only makes the tool overlays visible when you hover over the Content area. In other words, the crop guides, Red Eye Correction circles, Spot Removal circles and Adjustment brush pin markers disappear from view when you roll the mouse cursor outside the image area such as to the top panel menu.

Another way to work with the tool overlay show/hide feature is to use the ⌘Shift H (Mac), Ctrl Shift H (PC) keyboard shortcut, which will act as a toggle for switching between the Always Show and Never Show options. An easier-to-remember (and more flexible) shortcut is to simply use the H key. This will toggle between the Auto Show and Never Show modes or toggle between the Always Show and Never Show modes (depending on whether you have Auto Show or Always Show selected first).

Histogram panel

When you are in the Develop module, the Histogram panel is always displayed in the top-right corner (there is also a Histogram panel in the Library module, but the Develop module histogram has more direct relevance when making Develop adjustments). Histogram information is only useful if you know how to interpret it correctly. For example, if you shoot using raw mode, the histogram display on a digital camera is misleading because it is based on what a JPEG capture would record, and the dynamic range of a JPEG capture will always be less than that available from a raw file. If you are shooting raw, the only way to tell if there is any clipping is to inspect the raw image in Lightroom, or via the Photoshop Camera Raw plug-in. In other words, don't let the camera histogram unduly sway your judgment if you have good reason to believe you are shooting with a correct camera exposure. If you are editing an imported JPEG, PSD, or TIFF image, the Lightroom histogram represents the tone range based on the file's native color space. If you are editing a raw capture, there are no gamut constraints until you export the image as a JPEG, TIFF, or PSD file, at which point the gamut space limits will be determined by the choice of RGB output space. sRGB has a small gamut and many of the colors will be clipped when you export (**Figure 6.20**). Adobe RGB is a popular, commonly used color space, and ProPhoto RGB has the widest gamut of all. Incidentally, Lightroom uses a wide gamut RGB space similar to ProPhoto RGB to do all the image calculations, and the histogram and RGB percentage readouts are based on the native Lightroom RGB space. To find out more about the Lightroom RGB space, refer to Appendix B.

NOTE

For those working on a computer with a small pixel size display, you will be pleased to know that you can collapse both the Navigator and the Histogram displays. This can make quite a big difference when working with the right panel displays because it allows you to observe both the Basic and Tone Curve panels simultaneously. Note also that the other panels slide beneath the Histogram and Tools panels as you scroll down the panel list. This too can be helpful for those who have limited screen real estate, because it allows you to see the Histogram and Tone Curve panels at the same time.

TIP

Press ⌘ 0 (Mac) or Ctrl 0 (PC) to toggle between collapsing and expanding the Histogram panel.

Figure 6.20 *One way to preview the image with a clipping warning is to roll over or click the buttons circled here. Clicking these buttons toggles displaying the color overlays shown here. Blue indicates the shadow clipping and red indicates the highlight clipping. The clipping warning triangles indicate initial clipping in the colors that are being clipped most and then change to white as all channels are clipped.*

Figure 6.21   *The Basic panel.*

NOTE

Increasing the contrast in Lightroom does not produce the same kind of unusual color shifts that you sometimes see in Photoshop when you use Curves. This is because the Lightroom/Camera Raw processing manages to prevent such hue shifts from occurring when you pump up the contrast.

TIP

When setting the Exposure slider, you need to be aware of the difference between reflective (specular) and nonreflective highlights, and how the highlight clipping you choose affects the way the image will eventually print (see page 266).

Basic panel controls

If you have ever used the Adobe Camera Raw plug-in with Photoshop and Bridge, you'll already be familiar with some of the Basic panel sliders (see **Figure 6.21**). The Color controls include the Temp and Tint sliders in the White Balance tools (WB) section, which can be used to precisely adjust the white balance of a photograph. With these, you can color-correct most images, or apply different white balances. The Exposure slider sets the highlight point, determining where the image highlights get clipped, and is also a primary tool for adjusting the overall brightness of an image. You may be aware that the Exposure slider is sometimes used as a negative exposure adjustment to rescue highlight detail. The problem here is that you can often end up setting the exposure a lot lower than is ideal, and end up making the image darker than necessary. The Recovery slider is a highlight recovery control. It is not a tool for darkening highlights in the same way or to the same extent that the Fill Light can compensate for dark shadows. Rather, the Recovery slider can be used to let you bring back highlight detail without having to drag the Exposure slider too much to the left. My advice is to start with the Recovery set to zero, adjust the Exposure first but without dragging the Exposure too far to the left, and use Recovery only when necessary to bring back important highlight detail. Note that if you hold down the Alt key as you drag the Recovery slider, you see a Threshold mode view of the highlight clipping. The Blacks slider controls the shadow clipping, and although setting the shadows is not as critical as setting the highlights, you still need to be aware of how much is safe to clip when adjusting the Blacks slider. The Fill Light can be used to dramatically lighten the shadow areas. As with Recovery adjustments, I recommend that you always adjust the Blacks first before you add a Fill Light adjustment. The Brightness and Contrast controls allow you to make basic adjustments to all the tones between the shadow and highlight clipping points. Clarity can be used to enhance the midtone contrast and make pictures appear less flat. At first, the Vibrance slider appears to be very similar to the Saturation slider. And it is, except that the Vibrance slider applies a nonlinear saturation adjustment. This means that lower saturated pixels get more of a saturation boost than the higher saturated pixels. The advantage here is that colors can be given a saturation boost, but with less risk of clipping. Vibrance also contains a skin tone protector that prevents skin tone colors from being boosted. Vibrance is therefore a useful alternative to the comparatively cruder Saturation slider.

Camera exposures

A typical CCD or CMOS sensor in a digital camera is capable of recording over 4,000 levels of information. If you are shooting in raw mode, the ability to record all these levels very much depends on a careful choice of exposure. The ideal camera exposure should be bright enough to record all the tonal information without clipping important highlight detail. This is because half the levels information is recorded in the brightest stop range. As shown in **Figure 6.22**, for each stop decrease in exposure, the number of levels that can be recorded are potentially halved. The upshot of this is that you do not want to deliberately underexpose an image unless to do otherwise would result in the loss of important highlight detail. Deliberate underexposure will have a dramatic impact on the deep shadow detail, since relatively fewer levels are left to record the shadow information. **Figure 6.23** shows how you can easily lose detail in the shadow areas due to an underexposure at the capture stage.

If you are shooting raw, it is unwise to place too much emphasis on the camera histogram. It is best to either trust the exposure system in the camera to get it right or rely on the histogram in Lightroom.

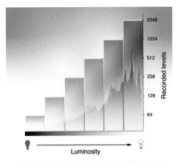

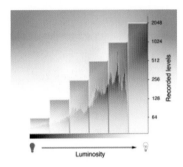

Figure 6.22   *If you don't optimize the camera exposure, you may be missing the opportunity to record a greater number of levels via the sensor. The top diagram shows how a correctly optimized exposure makes maximum use of the sensor's ability to record the fullest amount of levels information possible. In the lower diagram you can see how recording the exposure just one stop darker than the ideal exposure results in only half as many levels being recorded by the sensor.*

Figure 6.23   *This image is divided diagonally. The top section shows the enhanced shadow detail using an optimum camera exposure setting, and the bottom section shows the same scene captured at minus two stops camera exposure and then processed to match the luminance of the normal exposure. Notice that there is more noise and less tonal information in the underexposed version.*

Basic image adjustment procedure

The main purpose of the Basic Develop controls is to make a first-pass adjustment to set the overall color balance and optimize the tone information in the source image. It does not necessarily matter which order you apply the Basic adjustments in, but you will find it best to work through them from the top down. Usually the main goal is to set the white balance first. If you can get this right, you'll usually find that all the other colors easily fit into place. Next, adjust the Exposure slider as you would when judging film exposures: Exposure can be used to compensate where a photograph initially appears too light or too dark, and it is always best to set the Exposure first before you adjust the Brightness (we'll come on to why later). You then set the Blacks slider to clip the shadows so that the darkest black just begins to get clipped. Once these first three steps have been applied to the source image, you should end up with a photograph that has a full contrast range from solid black to the lightest printable highlights. However, sometimes the Exposure and Blacks adjustments are not enough on their own and it is necessary to use the Recovery and Fill Light sliders to bring out more detail in the highlight and shadow regions of a picture. When you have finished adjusting all these sliders, you can then fine-tune with Brightness and Contrast. And lastly, the Presence group of sliders can be used to add contrast in the midtones (which will bring out more image detail in flat tone areas) and pump up the color saturation using Vibrance. **Figure 6.24** shows the Develop panel in expanded form.

Modify: Highlight Recovery

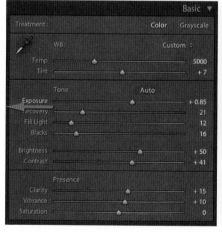

Figure 6.24   *The Lightroom panels can be expanded by dragging on the side edge. An expanded Develop panel offers greater precision when making adjustments. As you switch from one setting to another (you can also use the ⟨ , ⟩ keyboard shortcuts) the setting name and adjustment shows up in the Content area.*

White Balance tool

The White Balance tool is located near the top of the Basic panel (**Figure 6.25**). You can activate the tool by clicking it (or press W), which unlocks the tool from its location and allows you to click anywhere in the image to set the white balance. The floating pixel magnifier provides an extreme close-up of the pixels you are measuring, which can really help you select the correct pixel reading. As you hover over an image, you see the RGB readout values for the point in the picture beneath the cursor (**Figure 6.26**). These RGB readings are shown as percentage values and can help you locate and check the color readings (if the RGB values are all close enough to the same value, the color can be regarded as neutral). If the Auto Dismiss option is disabled, you can hold down the W key and continue clicking with the tool until you get the right balance setting, while the Esc key can be used to cancel and return the tool to its normal docked position.

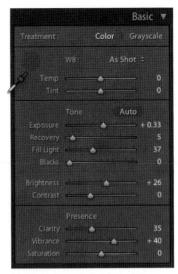

Figure 6.25   *To activate the White Balance tool, click the tool to undock it from the panel.*

Figure 6.26   *Instead of using the traditional 0–255 scale, the RGB readouts are given as percentages. You can determine the neutrality of a color by how close the readout numbers are to each other.*

1. To make a white balance adjustment, select an area of the picture that should be neutral in color (but not a bright white area of the photo). The light gray stones in this picture are a perfect spot to sample from. If the Auto Dismiss box (circled) in the toolbar is checked, the White Balance tool automatically returns to its docked position in the Basic panel. If the Auto Dismiss box is unchecked, you can click and keep clicking with the White Balance tool until you are completely satisfied with the white balance adjustment that you have made.

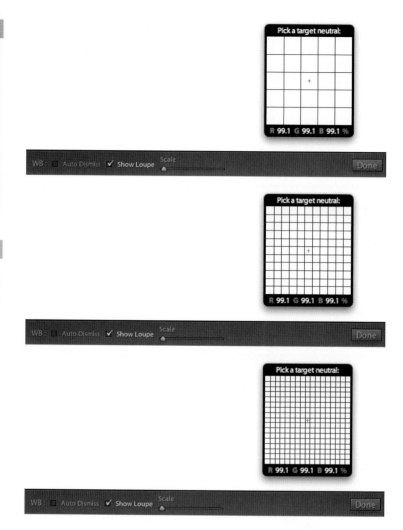

2. The Show Loupe check box allows you to toggle displaying the loupe that appears just below the White Balance tool cursor. You can adjust the loupe scale setting by dragging the slider next to the Show Loupe item in the toolbar. This slider adjusts the sample grid pixel size, and dragging the slider to the right will increase the number of pixels used when sampling a white balance point measurement. Increasing the pixel sample size can be beneficial if you want to aggregate the pixel readings more, such as when you're sampling a really noisy image and you don't want a white balance measurement to be unduly affected by the pixels that contain color noise.

White Balance corrections

In most shoot situations, once you have found the right white balance, all the other colors will tend to fit into place. The As Shot camera Auto White Balance setting may do a good job, but it really depends on the camera you are using (**Figure 6.27**). Even the best camera won't know how to handle every lighting situation it meets. In **Figure 6.28**, we see a scene where there were mixed lighting conditions. This photograph could be processed for either the daylight lighting or the tungsten lighting indoors, and each could be said to be correct. In situations like this you can't always rely on the camera's Auto White Balance setting; you have to decide for yourself which setting looks the best. This is where the White Balance tool can come in handy. The trick is to analyze the picture and look for colors in the scene that should be a neutral, nonspecular, textural highlight. You should try to select a neutral light gray, because if you select a white that is too bright, there may be some clipping in one or more of the color channels, and this can result in a false white balance measurement and adjustment.

Figure 6.27 *Among other things, the X-Rite Gretag Macbeth ColorChecker chart is useful for taking white balance readings under the same lighting conditions as those you are about to shoot with. To take a white balance reading in Lightroom, click on the light gray patch next to the white patch.*

NOTE

It is tempting to assume that the grayscale patches in the X-Rite Gretag Macbeth ColorChecker chart shown in Figure 6.27 correspond to the full tonal range that you are trying to optimize using the Basic and Tone Curve panel controls. This is a dangerous assumption to make because in a properly optimized image, the white and black patches rarely ever equate to the respective highlight and shadow points in the image. For example, the black patch in the ColorChecker is really a dark gray, and if you were to clip the shadows using this patch as your guide you could end up clipping a lot of important shadow information.

Figure 6.28 *The white balance can be measured manually by selecting the White Balance tool (✐) and clicking a color in the image that should be near white in color. This image shows two possible white balances: one measured for the indoor lighting (left) and one measured for the outside daylight (right).*

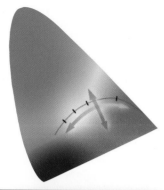

Figure 6.29 *The White Balance slider controls in the Basic panel allow you to manually adjust the white point in an image. The Temperature slider adjusts the white point from warm artificial lighting conditions to cool daylight and beyond. The Lightroom slider represents this as a progression going from blue to yellow. The Tint slider allows you to fine-tune the white point for any green/magenta bias in the white point.*

The White Balance slider controls in the Basic panel have the greatest impact on the color appearance of an image (**Figure 6.29**). The numbers used in the Temp slider refer to the temperature scale measured in degrees Kelvin, which in photography is commonly used when describing the color temperature of a light source.

Artificial lighting, such as a tungsten lamp light source, has a color temperature of around 2800–3200 K, whereas average daylight is notionally rated as being 5000 K and overcast daylight is somewhere around 10000 K. Photographers often describe higher color temperature lighting conditions as being cooler and the lower color temperature lighting conditions as being warmer, because most people equate blue colors with coldness and reddish colors with warmth (although technically speaking, a bluer color temperature is actually hotter). The Temperature slider scale allows you to set what "should be" the white point of the image based on the Kelvin scale. The key point to emphasize here is that the White Balance controls are used to "assign" the white point as opposed to "creating" a white balance. Some people get confused on this point because they assume that if 3200 K equates to tungsten-balanced film and 5500 K equates to daylight-balanced film, they wrongly expect that dragging the Temperature slider to the right makes the image cooler and dragging to the left makes it warmer. The opposite is true, because you are using the Temperature slider to assign a color temperature to the image. Dragging the slider to the right will make the image warmer and dragging to the left will make it cooler. Try thinking of it this way: If you have a photograph shot under average daylight conditions and assign the image a lower color temperature more suited for tungsten lighting conditions, such as 3200 K, then naturally enough, the colors in the image will appear blue. This is the same as using a tungsten-balanced film emulsion to record a daylight scene.

Tint adjustments

The Tint slider adjustments can usually be quite minor, except for those situations where the light source emits uneven spectral wavelengths of light, such as when shooting under fluorescent lighting. It is hard to set an accurate white point for these types of lighting conditions, but fluorescent lighting conditions will usually require a heavy magenta tint bias to the white point to remove a green cast.

Creative white balance adjustments

Who is to say if a correct white balance is any better than an incorrect one? Before digital capture came along, photographers could only choose between shooting with daylight-balanced or tungsten-balanced film emulsions. A lot of photographers would simply accept whatever colors the film produced, although some professionals had the know-how to measure the color temperature and would place filters over the camera lens to correct for color shifts in the lighting. With a digital camera it is easy to set the white balance precisely. There may be times, such as when shooting catalog work, when it is critical to get the color exactly right from camera to screen. But you don't always have to obsess over the color temperature at the capture stage on every type of shoot. You now have the freedom to interpret a master raw file any way you like, and you can change the mood in a photograph completely by setting the white balance to an incorrect setting (**Figure 6.30**).

TIP

Warning! If you shoot using a studio flash system (not the built-in flash) and have the camera set to automatically white balance, there is a high probability that the white balance reading will be influenced by the tungsten modeling lights instead of the strobe flash.

Figure 6.30 *Here is an image processed using two different white balance settings. It is often largely a matter of personal judgment when deciding which version you prefer, since neither of these of these examples uses what could be described as a "correct" white balance.*

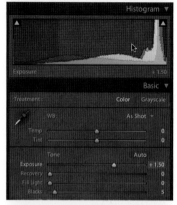

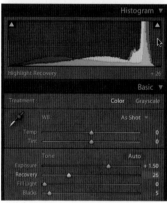

Figure 6.31 *In the top histogram, the highlights need to be expanded to fill the width of the histogram. In the middle example, I adjusted the Exposure slider to make the image brighter, while keeping an eye on the clipping indicator so as not to go beyond the clipping limits for the highlights. In the bottom example, I compensated with the Recovery slider to reduce the extreme highlight clipping, preserving more highlight detail but without compromising on the exposure brightness.*

Basic adjustments and the Histogram panel

You normally use the Exposure slider to set the highlight clipping and the Blacks slider to adjust for the shadow clipping. These two Basic tone adjustments can make the biggest difference to the appearance of an image. Get the highlights and shadows right and you will often find that all the in-between tones will look right too. But while the Exposure slider is seen as the key tool for controlling the highlight clipping, it acts as a brightness control as well. This is where the Histogram panel comes in useful, because as you make an exposure adjustment you can observe the image levels expand to the right, just to the point where the highlights should begin to clip. **Figure 6.31** shows how the levels were expanded as the Exposure was increased. But notice also how the highlight clipping indicator lit up as I came within range of where the highlights were about to clip (the color indicates which colors are clipped). You can use the highlight indicator as a guide to the range of exposure settings that are suitable to use on a particular image. You can then use the Recovery slider to compensate for any unwanted highlight clipping. As you drag the Recovery slider to the right the highlight end of the histogram compresses to recover the clipped highlight detail, and the highlight clipping indicator will turn off at the optimum point where there is no more clipping. As you experiment with these two slider controls, you soon discover how it is possible to use Exposure to set what looks like the best exposure setting for the image brightness (but within the range of clipping tolerance), and then compensate separately for the precise clipping by using the Recovery slider.

The Blacks and Fill Light sliders appear to do the same thing in reverse, but their behavior is in fact different. For raw camera files, the default Blacks setting is "5." This should be about right for most images. You can set this lower, but even with an underexposed image it is unlikely you will want to set the Blacks lower than say 2 or 3. The shadows clipping indicator also lights up to indicate the range of appropriate Blacks settings to use as you try to determine where best to clip the shadows. The Fill Light slider is not a shadow recovery control in the same way as the Recovery slider is used to rescue the highlights, but is ideal for lightening the dark tone areas, and it can certainly make quite a dramatic difference on a photograph that has heavy shadows. As you adjust the Fill Light, the clipping indicator again hints at the ideal range of settings to use. You can extend a Fill Light adjustment beyond this range, but overdoing the Fill Light won't always produce the most natural-looking results.

But what's really cool is that the histogram is more than just an information display. You can also use it to actively adjust the four main Basic panel tone slider controls: Exposure, Highlight Recovery, Fill Light, and Blacks (**Figure 6.32**). As you roll the mouse over the histogram, you will see each of these four sections highlighted in the histogram. And if you click and drag, you can actively mold the shape of the histogram and levels output by dragging with the mouse inside the Histogram panel.

The Brightness and Contrast controls are partly there for legacy reasons, because customers have grown accustomed to working with them in the Adobe Camera Raw plug-in and are familiar with and like the control that they give. In practice I find that Brightness is the more useful of the two, because an Exposure adjustment won't always do enough to lighten or darken every image I encounter. If you are familiar with the legacy Camera Raw method for processing raw files and want to continue using these same adjustment methods, then use the Contrast slider. Basic panel Contrast adjustments can work great for many simple contrast tweaks, but the slider controls in the Tone Curve panel offer a more precise way of adjusting the contrast.

The overall objective with Basic panel editing is to adjust the raw (or pixel image) data to produce an image that is more or less correct for tone and color. The separation between the Basic and Tone Curve panels is there because the Tone Curve controls are designed to pick up from where the Basic panel adjustments left off. It is important to understand this distinction, because the image data is processed through the Basic panel first before being fed through the Tone Curve panel, where you can make fine-edit adjustments to the tone contrast in the image. For example, if you look carefully in the Tone Curve panel you will notice how the histogram from the Histogram panel is mirrored in the background of the Tone Curve edit box. We will be discussing the Tone Curve panel shortly, and we'll also take a look at a step-by-step example of how to work with the Basic and Tone Curve panels.

Auto Tone setting

The new, improved Auto Tone (⌘ U [Mac], Ctrl U [PC]) works well on a great many images as a quick-fix tone adjustment (see **Figure 6.33**). It automatically sets the Recovery, Blacks, Brightness, and Contrast (always resetting Exposure and Fill Light to zero). From there you can adjust the Exposure and Fill Light manually to fine-tune an adjustment. Auto Tone can also be included in Develop presets, allowing you to import images with Auto Tone applied right from the start.

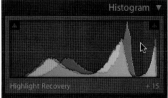
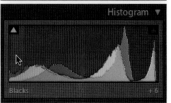

Figure 6.32 *The Basic panel adjustments shown here were all achieved by clicking on different sections of the histogram and dragging right or left to increase or decrease the setting represented by that particular section of the histogram. Double-click on these areas of the histogram to reset these values.*

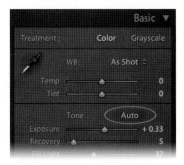

Figure 6.33 *The Auto Tone button.*

Figure 6.34 *In the top image the highlights are all reflective. They contain no information, and you would normally want to clip these highlights to achieve the optimum image contrast. In the lower image you also have reflective highlights in the hubcap, but it is essential to ensure that the nonreflective highlights of the white tire wall do not get clipped.*

The main objective when optimizing an image is to ensure that the fullest tonal range can be reproduced in print. With this in mind, it is vitally important that you set the highlights correctly. If the highlights are clipped too much, you risk losing important highlight detail in the finished print. And if you don't clip them enough, you end up with a flat-looking print that lacks sparkle.

The important thing to appreciate here is the difference between reflective and nonreflective highlights. The two examples shown in **Figure 6.34** help explain what these are. A reflective highlight (also referred to as a specular highlight) is a shiny highlight, such as the light reflecting off a glass or metal surface that contains no highlight detail. It is therefore advisable to clip the highlights so that these highlights are the brightest part of the picture and print using the maximum white value.

Nonreflective highlights (also known as nonspecular highlights) need to be treated more carefully, because they mostly contain important detail that needs to be preserved. Each print process varies, but in general, whether you are printing to a CMYK press or printing via a desktop inkjet printer, if the nonreflective highlights are set too close to the point where the highlights clip, there is a real risk that the detail in these highlights may print to the same paper white as the clipped highlights.

It is not too difficult to learn how to correctly set the Exposure slider to clip the highlights, especially when you are aware of the difference between a reflective and nonreflective highlight, and the clipping issues involved. Most images will contain at least a few reflective highlights, and in practice I use the Threshold mode (see page 269) to analyze where the highlight clipping takes place and toggle between the Threshold mode and Normal image view to determine if these highlights contain important detail. Alternatively, you can use the clipping gamut warning in the Histogram panel. I usually try to set the Exposure to clip the reflective highlights, but I carefully check the nonreflective highlights as well and ensure that I nudge back a little on the Exposure slider so that they have a lightness value that is a little less than the brightest white.

Setting the Blacks

Setting the Blacks is not nearly as critical as when you are adjusting for the highlights. It really all boils down to a simple question of how much you want to clip the shadows. Do you want to clip them a little or do you want to clip them a lot?

I know some Photoshop books and tutorials instruct you to set the shadow point to a specific black value that is lighter than a zero black, but this advice is only useful if you are working toward a specific, known print output. And even then this should not really be necessary, since both Lightroom and Photoshop are able to automatically compensate the shadow point every time you send a file to a desktop printer, or each time you convert an image to CMYK. Just remember this: Lightroom's internal color management system always ensures that the blackest blacks you set in the Basic panel will faithfully print as black and preserve all the shadow detail. When you convert an image to CMYK in Photoshop, the color management system in Photoshop will similarly make sure that the blackest blacks are translated to a black value that will print successfully on the press.

On page 270 I show an example of how to use the Threshold mode to analyze the shadows and determine where to set the clipping point with the Blacks slider. In this example, the objective is to clip the blacks just a little so as to maximize the tonal range between the shadows and the highlights. Some photographs may contain important information in the shadows; the photograph of the car tire and black bodywork in Figure 6.34 is a good case in point, because there is a lot of information in the shadow region that needs to be preserved. This is where the Brightness and Contrast sliders come in handy, and more important, the Tone Curve controls, which I will discuss shortly. The Tone Curve controls provide you with really precise control over tonal detail in the shadows and highlight areas.

It is rarely a good idea to clip the highlights unnecessarily, but clipping the shadows can greatly enhance the contrast. **Figure 6.35** shows a classic example of an image where the shadows have been deliberately clipped. A great many photographers have built their style of photography around the use of deep blacks in their pictures. For example, Photographer Greg Gorman (whose work appears on pages 378–381), regularly processes his black and white portraits so that photographs shot with a black background print with a solid black.

Figure 6.35   *In this example, I dragged the Blacks slider to 17 because I deliberately wanted to clip the shadows to a solid black.*

1. Here is a before image in which the Lightroom Basic adjustments have been set to the Lightroom defaults and the White Balance setting is As Shot White Balance (as recorded by the camera). I began by selecting the White Balance tool and clicked on the white paint work of one of the boats to select what should have been a nonreflective neutral color. Note that if you uncheck the Auto Dismiss option in the toolbar, you can hold down the W key and keep clicking with the White Balance tool to produce a new White Balance setting (release the mouse to cancel).

2. Here is the same photograph after I had applied a white balance correction. The RGB percentage readouts where I had clicked with the White Balance tool now show a more neutral balance.

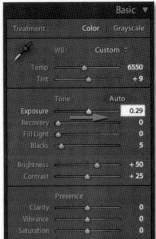

3. I then used the Exposure slider to expand the tonal range. This step sets the highlight clipping point and lightens the image.

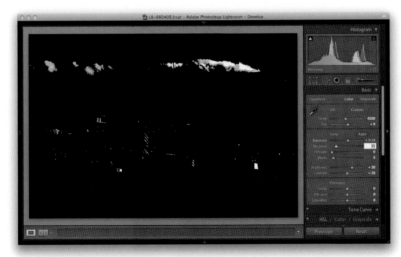
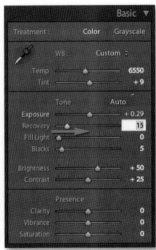

4. The Recovery slider helps prevent any highlight clipping. If you hold down the Alt key as you drag the Recovery slider, the image is displayed in Threshold mode. If there is highlight clipping, you see a posterized image that shows where the highlights start to get clipped. If the highlights you see being clipped are specular (reflective) highlights, it is okay to clip them. But if the highlights contain nonreflective highlight detail, it's best to nudge the Recovery slider more to the right to reduce such clipping.

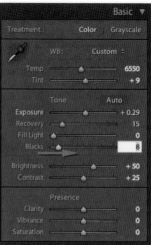

5. Similarly, when you use the Blacks slider to set the shadow point in an image, you can hold down the [Alt] key again to see the image displayed in the Threshold mode. If there is no clipping, the image displays as white. As you gradually move the Blacks slider to the right, a posterized image starts to appear. It is usually best to set the Blacks slider so that there is always some clipping in the shadows.

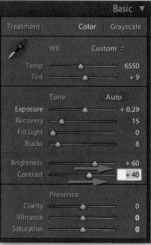

6. The Basic Develop controls generally allow you to make big enough improvements to the appearance of an image so that you won't always need to do anything else to a photograph. In this example, I added a little more overall Brightness and Contrast.

Vibrance and Saturation

The Vibrance and Saturation sliders can both be used to boost the saturation in an image. The difference between the two is that the Saturation slider applies a linear adjustment to the color saturation, whereas a Vibrance adjustment uses a nonlinear approach. In plain English, this means that when you apply a Vibrance adjustment, the less saturated colors get more of a saturation boost than those colors that are already saturated (**Figure 6.36**). This can be of real practical benefit when you're applying a saturation adjustment to a picture and you want to make the softer colors look brighter but don't want to brighten them at the expense of losing important detail in the already bright colors (in **Figure 6.37**, I demonstrate how a saturation boost can easily damage the color information in an image). The other benefit of working with Vibrance is that it has a built-in skin color protector that should filter out colors that fall within the skin color range. This can be useful if you are editing a portrait and you want to boost the color of someone's clothing, but at the same time, you don't want to oversaturate the subject's skin tones. Vibrance is the only saturation control you ever really need. However, the Saturation control still remains useful. A Saturation adjustment can be used to make big shifts to the saturation, such as when you want to dramatically subdue the colors in a photograph (**Figure 6.38**).

Figure 6.36 *In this example, the left half of the photograph shows a normally corrected version and the right half shows a version in which I applied a +60% Vibrance adjustment, which boosted the subtle colors in this scene.*

Figure 6.37 *In the top screen shot I increased the Saturation to +60%. The Saturation boosts all colors equally, and as you can see here, there is a lot of clipping in the saturated red colors. In the lower screen shot I increased the Vibrance to 60%. This resulted in the flowers appearing more saturated, but without oversaturating to the point where the tonal detail was lost.*

Figure 6.38 *In the top screen shot I applied a negative Vibrance of –100%. As you can see, the effect is quite subtle. This is an effective tool for making gentle reductions in the color saturation. In the bottom screen shot, I reduced the Saturation to –80%, which produced a pastel color version of the image. If you move the Saturation slider all the way to –100%, you will end up with a monochrome image.*

NOTE

Clarity is a hybrid based on two separate contrast enhancing techniques. One is a local contrast enhancement technique, devised by Thomas Knoll, using a low amount and high radius setting in the Photoshop Unsharp Mask filter. The other is a midtone contrast enhancement Photoshop technique that was originally devised by Mac Holbert of Nash Editions. He found that it helped him to bring out crisper detail in his landscape prints. I think most photographs can gain from adding a little bit of Clarity.

Clarity slider

The Presence section of the Basic panel includes the Clarity slider, which is essentially a midtone contrast adjustment slider. Clarity cleverly applies an adaptive contrast adjustment that is similar to the low Amount/high Radius unsharp mask technique referred to in the accompanying note. This is achieved by adding wide halos to the edges in the photograph, and these build up the contrast in the midtone areas based on the edge detail in the photograph. The net effect is that a positive Clarity adjustment boosts the apparent contrast in the midtones, but without affecting the overall global contrast. Normally, you would want to start around 10 and try not to overdo the effect. But as you increase the amount, the halos get wider, strengthening the midtone contrast effect and making the midtone areas look sharper. You can see the halos forming as you drag the slider left and right.

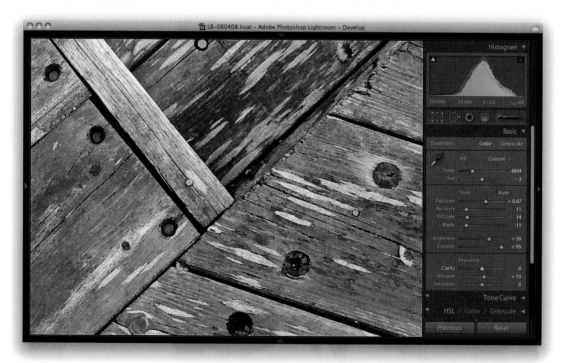

1. Here is a screen shot showing a close-up 1:1 view of a photo. A few adjustments have been made to the basic tone controls and sharpening has already been added via the Detail panel. You don't have to necessarily be viewing the image at 1:1 in order to evaluate the results, but this is usually the best way to view your work.

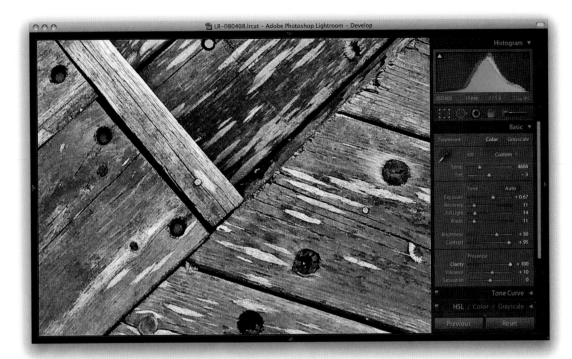

2. In this next screen shot you can see how the wood floor looked after adjusting the Clarity slider. In this example I have taken the slider to the maximum setting in order to show the most dramatic difference between this and the previous screen shot.

Levels decompression

All image adjustments are destructive in one way or another. You end up either expanding the tones in an image, which stretches the levels further apart, or compressing the tones by squeezing the levels closer together. For example, some Tone Curve adjustments flatten portions of the curve, and as you compress the detail in these areas, you lose some of the tonal separation that was there originally.

When you edit a raw image, there should be plenty of levels information waiting to be used. So, despite the apparent compression you may get when you use the Tone Curve, this is where Clarity can be beneficial because a positive Clarity adjustment can be used to reach into these areas of flat tone and enhance the detail that's still lurking in the original capture image.

Negative Clarity adjustments

A less obvious innovation in Lightroom 2 is the ability to apply a negative Clarity adjustment (see **Figures 6.39** and **6.40** for an example). But now that it is implemented, I can foresee quite a few creative possibilities. Negative Clarity does the opposite of a normal Clarity adjustment because it softens the midtones, and does so in a way that produces an effect not too dissimilar to a traditional darkroom diffusion printing technique. The net result is that you can create some quite beautiful diffuse soft focus image effects that are particularly suited to black and white photography. It's a bit like being able to add a cloudy sky lighting effect.

Figure 6.39   *This shows how the photograph I was about to work with looked before applying a negative Clarity adjustment. It's a nice picture with lots of sharp detail, but also a good candidate for this "pseudo" diffusion printing technique.*

Figure 6.40 *This screen shot shows the photograph in Figure 6.39 where I applied a −100% Clarity adjustment in the Presence section. As you can see, the negative Clarity creates a kind of diffuse printing effect.*

Correcting an overexposed image

Lightroom has the ability to reveal highlight detail that might otherwise have remained hidden. You can often recover seemingly lost highlight information by combining a negative Exposure adjustment with the use of the Recovery slider. It may be possible to use this technique on a JPEG image to darken the highlights a little, but this method really only works best with raw images. This is because Lightroom is able to use all of the luminosity information contained in a raw file that is simply waiting to be discovered. In the accompanying example, I was able to recover one and a half stops of overexposure, but in some cases it is possible to recover as much as two stops. As mentioned on page 257, it is often better to optimize the camera exposure to capture as much of the shadow detail as possible, but without overexposing to the point where you are unable to process important highlight information. I will often ignore the camera or light meter readings and deliberately overexpose at the time of capture to record the maximum amount of levels information and use the combination of a negative Exposure and a positive Recovery shift when processing the image.

1. The photograph on the facing page was first processed using the default Basic panel settings in the Develop module. The histogram shows clipping in the highlights, and you can see how there is very little detail in the sky or building. A histogram like this can appear disconcerting until you realize that there is a lot more information contained in the image than there appears at first sight. Although Lightroom can work its magic on all images, it has a limited effect on pixel-based images such as JPEGs or TIFFs. For best results, you should use this technique when processing raw master files.

2. Highlight recovery can be achieved by applying a combination of a negative Exposure value combined with a positive Recovery adjustment. If you drag the Exposure slider to the left, you can effectively recover at least a stop worth of information, and maybe even as much as two stops. The downside is that you usually end up making the overall image darker. But when you combine this with a positive move with the Recovery slider, you see highlight information that would otherwise be clipped. I also adjusted the Fill Light, Blacks, Brightness, Contrast, and Vibrance in this shot, but the main highlight adjustment was all achieved using Exposure plus Recovery.

Correcting an underexposed image

Underexposed images represent a bigger problem because there are fewer levels available to manipulate, particularly in the shadows. The Basic panel controls in Lightroom can be used to brighten an image and lift out the shadow detail. But it is important that you work through the Basic image adjustments in the right order, as described in the following images. When adjusting the tones in an underexposed photograph, you will notice that the Blacks adjustment can be very sensitive and a small shift of the Blacks slider can make a big difference to the shadows brightness. In the example shown here I could have opened the shadows more by setting the Blacks slider to 1 or 2. But by choosing 4, I was able to preserve more of the overall contrast.

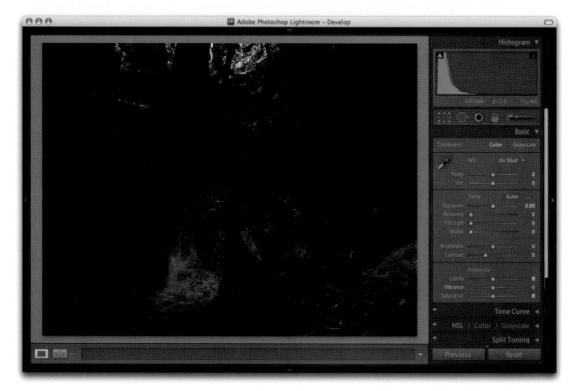

1. As with the highlight recovery method earlier, corrections for underexposure should mainly be done by adjusting the Exposure slider first to set the highlight clipping. This should be followed by an adjustment to the Blacks, and then an adjustment to the Brightness and Contrast.

2. In this example I dragged the Exposure slider to the right, which enabled me to preserve all the information in the highlights. I then adjusted the Blacks so that the shadows were just clipped and used the Fill Light adjustment to radically lighten the dark shadow areas. Finally, I used the Brightness and Contrast sliders to lighten the midtones further and add more contrast depth. What you don't want to do here is to adjust the Brightness slider before you adjust the Exposure slider. Although similar results can be achieved in this way, you will end up stretching the shadow tones far more than is good for the image. For best results, always approach the Basic controls in the order that I just described.

Match Total Exposures

You can use this command to match the exposure across a series of images that have been selected via the Filmstrip. Match Total Exposures calculates a match value by analyzing and combining the shutter speed, lens aperture, the ISO speed the photos were captured at, plus any camera-set exposure compensation. It then factors in all these camera-set values, combines them with the desired exposure value (as set in the most selected image), and calculates new Lightroom exposure values for all the other selected images. I find that this technique can often be used to help average out the exposure brightness in a series of photos where the light values were going up and down during a shoot, which is probably why the chief Lightroom architect Mark Hamburg also likes to describe this as a a "de-bracketing" command.

So in effect, if you highlight an individual image in the series and select Match Total Exposures, the other images in that selection automatically balance to match the exposure of the target image.

1. In this example, I made a selection of photographs in the Library module Grid view, where you can see that some of the pictures in the sequence are more underexposed than the others.

2. I selected the photo with the correct-looking exposure and made this the most selected image. I then went to the Develop module and chose Match Total Exposures from the Settings menu.

3. In this Library Grid view you can see how the exposure appearance of the other photos is now more evenly balanced compared to the Library Grid view in Step 1.

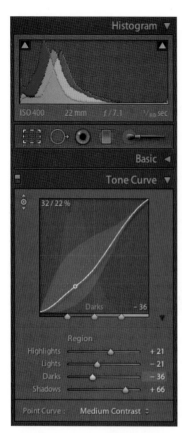

Figure 6.41 *The Tone Curve panel controls are shown here with an adjustment in progress being made to the Darks. Notice how the histogram in the Histogram panel is mirrored in the curve graph and both are updated as you edit the Tone Curve controls.*

NOTE

In Target Adjustment mode you can use the up and down arrow keys to increase or decrease the settings. Holding down the [Alt] key as you adjust the values applies smaller incremental adjustments. Holding down the [⇧ Shift] key as you adjust the values applies larger incremental adjustments.

Tone Curve controls

The Tone Curve controls offer a new approach to tone curve mapping (known as "parametric curves" in Lightroom and Camera Raw 4.0 or later), where the tone curve is modified through slider control adjustments. The reason the Tone Curve controls are presented in this way is to encourage people to make tone curve adjustments based on descriptive criteria. If you are used to working with point curves in Photoshop, the Lightroom method may appear restrictive at first, but the Tone Curve slider controls in Lightroom can often inspire you to create tone curve shapes that are quite unlike the curve shapes you might have applied when adjusting them manually. The slider controls also recognize that a lot of photographers just didn't get how to work the curves adjustment in Photoshop. The Tone Curve sliders will hopefully make curves adjustments accessible to everyone now, but the good news is that you can still manipulate the curve graph directly by clicking on a point on the curve and dragging up or down to modify that particular section of the curve. Best of all, you can also edit the curve by targeting an area of interest in the actual picture. If you click the Target Adjustment tool button, you can then click over any part of the image and drag the mouse up or down to make the tones there lighter or darker. When you start using this method of tone editing to refine the tones in an image, you won't even need to look at the Tone Curve panel. You can also use the keyboard arrow keys: The up and down arrows adjust the tone values (note, the left and right arrow keys are reserved for navigating images in the Filmstrip). You can turn off the Target Adjustment tool by clicking the button again or by pressing ⌘ Alt Shift N (Mac) or Ctrl Alt Shift N (PC).

The four main slider controls for controlling the tone curve are Highlights, Lights, Darks, and Shadows. The slider controls also provide a shaded preview of the range of shapes an individual Tone Curve slider adjustment will make. In **Figure 6.41**, I was in the process of adjusting the Darks slider. The gray shaded area represents the limits of all possible tone curve shapes I can create with this particular slider in conjunction with the other current slider settings. For those who understand curves, this provides a useful visual reference of how the curve looks. Plus, you can edit it by clicking anywhere on the curve and moving the mouse up or down to make that section of the tone curve lighter or darker.

As mentioned earlier, the Basic panel is used to apply the main tone adjustments. It important to understand that these are all applied upstream of the tone curve, so Tone Curve is an image adjustment control that you always apply after making the initial Basic panel adjustments. The layout of the tools in both the Basic and Tone Curve panels are also influenced to some degree by the legacy constraints of the Adobe Camera Raw plug-in. For example, recall that the Contrast control in the Basic panel is mainly there to provide a slider equivalent to the one found in the Camera Raw plug-in. So those people who prefer using the simpler Camera Raw method of adjusting contrast can continue to do so. But more important, it has been necessary to ensure that settings applied to an image via Camera Raw in Photoshop will also be recognized (and made accessible) when the same image is opened via the Develop module in Lightroom. I mention all this as an explanation for the presence of the Point Curve menu at the bottom of the Tone Curve panel (**Figure 6.42**). In the early days of Camera Raw, some purists argued that the tone curve should always default to Linear, and if you wanted to add contrast, it was up to the user to edit the curve. Meanwhile, almost every other raw converter program was applying a moderate amount of contrast to the curve by default. The reason for the default application was that photographers liked their pictures to have a more contrasty and film-like look as the standard setting. Consequently, the Adobe Camera Raw plug-in has evolved to offer three choices of curve contrast; Medium Contrast is the default setting. So the Point Curve menu in the Tone Curve panel is mainly there to match up raw files that have been imported with legacy Camera Raw settings. The Medium Contrast curve applies more of a kick to the shadows to make them slightly darker and lightens the highlights slightly (which you can see by looking at the shape of the curve). The Point Curve is therefore nothing more than a curve shape setting that can be used as a starting point for making further edits to the tone curve, and is mainly there for compatibility reasons.

The Tone Range Split Points at the bottom of the tone curve allow you to restrict or broaden the range of tones that are affected by the four Tone Curve sliders (**Figure 6.43**). Adjusting each of the three Tone Range Split Points enables you to further fine-tune the shape of the curve. For example, moving the Dark Tone Range Split Point to the right offsets the midpoint between the Shadows and Darks adjustments. These adjustment sliders are particularly useful for those instances where you are unable to achieve the exact tone localized contrast adjustment you are after when using the Tone Curve sliders on their own.

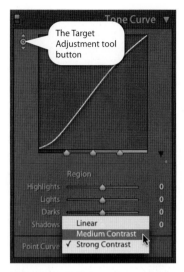

Figure 6.42 *The Point Curve menu offers a choice of three curve settings.*

TIP

If you like using the on-image tone curve editing and screen real estate is at a premium, you can collapse the Tone Curve sliders by clicking the arrow icon next to the Tone Curve graph.

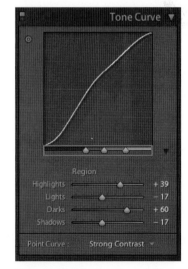

Figure 6.43 *The Tone Range Split Point controls.*

The Tone Curve zones

The Tone Curve zones are evenly split between the four quadrants of the tone curve. In the following step-by-step example, I wanted to show a series of tone curve adjustments in which each of these zones is adjusted. To emphasize how the Tone Curve Zone sliders operate, I have highlighted the active quadrants in green to accentuate the zone regions, and to show which areas of the curve are being adjusted.

1. I began by adjusting the Highlights slider to make the brightest portion of the image darker and set Highlights to –80. This could have been done in a number of ways: I could drag the Highlights slider in the Tone Curve panel to the left, or make the Highlights field active and use the down arrow key to reduce the value. I could click anywhere in the green shaded section of the Tone Curve and drag the curve downward, or click on this portion of the curve and use the down arrow key on the keyboard to darken the highlights. But in this instance I clicked the Target Adjustment tool button (circled) to make it active, moved the cursor over the image, and hovered over a highlight area on the plate. I then clicked and dragged downward to darken the tones in this selected portion of the curve. Note that you need to drag the mouse up to lighten and down to darken.

2. Next I wanted to concentrate on darkening the tones within the Lights zone of the curve. I placed the cursor over the table area and again dragged downward with the mouse.

3. I then darkened the Darks zone by moving the mouse over one of the chili peppers and dragged the mouse downward. If you are using the arrow keys, you can use the [Alt] key to apply small incremental shifts and the [Shift] key to apply bigger shifts.

4. Lastly, I adjusted the Shadows, which again could be done by dragging the Shadows slider and clicking on the curve to directly edit the shape of the tone curve. But in this case, I placed the mouse over a shadow area in the image and dragged the mouse upward to lighten.

Combining Basic and Tone Curve adjustments

So far, I have shown you how Tone Curve adjustments are made in isolation. But in a typical develop session, you will normally work using a combination of both the Basic and Tone Curve adjustment panels. Over the next few pages, I provide a step-by-step example in which the Basic panel adjustments are applied first in order to correct the white balance, recover lost highlight detail, and improve the overall contrast in the photograph. This is followed by some Tone Curve adjustments to fine-tune the tonal balance and bring out more detail in the highlights and shadows. You can do a lot to improve the appearance of a photograph by making just a few Basic and Tone Curve adjustments. But with careful use of these Develop module controls, it is possible to edit the tones in a picture so that you won't always have to apply localized adjustments to get the look you are after.

1. Here is a raw image where just the default Lightroom Develop settings have been applied. I first corrected the As Shot white balance by selecting the White Balance tool and rolling the cursor over an area that I wanted to make neutral.

2. I clicked with the White Balance tool and was pleased with the cooler color temperature setting this gave me. I then proceeded to darken the Exposure setting, which I did by clicking on the midsection of the histogram, holding the mouse button down, and dragging to the left.

3. The Exposure slider can mainly be used to get the image brightness right without worrying too much about the highlights. Next, I adjusted the Blacks to set the shadow clipping point. I clicked on the shadow end of the histogram graph and again held the mouse button down, and dragged to the left (dragging to the left in the histogram increases the amount of clipping in the Blacks).

4. In this step, I applied a Recovery setting of +60, which helped prevent the highlights from becoming too clipped.

5. I wanted to preserve as much shadow detail as possible, so I clicked on the Fill Light zone of the histogram and, while holding down the mouse button, dragged the mouse to the right to add more Fill Light in the shadows.

6. At this point I could have completed all the Basic panel tone edits by reducing the Brightness and increasing the Contrast to achieve what could be considered an acceptable finished result.

7. Instead of using Brightness and Contrast, I reverted back to the settings in Step 5. I opened the Tone Curve panel and used the Tone sliders to improve the brightness and contrast. With the Tone Curve panel in Target mode, I clicked on the clouds, held down the mouse button, and dragged the Highlights to +72. I then clicked on the shaded spray and dragged the Lights down to –84. Notice how the steep curve increases the contrast in the Lights and Highlights zones.

8. I then clicked on the rocks and dragged downward to take the Darks zone down to –24%.

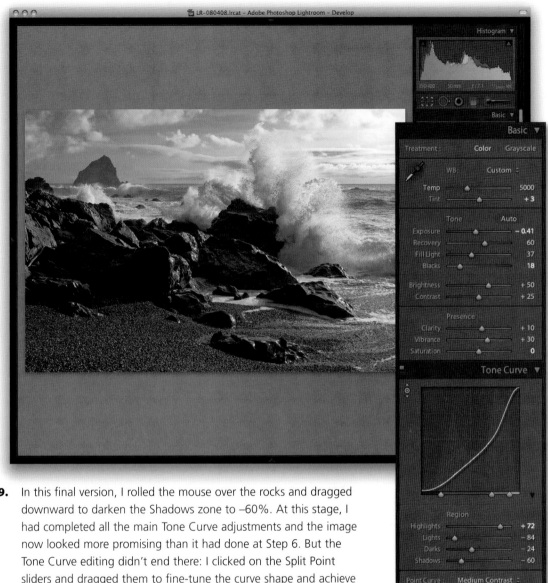

9. In this final version, I rolled the mouse over the rocks and dragged downward to darken the Shadows zone to –60%. At this stage, I had completed all the main Tone Curve adjustments and the image now looked more promising than it had done at Step 6. But the Tone Curve editing didn't end there: I clicked on the Split Point sliders and dragged them to fine-tune the curve shape and achieve the exact tone mapping I was after. Finally, I added some Clarity and Vibrance. If you compare the version shown here with the one in Step 6, the earlier version is perfectly acceptable, but the Tone Curve panel provides us with almost complete control to shape the curve any way we like using just the four Tone Range controls plus the Split Point adjustment sliders.

Tone Range split point adjustments

The Tone Range Split Points are located at the bottom of the tone curve. Note that I have added emphasis to the figure diagrams shown below to underscore this feature (**Figures 6.44**, **6.45**, and **6.46**).

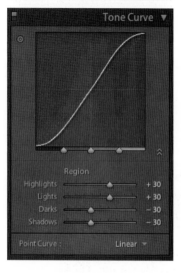 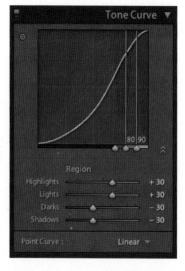 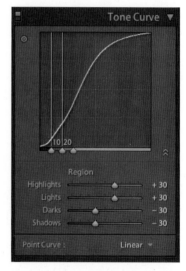

Figure 6.44 *The screen shot on the left shows a tone curve with the Tone Range Split Points in their normal positions with equal spacing for the Shadows, Darks, Lights, and Highlights zones. The middle example shows the Shadows zone set to its widest extent, compressing the other three zones. The example on the right shows the Highlights zone set to the widest point allowed.*

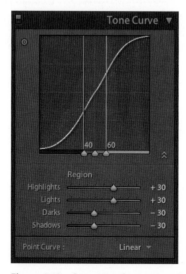 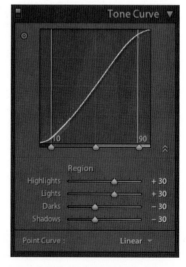

Figure 6.45 *By moving the two outer Tone Range Split Points in closer, you can increase the midtone contrast, and reduce the contrast by moving them farther apart.*

Figure 6.46 *These screen shots show a photograph where the Tone Curve zone settings have been adjusted to fine-tune the Tone Curve contrast. In the top screen shot, the Tone Range Split Points are in their default positions and the Tone Curve zones are evenly divided. In the lower screen shot I moved the middle and outer right sliders to the right, which compressed the width of the Lights zone and thereby increased the contrast in the Lights zone area and revealed more tone detail in the face.*

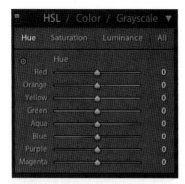

Figure 6.47 *The HSL / Color / Grayscale panel with the HSL mode selected.*

Figure 6.48 *The HSL / Color / Grayscale panel with the Color mode selected.*

HSL / Color / Grayscale panel

The HSL / Color / Grayscale panel is an all-in-one panel for fine-tuning targeted color adjustments and grayscale conversions. The HSL component (see **Figure 6.47**) is kind of equivalent to the Hue/Saturation dialog found in Photoshop, except in Lightroom you can now apply these types of adjustments to raw photos, not just pixel images (although you can do this now in Photoshop as well). Essentially, you have three color adjustment sections for controlling the Hue, Saturation, and Luminance over eight color band ranges with Target Adjustment tools available for each. The Color section of this panel (see **Figure 6.48**) provides a more simplified version of the HSL controls that has button selectors at the top for choosing the colors, with Hue, Saturation, and Luminance sliders below. The Grayscale section is for carrying out monochrome conversions, which I'll be discussing separately in the next chapter.

The sliders in the Hue section control the hue color balance and allow you to make subtle (or not so subtle) hue color shifts in each of the eight color band ranges. For example, if you start with the Green Hue slider, dragging to the right makes the greens more cyan, while dragging to the left makes the greens more yellow. The sliders in the Saturation section control the color saturation. Dragging a slider to the right increases the saturation, while dragging to the left decreases the saturation to the point where if all the Saturation sliders were dragged to the left, you could convert the whole of the image to monochrome. The sliders in the Luminance section darken or lighten the colors in the selected color ranges.

If you click the All button, the panel expands to reveal a complete list of all the sliders. As with the Tone Curve panel, the HSL controls can be applied in a Target Adjustment mode. Just click to select an HSL section such as Hue, Saturation, or Luminance, and then click the Target Adjustment tool button to switch to Target Adjustment mode. Click and drag up or down with the mouse to adjust the tones that match where you are dragging. The Target Adjustment controls are specific to each section of the HSL panel, so be careful when switching between Hue, Saturation, and Luminance to activate the Target mode in whichever section you are editing with. You can turn off the Target Adjustment tool by clicking the button again, or pressing ⌘ Alt Shift N (Mac) or Ctrl Alt Shift N (PC). Overall, the HSL / Color / Grayscale panel should be considered a color adjustment tool for use in those situations where you need to target specific colors and creatively fine-tune the color adjustments.

1. If you shoot a lot of skin tones, you might consider creating a
custom camera calibration (see page 310). But if you shoot a
mixture of subjects with the same calibration, you can also
use the HSL Color Tuning panel to compensate for reddish skin
tone colors.

2. In this example, I went to the Hue section and clicked to activate
the Target Adjustment tool. I then clicked on a skin tone area in
the picture and dragged the mouse upward to make the skin tones
less red and more yellow.

TIP

The Target Adjustment tool can also be activated using the following shortcuts: Press ⌘ Alt Shift H (Mac) or Ctrl Alt Shift H (PC) to turn on the Hue Target Adjustment tool. Press ⌘ Alt Shift S (Mac) or Ctrl Alt Shift S (PC) to turn on the Saturation Target Adjustment tool. Press ⌘ Alt Shift L (Mac) or Ctrl Alt Shift L (PC) to turn on the Luminance Target Adjustment tool. And press ⌘ Alt Shift N (Mac) or Ctrl Alt Shift N (PC) to turn off the Target Adjustment tool.

TIP

To create more extreme hue shifts, you may need to shift more than one Hue slider. For example, you could create some Develop settings in which all the Hue sliders are shifted by equal amounts. Set all the Hue sliders to +30 and save a setting, set them all to +60 and save, and so on. I suggest this as a way to create creative hue shift coloring effects.

Selective color darkening

At first glance, the HSL controls in Lightroom appear to be the same as those in Photoshop's Hue/Saturation dialog, but if you experiment a little further with the HSL controls, you will notice some distinct differences. Although the hue shift increments are the same as those in the Photoshop Hue/Saturation dialog, the Lightroom Hue slider adjustments are somewhat tamer than their Photoshop cousins. In Lightroom you are limited to a hue shift of just 30 degrees in either direction. Looking back at the example on the previous page, if I were to drag the Red hue slider fully to the left, I could make the skin tones more magenta, and if I dragged it to the right, I could make them more yellow (if you wish to make the hue shifts more extreme, you can follow the tip advice in the side panel). There is still some room to go crazy and do things like turn blue skies purple, but the hue adjustments in Lightroom are definitely more constrained. The Saturation sliders respond more or less the same as they do in Photoshop, but the most marked differences are revealed when working with the Luminance controls. When you adjust the Lightness in the Photoshop Hue/Saturation dialog, the colors mostly tend to lose their saturation, and to selectively darken a color in Photoshop, you often have to search for a magic combination of saturation and lightness that will achieve the desired result. But the Lightroom sliders really do respond the way you would expect them to. The Luminance sliders provide you with complete control over the luminance of any color range, as shown in the accompanying screen shots.

1. In the image at the top of the facing page, the challenge is to simulate the effect of a polarizing lens filter and darken the blue sky without affecting the tonal balance of any of the other colors. If I was working on this image with the Hue/Saturation adjustment in Photoshop, it would be tricky to find the exact Saturation and Lightness values that would make the blue sky go darker.

2. If I want to darken the sky in Lightroom, all I have to do is switch to the Target Adjustment mode in the Luminance section, and click on an area of sky and drag downward. As you can see in the image at the bottom of the facing page, this mainly reduces the Blue slider luminance. A word of caution, though: You may need to adjust the Detail panel controls to reduce unwanted halos. In this example I reduced the Color noise to prevent this from happening.

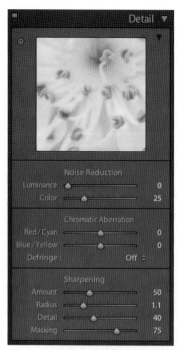

Figure 6.49 *The Detail panel controls including the Chromatic Aberration sliders.*

Detail panel: Chromatic aberration

In this next section I'm just going to discuss the Lens Corrections sliders in the Detail panel. This is because there is so much to write about the Noise Reduction and Sharpening sliders, and I have devoted the whole of Chapter 8 to this particular subject.

Chromatic aberration adjustments

The sensors in the latest digital SLRs and medium format camera backs are able to resolve a much finer level of detail than was possible with film. As a consequence, any deficiencies in the lens optics can be made even more apparent. To address these problems, some camera companies have designed "digital" lenses that are specially optimized to provide finer image resolution or in the case of non-full frame sensor cameras, lenses that are optimized for a smaller-sized sensor chip.

Where lens aberrations are a problem, the Chromatic Aberration sliders in the Detail panel are able to address and correct such optical lens deficiencies (**Figure 6.49**). Chromatic aberrations are caused by the inability to focus the red, green, and blue light wavelengths at the same distance along the optical axis. As a result, in an image where some color wavelengths are focused at different points, you may see color fringes around edges of high contrast. This can be particularly noticeable when shooting with some wide angle lenses (especially when they are being used at wider apertures), where you may well see color fringing occur in areas of high contrast toward the edges of the frame. The Red/Cyan and Blue/Yellow Chromatic Aberration sliders are able to correct such lens problems by very slightly expanding or shrinking one of the RGB channels relative to the other two. So if you adjust the Red/Cyan slider, the red channel expands or shrinks relative to the green and blue channels. If you adjust the Blue/Yellow slider, the blue channel expands or shrinks relative to the red and green channels. If you hold down the [Alt] key as you drag on the Chromatic Aberration sliders, you will see a more neutral color image in which the color fringe edges are easier to detect. As with the other Detail panel controls, you must inspect the image at the actual pixels view size to gauge these adjustments correctly. In particular, you will need to scroll the image to carefully examine the corner edges where fringing will more likely be at its worst. As just mentioned, these problems are more common with wider angle lenses, so you may find you need to share the aberration correction settings made for one image across several others in a series (providing that they were all shot with the same lens at the same zoom setting and same aperture).

1. I don't usually expect to see color fringing when I shoot using my 70–200 mm lens, but this is a genuine example where color fringing was seen around the edges of the bright pink flower petals.

2. This was resolved by adjusting the Chromatic Aberration sliders in the Detail panel. I adjusted both the Red/Cyan and Blue/Yellow sliders as shown here to remove the blue/purple fringe.

Defringe controls

The Chromatic Aberration section also features two automatic defringe controls. The first one is called Highlight Edges, which is able to correct for the color fringing that you sometimes see in extreme burned-outhighlight areas. This type of color fringing is caused by extreme light exposure hitting the camera sensors, which can overload individual photosites with too many photons, in turn creating problems in the demosaicing process. The Highlight Edges Defringe option is therefore carrying out a different kind of calculation in order to correct the magenta fringing that is sometimes seen around the highlight edges. I have to say that the effect is really subtle. It has not been easy to find a photograph where I can show a significant amount of difference between the before and after, but **Figure 6.50** shows a picture taken of sunlight reflecting off the sea, a typical example of the sort of shot that could benefit from a Highlight Edges correction.

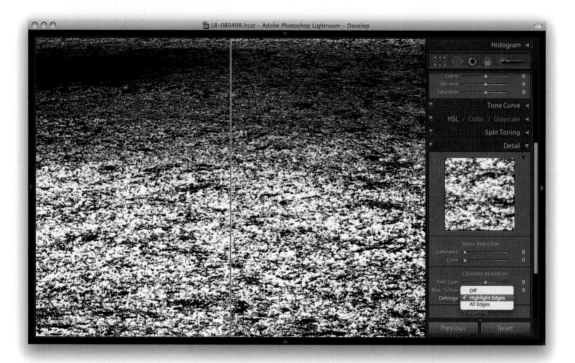

Figure 6.50   *The Highlight Edges Defringe command can be used to autocorrect color fringing in the extreme highlights. This example shows an uncorrected version in the left half of the preview and a Highlight Edges correction in the right half.*

All Edges corrections

The All Edges correction also offers a rather subtle autocorrection, but I do find that it can be useful if you need to improve an image with chromatic aberration that is proving tricky to remove using the manual sliders in the Lens Corrections panel. If you are experiencing problems trying to remove chromatic aberration, then selecting the All Edges defringe option may do a decent job of cleaning up the edges further, removing all traces of fringing.

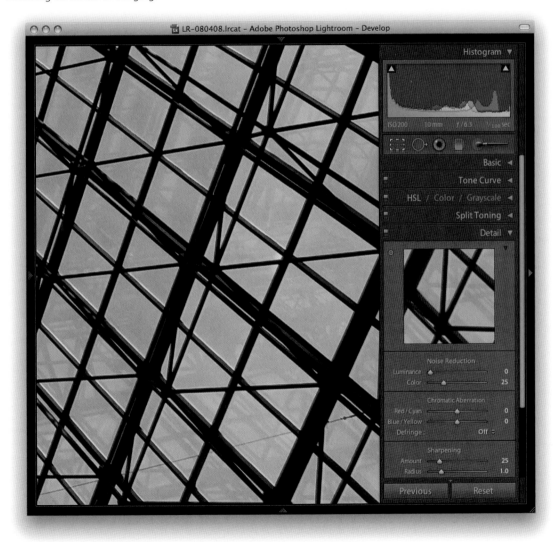

1. Here is a photograph where there was a problem with chromatic aberration toward the corner edges of the frame.

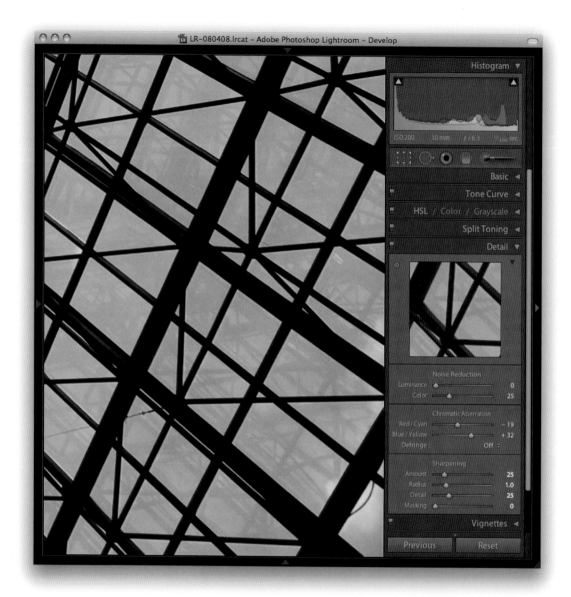

2. This photograph mainly required the use of the Chromatic Aberration sliders to remove the color fringes. In this example I set the Red/Cyan slider to −19 and the Blue/Yellow slider to +32. This seemed to be the optimum setting to use, but there was still a little bit of fringing around the high-contrast edges that I could not get rid of completely.

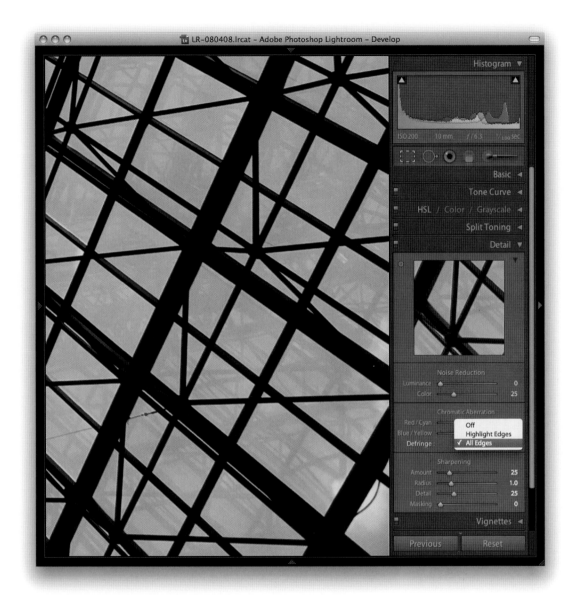

3. In this step I selected the All Edges Defringe option. The difference between this and the previous screen shot may appear quite subtle, but when I compared the before and after by toggling the effect in Lightroom I was able to see a distinct improvement. I therefore like to look upon the All Edges defringe setting as a way to polish up the edges and remove chromatic aberration that the slider settings can't manage on their own.

Figure 6.51 *The vignette controls can also be used to compensate for light falloff in a studio shot.*

Vignettes panel

Lens vignetting is also more common with wider angle lenses and is particularly noticeable if the subject you are photographing contains what should be an even shade of tone or color. For example, if you are photographing a landscape with a large expanse of sky or viewing a photograph taken against a plain wall, it is in these types of situations that you may become more aware of any lens vignetting problems that can be seen as a darkening of the image toward the corner edges.

The Vignettes panel consists of two sections. The first contains the Amount slider, which can be used to lighten the outer corners relative to the center, and a Midpoint slider. By using these two controls, you can usually find an optimum setting that will correct for the light falloff in a photograph, such as in the landscape photograph example shown on the right. Most of the correction is done by first adjusting the Amount slider, followed by a fine-tuning with the Midpoint slider to balance the vignette from the center to the edges. With these two slider controls, you should be able to precisely correct for the vignetting in almost any photograph. Once you have found the settings that are right for a particular lens, you might want to save these Vignette panel settings as a preset that can be applied to other pictures shot using the same lens focal length and aperture.

The Vignette Amount and Midpoint sliders can also be used to compensate for the light falloff in studio lighting sets. In **Figure 6.51** you can see an example of a studio shot in which the model was photographed against a white background using a wide angle lens. Although I tried to light the background and foreground as evenly as I could, there was some inevitable light falloff toward the edges of the frame. In situations like this it can be useful to adjust the Lens Correction sliders so that the darker corner edges of the frame are lightened slightly. You might even want to copy what I did with this set of photos and create a default setting for all the photographs that are taken using a particular lighting setup that includes lens correction adjustments.

1. Vignetting is always more noticeable in photographs where there is a large area of flat continuous color or tone, such as a deep blue sky. The increase in darkness toward the corner edges is quite noticeable here.

2. Here I applied some lens correction adjustments via the Detail panel, in which I used a positive Amount setting to lighten the corners and fine-tuned this anti-vignetting adjustment by tweaking the Midpoint slider.

Post-crop vignettes

Just as you can use the Lens Correction sliders to remove a vignette, you can use them to apply a vignette as well. I often like to deliberately darken or lighten the edges of a photograph and use the Lens Correction sliders as basic dodge or burn tools for the corners of a photograph.

In Lightroom 2, we now have Post-Crop vignette controls (see **Figure 6.52**) that can do the same thing as the Lens Corrections sliders, except they are applied relative to the proportions of the cropped photograph and feature a Feather slider that allows you to soften or harden the vignette edge. This is very much a tool for making creative effects. To give you some inspiration I have taken the photograph shown in **Figure 6.53** and applied four different Post-Crop vignette settings (**Figure 6.54**). The main thing to point out here is that the Post-Crop sliders work just as well on uncropped images and the ability to apply both a global and a local vignette means that you can even experiment with combinations of the two settings when editing a cropped photograph. For example, in the bottom-right image in Figure 6.54, I combined a negative global vignette with a positive Post-Crop vignette.

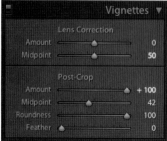

Figure 6.52 *At zero Roundness, the vignette shape matches the proportions of the cropped image. At +100, the Roundness slider makes the post-crop vignette more circular.*

NOTE

When you use the Crop Overlay mode to edit the crop setting, the vignette effect is temporarily disabled.

Figure 6.53 *This shows the original photograph used to create the examples shown in Figure 6.53, as the image was in the process of being cropped.*

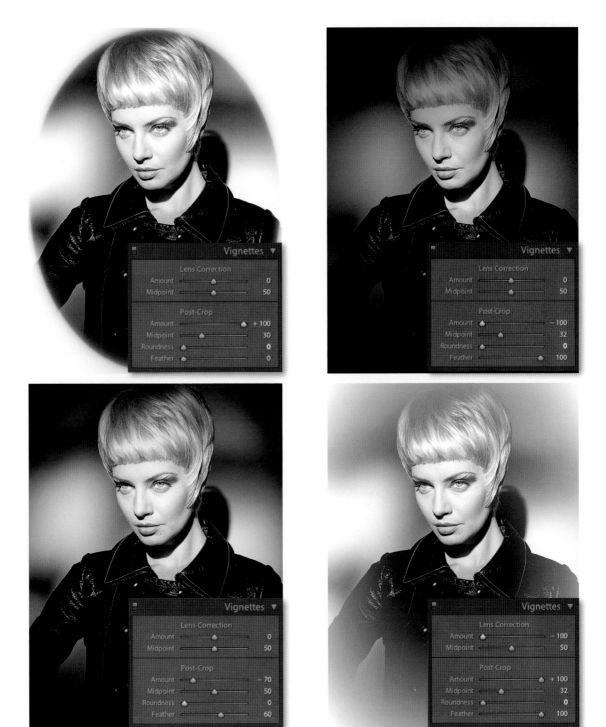

Figure 6.54 *Examples of different post-crop settings applied to the image in Figure 6.52.*

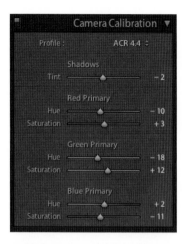

Figure 6.55 *The Camera Calibration panel controls.*

Camera Calibration panel

The Camera Raw conversions in Lightroom are the result of many years of painstaking work, in which Thomas Knoll (who with his brother John created the original Photoshop program) evaluated the color response of lots of different cameras. Basically, for each camera raw format that is supported, Thomas made two profiles that measure the camera sensor's color response under controlled daylight and tungsten lighting conditions. Using this data, it has been possible to extrapolate what the color response will be for all white balance lighting conditions that fall between these two setups and beyond.

Over 175 different cameras are supported by Adobe Camera Raw (ACR) and Lightroom, and in some instances several camera samples were tested to obtain a representative average set of measurements. Other times only one camera model was actually used. But in all cases it is clear that the measurements made by Thomas can only ever be as good as the camera or cameras from which the measurements were made (and how representative these were of other cameras of the same make). However, the sensors in some cameras can vary a lot in color response from camera to camera, and this variance means that although a raw file from your camera may be supported by Lightroom, there is no guarantee it will be exactly similar in color response to the raw files from the cameras Thomas evaluated. This is where the Camera Calibration panel comes in. The Camera Calibration panel sliders can be used to make fine-tuned adjustments to the color response (**Figure 6.55**).

Creating a custom calibration via Photoshop

If you have Photoshop CS or later, you can automatically create a custom calibration for your camera that involves the use of Thomas Fors' ACR Calibrator script. This script works for Mac or PC and can be downloaded from http://fors.net/chromoholics. Install the script in the Photoshop application/Presets/Scripts folder, then restart Photoshop and follow the step-by-step instructions shown here. The script will open a new ACR Calibrator Status window (**Figure 6.56**) and run through a series of procedures, in which the raw image containing the Color Checker chart is opened many times using different settings to measure the results. This process can take a long time to complete, which is why it is important to keep the bit depth at 8-bits per channel and keep the image size small. It will also help if you hide all the palettes before you run the script.

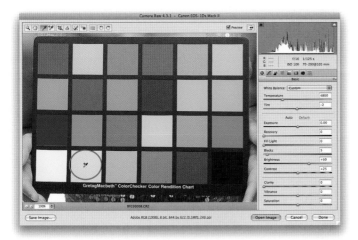

1. To use the ACR Calibrator script, photograph an X-Rite Gretag Macbeth ColorChecker chart and open the raw file in Photoshop. Use the White Balance tool to measure the circled patch. Crop the image tightly around the ColorChecker chart, and set the crop size to the smallest resolution possible and the bit depth to 8-bits per channel. Click Open Image to open the image in Photoshop.

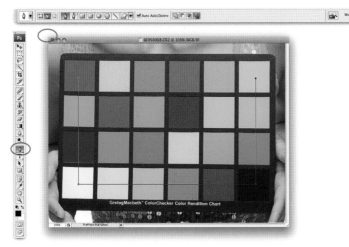

Figure 6.56 *Here is the ACR Calibrator Status window after the script has run its full course. I have highlighted the calibration settings in yellow. You need to write these figures down, enter them in the Calibration panel in Lightroom, and save them as a custom calibration setting for your camera. You may also want to make a note of the Color Temp (temperature), White Balance, and Tint settings, and save them as part of your custom calibration setting.*

2. In Photoshop, select the Pen tool with the Paths mode option selected in the Tool Options bar. Use the Pen tool to click first the brown, then the white, black, and blue-green patches, in that order. Choose File ⇨ Scripts and select the ACR Calibrator script. The script automatically opens the raw file many times over and builds a status report. (Figure 6.56). **Figures 6.57, 6.58,** and **6.59** show examples of using the Camera Calibration panel to produce creative coloring effects.

Creative use of Camera Calibration panel

Figure 6.57 *The top screen shot is a standard version of an image with zeroed Camera Calibrate settings. The lower screen shot is a vivid color setting that was created using the Camera Calibration settings shown here.*

Figure 6.58 *To create this color infrared effect, I used the Camera Calibration settings shown here (you may want to turn down the Vibrance as well).*

Figure 6.59 *To create this magenta sky effect, I used the Camera Calibration settings shown here. In addition, I set the Yellow luminance in the Color Settings panel to +35 and the Greens luminance to +35.*

Assessing your images

Comparing before and after versions

While you are working in the Develop module, you can simultaneously compare the before and after versions of any photograph you are working on, which allows you to compare the effect of the Develop settings adjustments, as they are applied to the image. To view the before and after adjustments, click the Before/After view mode button and then click on the disclosure triangle, circled in **Figure 6.60**, to select one of the Before/After viewing modes from the fly-out menu. These viewing modes let you display two identical views of the currently selected image, splitting the screen vertically, when using a Left/Right

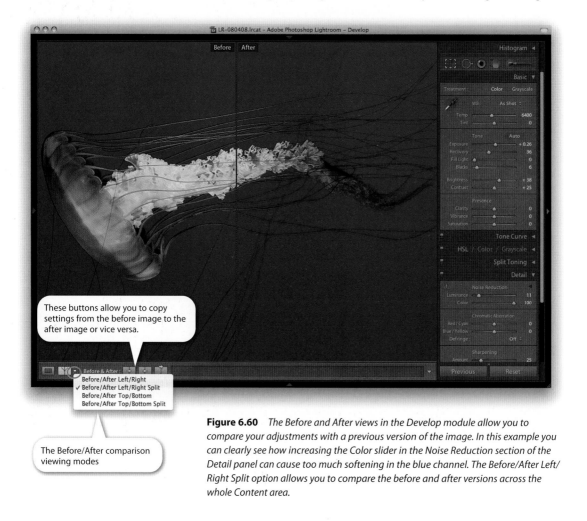

These buttons allow you to copy settings from the before image to the after image or vice versa.

The Before/After comparison viewing modes

Before/After Left/Right
✓ Before/After Left/Right Split
Before/After Top/Bottom
Before/After Top/Bottom Split

Figure 6.60 *The Before and After views in the Develop module allow you to compare your adjustments with a previous version of the image. In this example you can clearly see how increasing the Color slider in the Noise Reduction section of the Detail panel can cause too much softening in the blue channel. The Before/After Left/ Right Split option allows you to compare the before and after versions across the whole Content area.*

view, or split horizontally, when using a Top/Bottom view. Meanwhile, the Split views divide the image in half, displaying a Before view on the left and an After view on the right (or a Before view on top and an After view below [**Figure 6.61**]). Alternatively, you can repeat click the Before/After button to cycle through all the available views. You can use the Y key to toggle the standard Left/Right view mode, press Alt Y to toggle the standard Top/Bottom view mode, and press Shift Y to then go to a Split screen version of either of the above (pressing D returns to the default Loupe mode view). While you are in any of the Before/After view modes, you can also zoom in to scroll the image and compare the results of your adjustments up close.

TIP

You can switch between the before and after versions in the Develop module by going to the View menu and choosing Before / After ⇨ Before Only. Or, use the backslash key (\) shortcut to quickly toggle between these two viewing modes.

Figure 6.61 *These two screen shots show you the two main viewing modes for comparing before and after versions of an image. The top image shows a photograph in the Before/After Left/Right view mode and the bottom image in the Before/After Top/Bottom Split view mode.*

TIP

The Copy After's Settings to Before keyboard shortcut is ⌘ Alt Shift ← (Mac) or Ctrl Alt Shift ← (PC). The Copy Before's Settings to After keyboard shortcut is ⌘ Alt Shift → (Mac) or Ctrl Alt Shift → (PC).

Swap Before and After settings

Copy settings from the after photo to the before photo.

Copy settings from the before photo to the after photo.

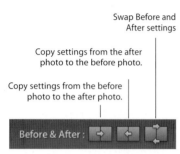

Figure 6.62 *The Copy settings buttons only appear at the bottom of the Develop module when either the Left/Right or Top/Bottom view modes have been selected. The buttons shown here appear when the Left/Right view mode is selected.*

NOTE

The before version of a photo uses either the Develop settings that were applied when it was first imported into Lightroom or the last assigned Before state. When you click the "Copy settings from the after photo to the before photo" button, you are assigning a new Before state to the photo.

Managing the before and after previews

When you edit an image in one of the Before/After viewing modes, you can make umpteen adjustments via the Develop module and at all times be able to compare the revised after version with a before version. But suppose that you want to make the current after version the new before. You can do this by clicking the "Copy settings from the After photo to the Before photo" button. This updates the before image with the after image settings. What you are effectively doing is making a snapshot of the settings at a certain point in the Develop adjustment process, which lets you make further new adjustments and compare them with a new before version. Let's say at this point that you continue making more tweaks to the Develop panel settings, but decide that these corrections have not actually improved the image and the interim before version was actually better. You can reverse the process by clicking the "Copy settings from the before photo to the After photo" button. Basically, the Before and After compare mode controls (**Figure 6.62**) let you take a snapshot of an image mid-correction and compare it with whatever settings you apply later. The following steps illustrate one such workflow.

1. This screen shot shows a photo in the Develop module Loupe view with the image settings that were applied at the import stage.

2. I clicked the Before/After view YY button (you can also use the Y keyboard shortcut) and made a few Develop adjustments, and I altered the white balance so that the modified after version was bluer in color.

3. I then went to the Before/After viewing mode menu and switched view modes, selecting the Before/After Left/Right Split view. I then magnified the image to display the photo at a 1:4 zoom view (notice that Before/After button changes to Y).

4. I then clicked the Develop module Loupe view button to switch out of the Before/After view mode so that I could work on the picture in a normal full-screen mode.

5. While working in the standard Develop module Loupe view mode, you can easily compare the current Develop settings with the before version, using the ⟨\⟩ keyboard shortcut. This will switch to show the Before view. Press ⟨\⟩ again to revert to the After view.

6. I then clicked the Before/After view button again (you can use the Y keyboard shortcut) and clicked the "Copy After's settings to Before photo" button (⌘ Alt Shift ← [Mac], Ctrl Alt Shift ← [PC]) to make the current version the new Before setting.

7. The blue version is now the new Before setting associated with this photo. I could then make further edits, such as converting the photo to grayscale and comparing it with the new saved before version.

Figure 6.63 *The retouching tools are all located just below the Histogram panel in the Develop module. From left to right: Spot Removal, Red Eye, Graduated Filter, and Adjustment brushes. This screen shot shows the Spot Removal tool panel options. Click the Close button to collapse this panel (or click the tool icon, or press the* D *key).*

TIP

Use the On/Off button at the bottom to toggle showing and hiding all Spot Removal tool edits. The Reset button can be used to cancel and clear all the current spots tool edits.

Image retouching tools

The retouching tools in the Develop module (**Figure 6.63**) can be used to retouch a photograph in Lightroom without actually editing the pixel data. When you work with the Spot Removal, Red Eye, Adjustment Brush, or Graduated Filter tools, their actions are recorded as sets of instructions and the pixel image data in the original master file remains untouched. It is only when you choose to export a file as a TIFF, JPEG, or PSD, or carry out an "Edit in external editor" command, that the retouching work is physically applied to the exported image.

Spot Removal tool

The Spot Removal tool (N) has a Clone mode and a Heal mode. In Clone mode, the Spot Removal tool copies and repairs from a sampled area without trying to blend the result with the surrounding pixels. In Clone mode a soft-edged selection is used, and this is the most appropriate mode to work with when removing spots that are close to an edge. For all other retouching work, I suggest using the Heal mode, which blends the results of the retouching with the image information that is just outside of the area you are trying to repair. The Heal mode is usually successful in hiding the blemish removal areas by invisibly blending the healed area with the surrounding pixels.

To work with the Spot Removal tool, start by adjusting the Spot Size slider in the Remove Spot tool options (Figure 6.63) so that it matches the size of the areas you intend to repair. Perhaps the quicker method is to use the square bracket keys on the keyboard. Click or hold down the] key to make the spot size bigger and use the [key to make the spot size smaller. Next, locate the spot or blemish you wish to remove and click on it with the Remove Spot tool. If the cursor size is larger than 75, you see a small crosshair in the center of the cursor circle. You can use this to help you target the dust spot you want to remove by centering the cursor precisely. Then drag outward to select an image area that you'll use to "cover" the spot. At this stage you'll notice that the original (destination) circle cursor disappears so that you can preview the effect of the clone action without a distraction of the spot circle. A linking arrow also appears to indicate the relationship between the source circle and destination areas (**Figure 6.64**). When you have finished applying a spot removal, the destination cursor circle remains as a thin, white circle on the screen for as long as the Spot Removal tool is active in the Develop module.

Because Lightroom is recording all these actions as edit instructions, you have the freedom to fine-tune any clone and heal step. Do this by clicking inside a Spot Removal circle (to reactivate it) and reposition either the source or destination circles. Carefully place the mouse over either of the cursor circle edges (a bar with a bidirectional arrow appears), and click and drag to dynamically adjust the spot size of both the source and destination circles. Another way to work with the Spot Removal tool is to click and drag with the ⌘ key (Mac) or Ctrl key (PC) held down. This allows you to define a different spot size each time you drag with the tool, but the sample cursor will pick anywhere that surrounds the area you define for spot removal. When using this method of spotting, the source selection may appear quite random, but Lightroom is using the same logic as used by Photoshop's Spot Healing brush. In Figure 6.64 I have illustrated several of the ways you can work with the Spot Removal tool. Some of the behavioral changes are quite subtle. On the next page is a summary of the ways you can work with the Spot Removal tool.

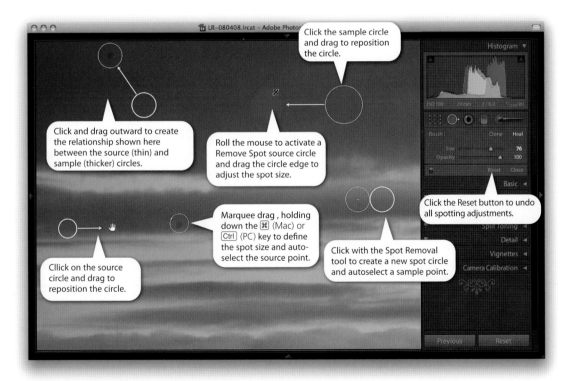

Figure 6.64 *This figure shows a combined series of snapshots taken of the Spot Removal tool in action to illustrate the different ways you can use this tool.*

NOTE

Dust marks are the bane of digital photography, and ideally you want to do as much as you can to avoid dust or dirt getting onto the camera sensor. I have experimented with various products and found that the Sensor Swabs used with the Eclipse cleaning solution from Photographic Solutions Inc. (www.photosol.com) are reliable products. I use these from time to time to keep the sensors in my cameras free from marks. It is a bit scary when you first try to clean a sensor. Just remember to follow the directions and don't use too much solution on the sensor swabs, because you don't want to drench the sensor surface with cleaning solution.

Clone or Heal

In Clone mode, the Spot Removal tool copies pixels using a feathered circle edge. In Heal mode the Spot Removal tool copies pixels and blends them around the inner edge of the circle. You can also use the Clone/Heal buttons in the tool options panel to change the spotting mode for any Spot Removal circle. Another important thing to be aware of is that if you click with the Spot Removal tool in Heal mode (or ⌘ [Mac], Ctrl [PC] drag with the mouse), rather than just drag to set the sample point, the Spot Removal tool behaves like the Spot Healing brush in Photoshop. This behavior is well worth noting when using the Synchronize Settings to synchronize your spotting work, which I'll be coming to shortly, on page 324.

Spot size

You can adjust the size of the Remove Spot cursor circle by adjusting the size slider in the Spot Removal tool options (Figure 6.63). You can do this before you apply the tool, or you can use the slider to readjust the size of a selected circle. You can also use the square bracket keys to adjust the spot size of the cursor before you use it to create a new spot. Use the left bracket ([) to make a spot size smaller and the right bracket (]) to make a spot size bigger.

Click and drag

Place the Spot Removal cursor over the area you want to remove and center the cursor using the crosshair. Hold down the mouse and drag outward to set the source circle position. As you do this, the preview area inside the source circle is updated as you drag to set the position of the sample circle. The circle itself is hidden so that you aren't distracted by seeing the cursor on the screen as you work with this tool.

Click only

You can just click with the Spot Removal tool to remove a mark or blemish. In this respect you could say that the Spot Removal tool is able to work a bit like the Spot Healing brush that is found in Photoshop and Photoshop Elements. That is to say, Lightroom will automatically select the best point to sample from. When you click with the Remove Spot tool in Lightroom, it automatically places the sample circle for you and uses a certain amount of built-in intelligence to choose a suitable point to sample from.

Editing the spot circles

The Spot Removal circles always remain fully editable. You can click on a sample circle and drag to move the sample area. But you can only resize the spot size by dragging the slider in the toolbar or by holding the mouse down on the edge of a source circle only and dragging. Note, too, when you drag on a source circle to resize it, that the thin circle cursor conveniently disappears, allowing you so see more clearly the effect these changes are having on the photo. Similarly, if you hold the mouse down inside a spot circle, the thin circle disappears and changes to show a hand icon that allows you to drag and reposition the source spot circle.

Hiding the spot circles

The most convenient way to hide the spot circles and inspect a photo without seeing them overlay the image is to use the H keyboard shortcut. Pressing H hides the spot circles, but as soon as you begin work with the Spot Removal tool, the spot circles are revealed again.

Undoing/deleting spot circles

Use ⌘ Z (Mac), Ctrl Z (PC) to undo the last spot circle. To delete a spot circle, click to select it and then hit the Delete key. And to remove all spot circles from an image, click the Reset button in the tool options panel.

Heal mode synchronization

As I mentioned previously, if you click with the Spot Removal tool in Heal mode (or ⌘ [Mac], Ctrl [PC] drag with the mouse), Lightroom automatically chooses the best area of the photo to sample from. As long as you don't try to edit the sample point (by manually dragging the sample circle to reposition it), the spot circle will remain in its "autoselect sample point" mode. If you therefore carry out a series of spot removals using only the Heal mode and always click with the tool rather than drag, you can set up Lightroom to synchronize the spot removal more efficiently. If you synchronize a series of photos in this way, the Lightroom spot circles will autoselect the best sample points in each of the individual synchronized photos. This does not guarantee 100% successful spot removal synchronization across every image, but if you follow this advice your spot removal synchronization results should generally be successful.

TIP

The Tool Overlay options are accessed via the View menu. These refer specifically to things like the Spot Removal circles, and the Adjustment brush and Graduated Filter tool pin markers. If you select the Always Show menu option, the tool overlays remain visible at all times. If you want to hide the tool overlays, select Never Show from the menu. When this menu option is selected, the overlays remain hidden, even when you roll the mouse cursor over the image. But as soon as you start working with a tool, the tool overlay behavior automatically switches to the Auto Show mode.

TIP

If you have made a selection of images via the Filmstrip (or in the Library Grid view) you can also use the [Cmd][Shift][S] (Mac), [Ctrl][Shift][S] (PC) shortcut to open the Synchronize Settings dialog.

Synchronized spotting

One of the best things about the Spot Removal feature is that you can continue to edit the tones and colors in the photograph and the spotting adjustments update accordingly. As you will read later, you can also synchronize the settings in one image with others from the same sequence; this includes synchronizing spot removals. So if you get the spotting work right for one image, you can use a synchronization to copy the spot removal work to all the other pictures. There are two ways you can do this. One method is to apply the Spot Removal tool on one photo and synchronize the spotting with other photos later. Or, you can Auto Sync a selection of photos and update all the selected images at once as you retouch the most selected photo.

1. Make sure the photo that has had all the spotting work done to it is the one that is the most selected, or "target" photo (the one with the lighter gray border). Then click the Sync button.

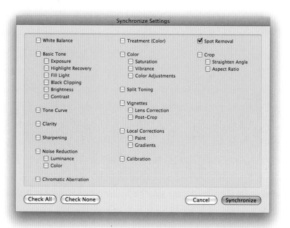

2. This opens the Synchronize Settings dialog. If you first click the Check None button, then check the Spot Removal check box and click the Synchronize button, Lightroom will synchronize the spot removal settings across all the selected images.

Auto Sync spotting

NOTE

Copying the Spot Removal settings or working with the Auto Sync feature can work well on some photo series better than others. In the example shown here, I was careful to use the Spot Removal tool in Heal mode by clicking only to remove the dust spots (rather than clicking plus dragging). This is because when you synchronize in Heal mode with a click-only action, the click "Heal" instruction automatically selects the best area to clone from. The net result is that for each heal clone spot, Lightroom will clone from wherever it thinks is the best portion of the picture to sample from and do so differently with each individual image. It won't work perfectly in every instance, and it may be necessary to review each image individually to fine-tune the clone source points (with Auto Sync disabled). But on the whole, Auto Sync cloning can still save you time when repetitively cloning out spots from areas such as skies or plain studio backdrops.

1. An alternative method is to make a selection of the photos, hold down the ⌘ key (Mac), Ctrl key (PC), and click the Sync button, which sets the selected photos to Auto Sync mode.

2. You can then start editing any of the pictures and *all* the Develop settings will automatically synchronize to the target photo. Here, I used the Spot Removal tool in Heal mode to remove the dust marks from the photo shown in Step 1. The Spot Removal tool settings were automatically applied to all the other photos in the selection. Remember to click the Auto Sync button to revert back to the standard Sync mode behavior.

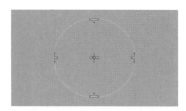

Figure 6.65   *The Red Eye Correction tool cursor design.*

Figure 6.66   *The Red Eye Correction tool panel options.*

TIP

If you know Lightroom can repair red eye so neatly, do you really need to continue using the anti-red eye flash mode? I know what I propose here may sound like a lazy approach to photography, but bear with me. In my experience, the anti-red eye flash mode can really kill all opportunities to grab the best, most spontaneous snapshots. There is nothing worse than seeing a great expression or something special going on between a group of people in the frame and then have to wait several seconds for the camera to get up to speed while it fires a few pre-flashes before taking the full flash exposure. These days I prefer to shoot using the normal flash mode and let Lightroom fix any red eye problems that occur.

Red Eye Correction tool

There are many ways you can prevent red eye from happening. You can use a flash gun where the flash source is not so close to the lens axis, or you can set the flash on most compact cameras to an anti-red eye mode. But for those times you can't, the Red Eye Correction tool corrects photographs in which the direct camera flash has caused the pupils in people's eyes to appear bright red.

Begin by targeting the center of the pupil using the crosshair in the middle and drag outward to draw an ellipse that defines the area you wish to correct (the Red Eye Correction tool cursor is shown in **Figure 6.65**). Lightroom automatically detects the red eye area that needs to be repaired and fixes it. You don't have to be particularly accurate, and it really is rather neat the way Lightroom does this! It's interesting to watch how this tool behaves when you lazily drag to include an area that is a lot bigger than that you need to define with the Red Eye Correction tool cursor. Lightroom always seems to know precisely which area to correct, because the cursor shrinks to create an ellipse overlay representing the area that has been targeted for the red eye correction. After you have first applied the tool to a photo, the Red Eye tool options (**Figure 6.66**) appear below in the Tools panel selection. These options allow you to adjust the sliders to fine-tune the Pupil Size area you want to correct and decide on the amount you want to darken the pupil. You can revise the Red Eye removal settings by clicking on a circle to reactivate it, or use the Delete key to remove individual red eye corrections. If you don't like the results, you can always click the Reset button in the tool panel options to delete all Red Eye Correction retouching and start over again.

Adjusting the cursor size

Before applying the Red Eye Correction tool you can adjust the size of the cursor by using the square bracket keys. Use the left bracket ([) to make the cursor size smaller and the right bracket (]) to make the cursor size bigger. To be honest, the cursor size doesn't always make much difference because big or small, once you click with the tool you can drag the cursor to define the area you wish to affect. The cursor size is probably more relevant if you are using the Red Eye tool to click on the pupils to correct them rather than dragging. But the tool seems to do such a great job anyway of locating the area that needs to be corrected.

1. Here is an example of the Red Eye Correction tool in action. In this screen shot you can see that I selected the Red Eye Correction tool and dragged the cursor over the left eye, moving from the center of the pupil outward. Alternatively, I could simply have clicked on the pupil using the Red Eye Correction tool. Either method will work.

2. After I released the mouse, a Red Eye Correction tool ellipse overlay shrank to fit the area around the eye. As I just mentioned earlier, you don't have to be particularly accurate with the way you define the eye pupils. In this screen shot you can see that I first applied a red eye correction to the eye on the right before correcting the left eye. Notice here how the first ellipse overlay has a thinner border and the current ellipse overlay is thicker, indicating that this one is active. When a red eye ellipse is active, you can then use the two sliders in the toolbar to adjust the Red Eye Correction settings. Use the Pupil Size slider to adjust the size up or down for the area that is being corrected. Next to this is the Darken slider that you can use to fine-tune the appearance of the pupil. I tend to find that the Lightroom autocorrection (using the midway settings of 50) is usually perfect in most instances.

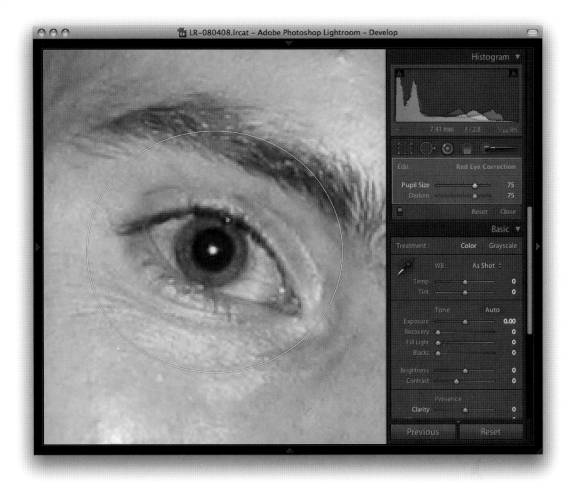

3. If you then move the mouse over to the edge of an ellipse and drag to resize the area, or drag from inside to reposition the ellipse, the behavior is quite different from what happens when you try to edit a Remove Spot circle. When you drag the overlay edge to resize a Red Eye Correction overlay, this allows you to fine-tune the shape and size of the red eye adjustment. You know how it is said that there are no layers in Lightroom? Well, this is so far the first example of what you could call a Lightroom layer. The benefit is that you can get the red eye correction coverage to match the eye pupil precisely. If you need to redo a red eye adjustment, the best thing to do is to make an ellipse overlay active, hit the Delete key to remove it, and apply the Red Eye Correction tool again.

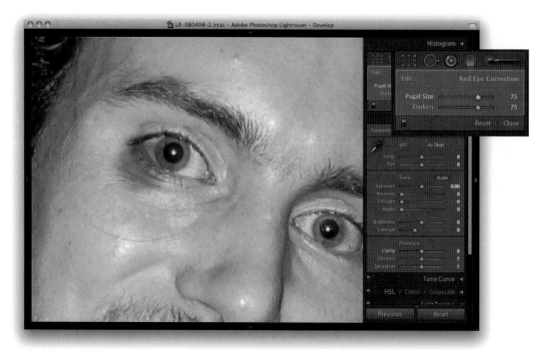

4. All will become even clearer if you hold down the mouse over the ellipse circle and drag the ellipse overlay away from the pupil. Basically the ability to resize the shape of the red eye correction and reposition it provides you with a lot of scope to fine-tune any red eye adjustment.

Localized adjustments

Let's now take a look at the true stars of Lightroom 2: the Adjustment brush and Graduated Filter tools. These are not just tools for dodging and burning, because you have a total of seven effects to choose from, not to mention dual brush settings and an Auto Mask option. Just like the Spot Removal and Remove Redeye tools, the Adjustment brush and Graduated Filter tools are completely nondestructive. There is no need for Lightroom to create an edit copy of the master image first (if that is what you want to achieve, then you can always use the Edit in Photoshop command discussed in Chapter 9). The unique thing about these tools is that when localized adjustments are applied to an image, the adjustments are saved as instruction edits that automatically update as you make further adjustments to the tool and other Develop module settings. You can even synchronize localized adjustment work across multiple images using the Sync Settings command.

Initial Adjustment brush options

When you first start working with the Adjustment brush, the panel options will look like those in **Figure 6.67** or **6.68**. To begin with, you will be in New mode, ready to create a fresh set of brush strokes, but first you need to choose a paint effect: Exposure, Brightness, Contrast Saturation, Clarity, Sharpness, or Color. In Figure 6.67, I clicked the Exposure button, which meant I could set an Exposure setting to paint with, such as a positive value to lighten or a negative value to darken (these are your basic dodge and burn tool settings). In Button mode, you can select one paint effect at a time and use the Amount slider to adjust the effect setting. To switch to the Effect Slider mode, click on the switch that's circled in Figure 6.68. In this mode you can use any combination of the available slider adjustments for the Adjustment brush effect and save them as a custom setting that can be accessed via the Effect menu (also circled in Figure 6.68).

Below this are the Brush settings, where you have three sliders. The Size slider controls the overall size of the brush cursor (**Figure 6.69**), or you can use the ⬚ and ⬚ to make the cursor circles bigger or smaller. The reason for the two circles is to show the hardness of the brush. The inner circle represents the core brush size, while the outer circle represents the feathering radius. As you adjust the Feather slider, the outer circle expands or contracts to indicate the hardness or softness of the brush. Or, you can use Alt ⬚ to make the brush edge harder or Alt ⬚ to make the edge softer. The Flow slider is kind of like an airbrush control: by selecting a low Flow setting you can apply a series of brush strokes that successively build to create a stronger effect. You will notice that as you brush back and forth with the Adjustment brush, the paint effect gains opacity (if you are using a pressure-sensitive tablet such as a Wacom™, the flow of the brush strokes is automatically linked to the pen pressure that is applied). The Density slider at the bottom limits what the maximum brush opacity can be. At 100% Density, the flow of the brush strokes builds to maximum opacity, but if you reduce the Density, this limits the maximum opacity for the brush. In fact, if you reduce the Density and paint, this allows you to erase the paint strokes back to a desired Density setting. When Density is set to zero, the brush acts like an eraser. The A and B buttons enable you to create two separate brush settings so that you can easily switch between two different brushes as you work.

We are now ready to start painting with the Adjustment brush (K). Where you first click adds a pin marker to the image. This is just like any other overlay, and you can hide it using the H key (or use the

Figure 6.67 *The standard Adjustment brush options in Button mode.*

Figure 6.68 *The Adjustment brush options in Slider Control mode.*

Figure 6.69 *The Adjustment brush cursor.*

Figure 6.70 *This shows the Adjustment brush panel Edit options (note as you scroll the other panels these slide beneath the tool options).*

Figure 6.71 *The Effect settings menu.*

View ⇨ Tool Overlay options discussed earlier to govern the show/hide behavior for these overlays). The pin overlay is therefore like a marker for the brush strokes you are about to add and can later be used as a reference marker when you need to locate and edit a particular group of brush strokes. The important thing to understand here is that you click once and start painting away on an area of the picture to form a collection of brush strokes (identified by the marker). When you edit the brush strokes, you can adjust the parameter settings for the group as a whole. So you can come back later and say "Let's make this series of brush strokes a little stronger," or "Let's try making the Exposure darker and add some more saturation too." Consequently, when you use the Adjustment brush you should work with this in mind and create new brush stroke groups whenever you need to shift the focus of your retouching from one part of the photograph to another. Therefore, always click the New button in the Adjustment brush's panel when you need to create a new (separate) group of brush strokes.

Editing the Adjustment brush strokes

To edit a series of brush strokes, click on an existing pin marker to select it (a black dot appears in the center of the pin). This takes you into Edit mode, where you can start adding more brush strokes and edit the current brush settings (**Figure 6.70**). If you didn't get the slider settings right when you were painting, you now have complete control to edit them. Also, as you edit a localized adjustment, you can click on the pin marker, hold down the Alt key, and drag the cursor left or right to decrease or increase the strength of an effect. When you are done editing, hit ↵Enter or click the New button to return to the New adjustment mode, where you can click on the image and add a new set of brush strokes. As you work with the Adjustment brush, you can undo a brush stroke or series of strokes using the undo command (⌘Z [Mac] Ctrl Z [PC]), and you can erase brush strokes by clicking the Erase button to enter Eraser mode, or simply hold down the Alt key as you paint to erase any brush strokes.

Saving effect settings

As you discover combinations of effect sliders that you would like to use again, you can save these via the Effect menu (**Figure 6.71**). For example, there is a preset setting called Soften Skin that uses a combination of negative Clarity and positive Sharpness.

1. This shows a photograph where Basic adjustments have been applied to set the highlights and shadows and optimize the contrast.

2. In this example I added several groups of brush strokes. I included a series of negative Exposure brush strokes to darken the brightest highlight areas and (shown here), a series of positive Exposure lightening brush strokes to lighten the logs that were in the shade.

Figure 6.72 *Often, all you need to do is to click on an area of a picture with the color you wish to target and drag the Adjustment brush in Auto Mask mode to quickly adjust areas of the picture that share the same tone and color.*

Automasking

The Auto Mask option cleverly masks the image as you paint with the Adjustment brush. It works by analyzing the color and tone of the area where you click with the Adjustment brush and only applies the effect to those areas that match the same tone and color. The paint strokes in a pin group don't have to all be based on the same color; the Auto Mask resamples continuously as you paint to calculate the mask. **Figure 6.72** shows an example of how you can click (on the warm-colored backdrop) and drag the brush around the areas you wish to paint in one swoop, and the brush adjustment won't bleed into the flower petals or stems. In the next exercise, I show how you can use successive strokes to neutralize all of the warm-colored backdrop. The Auto Mask feature does appear to work remarkably well at autoselecting areas of a picture based on color, but to fine-tune the edges, you may need to do what I did here, and switch back and forth with the Alt key to erase areas where the Adjustment brush effect spills over the edges.

You can also hold down the ⌘ key (Mac) Ctrl key (PC) to temporarily switch the Adjustment brush into Auto Mask mode (or revert back to Normal mode if Auto Mask is already selected).

1. This shows the original photograph with a warm-toned backdrop. I began by clicking on the Adjustment brush to reveal the tool options.

2. I selected the Saturation mode, set the Effect slider to −100% (to desaturate completely), and started painting. Because Auto Mask was checked, the brush only adjusted the backdrop colors.

3. After finishing the main brush work, I switched to Edit mode, so that I could fine-tune the settings. In this example, I adjusted the Brightness, which meant I could also darken the painted area.

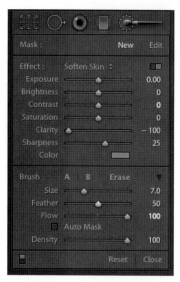

Figure 6.74 *This shows the Soften Skin Adjustment brush settings that were used to work on the photograph shown in Figure 6.74.*

Previewing the brush stroke areas

As you roll the cursor over a pin marker, you will see a temporary overlay view of the painted regions (**Figure 6.73**). This shows a gray overlay that represents the areas that have been painted. You can also press O to switch the mask on or off and Shift O to cycle the mask display.

Figure 6.73 *This shows an overlay view of the Adjustment brush stokes.*

Beauty retouching with negative clarity

On pages 276–277 I showed an example of how to use a negative Clarity adjustment on a black and white image to create a diffuse printing type effect. Meanwhile a couple of Lightroom beta testers, Clicio Barroso and Ettore Causa, came up with the suggestion that you could use a negative Clarity effect as a Adjustment brush effect for softening skin tones. Personally, I have an aversion for the over-retouched look of some fashion beauty portraits, but painting with the Soften Skin effect setting with Clarity set to –100% and Sharpness to 25 works really well as a skin-smoothing Adjustment brush. To illustrate how well this works, I painted with the Adjustment brush using the settings shown in **Figure 6.74** to create the before and after close-up view of a beauty photograph (**Figure 6.75**). I didn't need to use the Auto Mask mode; I just painted over the areas of the face that I felt needed softening. After applying the Soften Skin effect, I used the Spot Removal tool to clean up the photograph further, but most of the difference you see here is a result of using the Soften Skin effect with the Adjustment brush.

Figure 6.75 *The top photograph shows the unretouched, before image and the lower photograph shows the retouched version that was mainly edited using the Adjustment brush with the Soften Skin effect setting.*

Hand-coloring in Color mode

The Color effect allows you to brush with color on your photographs and can be likened to working with the Brush tool in Photoshop with the Color blend mode. There are lots of potential uses for this tool: you could use it to make someone's hair a different shade of color or change the eye color, or you might want to cool an area of the picture such as in the Graduated Filter example later, where I used a blue Color Graduated Filter to make the sky bluer. In the example shown here, I started with an image that had been converted to black and white by desaturating the colors. The main thing to point out here is that I used the Adjustment brush in Color mode with Auto Mask selected. Although the previewed image was in black and white, it did not matter which black and white conversion method was used, since Lightroom always references the underlying color data when calculating the Auto Mask. The Auto Mask feature was therefore able to do a good job of detecting the mask edges based on the underlying colors of the flower heads, stems, and leaves.

1. This photograph was converted to monochrome by desaturating all the Saturation sliders in the HSL panel (you could also drag the Basic panel Saturation slider to zero, or convert to grayscale). I selected the Tint effect and clicked on the main color swatch to open the color picker shown here and selected a green color to paint with.

2. With Auto Mask checked, I brushed along the stems and leaves, switching between a broad brush A and smaller brush B. I also used the Edit sliders to modify the color and increase the saturation.

3. I pressed ⏎Enter to OK these brush strokes and started a new set of paint strokes. This time I selected a yellow color and began painting the flower petals, again with the Auto Mask option selected.

Positive Sharpness is using a cross between the old (Lightroom 1.0) and new (Lightroom 1.1) sharpening logic. Basically, the Amount slider sets the level of detail that is applied, but unlike the Detail panel controls, no edge masking used. Negative sharpness undoes the sharpening and at its maximum strength takes you to a slightly blurred version of the original image.

Sharpening and blurring

A positive Clarity Adjustment brush setting can be used to paint in mid-tone contrast. In **Figure 6.76**, I used a Positive Clarity brush to brush over the areas of flat tone (avoiding the sharp edges) to bring out more detail in the rock surface. As well as Clarity, we also have a Sharpness effect that with a positive value can be used to add sharpness, and with a negative value can be used to add blur.

In **Figure 6.77** I have shown a before and after version of a beauty photograph where the top version was treated with a standard portrait sharpen setting. When I shoot beauty pictures I am faced with the dilemma of what do you sharpen for, the face or the hair? Usually, I sharpen for the eyes and skintones. I used the Detail panel settings shown in the bottom example, employing a higher than 1.0 Radius to enhance the face features and a high Masking value to protect the skintones. But the problem with this approach is that the fine hair strands don't get the appropriate level of fine-edge sharpening that can make the hair stand out more. What you can do now is mainly sharpen for the skintones, eyes, and lips, and use just a gentle Sharpen Adjustment brush to locally add more sharpness to the hair.

Figure 6.76 *This shows a photograph of a rock surface where I used a positive Clarity Adjustment brush to bring out detail in the areas of flat tone.*

Figure 6.77 *The top version shows the photograph with default sharpening settings for portraits. In the lower version I modified the Detail panel settings to achieve a more desirable sharpening for the face features. Meanwhile, I used a Sharpen Adjustment brush at 60% to add more sharpness to the hair and later faded this to 33% to achieve the right balance between the sharpening for the hair and face.*

Figure 6.78 *The Graduated Filter tool options in Button mode.*

Figure 6.79 *The Graduated Filter tool options in Sliders mode.*

TIP

Double-clicking the slider names resets them to zero, or to their default values.

TIP

As you edit a localized adjustment, click on the pin marker, hold down the [Alt] key, and drag the cursor left or right to decrease or increase the strength of an effect.

Graduated Filter tool

Everything that I have described so far about working with the Adjustment brush more or less applies to working with the Graduated Filter tool as well. The Graduated Filter tool (see **Figures 6.78** and **6.79**) allows you to add linear Graduated Filter fade adjustments. To use the tool you click in the picture to set the start point for the Graduated Filter (the point with the maximum effect strength), drag the mouse to define the spread of the Graduated Filter, and release at the point where you want the Graduated Filter to finish (the point of minimum effect strength). The Graduated Filter tool therefore allows you to apply linear fadeout adjustments between these two points. There is no midtone control with which you can offset a Graduated Filter effect, and there are no Graduated Filter options other than a linear Graduated Filter. A radial Graduated Filter would be nice, but I suppose we do at least have the post-crop vignette feature.

Graduated Filter effects are indicated by a pin marker, and you can move a Graduated Filter once it has been applied by clicking and dragging the pin. The parallel lines indicate the spread of the Graduated Filter, and you can change the width of the Graduated Filter by dragging the outer lines. If you want to edit the angle of a Graduated Filter effect, you can do so by clicking and dragging the middle line. Oh, and in case you were wondering, the Graduated Filter tool icon is meant to represent a Cokin™ type grad filter attached to a camera lens!

1. This shows how the original photograph looked after I had applied just the main Basic panel adjustments to optimize the highlights, shadows, and contrast.

2. I clicked the Graduated Filter tool to reveal the Graduated Filter options, selected a negative Exposure as the effect to use, and dragged the Graduated Filter tool from the middle of the sky downward.

3. I then decided to strengthen this darkening Exposure Graduated Filter by decreasing the Amount to –1.90.

TIP

Click on the circled switch to go from
the Button edit mode (where you
can only adjust a single effect) to the
Sliders edit mode shown in Step 5.

4. Next, I selected a Color effect, sampled a blue color to use as the
color effect, and added a new Graduated Filter by dragging from
the top of the photograph downward to the horizon. As you
would expect, this made the sky appear bluer in color.

5. Lastly, in the Graduated Filter tool Edit (Sliders) mode, I lowered
the Brightness to –25 and boosted the Saturation to 59.

History panel

Every step you apply in the Develop module is recorded as a separate history state in the History panel (**Figure 6.80**), which is located just below Presets and Snapshots. The History feature in Lightroom has the unique advantage over Photoshop in that all history steps are preserved after you quit Lightroom. When you relaunch the program, the last selected history step is applied to the image and all the other history states are preserved. History is therefore useful because it allows you to revert to any previous Develop module setting (even after you have quit), and you can access an unlimited number of history states via the History panel, without incurring the efficiency overhead that is normally associated with Photoshop image editing and History. There are several ways you can navigate through a file's history. You can go to the History panel and click to select a history step, which will allow you to jump quickly to a specific state, or you can roll the cursor over the list of history states in the History panel to preview them in the Navigator panel before selecting one. **Figure 6.81** shows an example of how the History panel looked after I had made a series of Develop adjustments to the image.

Figure 6.80 *In this close-up view of the History panel in Figure 6.81, you can see the original history state that was date stamped at the time of import. The subsequent history states are listed in ascending order. The numbers in the middle column show the number of units up or down that the settings were shifted, and the right column lists all the new setting values.*

Figure 6.81 *In this example you can see that the sequence of steps applied to the image are recorded in the History panel in the order they were applied.*

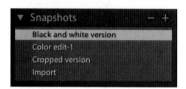

Figure 6.82   *The Snapshots panel is used to store saved history steps as variations.*

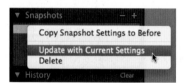

Figure 6.83   *Use the contextual menu to choose Update with Current Settings.*

You can also select Edit ⇨ Undo or press (⌘Z) (Mac) or (Ctrl)(Z) (PC) to undo the last step. As you repeatedly apply an undo, the history steps will be removed from the top of the list one by one. You can restore these steps by selecting Edit ⇨ Redo or using the (⌘)(⇧Shift)(Z) (Mac), (Ctrl)(⇧Shift)(Z) (PC) shortcut, but be warned that if you carry out a series of undos and then quit Lightroom, you will be unable to recover those later history steps. If you click the Clear button in the History panel, you can also delete all history steps associated with a photo. Clearing the list of history steps is a useful thing to do if the number of history steps is getting out of control and you want to manage the history list better.

Snapshots panel

Another way to manage your history states is to use the Snapshots feature. Snapshots can be used to store your favorite history states as a saved variation image setting (**Figure 6.82**). It is often more convenient to use snapshots to save specific history states in the Snapshots panel, as this can make it easier for you to retrieve history states that are of particular importance or usefulness, rather than use the History panel to wade through a long list of previously recorded history states.

To use the Snapshots feature, select a history state from the History panel that you want to record as a snapshot and click the plus button in the Snapshots panel. This creates a new untitled snapshot (if you want to delete a snapshot, click the minus button). Give the snapshot a name and press (Enter) to confirm the new Snapshot name. Snapshots are always arranged alphabetically in the Snapshots panel, and the preview in the Navigator panel updates as you roll the mouse over the snapshots in the list. To open a Snapshot, simply click on the snapshot to select it. If you want to update the settings for a particular snapshot, you can do so via the contextual menu: right-click on a snapshot and select Update with Current Settings (**Figure 6.83**). This will update any snapshot with the current history state.

You can use the Snapshots panel to save multiple variations of a master photo, such as a color-enhanced or a grayscale version of the original master (**Figure 6.84**).

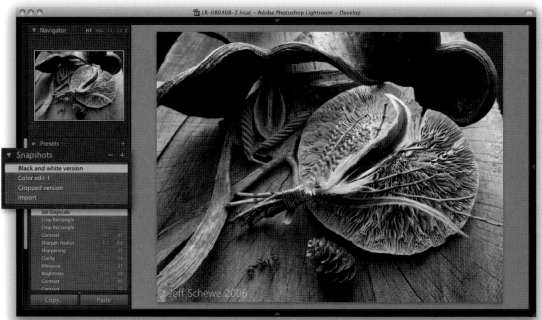

Figure 6.84 *In the top screen shot I saved a cropped version of the master image as a new snapshot titled "Cropped version." I then made a few adjustments using the Grayscale Mix settings and titled this Snapshot "Black and white version."*

Synchronizing snapshots

1. Here is an example of a photograph that has been optimized in the Develop module and the settings saved as a new snapshot.

2. I continued editing the photo and saved a new Color Enhanced snapshot. But you will notice that this snapshot included a lot of spotting work that had been carried out since saving the earlier snapshot.

3. It is quite likely you'll always be making late changes to the Develop settings that earlier saved snapshots could benefit from sharing. To resolve this you can do what I did here: go to the Settings menu and choose Sync Snapshots.

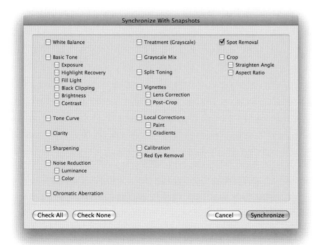

4. This will open the Synchronize With Snapshots dialog. In this instance I clicked the Check None button to deselect all the check boxes and then checked the Spot Removal option. I clicked Synchronize to update all the other snapshots in the Snapshots panel with the most recent Spot Removal settings.

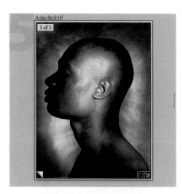

Figure 6.85 *Virtual copy images are automatically stacked with the master file. When viewing in the Library Grid view or Filmstrip, you can tell which images are virtual copies by the turned-page badge in the bottom-left corner.*

TIP

Once you have created one or more virtual copies, you can then choose the new **Set Copy as Master** command to make any virtual copy version of an image become the new master version (and make the old master version a virtual copy).

Easing the workflow

Making virtual copies

As well as making snapshot versions, you can also create virtual copies of your master photos by going to the Library module and choosing Photo ⇨ Create Virtual Copy (⌘ ' [Mac], (Ctrl) ' [PC]). This creates a virtual copy version of a master image that will automatically be grouped in a stack with the master photo (see **Figures 6.85** and **6.86**). As the name suggests, you are making a proxy version of the master. It may look and behave like a separate photo but is in fact a virtual representation of the master that you can edit in Lightroom as if it were a normal image.

So what is the difference between a virtual copy and a snapshot? A snapshot is a saved history state that's a variation of the master. You have the advantage of synchronizing specific edit adjustments across all the snapshot versions but lack the potential to create multiple versions as distinct entities that behave as if they were real copies of the master image. A virtual copy is therefore like an independent version of a snapshot, because when you create a virtual copy, you have more freedom to apply different types of edits and preview these edits as separate image versions. You could, for example, create various black and white renderings and experiment with alternative crops on each virtual copy version. **Figure 6.87** shows how you might use the Compare view mode to compare virtual copy versions of a photo alongside the master version. Virtual copies also make it possible for you to create collections that have different settings. For example, you could use the Create Virtual Copy command to create black and white versions as well as colorized versions from a master image, and then segregate these virtual copies into separate collections.

You also have the freedom to modify the metadata in individual copies. For example, you may want to modify and remove certain metadata from a virtual copy version so that when you create an export from the virtual copy, you can control which metadata items are visible in the exported file. Let's say you are running a location scouting service and send out images to clients that show the properties you recommend as photographic locations. You would normally store all relevant metadata about the location such as the address and zip code, but you would want to remove such commercially sensitive information when distributing these images to prospective clients.

Figure 6.86 *As you make new virtual copies of a master file, they are automatically stacked with the original master image.*

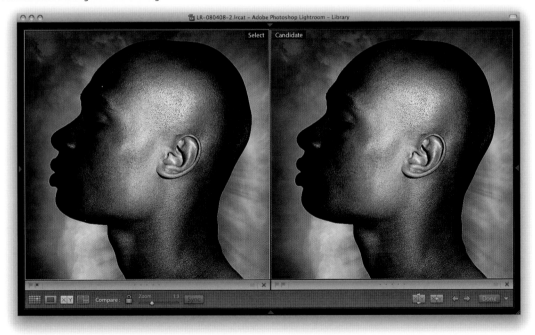

Figure 6.87 *One of the advantages of having virtual copy versions of a master file is that you can experiment with different treatments and use the Compare view to check them against the original master.*

Figure 6.88 *When more than one image is selected via the Filmstrip, the Sync button (with an ellipsis) lets you synchronize images in that selection via the Synchronize Settings dialog. When you hold down the* Alt *key, the ellipsis disappears, and clicking this button bypasses the Synchronize Settings dialog. Or you can hold down the* ⌘ *key (Mac) or* Ctrl *key (PC) to switch to the Auto Sync mode (bottom).*

Synchronizing Develop settings

Now that we have covered all the main Develop controls, let's look at ways Develop settings can be applied to multiple images. Whenever you have a selection of images active, the Previous button changes to show Sync... (**Figure 6.88**), and clicking this button will allow you to synchronize the Develop settings across two or more photos, based on the settings in the target (most selected) photo. In **Figure 6.89**, a number of photos have been selected in the Filmstrip and if you click the Sync... button, this will open the dialog shown in **Figure 6.90**, where you can then decide which settings you want to synchronize. If you click the Check All button, everything will be checked, which in some cases is the easiest and most practical option. If you click Check None, you can then pick and choose any subset of synchronization settings. Whether you choose to save everything or just a subset of settings, this will have important consequences for how the photos are synchronized. If you choose Check All, everything in the selected image will be copied and pasted. This might include the White Balance or Crop settings, and while these settings may be relevant for the target image, you won't necessarily always want to share them with all the other photos. Sometimes you need to think carefully about which specific settings you should synchronize. If not, you can end up overwriting settings that should have been left as they were (although you can always recover the previous image version via the History panel on an image-by-image basis). For example, if your imported photos have the Camera Default settings applied for Sharpening, Noise Reduction, and Calibration, you will want to be extra careful not to overwrite those settings.

If you hold down the Alt key, the Sync button loses the ellipsis, and clicking it bypasses the Synchronize Settings dialog and applies a synchronization based the last used Synchronize settings. If you ⌘–click (Mac), Ctrl–click (PC) the Sync button, it switches to Auto Sync mode and stays as such until you click the Auto Sync button to revert back to Sync mode again. In Auto Sync mode you first make a selection of photos, and then as you adjust the Develop settings for the most selected image, you will see these adjustments propagated across all the images in the selection. Auto Sync therefore behaves a bit like a Quick Develop panel mode for the Develop module. Lastly, there is the Reset button, which can be used whenever you want to reset photos back to their Lightroom default settings.

Figure 6.89 *The Develop settings in the most selected photo can be synchronized with all the other photos in a selection by clicking the Sync (with an ellipsis) button. The selected photos in the Filmstrip are indicated with a gray surround, and the most selected photo is the one with the lightest gray color.*

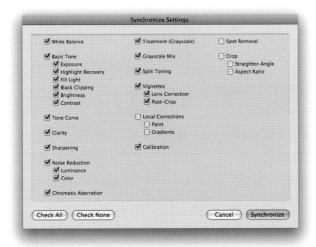

Figure 6.90 *The Synchronize Settings dialog. Use the Check All settings option with caution since synchronizing everything may overwrite some settings in the selected photos.*

TIP

You can also use ⌘⇧Shift S (Mac) or Ctrl ⇧Shift S (PC) to open the Synchronize Settings dialog.

NOTE

To access the latest version of Camera Raw for Photoshop and Bridge, go to the Adobe website: www.adobe.com/products/Photoshop/cameraraw.html.

NOTE

Camera Raw development is mainy linked to specific versions of Photoshop. At the time of this writing, the latest version of Camera Raw is version 4.4.1 for Photoshop CS3 only. This version of Camera Raw supports all the latest cameras and Camera Raw features for CS3. When a new version of Photoshop comes out, there will be an update to the Camera Raw spec that we would expect to include the features that are new to Lightroom 2. Now, although the Camera Raw plug-in for Photoshop CS3 allows CS3 users the ability to read Lightroom 2 edits, there won't be any further functionality added to the Camera Raw plug-in for for Photoshop CS3 users. The upshot of this is that if you want Camera Raw to allow full editing as you have in Lightroom 2, you will need at some point to upgrade Photoshop.

Lightroom and Camera Raw

As you are probably aware, Adobe Photoshop Lightroom and Adobe Camera Raw (as part of the Adobe Photoshop program) both share the same Camera Raw processing engine. This means that any development adjustments that are applied in one program can be recognized and read by the other. However, there are a few things you need to bear in mind here.

Viewing Lightroom edits in Camera Raw

The first point to remember is to always save the metadata edits out to the files' XMP space if you want Camera Raw to be able to read the Develop adjustments that have been applied in Lightroom. If you don't save the metadata to the files' XMP space, the edit changes you make will not be read by Camera Raw. But the second and more important point is that only the latest versions of Camera Raw are going to be capable of reading all the Develop adjustments that have been applied in Lightroom. To coincide with the launch of Lightroom 2, a new version of Camera Raw (version 4.5) has been released for Photoshop CS3, which while it does not include all the new Develop controls found in Lightroom 2, is capable of reading and processing all Lightroom 2 edits. So if you are using Photoshop CS3 and have just acquired Lightroom 2, you will want to download the latest free Camera Raw update for CS3. This will then allow you to open up Lightroom 2 edited images via Camera Raw, which can read things like localized corrections, negative Clarity, and post-crop vignettes, but you just won't have the tools to edit these settings. I think it is fair to assume that the new Lightroom 2 Develop features will eventually be included in a later version of Photoshop, at which point there will also be a later version of Camera Raw for those Photoshop users only.

Viewing Camera Raw edits in Lightroom

If you want your Camera Raw edits to be visible in Lightroom, you need to make sure that the image adjustments applied in Camera Raw are also saved to the file's XMP space. To do this, launch Bridge and choose Camera Raw Preferences from the Bridge menu. This will open the dialog shown in **Figure 6.91**. Select "Sidecar .xmp files" from the "Save image settings in" menu. This ensures that Camera Raw settings are always saved to the XMP space by default.

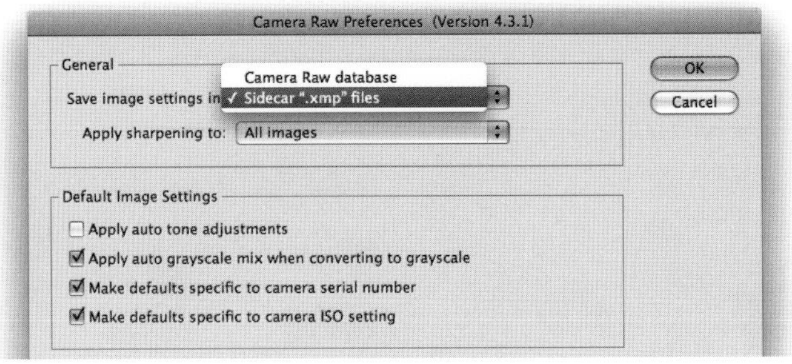

Figure 6.91 *To keep the Camera Raw edits in sync with Lightroom, you need to make sure that the Camera Raw settings are always saved to the .xmp files.*

Keeping Lightroom edits in sync

If Lightroom detects that a file's metadata has been edited externally, it should display a metadata status conflict warning in the grid cell with an upward arrow. A click on this arrow opens the dialog shown in **Figure 6.92**. If you see no warning icon, but have good reason to believe that the metadata has been updated, then choose Metadata ⇨ Read Metadata from files (in the Library module), or Photo ⇨ Read Metadata from file (in the Develop module). Alternatively, choose Library ⇨ Synchronize Folder (**Figure 6.93**). The Synchronize Folder command also runs a quick check to make sure that everything is in sync between Lightroom and any edit changes that may have been applied externally.

Figure 6.92 *The metadata status change warning dialog.*

Figure 6.93 *The Synchronize Folder command can run a quick scan for updates.*

Synchronizing Lightroom with Camera Raw

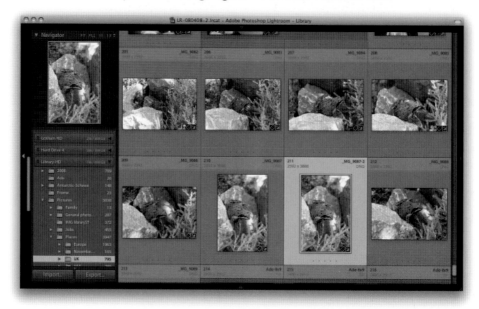

1. This shows a simple illustration of how to keep a set of photos in sync when switching between Lightroom and Camera Raw. In this first screen shot we see a folder view of photos in Lightroom that have been optimized for the best tone contrast and color.

2. Over in Camera Raw, I opened the same selection of photos, converted one of the pictures to grayscale, and synchronized this setting change across all the selected images.

3. When I returned to Lightroom, the "out-of-sync" photos displayed a metadata status change warning icon with an exclamation mark, indicating a metadata conflict. I clicked the warning icon and then clicked the Import Settings from Disk button in the dialog shown here to import the Camera Raw adjusted settings into Lightroom.

TIP

If you don't see a metadata status warning where there should be (this can happen), then choose Metadata ⇨ Read metadata from file.

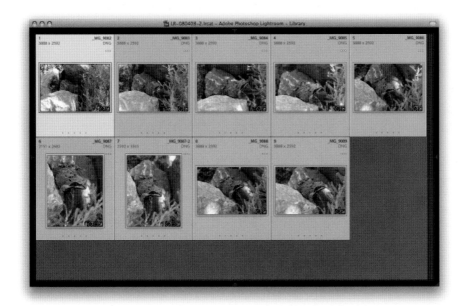

4. The externally adjusted settings now appear updated in Lightroom.

Figure 6.94 *The Copy and Paste buttons are located in the bottom left in the Develop module.*

Copying and pasting Develop settings

Another way to synchronize images is to copy and paste the Develop settings from one photo to another (**Figure 6.94**). In the Develop module, select a photo from the Filmstrip and click the Copy button (or use the ⌘C [Mac], Ctrl C [PC] shortcut). The Copy Settings dialog shown in **Figure 6.95** opens, which allows you to specify the settings that you want to copy. Note that if you Alt-click the Copy button, you can bypass this Copy Settings dialog completely (or use ⌘ Alt C [Mac], Ctrl Alt C [PC]). So if you had previously clicked the Check All button to check all the settings in the Copy Settings dialog, Alt-clicking the Copy button will copy all settings without showing the dialog. Once you have copied the Develop settings, you can then select a photo or a selection of photos via the Library module Grid view or Filmstrip and click the Paste button to apply the current copied settings (or use the ⌘V [Mac] or Ctrl V [PC] shortcut).

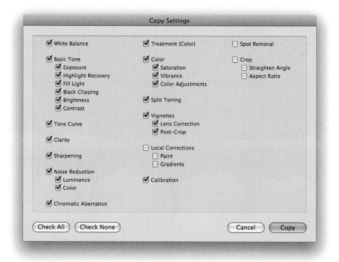

Figure 6.95 *The Copy Settings dialog copies all the settings except the Spot Removal and Crop.*

Copying and pasting settings in the Library module

When working in the Library module you need to rely on the following shortcuts: press ⌘ ⇧ Shift C (Mac) or Ctrl ⇧ Shift C (PC) to copy the settings, ⌘ ⇧ Shift V (Mac) or Ctrl ⇧ Shift V (PC) to paste, and use ⌘ Alt V (Mac) or Ctrl Alt V (PC) to apply previous settings.

Applying a previous Develop setting

As you navigate the Filmstrip, Lightroom temporarily stores the Develop settings for each photo you click on and thereby allows you to apply a previous Develop setting to any photo.

NOTE

When applying a previous Develop setting there is no Copy Setting dialog. A previous setting applies all the Develop settings from the previously selected photo.

NOTE

If more than one photo is selected in the Filmstrip, the Previous button will change to say Sync... If you wish to override this behavior you can do so by holding down the Shift key, as this reverts the button to the previous mode of operation. Lightroom then applies a copy of all the settings from the previously selected photo to the selected photos.

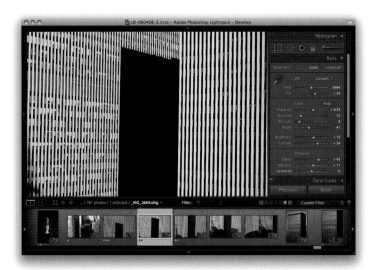

1. Select a photo in the Filmstrip and Lightroom automatically stores the Develop settings as a Copy All setting.

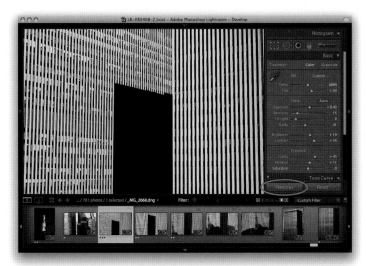

2. If you select another photo in the Filmstrip, such as the one next to it, and click the Previous button, this will paste all the Develop settings from the previously selected photo.

Saving Develop settings as presets

Copying and applying settings is useful in the short term, but if you create a setting that you are likely to reuse again, it is a good idea to save it as a preset. **Figure 6.96** shows an expanded view of the Develop module Presets panel in which you can see a list of custom preset settings. The Lightroom Presets folder is installed with Lightroom and has enough presets to help get you started, but you can add your own Develop presets by clicking the plus button at the top the Presets panel. This opens the New Develop Preset dialog shown in **Figure 6.97**, where you can choose which settings you want to have included in the preset. When you have decided which settings to check, give the preset a name, choose a folder location to save the preset to, and click the Create button to add it as a new preset to the list.

The default Lightroom Presets folder cannot be edited—you can't delete or add presets to this folder. But any new presets that you add are automatically added to a folder called *User Presets*. If you want to better organize your Develop settings, organize your presets into different folder groupings. You will notice in Figure 6.97 that I have a number of added preset folders and they always appear listed in alphabetical order below the Lightroom Presets folder.

Figure 6.96 *As you roll the cursor over the Presets list, the Navigator updates to show you a quick preview of how the Preset settings will affect the image. You can update existing settings by holding down the* Ctrl *key (Mac) or right-clicking (PC) to reveal a contextual menu for the presets. Click the minus button to remove a selected preset from the list.*

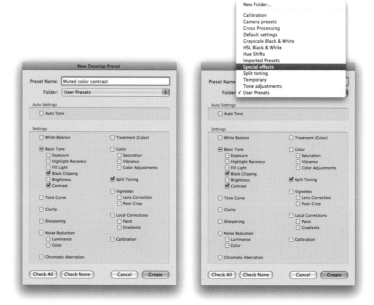

Figure 6.97 *In the New Develop Preset dialog, check the items you want to include in a preset, give the preset a name, and decide which folder to save the preset to.*

To add a new folder to the Presets list, right-click anywhere inside the Presets folder to open a contextual menu like the one shown in **Figure 6.98**, and choose New Folder, which opens the New Folder dialog (**Figure 6.99**). Give the folder a name and it will appear added to the Presets list. You can now organize your presets by dragging them into the folders that you have just created.

Auto Tone preset adjustments

The Auto Tone option is potentially useful for those times when you want to include an Auto Tone adjustment as part of a preset. In some instances this might be considered a useful item to include in a preset because you can get Lightroom to combine an autocorrection in combination with other types of Develop adjustments. On the other hand, because it can lead to different tone settings being applied to each image, this might not always produce the results you were after, even though the Auto Tone logic has been improved in Lightroom 2. So just be aware of this when you include Auto Tone in a saved Develop preset setting and that the results may sometimes be unpredictable.

The art of creating Develop presets

Develop presets have proved incredibly popular. Lots of Lightroom users have got into sharing their preset creations. If you are looking for inspiration, visit Richard Earney's *Inside Lightroom* site where there are lots of different presets that you can download and import into the Develop Presets panel: http://inside-lightroom.com/. While it is impossible to encapsulate a complete Develop module look in a single preset, it seems to me that the best way to use Develop presets is to break them down into smaller chunks. In my experience the trick is to save as few settings as possible when you create a Develop preset. What we often see are Develop presets where the creator checks too many boxes and ends up with a preset that adjusts not just the settings it needs to adjust, but other settings as well. In many cases it is not always obvious which settings a Develop setting is meant to be altering, and applying the preset overwrites settings that it shouldn't. Or the creator includes White Balance or Exposure settings that may have been relevant for the pictures the creator tested the setting with, but are not necessarily suited for other people's photographs. On the next page I provide a quick guide for creating neatly trimmed Develop presets.

Figure 6.98 *You can use the contextual menu to import new presets. If you have been sent a Develop preset or have just downloaded one, use the contextual menu shown here to select Import and then locate the preset (or presets) you wish to add.*

Figure 6.99 *You can also use the above contextual menu to add a new folder to the Presets list.*

1. Here is a photograph that I had tweaked in the Develop module and that was ready for me to save as a new preset.

TIP

The most important lesson to learn here is this: Only save the settings that you need to save when creating a preset.

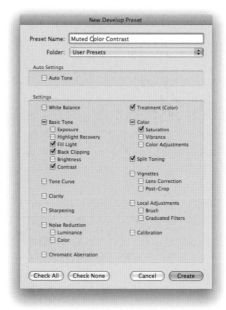

2. I clicked the Presets panel's plus icon to open the New Develop Preset dialog and checked only those settings that were key to applying the desired color effect. I named the Preset setting *Muted Color Contrast* and saved it to a folder in the Presets panel called *Special effects*.

Understanding how presets work

Even with a Develop setting like the one shown in **Figure 6.100**, it can still get confusing, because this Develop preset is doing several things in one shot. It is raising the threshold for the black clipping point and boosting the contrast, and it is reducing the color saturation and applying a split tone color effect. Including all this in one preset has its disadvantages and can also lead to messy situations like that shown in **Figure 6.101**.

TIP

A safe way to work with Develop presets is to apply a preset and then use ⌘ Z (Mac), Ctrl Z (PC) to undo it before trying out another one.

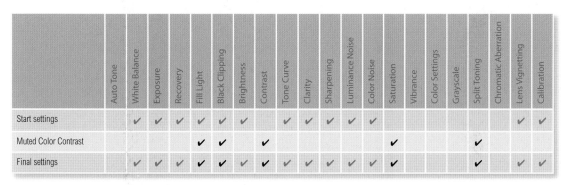

	Auto Tone	White Balance	Exposure	Recovery	Fill Light	Black Clipping	Brightness	Contrast	Tone Curve	Clarity	Sharpening	Luminance Noise	Color Noise	Saturation	Vibrance	Color Settings	Grayscale	Split Toning	Chromatic Aberration	Lens Vignetting	Calibration
Start settings		✔	✔	✔	✔	✔	✔		✔	✔	✔	✔	✔							✔	✔
Muted Color Contrast						✔	✔	✔						✔				✔			
Final settings		✔	✔	✔	✔	✔	✔	✔	✔	✔	✔	✔	✔	✔				✔		✔	✔

Figure 6.100 *This chart summarizes the outcome of a single Develop preset adjustment. In the Final settings row, the green tick marks represent the settings that were adjusted in the original image version and remained unaltered afterward. The black tick marks represent those settings that are new and have been changed.*

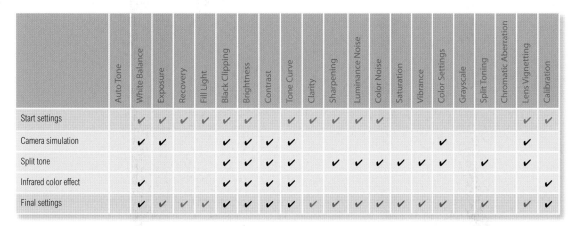

	Auto Tone	White Balance	Exposure	Recovery	Fill Light	Black Clipping	Brightness	Contrast	Tone Curve	Clarity	Sharpening	Luminance Noise	Color Noise	Saturation	Vibrance	Color Settings	Grayscale	Split Toning	Chromatic Aberration	Lens Vignetting	Calibration
Start settings		✔	✔	✔	✔	✔	✔		✔	✔	✔	✔	✔							✔	✔
Camera simulation		✔	✔			✔	✔	✔	✔							✔				✔	
Split tone						✔	✔	✔	✔		✔	✔	✔	✔	✔	✔		✔		✔	
Infrared color effect		✔				✔	✔	✔	✔												✔
Final settings		✔	✔	✔	✔	✔	✔	✔	✔	✔	✔	✔	✔	✔	✔	✔		✔		✔	✔

Figure 6.101 *This chart shows you what can happen when you apply a series of Develop presets. In the Final settings row, the green tick marks represent the settings that were adjusted in the original image version and remained unaltered at the end. The black tick marks again represent the settings that are new or have been changed. However, the red tick marks represent the settings that have changed cumulatively during the process of trying out different Develop presets (but were not part of the last applied preset). What this highlights is the fact that when "Infrared color effect" was selected as a final setting, the Develop settings had already been contaminated by the previously selected Develop presets.*

How to prevent preset contamination

As I mentioned earlier, one way I like to work with presets is to trim them down so that each preset performs a discrete task, such as a grayscale conversion or a split tone coloring effect. That way I have more options to mix and match the preset settings and prevent getting into a situation like the one shown in Figure 6.101 where the end result is a contaminated mess. For example, I may apply one preset to modify the contrast and another preset to apply a coloring effect. I then keep these stored in separate preset folders so that it is easy for me to locate all the presets that can be used for applying different grayscale conversions or cross processing effects. The chart shown in **Figure 6.102** summarizes the steps that are described over the next few pages. You will notice how I added a series of presets to build an effect. Therefore, when applying different split tone effects I can click on all the presets in turn to see a full-screen view of what the result will look like.

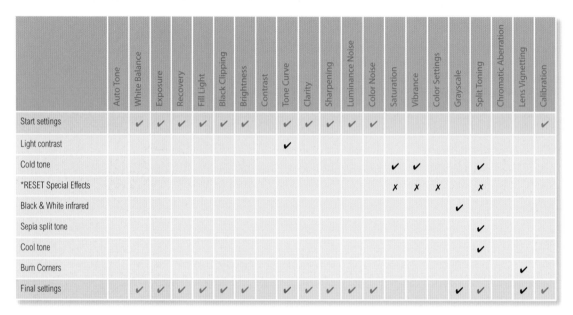

	Auto Tone	White Balance	Exposure	Recovery	Fill Light	Black Clipping	Brightness	Contrast	Tone Curve	Clarity	Sharpening	Luminance Noise	Color Noise	Saturation	Vibrance	Color Settings	Grayscale	Split Toning	Chromatic Aberration	Lens Vignetting	Calibration
Start settings		✔	✔	✔	✔	✔	✔		✔	✔	✔	✔	✔								✔
Light contrast									✔												
Cold tone														✔	✔			✔			
*RESET Special Effects														✗	✗	✗		✗			
Black & White infrared																	✔				
Sepia split tone																		✔			
Cool tone																		✔			
Burn Corners																				✔	
Final settings		✔	✔	✔	✔	✔	✔		✔	✔	✔	✔	✔				✔	✔		✔	✔

Figure 6.102 *The alternative approach is to break the Develop presets down into smaller chunks so that you use a sequence of Develop presets to build an effect. This chart summarizes the series of Develop preset steps that begin on the opposite page. The final settings include a couple of red tick marks where the settings have changed cumulatively, but this does not matter as much as in the Figure 6.99 example because the whole point is to build up the settings one step at a time. You will notice that I included a *RESET Special Effects step. This preset is designed to cancel out previous preset settings and therefore acts like a "clear settings" button. To illustrate this I have used crosses to indicate that these items are returned to their default settings.*

1. To begin with I tried out some tone adjustment presets and chose a Light Contrast tone curve preset to apply a moderate contrast boost to the original color version of this image.

2. I also wanted to try out some special effect coloring presets, so selected a "Cold tone" preset from my Special Effects preset folder. Should I wish to reset the preset settings used here and move on to try something different, I have included a RESET setting in each folder that can be used to reset the relevant sliders to zero.

3. After resetting the Cold tone preset I expanded the Grayscale Black & White preset folder and applied a Black and White Infrared grayscale preset to see what a monochrome conversion looked like.

4. Next I went to the Split Tone folder and tried different Split Tone presets. Note that if you have the Navigator panel open, you can hover the mouse over the preset list to preview each preset effect before applying.

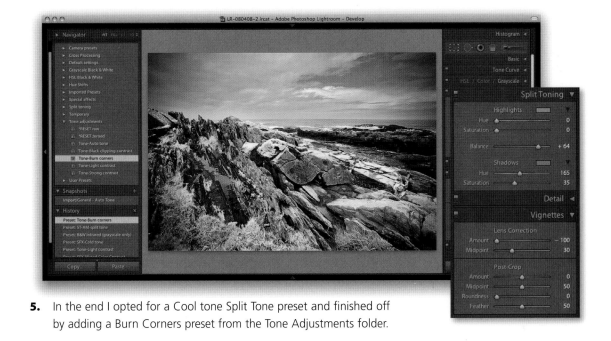

5. In the end I opted for a Cool tone Split Tone preset and finished off by adding a Burn Corners preset from the Tone Adjustments folder.

Reset settings

I will end this section by elaborating a little more on the use of the Reset preset settings such as the one referred to in Step 2. With the Develop preset folder method I use here, I have added a preset to each folder that is named *RESET*. This is a preset setting that undoes any of the presets that have been applied in that particular folder. In the case of the Grayscale Black & White folder, I have a preset called *RESET grayscale* that switches from Grayscale to Color mode. I created it by selecting a photo in color mode and created a new preset in which I checked only the Treatment (Color) check box (as shown in **Figure 6.103**). For all the other preset folders I similarly created presets such as a *RESET Split Tone* setting that uses zero Split Tone Saturation settings. The naming of these presets isn't critical; I prefer to use all caps so that the reset presets stand out more and I place an asterisk at the beginning of the name so that the reset preset always appears listed first in each folder.

Figure 6.103 *Here is an example of a preset that I created for converting a grayscale setting back to Color mode again. All I had to do was select any Color mode image and save a preset with the Treatment (Color) box checked.*

How to set default camera Develop settings

Any feature that saves you time is always welcome. Very often you will find that as you import pictures from a particular camera shot at a certain ISO speed, you end up wanting to apply the same Develop settings. For example, if you shoot with more than one digital camera you may want to create a custom camera calibration setting for each separate camera body. In addition, you may want to adjust the noise reduction settings in the Detail panel to set the level of noise reduction that is likely to be required at specific ISO settings.

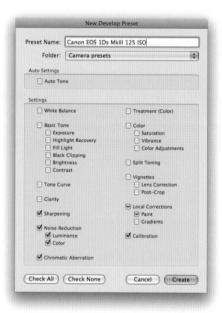

1. One way you might use this feature would be to create a new preset folder called "Camera Presets" and within that save the Develop settings for all the different ISO settings associated with a particular camera. Gather together a collection of sample photos shot with a particular camera that are representative of how the camera performs at different ISO settings. Work on each photo to achieve the best Sharpening, Noise Reduction, and Camera Calibration (see page 310–311), and as you do this, save the settings as new presets. Be sure to check only the items that are relevant for inclusion in the Develop preset setting such as Sharpening, Noise Reduction, and Camera Calibration. You don't want to check any of the other items that are available here because you don't want a camera-specific Develop setting to affect more than the above Develop settings.

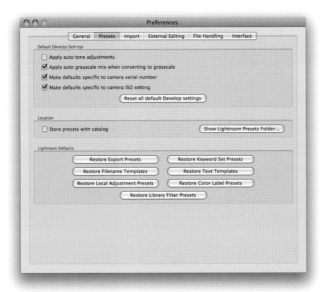

2. Go to the Lightroom Presets preferences and make sure that "Make defaults specific to camera ISO setting" is checked. It is important that you do this first before proceeding to the next step. You can also check "Make defaults specific to camera serial number" if you want the settings to be camera body specific.

3. Now go back to the photos you worked on at Step 1 and select each in turn. As you do so, choose Develop ⇨ Set Default Settings. This will open the dialog shown here, where you need to click the Update to Current Settings button. Do this and Lightroom automatically makes this the default setting for all newly imported photos that match the same criteria of matching camera model, serial number, and ISO setting. But remember that you have only created what amounts to a default setting. If you were to choose a specific setting in the Import Photo dialog, or apply a Develop setting later that included Sharpening, Noise Reduction, or Calibration subsettings, those settings would override the camera default setting values.

Photograph: L Train, Chicago © Martin Evening 2006
Canon EOS 1Ds Mk II | 44 mm | 640 ISO | f9.0 @ 1/200th

7 The art of black and white

How to achieve full creative control over your black and white conversions

I began my photographic career learning how to photograph and print in black and white and ever since then I have retained an enduring passion for black and white photography. In this respect, Lightroom does not disappoint because the Develop module tools provide the best environment I can think of to get the most creative control possible out of your color to black and white conversions.

The techniques described in this chapter will show you the three main ways to convert a photo to black and white; where you will find out how to master the Grayscale sliders in manual, auto, and target adjustment mode; how to work with the White Balance sliders while in grayscale mode; and how to use the HSL panel controls as an alternative approach to grayscale conversions. I also show how to achieve particular styles such as the black and white infrared look as well as how to work with the Split Tone panel to colorize not just for black and white images, but color photographs too.

There is one other method of
converting a color image to black
and white that isn't covered in this
chapter: using the Saturation slider.
It is possible to convert an image
from color to black and white by
dragging the Saturation slider fully
to the left. You can then modify the
color to black and white conversion
by adjusting the color controls such
as the White Balance Temperature
sliders and Calibration panel controls.
This works, but in my opinion it is an
unnecessarily convoluted approach
when you have all the controls you
need in the Grayscale Mixer panel as
well as the HSL desaturate method I
describe at the end of this chapter.

Black and white conversions

Black and white Develop controls

The easiest way to convert a color image to monochrome is to click
the Grayscale button in the Basic panel. Or, you can click Grayscale
in the HSL / Color / Grayscale panel, or use the V keyboard shortcut.
Any of these methods immediately activates the Grayscale controls
and converts the photograph to black and white (**Figure 7.1**). The
term "grayscale" is a little misleading, since Lightroom is not actually
converting a color image to grayscale mode. Rather, it is creating a
desaturated version of the color original that remains in RGB mode.
Lightroom blends the grayscale information contained in the individual
red, green, and blue channels that make up a composite RGB image.
If you have ever played with the Channel Mixer controls or the Black &
White adjustment in Photoshop, the Grayscale controls and conversion
process will appear familiar. In Lightroom, there are eight color slider
controls to play with, and they provide you with some nice, subtle
control over how the color component channels are blended in the
conversion process. But more subtle can also mean more complex, so
to make things a little easier, the Grayscale panel offers an Auto button
that, when you click it, applies an automatic monochrome conversion
that is determined by the White Balance setting in the Basic panel. You
can then vary the grayscale conversion by adjusting the Temperature
and Tint sliders up in the Basic panel.

When you switch to Grayscale mode you have full control over the individual sliders, and they can be adjusted any way you like to create custom black and white conversions. The great thing about the Lightroom
Grayscale panel is how the tonal balance of the image automatically
compensates for any adjustments you make. Even so, it may still be
necessary to revisit the Basic panel and readjust the Tone controls such
as the Exposure, Brightness, and Contrast after you have made a major
Grayscale panel adjustment. The Split Toning panel can be used to add
split tone color effects to a black and white image, but can also be
used on color originals to produce cross-processing effects. As always,
favorite Develop settings can be saved as presets in the Presets panel,
and a couple of black and white presets are there for you to play with,
such as the *Antique Grayscale* preset highlighted in Figure 7.1.

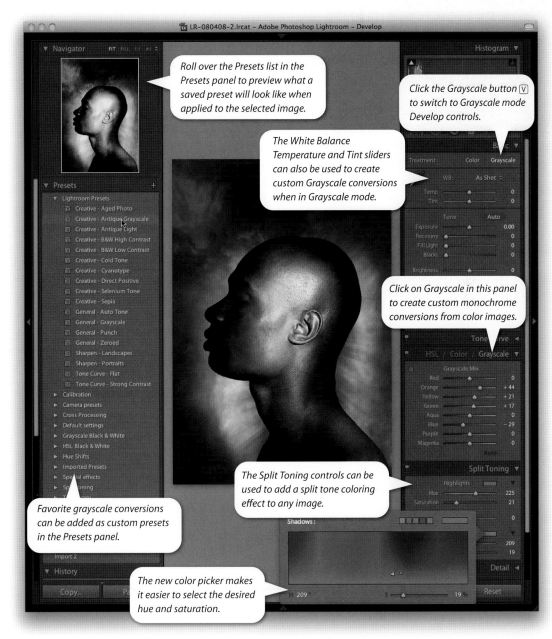

Roll over the Presets list in the Presets panel to preview what a saved preset will look like when applied to the selected image.

Click the Grayscale button ⓥ to switch to Grayscale mode Develop controls.

The White Balance Temperature and Tint sliders can also be used to create custom Grayscale conversions when in Grayscale mode.

Click on Grayscale in this panel to create custom monochrome conversions from color images.

The Split Toning controls can be used to add a split tone coloring effect to any image.

Favorite grayscale conversions can be added as custom presets in the Presets panel.

The new color picker makes it easier to select the desired hue and saturation.

Figure 7.1 *In this screen shot of the Develop module, I have highlighted the main black and white adjustment controls.*

Figure 7.2 *An RGB image consists of three grayscale channels that describe the red, green, and blue color information at the time of capture. The red, green, and blue information is then combined together to describe the RGB component image. Here already you can see three quite different black and white interpretations of the original color photograph.*

Black and white conversion options

In the early days of black and white photography, film emulsions were limited in their color response. Most of these film emulsions were mainly sensitive to blue light only, which is why the skies in old photographs often appear white, and the photographer could process their films in the darkroom using a red safe light. As film emulsion technology improved, panchromatic black and white films began to emerge, and film photographers were able to creatively exploit the improved color sensitivity in these modern film emulsions. This next section shows you how to continue that tradition when working with digital captures.

An RGB color image such as a raw-processed digital capture is made up of three grayscale images that are based on the luminance information recorded of the original scene as it passed through red, green, and blue filters overlaying the photosites on the camera sensor. The RGB color image you preview on the computer screen is a composite of those three grayscale channels as displayed through the tiny red, green, and blue filters in the LCD screen. **Figure 7.2** shows the individual color channels that make up the RGB full-color image. Before I explain how to use the Grayscale controls, I want to convey the general principle of how the three RGB color channels can be blended to produce different types of black and white conversions such as those in **Figure 7.3**.

How not to convert

I often hear of photographers who unnecessarily limit their black and white options, because they are simply unaware of the grayscale conversion techniques that use all the color channels in a color image. For example, some people set their cameras to shoot in a black and white JPEG mode. This restricts not only the tone adjustment options, but also the black and white conversion options. The camera's onboard image processor decides on the fly how to blend the color channel information and produce a fixed color to black and white conversion. You are consequently left with no room to maneuver, because all the color data is thrown away during the in-camera JPEG conversion process. Then there is the RGB to Lab mode method in which you delete the a and b channels and convert the remaining Lightness channel to Grayscale mode. I suppose I better be careful of what I say about Lab mode editing because of late there has been a resurgence of interest in the Lab color space. But I would say that there is nothing to be gained from this approach, because yet again, you are throwing away all the color data before you make the conversion.

Grayscale adjustments

There are eight Grayscale panel sliders: Red, Orange, Yellow, Green, Aqua, Blue, Purple and Magenta. Adjusting these sliders will allow you to lighten or darken these respective colors in the original color image when calculating the grayscale conversion.

Figure 7.3 *Figure 7.2 showed how an RGB image is composed of three separate grayscale channels representing the red, green, and blue colors in the final composite. The Grayscale Mix allows you to blend the color channel information in all sorts of ways to produce very different monochrome conversions from a color original.*

Temperature slider conversions

Let's now look at how to use a Grayscale conversion in Lightroom to convert a color image (**Figure 7.4**) to black and white. As just mentioned, one method is to click the Grayscale button in the Basic panel and adjust the White Balance settings. **Figure 7.5** shows two possible black and white outcomes that can be achieved by dragging the temperature (Temp) slider in the Basic panel and then clicking the Auto-Adjust button in the Grayscale section of the HSL / Color / Grayscale panel. The top version in Figure 7.5 shows a white balance with a warm bias. Notice that the blue sky tones appear darker when they are converted this way. When the Temp slider is dragged in the opposite direction as seen in the bottom picture, the blue sky tones and the cactus plants look lighter. You can also adjust the Tint slider as well. For example, dragging the Tint slider to the left (for a greener white balance) would make the cactus plants appear even lighter relative to the other tones. The optimum settings very much depend on the subject matter. In our next exercise, I show you how to optimize a black and white conversion for a color portrait using just the White Balance and Grayscale sliders.

Figure 7.4 *Here is a color original. Compare the monochrome conversions on the next page with the red, green, and blue colors in this photograph.*

Figure 7.5   *Here are two grayscale mode versions of the color image shown in Figure 7.4. If you adjust the White Balance settings and then click the Auto button in the Grayscale panel, the Grayscale sliders will adjust accordingly. The top version shows a warm white balance temperature conversion followed by an auto grayscale adjustment and the bottom version shows a cool white balance temperature conversion followed by an auto grayscale adjustment. Note the different outcomes in these grayscale conversions.*

Auto grayscale plus white balance adjustments

1. Let's look at how the Grayscale and White Balance Temp Slider controls can affect a conversion. Here is a color photograph of the actor Jonathan Jackson, photographed by Greg Gorman. This photograph uses the default Develop settings in Lightroom.

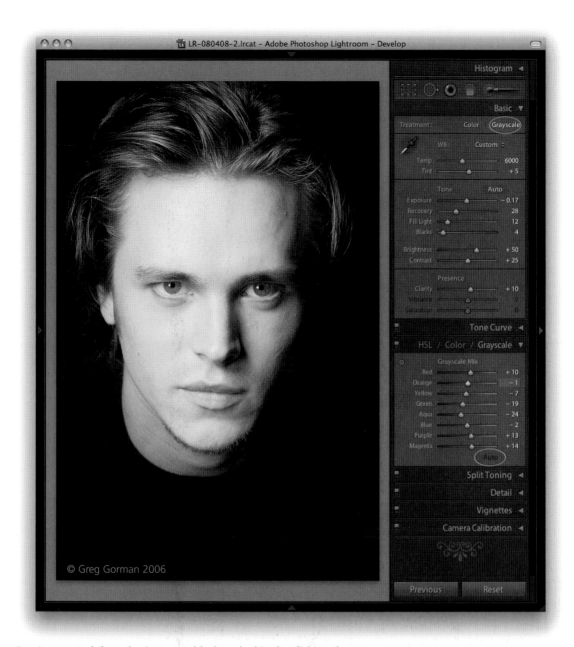

© Greg Gorman 2006

2. I converted the color image to black and white by clicking the Grayscale button in the Basic panel (circled). I then clicked the Auto button (also circled) in the Grayscale panel to apply an auto adjustment that was based on the current White Balance Temperature and Tint settings. As default conversions go, this is not a bad starting point to work from.

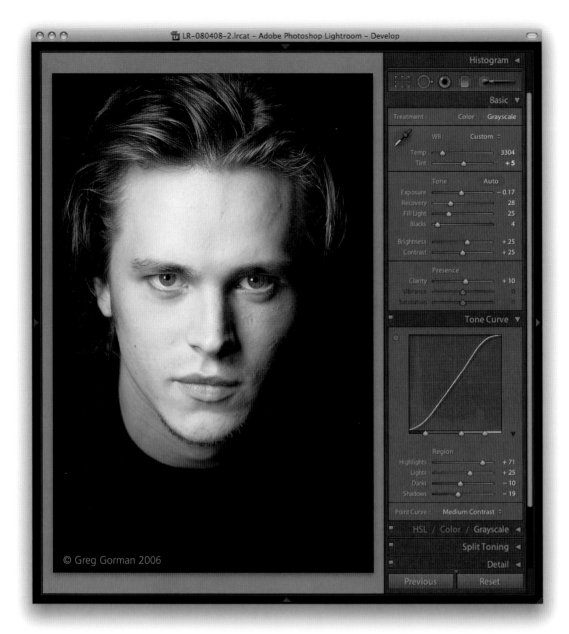

3. I then adjusted the White Balance Temp slider to find an optimum setting that would yield the best skin tone contrast and kept clicking the Auto-Adjust button to update the Grayscale settings. I also adjusted the Tone Curve. The goal here was to increase the tonal contrast to produce deep black shadows while preserving all the information in the skin tones.

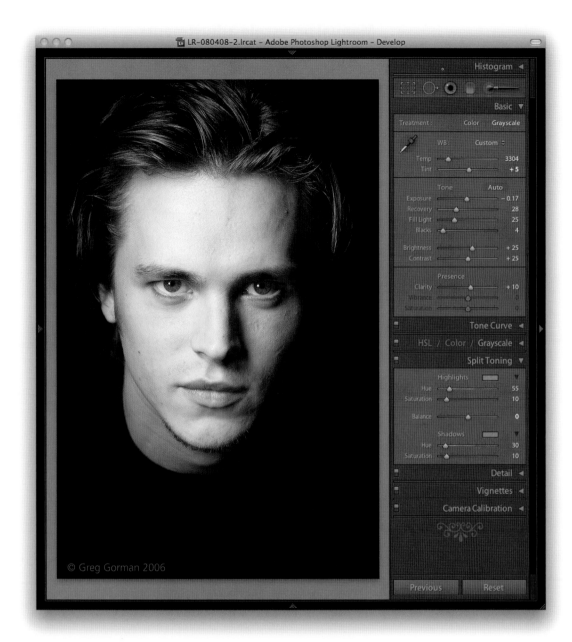

4. I also wanted to add some subtle color toning to the adjusted photo. So I used the Split Toning panel to add a red highlight and yellow shadow split tone (black and white split tones are covered in the next section).

Manual grayscale adjustments

In manual mode, the Grayscale panel gives you almost unlimited freedom to create custom blends that suit the photographs you are working on. This is where the real fun begins, because custom grayscale blends give you complete control over how light or dark certain colors will be rendered in the black and white converted version. The following steps show how I was able to maximize the contrast in the sky and the clouds. Notice that I gave the Aqua and Blue sliders negative values because I wanted these colors to render darker. Also notice how the combination of a cooler white balance plus the Grayscale adjustments further enhanced the sky contrast. Remember, the grayscale outcome is always influenced by the white balance setting, so it is often useful to try out different white balance adjustments as you search for the best combination, as shown in the following steps.

1. In this example the colors and tones were optimized using the Basic and Tone Curve panels. This screen shot shows the color original alongside a black and white version that used the Auto Grayscale setting. This default grayscale conversion was nowhere near as dramatic as I would have liked.

2. This second version shows the same image after I made some custom edits using the Grayscale sliders. I clicked the Target Adjustment Tool button (circled), moved the mouse over the rocks, and dragged upward to lighten selected colors. I then moved the mouse over the sky and dragged downward to darken and add more contrast to the clouds. Notice that I also adjusted the White Balance Temp slider to make the white balance setting cooler and this in turn made the grayscale-adjusted version look even more contrasty.

TIP

You can also press ⌘ Alt Shift G (Mac) or Ctrl Alt Shift G (PC) to enable the Tone Curve Target Adjustment tool in the Grayscale panel and press ⌘ Alt Shift N (Mac) or Ctrl Alt Shift N (PC) to turn it off again.

Grayscale slider tip

If you want to create dramatic black and white conversions, move the sliders farther apart and try moving two or more sliders in unison. In the above example, I moved the Aqua and Blues sliders to the left. This created the most dramatic tonal contrast based in the opposing colors of the warm rocks against a cloudy blue sky. The following section shows how to push Lightroom grayscale conversions to even greater extremes.

Black and white infrared effect

Now watch what happens when you take the White Balance settings to extremes before applying a Grayscale conversion. The following black and white infrared technique illustrates just one of the many ways you can make creative grayscale conversions in Lightroom.

1. Here is the before version, in which shows a country garden scene with a nice mix of foliage—ideal to to demonstrate the black and white infrared effect. All I did here was optimize the tones and apply a gradient at the bottom to darken the grass slightly.

2. To begin creating the fake black and white infrared look, I started with the image in Color mode, made the White Balance Temp slightly cooler, and applied a full negative Tint adjustment to the white balance to make the green colors, that is, the leaf foliage, as bright green as possible (but without actually clipping any important areas of detail).

3. I then clicked the Grayscale button in the HSL / Color / Grayscale panel to convert the photograph to black and white. To get the full infrared look you see here, it is important to note that I set the Yellow and Green sliders in the Grayscale panel to maximum and the Aqua slider to 50%. I also adjusted some of the Basic panel settings. In particular, I set the Recovery slider to –100%, which helped me preserve some of the delicate tone information in the leaves. I set the Clarity slider to –100%, because this created a diffused printing effect that added a nice, soft glow to the photograph.

4. Lastly, I went to the Split Tone panel to add a split tone coloring effect, which added some warmth to the highlights and a slight blue cast to the shadows. The settings shown here worked well for this particular image. If I wanted to apply this infrared effect to other photographs, I would need to save these settings as a custom preset. The main thing to remember is to lighten the greens by applying an extreme Tint slider adjustment in combination with the Grayscale panel settings shown here, plus a negative Clarity adjustment. The other tone settings will most likely need to be fine-tuned on an image-by-image basis.

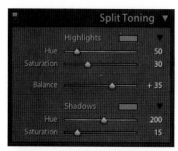

Figure 7.6 *The Split Toning panel.*

Figure 7.7 *To access the new color pickers, click on the swatches and click anywhere in the color ramp (or anywhere in the interface) to sample a new color (the current selected color is the one with the thicker border).*

TIP

To sample colors from anywhere in the image or interface screen area, open the color picker, click in the color ramp, and with the mouse held down, drag outside of the color ramp to anywhere on the screen.

TIP

You can save a new color swatch by [Alt]-clicking in the swatch boxes to the left of the main before/after color swatch box.

Fine-tuning black and white images

Split Toning panel

It should be fairly easy to produce a neutral gray print, as long as you have a good profile for your printer or are using a printer and ink combination specifically designed for black and white work. It should not even matter how well your monitor is calibrated. If an image is in black and white, you should be able to produce a perfectly neutral gray print regardless of how the photograph looks on the screen. If you are unable to achieve perfectly neutral black and white prints, there may be something wrong with your printer profiles, or if you're using an inkjet printer, the print heads may need cleaning.

The Split Toning controls (**Figure 7.6**) are mainly intended for use on photos after they have first been converted to grayscale, where you want to deliberately add some color to the monochrome tones in a photograph. The Hue sliders can be used to adjust the hue color in either the highlights or the shadows, and the Saturation sliders can be used in conjunction with the Hue sliders to apply varying strengths of color tone. Note that if you hold down the [Alt] key as you drag a Hue slider, you get a saturation boosted preview that can help you tell more clearly which hue color you are selecting without having to change the Saturation slider setting. With Lightroom 2 we have a new color picker (**Figure 7.7**) that now allows you to select hue and saturation more easily in one step. To choose a color, click on a swatch to open the color picker and then click anywhere in the color ramp, or anywhere in the image or interface even (providing you keep the mouse held down as you drag). You will notice that the color picker displays both the highlight and shadows color positions on the color ramp, so you can judge the relative positions of the two color sample points. There is also a slider at the bottom that you can use to adjust the saturation while keeping the hue value locked. The Balance slider lets you offset the balance between the shadow and highlight color toning and provides a really nice fine-tuning control for your split   tone effects.

With the Split Toning Controls in Lightroom, there are no hard and fast rules as to which color combinations to use. It can sometimes be useful to pick contrasting colors such as a blue color for the shadows and a warm color for the highlight tones. The following examples give you an idea of what's possible.

1. This photograph was converted to black and white in Lightroom using the Grayscale panel controls.

2. I then went to the Split Toning panel and used the new color picker to select a warm sepia color for the highlights and a cool color for the shadows. Lastly, I offset the split tone midpoint by adjusting the Balance slider.

Split toning a color image

The Split Toning controls work great on non-grayscale-converted, color images. If you want to give your photographs that distorted color look, here's how you can create a cross-processed effect in Lightroom. It is really easy to vary the effects shown here and save successful color split tone effects as presets.

1. Here is a standard version of a color original. No special effects have been applied just yet. This is a normal exposure photograph, processed using the default Lightroom Develop settings.

2. The color effect you see here was achieved by simply adjusting the Split Toning panel controls. In this example I tried to simulate a typical cross-processed film look, which I accomplished by setting the highlights hue to yellow and the shadows hue to cyan/blue. I could have achieved a more subtle effect than the one shown here by reducing the Saturation amount for the highlights and the shadows. I also offset the Balance slightly to add more weight to the cyan/blue coloring in the shadows.

Figure 7.8 *The HSL panel showing all controls with the Saturation sliders all set to –100.*

HSL panel: desaturated color adjustments

Lightroom offers another less obvious approach to converting color images to black and white. If you go to the HSL panel and drag all the Saturation sliders to –100, you can desaturate the color completely to create a grayscale version of a photo. On the face of it, this would appear to be the same thing as dragging the Basic panel Saturation slider all the way to the left, but the key difference here is that the Saturation slider applies its adjustment upstream of all the other color sliders, rendering them inoperable (apart from White Balance, Color Noise, and Calibration). But the HSL desaturate method cleverly gives you full access to *all* the color controls in the Develop module and this is where it can sometimes score favorably against basic Grayscale adjustments.

Here is how to get started. Go to the HSL panel and set all the Saturation sliders to –100, (as shown in **Figure 7.8**). That's it; don't adjust the Luminance sliders just yet, as you'll be doing that later. For now, I suggest you follow the advice given in **Figure 7.9** and save this HSL setting as a new preset. At the end of Chapter 6 I suggested that you use folders to organize your develop presets, and so my advice here is to save a setting like this to a dedicated folder for storing HSL grayscale presets such as the HSL Black & White folder used in Figure 7.9.

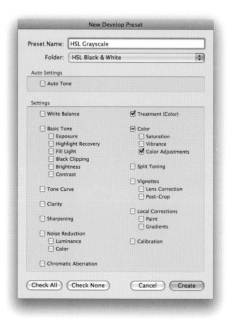

Figure 7.9 *When saving an HSL desaturate setting (such as the one shown in Figure 7.7) as a new develop preset, check the Color Adjustments box only, as shown here.*

The HSL grayscale method

With HSL grayscale conversions, all you need to do is apply the preset that was saved in Figure 7.9 and then adjust the HSL panel Luminance sliders. Don't bother editing the Hue sliders as these will have no effect on the grayscale conversion. The Luminance sliders can therefore be used to lighten or darken specific colors in the photo, just as you would when editing in the Grayscale panel. The Target Adjustment tool can also be used here. Click the Target Adjustment tool button to activate it, or use the ⌘ Alt Shift L (Mac) or Ctrl Alt Shift L (PC) keyboard shortcut to switch to Target Adjustment mode and ⌘ Alt Shift N (Mac) or Ctrl Alt Shift N (PC) to exit this tool mode behavior (Figure 7.8 shows how the HSL panel might look after you have finished adjusting the Luminance sliders). If you want, you can save an HSL grayscale setting as a new preset, in which case you would click the plus button in the Presets panel and again use the settings shown in Figure 7.9 when saving as a new custom preset.

So far you might think this a long-winded approach for producing exactly the same results as you can achieve with the Grayscale panel on its own. But as I mentioned earlier, when you work with the Grayscale panel, the Vibrance and Saturation sliders are grayed out. If you click on either of these two sliders, you can switch to color mode and adjust them for the color Develop settings, but they have *no active effect* on the grayscale conversion when you convert back to Grayscale mode. This is a shame, because you can potentially modify a grayscale conversion quite a bit using these two color controls, which is why I still advocate the HSL Grayscale workaround until the situation in Lightroom changes. In HSL desaturate mode, the Saturation slider in the Basic panel can act like an amplifier volume control for the HSL Luminance adjustments. So increasing the Saturation can therefore magnify the HSL slider settings. The Vibrance slider offers a more subtle, fine-tuning control. Interestingly, a Vibrance adjustment can sometimes appear to have an opposite effect to the Saturation slider, and decreasing the Vibrance can sometimes make certain colors (such as blue) appear darker when converted to black and white. This conversion method is perhaps more suitable for red contrast-type conversions where you might want to significantly darken a blue sky. I wouldn't say it is essential to use this approach in every case, because not all grayscale conversions are likely to require this alternative method. But the following steps illustrate a typical example of a grayscale conversion that might suit the HSL desaturate technique.

NOTE

Some readers may be aware that I used to promote the HSL desaturate grayscale conversion method as a way to beat noise creeping into your grayscale conversions. However, since version 1.4, Lightroom Grayscale conversions keep the Color Noise adjustment active, so you should no longer see this previously reported problem affecting your normal Grayscale panel conversions.

1. In this photograph just a few minor adjustments were made to the settings in the Basic panel and other panels.

2. This shows how the photograph looked when converted to black and white with the HSL Saturation sliders all taken to −100.

3. In the HSL panel I used the Luminance sliders to darken the Aqua, Blue, and Purple colors and lightened Orange, Yellow, and Green.

4. I then fine-tuned the conversion by reducing the Vibrance, which as you can see, made the sky go even darker.

Sharpening and noise reduction

How to make full use of the capture sharpening and noise reduction controls in the Detail panel

There are many reasons why it is necessary to presharpen an image. The process of converting the light information that hits the photosites on the sensor and subsequent digital data processing will result in an image with softer edge detail than would normally be considered desirable. It could be that the lens optics on your camera are not particularly sharp. Therefore, a little sharpening at the post-capture stage is usually necessary to produce an image that is sharp enough to look good on the screen, but without being overly sharpened. If a photograph is sharpened too much at this stage, you may end up with artifacts that will only be compounded as additional adjustments are made to the image. Presharpening should therefore be applied to raw capture images only and in moderation. It is about striking the right balance between compensating for the image softness in a raw file while avoiding the problems that can be caused by any oversharpening at this preliminary stage.

This chapter emphasizes the importance of presharpening digital photographs and how to reduce image noise. I explain how the sharpening sliders in the Detail panel work and offer suggestions on which settings to use for sharper, clearer photos.

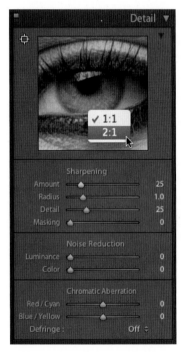

Figure 8.1 *The Detail panel, which now includes a preview window that can be set to a 1:1 or 2:1 view via the contextual menu.*

Capture sharpen for a sharp start

Before discussing the new sharpening controls in Lightroom, I should briefly explain the principle behind capture sharpening and the difference between this and output sharpening.

The Unsharp Mask filter in Photoshop has been around since the very earliest days of the program and has not really changed much since then. As Photoshop has matured, our understanding of sharpening and how to best use the Unsharp Mask filter controls has improved. Various techniques have evolved that cleverly use the Unsharp Mask filter to its best advantage. In his lifetime, author and Photoshop guru Bruce Fraser did the industry a great service with his research into Photoshop sharpening. His recipes for optimum sharpening, based on whether you were sharpening for input—that is, capture sharpening—or sharpening for output, have done a lot to improve our understanding of how to apply the most appropriate level of sharpening at each step of the image editing and printing process. It is also fair to say that Bruce's research and writing had an impact on the way some of the sharpening controls in Lightroom evolved. But more of this later.

Capture sharpening is all about adding sufficient sharpening to a photograph in order to correct for the inherent lack of sharpness that most digital images suffer from to a greater or lesser extent. If you shoot using raw mode, then your photographs will arrive untreated in Lightroom and they will most definitely need some degree of sharpening. If the photos you import have originated from a digital camera shot using the JPEG mode, then they will already have been sharpened in-camera. The Detail panel sharpening controls in Lightroom are therefore intended for use with photographs that are raw originals or non-raw files that have not been sharpened yet (see the section "Default Detail Panel Settings" on the next page).

The main goal with input/capture sharpening is to correct for the lack of sharpness in an image. Capture sharpening is therefore something that you should evaluate on the monitor (using a 1:1 view setting), and it is all about making the photograph look nice and sharp on the screen. At the same time, you don't want to oversharpen, since that can lead to all sorts of problems later at the retouching stage in Photoshop. The Detail panel controls (**Figure 8.1**) are therefore designed to let you apply such sharpening in a controlled way so that only the edge detail gets sharpened and the flat tone areas are preserved as much as possible.

Output sharpening

Output sharpening is something that is always done at the end, just prior to making a print, using the Print Sharpening options in the Print module Print Job panel. But note that Lightroom does not allow you to see on screen what the output sharpening looks like. The print sharpen processing is hidden from view, and the only way to evaluate print output sharpening is by judging the print. The amount of sharpening required at the print stage varies according to many factors, such as the print process, print size, print resolution, and the type of paper used. Fortunately, Lightroom 2 uses Pixel Genius™ Photokit Sharpener™ routines at the print stage, so this is now all handled automatically. But I am getting ahead of myself here. This section is all about the capture sharpening and what's new and special about the sharpening and noise reduction controls in Lightroom.

Default Detail panel settings

In Lightroom, the default behavior is to apply no Detail panel adjustments to an image unless it is recognized to be a raw capture. Raw capture images should always require some degree of sharpening and noise filtering, whereas JPEG captures already have had some level of sharpening and noise processing applied in-camera (see "Raw or JPEG?" on page 242). Other pixel images such as TIFFs and PSDs should not require any Detail panel processing either (unless you are working on an unsharpened scanned image). Basically, if a pixel image has already been sharpened, the last thing you want is for more sharpening to be applied after it has been imported into Lightroom, which is why the default sharpening is set to zero, all except for raw images.

Sharpen preset settings

Perhaps the easiest way to get started is to use either of the two new Sharpen presets found in the Develop module Presets panel shown in **Figure 8.2** (the Develop presets are also available via the Library module Quick Develop panel). All you have to do is decide which of these two settings is most applicable to the image you are about to sharpen. These presets can also be a useful starting point when learning how to sharpen in Lightroom. Start off by selecting one of these settings and fine-tune the settings based on the knowledge gained from reading the remainder of this chapter.

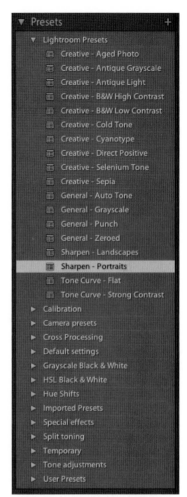

Figure 8.2 *The Develop module Presets panel contains two sharpening preset settings.*

Sharpen – Portraits

As you read the rest of this section it will become apparent what the individual sliders do and which combination of settings will work best with some photographs and not others. But to start with let's look at the two preset settings found in the Lightroom Presets subfolder. **Figure 8.3** shows a 1:2 close-up portrait of myself, shot by Seth Resnick, where naturally enough I chose to apply the *Sharpen – Portraits* preset. This combination of sharpening slider settings is the most appropriate to use for portraits, male or female, or any photo where you wish to sharpen the important areas of detail, such as the eyes and lips, but protect the smooth areas (like the skin) from being sharpened. You may wish to strengthen this setting by increasing the Amount. You may also wish to increase the Masking slider if the skintones are looking a little too "crunchy"—a higher Masking setting will help preserve the smooth tone areas.

Figure 8.3   *Here is an example of the Sharpen – Portraits preset in action.*

Sharpen – Landscapes

The other preset setting you can choose is *Sharpen – Landscapes*. This combination of sharpening slider settings is most appropriate for subjects that contain a lot of edge detail. You could include quite a wide range of subject types in this category. In **Figure 8.4** I used the Sharpen – Landscapes preset to sharpen a picture of a building on a rocky cliff. Basically you would use this particular preset whenever you needed to sharpen photographs that contained a lot of fine edges.

The two preset settings described here provide you with a great way to get started and get the most of the new sharpening settings without having to understand too much about how the sharpening in Lightroom works or what the individual sliders do.

Figure 8.4 *Here is an example of the Sharpen – Landscape preset in action.*

It is wonderful having tonal adjustment controls that allow you to pull more information out of the shadows, but as a result of this, Lightroom is more prone to emphasizing shadow noise problems. Many camera manufacturers are only too painfully aware of the problems of shadow noise and do their best to hide it by deliberately making the shadows darker to help hide any shadow noise. Some camera manufacturer raw processor programs apply a shadow contrast tone curve by default. If you use the Tone Curve controls in Lightroom to bring out more shadow information, just be aware that this may emphasize any shadow noise in the image. It is therefore always worth inspecting the shadows close-up after making such adjustments and check to see if the Luminance and Color sliders are needed to hide any noise (see pages 411–417).

Sample sharpening image

To help explain how the individual sliders work, I have prepared a test image that has been carefully designed to show some of the key aspects of Lightroom sharpening. You can access this image by going to *Lightroom-News.com* and downloading it from a feature story on Lightroom 1.1 sharpening.

The **Figure 8.5** image was specially designed to demonstrate several key aspects of sharpening. The eye and surrounding skin texture allows you to see the effects of portrait style sharpening where the objective is to sharpen detail like the eyelashes (but avoid sharpening the skin texture). Conversely, the patchy texture in the bottom-right corner allows you to test the ability to sharpen smooth texture content where you do want to emphasize the texture detail. The high-contrast detail content in the left section allows you to test the effects of sharpening on fine-detailed image areas, and the crisscross lines have been added to highlight the effects of the Radius slider adjustments.

Figure 8.5 *The sample image used in the final section of this chapter can be accessed at http://photoshopnews.com/stories/images/sharpen-test.jpg.*

Evaluate at a 1:1 view

The only way to properly evaluate the capture sharpening is at a 1:1 view. When you go to the Detail panel, a warning triangle (circled in **Figure 8.6**) appears if the selected photo is displayed at anything less than a 1:1 view. Click the triangle to open a preview window that displays a 1:1 view of the image, which you can scroll by clicking and dragging with the mouse. If you click the arrow to the right, this expands the Detail panel to reveal the preview window (**Figure 8.7**). You can then scroll this preview to analyze the image, or use the Detail panel target adjustment tool to roll the cursor over the image and quickly pinpoint areas of interest.

Luminance targeted sharpening

The first thing to say about Lightroom sharpening is that the sharpening is only applied to the luminance information in a photograph. Lightroom always filters out the color content when it applies its sharpening. This is a good thing because sharpening the color information would enhance any color artifacts. In the early days of Photoshop, people sometimes converted an RGB image to Lab mode and sharpened the Luminosity channel separately. This technique allowed the user to sharpen the luminance information without sharpening the color content. Ever since version 3.0 of Photoshop on, it has been easier (and less destructive) to sharpen in RGB mode and use the Luminosity blend mode to restrict the sharpening to the luminance information. Lightroom does a similar thing here: It filters out the color content when sharpening. For this reason it can be useful to inspect the image in luminance mode when working with the slider; do this by holding down the Alt key as you drag the Amount sharpening sliders in the Detail panel. Note that holding down the Alt key isolates the effects all the other slider controls are having. But it should be noted that the grayscale previews can't be accessed unless you are viewing the image at a 1:1 view or higher.

The sharpening effect sliders

Let's start by looking at the two main sharpening effect controls: Amount and Radius. These sliders control the how much sharpening is applied and how the sharpening is distributed. As I mentioned earlier, you can download the Figure 8.5 image, import it into Lightroom, and copy the steps described here. Note that all these screen shots were taken while holding down the Alt key as I dragged the slider controls.

Figure 8.6 *A warning triangle in the Detail panel indicates that the image is currently being viewed at a lower than 1:1 view. Click the triangle to enlarge the image to a 1:1 view.*

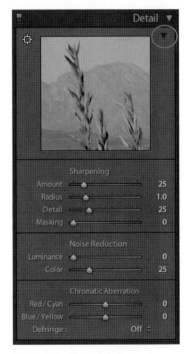

Figure 8.7 *If you click the arrow (circled), this reveals a preview window in the Detail panel and a target adjustment tool that can be used to pinpoint the area you wish to preview.*

Amount slider

1. Note that the previews shown here were captured with the Alt key held down as I dragged on the Amount slider, which is basically like a volume control. The more you apply here, the more you sharpen the image. In this respect it works in a similar way to the Amount slider in the Unsharp Mask filter. The Amount range can go from zero (no sharpening) to 150 (maximum sharpening, where the slider scale goes into the red). The 150 setting goes well beyond the 0–100 range that was available previously, but there is a reason for this: You can use the sharpen suppression controls (described a little later) to dampen the effect of the sharpening. Although you are rarely going to need to set the sharpening as high as 150, the extra headroom is available should you need it. In this example you can see what the sample image looked like using the default 25 sharpening.

2. As you increase the Amount sharpening to 100, you can see how all the detail in the image looks crisper. Used like this, the Amount slider is a fairly blunt instrument, but it is the newly included ability to modify the distribution of the sharpening and filter out the edge halos that makes Lightroom sharpening so special. The important thing to remember is not to overdo the sharpening. The intention is to find the right amount of sharpening to correct for the lack of sharpness that is in the original raw image and not let any sharpening artifacts be noticeable at a 1:1 view.

Radius slider

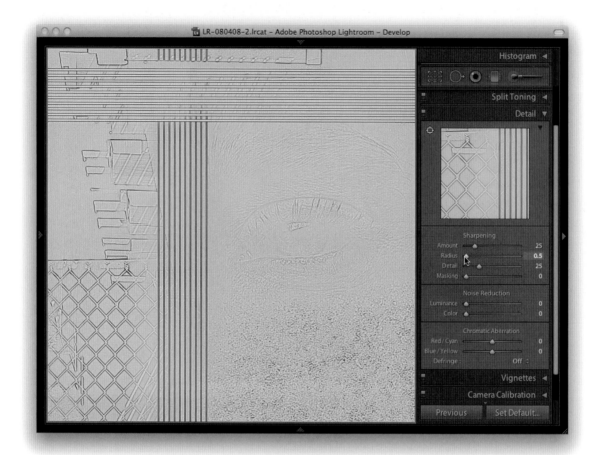

1. For this step and the next, I held down the [Alt] key again to isolate the effect that the Radius setting would have on the image. At the minimum Radius setting you can see how a small Radius has a greater effect on the narrow edge detail, such as the fence wire in the picture, and has very little effect on the soft edge detail, such as the eye and eyelashes. Notice also the effect a small Radius setting has on the crisscross lines. This demonstrates that for high-frequency detailed subjects such as architecture photographs or landscapes, you will often benefit from choosing a less than 1.0 size Radius setting.

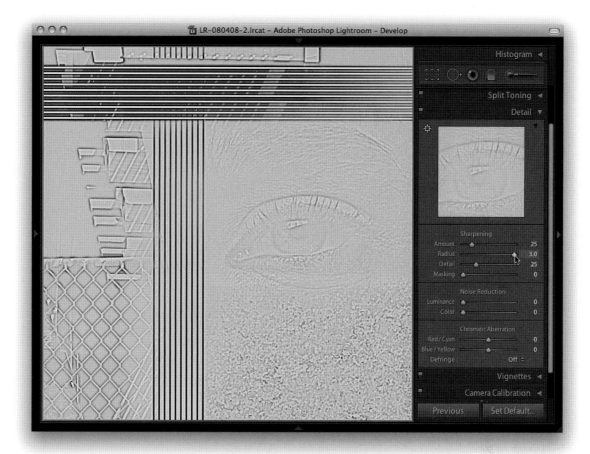

2. As the Radius slider is increased to its maximum setting, notice how the halo width increases to the point where the halos have less real sharpening effect on the fine edge detail. The sharpening around the wire fence area looks kind of fuzzy, but at the wider setting there is now more noticeable sharpening around the eyelashes and the eye pupil. For this reason you will find it is usually more appropriate to select a higher than 1.0 size Radius when sharpening photographs that contain a lot of soft-edged detail, such as portrait photographs.

The suppression controls

The next two sharpening sliders act as dampening controls that modify the effect that the Amount and Radius sharpening settings have on an image.

Detail slider

The Detail slider cleverly suppresses the halos effect and thereby allows you to concentrate the sharpening on the edge areas. This in turn allows you to apply more sharpening with the Amount slider, adding sharpness to the edges, but without generating noticeable halos around them. A setting of zero applies the most halo suppression, and a setting of 100 applies no halo suppression at all.

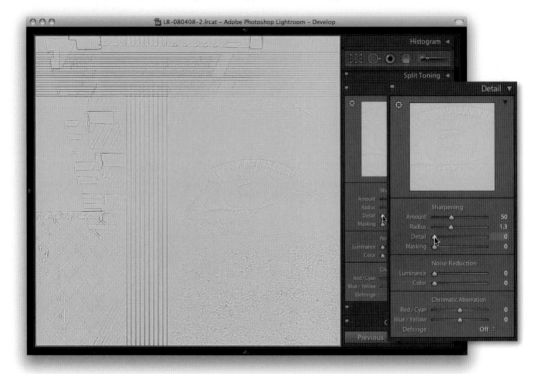

1. In this step the Detail slider was set to zero (I again held down the Alt key to preview in isolation the effect this slider adjustment was having). When the Detail slider is at this lowest setting, nearly all the edge halos are suppressed. The combination of a low Detail setting and a medium to high Radius setting allows you to apply a strong sharpening effect to bring out details like the eye and eyelashes while suppressing the halos on the smooth skintones.

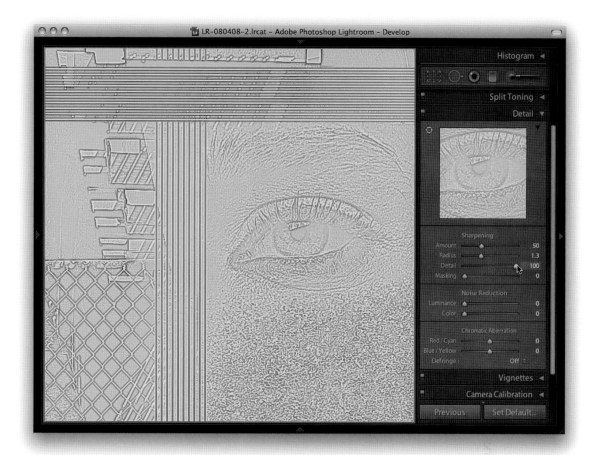

2. When the Detail slider is raised to the maximum setting, all of the sharpening effect is allowed to filter through, unconstrained by the effect the Detail slider would otherwise have on the sharpening effect. When Detail is set to 100, you could say that the Amount and Radius sharpening settings are allowed to process the image with almost the same effect as an Unsharp Mask filter in Photoshop.

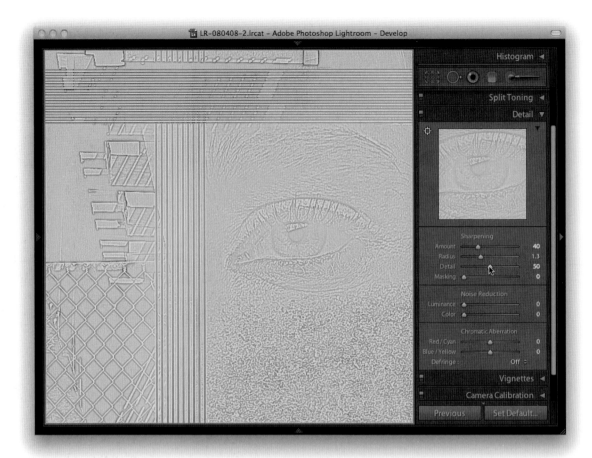

3. When the Detail slider is set to a midpoint value between these two extremes, we see how the Detail slider can be used to target the areas that need sharpening most. If you refer back to the sharpen preset used at the beginning, a lower setting of 20 is suitable for portrait sharpening because it does a good job of suppressing the sharpening over the smooth tone areas. A higher Detail setting will carry out less halo edge suppression and is therefore more suitable for emphasizing fine edge detail.

Interpreting the grayscale sharpening preview

This would be a good point for me to explain what the grayscale previews are actually showing us here. As I have already stated, if you hold down the (Alt) key as you drag the Amount slider, you see an accurate preview of the cumulative effect that all the sharpening sliders are having on the Luminosity information in an image. But when you (Alt)-drag on the Radius and Detail sliders, you are seeing a rather different kind of preview, because with these you are able to preview the sharpening effect in isolation.

What does this mean? The more experienced Photoshop users will understand better if I explain that this is a little (but not exactly) like previewing a duplicate layer of the Background layer after you have just applied the High Pass filter. You see, there is a Photoshop sharpening technique where you apply the High Pass filter to a duplicate of the Background layer to pick out the edge detail and set the duplicate blend layer to Overlay mode. The High Pass filter turns most of the image a mid-gray, but when you set the layer to the Overlay blend mode, the mid-gray areas have no effect on the appearance of the photograph, while the lighter and darker areas in the Overlay blend mode layer build up the edge sharpness. The Radius and Detail (Alt) mode previews are basically showing you the edge enhancement effect as if it were on a separate sharpening layer. And what these previews are showing you is an isolated view of the combined Amount, Radius, and Detail slider settings.

Masking slider

The Masking slider adjustment adds a final level of suppression control and was inspired by Bruce Fraser's written work on his Photoshop sharpening techniques. If you want to read more about Bruce's techniques for input and output sharpening plus his creative sharpening techniques, I highly recommend you check out *Real World Image Sharpening with Adobe Photoshop CS2* from Peachpit Press (it is still just as valid if you are working with later versions of Photoshop).

The basic concept of the masking control is that you can use this slider to create a mask that is based on the image content that protects the areas you don't want to have sharpened. If you take the Masking slider all the way down to zero, no mask is generated and the sharpening effect is applied without any masking. As you increase the Masking setting, more areas are protected. The mask is generated based on the image content; areas of the picture where there are high-contrast edges remain white (the sharpening effect is unmasked) and the flatter areas of the picture where there is smoother tone detail turn black (the sharpening effect is masked). The image processing required to process the mask is quite intensive, so if you are using an older computer it may seem slow as the preview takes its time to update. But on a modern, fast computer you should hardly notice any time delay.

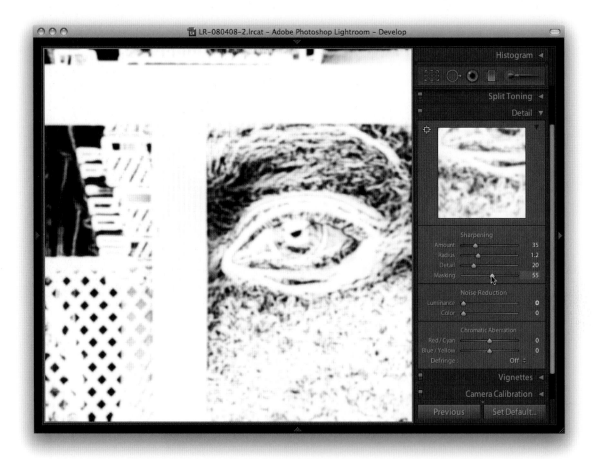

1. In this example, I set the Masking slider to 55 and held down the [Alt] key to reveal the mask preview. Again, always remember that the [Alt] previews will only work if the image is viewed at 1:1 or higher. At this midway setting you will notice how the flatter areas of the picture are just beginning to get some mask protection, such as the skintone areas around the eye.

2. As the Masking setting is increased to the maximum of 100, you can see how more of the flatter tone areas are now protected while the high-contrast edges are preserved. At this extreme setting, the Lightroom sharpening is only applied to the white mask areas. The black portions of the mask are completely protected and no sharpening is applied here.

Applying manual sharpening adjustments

Now that I have given you a rundown on what the individual sharpening sliders do, let's now look at how you would use them in practice to sharpen an image.

1. For this first step I adjusted the Sharpening sliders to provide the optimum amount of sharpening for the fine detail areas. I applied a Radius of 0.7 to add small halos around the edge details (such as the wire fence) and a Detail of 70, which acted to limit the halo suppression. I applied an Amount of 33 to make the fine edge detail nice and crisp and set the Masking slider to zero, which meant that no mask was used to mask the sharpening effect.

2. In this second step I adjusted the Sharpening sliders to provide the optimum amount of sharpening for the soft-edged detail around the eye. I applied a Radius of 1.5 to build wider halo edges around the eyelashes, but at the same time I used a Detail setting of 20 to suppress the edge halos. The Radius setting still has an effect on the sharpening, but the Detail slider is nicely suppressing the halo edge effect to produce a smoother-looking sharpening effect. I took the Masking slider all the way up to 85, so that I could target the sharpening on just those areas that needed sharpening most, that is, the details in the eye and eyelashes. You will note that the Amount was set to 45. This is a higher value than the default 25 setting, but this is because the sharpening is being substantially suppressed by the Detail and Masking sliders, so it is therefore necessary to apply a larger Amount setting.

TIP

As with the sharpening controls, you can only evaluate the effect of the noise reduction sliders by viewing the image at a 1:1 view or higher.

NOTE

The noise reduction in Lightroom may not be as spectacular as Noise Ninja or Noiseware. But it is now considerably more effective than it was in version 1.

Noise reduction

If you shoot with a good-quality digital camera at the standard ISO setting, you will be hard-pressed to see any noise in an image. But not all cameras are the same, and some camera sensors are particularly prone to showing noise, especially at the higher ISO capture settings. Image noise can be characterized in two ways: as luminance or color noise. With very noisy images, an electronic grain can be seen that is more like a fine speckled noise pattern. The Luminance slider in the Detail panel can help smooth out such luminance noise. The default Luminance setting is 0%, and you could try raising this to around 5–20%, but it shouldn't be necessary to go beyond 50% except in extreme circumstances. Improvements made since version 1.1 mean that Lightroom does a much better job now of reducing any white speckles in the shadows. Color noise is usually the most noticeable and ugliest aspect of a noisy image. The Color slider will get rid of most color noise, and you can, if necessary, take the slider all the way up to 100%. But avoid doing this for every high ISO, noisy image you encounter. The color noise reduction works by blurring the color channels (in particular the blue channel). So if you have important information in the blue channel, you may end up softening the image. Some photos can look worse if you try to remove all the noise with a high Color setting. **Figure 8.8** shows how setting the Color slider too high can adversely soften an image.

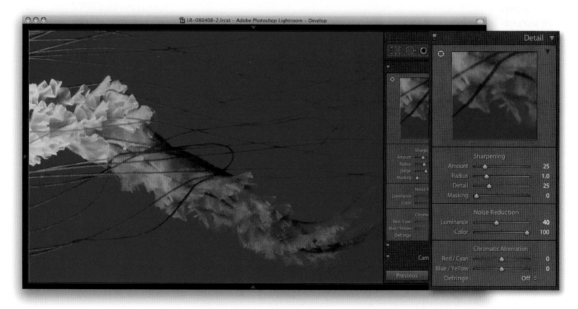

Figure 8.8 *Beware of setting the Color slider too high as this can blur image detail.*

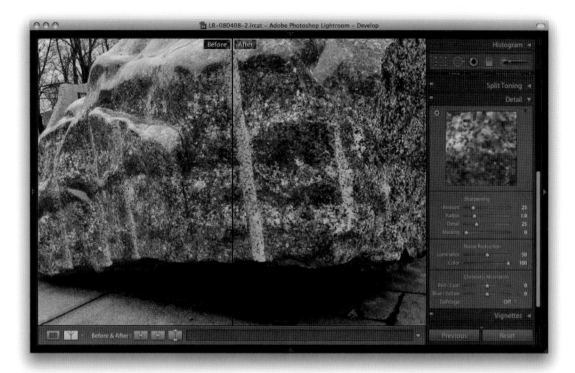

Figure 8.9 *This close-up view of an interior was shot at a 1600 ISO setting on the Canon EOS 400D camera. The image is shown in halves. On the left is the before view with no Detail adjustments and on the right the after version, where I applied a 50% Luminance and a 100% Color setting. The Color noise reduction removed nearly all of the color noise, and the Luminance setting removed most of the luminance noise. A higher Luminance setting would have smoothed out even more of the noise, but this might have resulted in a softer-looking image.*

Noise reduction tips

Get to know your camera and how the sensor responds to different lighting conditions. Some cameras fare better than others in low-light conditions: There will always be a trade-off between shooting at a medium ISO setting with a slower shutter exposure and shooting at a high ISO setting with a faster shutter exposure. Consider using a tripod or image stabilizing lenses as an alternative to shooting at the highest ISO setting. Where noise is a problem, I recommend using the Color slider first to remove the color noise followed by the Luminance slider to remove the fine luminance noise artifacts (**Figure 8.9**). Note that increasing the smoothness will compromise the sharpness. But don't be too paranoid about noise. There is no point in trying to remove every bit of noise, because the print process can be very forgiving!

TIP

Rather than tweak the Noise Reduction sliders on every individual image, you may find it worth following the tip advice on pages 368–369 in Chapter 6 about saving camera-specific defaults that include ISO specific defaults. This can help automate the process and avoid the need for multiple presets.

9

The Photoshop connection

How to get Lightroom and Photoshop to work together in harmony

The best way to view the Lightroom/Photoshop relationship is to see Lightroom as a program for managing and processing lots of images in a catalog and Photoshop as the program where you spend more time working on the individual photographs one at a time.

Although there is a fair amount of overlap between Photoshop, Camera Raw, and Lightroom, it is clear that Photoshop will remain the program of choice for retouching and layered image editing. The question then is, what is the most efficient way to work between these two programs? In this chapter I show you some of the various ways to take photographs from Lightroom and edit them in Photoshop, as well as how to use the Export module to process single images or batches of photographs. I will also show you how to use the post-processing section of the Export module to integrate complex Photoshop routines as part of the export process.

Opening images in Photoshop

So far I have covered all of the image processing that can be done exclusively in Lightroom using the Develop module controls. Remember, all Lightroom edits are nondestructive. The catalog contains the master images that are always preserved in their original state, and there can only be one master of each catalog image. Variations of the masters are made by creating virtual copies or saving snapshots. But if you want to edit a catalog photo outside of Lightroom in an image editing program such as Photoshop, the masters must be rendered as pixel images.

The Edit in Photoshop options

Before you do anything, first visit the Lightroom preferences and configure the External Editing preferences (**Figure 9.1**). There are now two ways to externally edit a Lightroom catalog image. The basic Edit command (⌘E [Mac] or Ctrl E [PC]) directly renders a pixel version of the master catalog image without adding a copy version or anything else to the catalog and does so in one of two ways. In the top section of the External Editing preferences, the external editing program will be

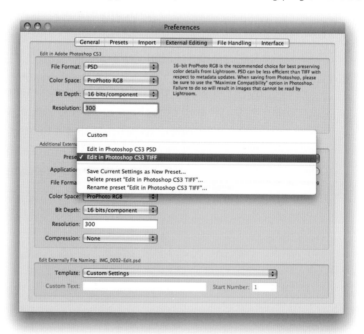

Figure 9.1   To change the external editing application, select Lightroom ➯ Preferences. Go to the Additional External Editor section and choose the File Format, Color Space, and Bit Depth options you want to use when creating an edit version of a master image in either Photoshop or an additional external editor program.

whichever is the most recent version of Photoshop on your computer and the options below allow you to establish the default file format, RGB space, and bit depth to use whenever you choose the ⌘E (Mac), Ctrl E (PC) command to edit a master image in Photoshop. If the photo you choose to open this way is a raw image and you have the latest version of Camera Raw (i.e., 4.4.1 or later) for Photoshop CS3 (or later), the Lightroom catalog image opens in Photoshop directly. If you don't have the latest Camera Raw plug-in, you will see the warning dialog shown in **Figure 9.2**, where you have the option to "Open Anyway" (maybe the applied Develop settings can all be read by an earlier version of Camera Raw). Or you can click "Render using Lightroom," to have Lightroom render a copy of the original that is automatically added to the Lightroom catalog as a copy version.

Figure 9.3   *If you open a non-raw image using the main Edit in Photoshop command, you will have the option Edit Original (which opens the image without adding it to the catalog), or you can choose one of the Edit copy options shown here.*

Figure 9.2   *If you don't have the latest version of Camera Raw for Photoshop CS3 or you're using an older version of Photoshop, this is the dialog you will see when choosing the main Edit in Photoshop command with a raw image.*

If the photograph you choose to open this way is a non-raw catalog image, then you will see the dialog shown in **Figure 9.3**, where you have the option Edit Original, which opens the original file directly. Or you can choose to edit a copy of the original (with or without Lightroom adjustments) and have Lightroom open a copy of the original photo and automatically add it to the catalog as a copy version. Lightroom highlights the Edit Original option by default because very often you will want Lightroom to open up the original image in Photoshop without creating a new copy version. The Edit Original option is therefore useful for editing layered masters or derivative versions of a master. You can choose Edit a Copy if you want to create an edit copy of the file in its original state (ignoring any Lightroom adjustments that might have been applied). And you can also choose Edit a Copy with Lightroom Adjustments if you want to open a JPEG, TIFF, or PSD image with the Lightroom adjustments applied. So if you are using Lightroom Develop adjustments to process a JPEG, TIFF, or PSD image, this would be the option to select if you want to open the photo with those settings applied to an edit copy of the image.

NOTE

When you open an image using the Edit in Photoshop command, it opens using the color space, bit depth, and resolution settings applied in the External Editing preferences. However, the file format choice only comes into play when you choose to save the image out of Photoshop. The default behavior is to save the file to the same folder as the original master, using the file format specified in the preferences (but the saved image won't be added to the catalog).

Figure 9.4 *This dialog appears when a raw image is selected and you choose Edit in Photoshop using* ⌘ Alt E *(Mac) or* Ctrl Alt E *(PC). The only available Edit option is to edit a pixel-rendered copy of the raw file and apply Lightroom adjustments. The "Stack with original" option autostacks the version images with the master.*

TIP

In the Edit in External Editor dialogs (Figures 9.4 and 9.6) you have the option to override file format, RGB space, and bit depth options set in the External Editing preferences.

The main point about the Edit in Photoshop command is that it provides you with a means to open Lightroom catalog images in Photoshop without generating new edit copy versions of the master each time you do so—that is, provided that (a) the image you are opening is a raw file and that you have installed the latest Camera Raw plug-in for Photoshop CS3 or later, or (b) the non-raw image you are opening (such as a JPEG, PSD, or TIFF) has not had any Lightroom Develop settings applied to it. Once you have opened a Lightroom catalog image this way, you can edit a raw original image in Photoshop and save it however you like. Likewise, with a non-raw image you can save a Photoshop-edited version however you like or simply choose Save to overwrite the original in the Lightroom catalog, or save a new edited version of the master to the same source folder. **Figure 9.4** shows the Edit Photo with Adobe Photoshop CS3 dialog box.

The Edit in External Editor options

The second section in the External Editing preferences allows you to select a pixel editing program to use as what is referred to as the "Additional External Editor." For this, you need to click the Choose button to select a program, which can be any pixel editing application, such as Adobe Photoshop Elements or Corel PaintShop Pro, or it can be the same version of Photoshop as was selected above.

Whichever program you select here, it then becomes available as a menu option when you go to the Photo ⇨ Edit in Photoshop menu, just below the main Edit in Photoshop command (**Figure 9.5**). The difference with opening catalog photos from Lightroom this way is that when you are shown an Edit Photo dialog (such as the ones in Figure 9.4 and **Figure 9.6**) it obliges you to create an edit copy version of the master and add these photos to the Lightroom catalog. To edit one or more Lightroom catalog photos in Photoshop using the Additional Editor method, select the image or images that you want to edit and choose Photo ⇨ Edit in Adobe Photoshop, or use the ⌘ Alt E (Mac) or Ctrl Alt E (PC) keyboard shortcut.

Whenever you select a raw image and you choose Edit in Additional Editor, the dialog in Figure 9.4 appears. In this situation only one option is available: Edit a Copy with Lightroom Adjustments. This renders a flattened pixel image and opens it in Photoshop (or other external editor program). The opened image will have *-Edit* appended to the original filename, and at the same time, this pixel rendered version is added to the Lightroom catalog as a new photo. The file naming applied here

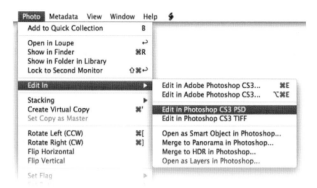

Figure 9.5 *Whichever program is selected as the Additional External Editor appears listed below the main Edit in Photoshop command in the Photo ⇨ Edit in Photoshop menu and can be invoked using the ⌘ Alt E (Mac) or Ctrl Alt E (PC) keyboard shortcut. Plus you can also select saved external editor presets (as shown in Figure 9.1).*

depends on what was set in the External Editing preferences (Figure 9.1). If you do nothing and leave this set to Custom Settings, the photo is renamed with the *-Edit* suffix. As you create more edit copies of the same image, these are appended with *-Edit-2, -Edit-3,* and so on. But you can choose any of the other file naming options or create your own when deciding how the external edit copy photos should be renamed. From there you can edit the photograph however you like. When you are finished, save and close the image. As you save the image from Photoshop, the Lightroom preview updates to reflect the changes made to the edited version of the image.

Whenever you select a non-raw image, such as a JPEG, a TIFF, or an existing Edit copy image, dialog shown in Figure 9.6 appears with the same option list, except all of the options are now available. This is essentially offering you the same options as you have when choosing the main Edit in Photoshop command (Figure 9.3). You can use either method to open an existing *-Edit* copy image, edit it some more in Photoshop, and close again without creating a new copy every time. The only real difference here between choosing ⌘ E (Mac) or Ctrl E (PC) or ⌘ Alt E (Mac) or Ctrl Alt E (PC) when opening a non-raw file is that when you take the Edit in External Editor route, you can choose to use a program other than Photoshop, or you can override the default file format saving options.

I realize that the summary I have given here does look rather complex, but that is only because I have aimed to cover all the different possible outcomes when you choose to edit a photo in Photoshop. The steps shown on the following pages demonstrate how simple editing in Photoshop really is.

Figure 9.6 *If a non-raw image is selected in Lightroom and you choose Edit in Adobe Photoshop using ⌘ Alt E (Mac) or Ctrl Alt E (PC), all the edit options will be available. You can create an edit copy of the original image with Lightroom adjustments applied, edit a copy (without Lightroom adjustments), or edit the original file (also without Lightroom adjustments).*

NOTE

If you select a program other than Photoshop or Photoshop Elements as the external editor, the PSD file format option may not be available.

How to use the external editing options

1. I selected a master raw image from the Filmstrip and used the Edit in Additional External Editor command (⌘ Alt E [Mac], Ctrl Alt E [PC]) to create an edit copy that could be edited in Photoshop. Notice that I checked the "Stack with original" option. This grouped the edited version in a stack with the original master.

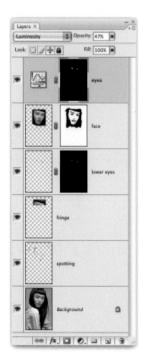

2. The edit copy of the original photograph opened directly in Photoshop and allowed me to retouch the photograph. When I was done, I chose File ➭ Save and closed the image.

3. Back in Lightroom you can see how the modifications made in Photoshop to the edit copy are reflected in the Filmstrip and main preview. The Edit Copy photo has now been added to the same folder as the original and is currently highlighted in the Filmstrip, where you can see the selected image identified as number 2 of 2 images in the stack that was just created.

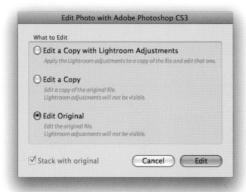

4. If I wanted to re-edit the image in Photoshop, I could use either ⌘E (Mac), Ctrl E (PC), or ⌘Alt E (Mac), Ctrl Alt E (PC) to show the Edit Photo dialog, where I would then choose Edit Original.

Photoshop as a sandwich filler for Lightroom

It is great that we have so many image adjustment tools in the Develop module. As you will recall, there are quite a few ways to produce interesting black and white conversions and different types of color processed looks. The question this raises is, when and where is the best time to apply such adjustments? Let's say you want to convert a photo to grayscale, but you also wish to carry out a significant amount of retouching in Photoshop. Should you convert the photo to Grayscale mode in Lightroom first and then choose to edit it in Photoshop? That could work, but once you have converted a photo to grayscale in Lightroom and edited it in Photoshop, there is no opportunity to go back to the color original. In my view, it is best to always edit photos in Photoshop in what I consider to be an optimized image state, and if you want to convert a photo to black and white or apply coloring effects, you can apply these adjustments to a master, Photoshop-edited image. Of course, the major problem with this approach is that you don't get to see what the image will eventually look like while you are working in Photoshop. However, the following steps suggest ways that you can make this transition between Lightroom and Photoshop more fluid.

1. We start here with a raw image and a virtual copy version of the photo in which I converted it to grayscale and applied a split tone and vignette to create the virtual copy version you see here.

2. Now if I want to edit this photo in Photoshop, I have two options here. I could select the virtual copy version and choose Photo ⇨ Edit in Photoshop, But as I pointed out in the introductory text, this method does limit my options. Suppose, for example, the client decided later that they didn't like the black and white look and wanted the color version instead? My preferred approach is to first create an optimized color of the raw photo and make a Photoshop Edit copy based on this setting. To do this I used the ⌘ Alt E (Mac), Ctrl Alt E (PC) method.

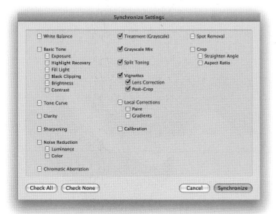

3. But how can you work on an optimized image in Photoshop and also see how the photo looks with the black and white effect? Select the virtual copy, "effect" version of the image and then the newly created Edit Copy image. Click "Sync settings" to open the Synchronize Settings dialog, where you can synchronize just those settings needed to create the black and white effect.

NOTE

When you follow this step, make sure that the virtual copy "effect setting" image is the one that is most selected (it will have a lighter gray cell border). This is important because you want to synchronize the effect settings from the "effect setting" image to the Photoshop-edited version.

4. In the screen shot shown here I synchronized the Grayscale, Split Toning, and Vignette adjustments from the virtual copy image on the right with the newly created Photoshop edit version on the left.

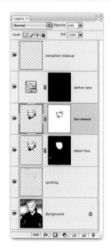

5. I continued editing the image in Photoshop by choosing Photo ⇨ Edit in Photoshop and selected Edit Original. Each time I did this, it would open the original optimized image version and allow me to carry out the retouching work on a normal, full-color version of the photo.

6. Meanwhile, back in Lightroom, you can preview a combination of the Photoshop edited image and the Lightroom applied adjustment. But you have to remember to keep saving the image in Photoshop in order to see the most currently updated version of the photo appear in the Lightroom Content area.

7. There are various ways you can toggle between the two programs. If you are on a Mac and using the latest Leopard operating system, you could allocate separate desktop spaces for Photoshop and Lightroom and toggle between them. If you have the luxury of a dual-monitor setup, you can display Photoshop on one screen and Lightroom on the other.

TIP

With a dual-monitor setup, you may need to force the Lightroom screen view to update by clicking on a photo next to it in the Filmstrip and then click back on the photo again.

NOTE

One disadvantage of processing panoramas via Lightroom is that you are always obliged to open the original images at their full size. If you are only merging three or four photos as a panorama this may not matter so much, but if you need to process a larger number of pictures, you might like to follow this tip that was suggested to me by Ian Lyons:

1. Select the pictures you wish to merge as a panorama and choose the "Photo ⇨ Edit in ⇨ Open as layers in Photoshop" command. This creates a single image in Photoshop where all the selected images are added as layers. In Photoshop you can then choose Image ⇨ Image Size and reduce the file size to, say, 50% (with constrain proportions checked).

2. Choose Select all Layers: ⌘ Alt A (Mac), Ctrl Alt A (PC).

3. Go to the Edit menu and choose Auto-Align. This opens the Auto-Align Layers dialog, which has the same Layout options as shown in Step 2. The Auto-Align command will align the photos correctly (but without blending them).

4. Now choose Auto-blend from the Edit menu. This carries out the finishing touches and applies the layer masking, as you can see in Step 4.

To make all this simpler, I suggest you record the above steps as a Photoshop action and replay the action after you have successfully exported the photos using the "Open as layers in Photoshop" command.

Extended editing in Photoshop

As well as editing photos directly in Photoshop, Lightroom now offers you the ability to hook up directly to Photoshop's extended editing features: Merge to Panorama, Merge to HDR, and Open as Layers. These commands use the same settings as the Edit in Photoshop command and allow you to process images out of Lightroom without adding a new photo to the catalog. The Merge to HDR method processes the selected files and opens the Merge to HDR dialog in Photoshop, from where you can save a 32-bit HDR file. The Open as Layers option places the selected photos as layers in a single Photoshop image. You can then autoalign the layers and if you have the Extended version of Photoshop, do things like convert to a Smart Object and run a Stack mode rendering process. To give you an idea of how these editing options work, I have provided on these pages a brief example of how to create a panorama image via Photoshop from a selection of photos in Lightroom. On the following pages is an example of how to merge two photos as Smart Objects to produce a composite image in Photoshop.

1. I started by making a selection of photographs in Lightroom that had been shot with the intention of creating a merged panoramic photograph. I went to the Photo menu in Lightroom and chose Edit in Photoshop ⇨ Merge to Panorama in Photoshop.

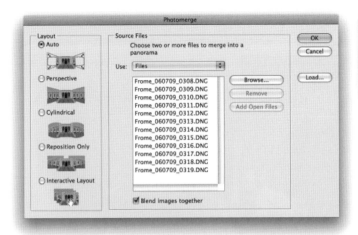

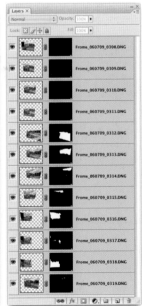

2. If the version of Camera Raw you are using is older than Camera Raw 4.4.1, you will see the warning message shown here. In this example, I opened using Photoshop CS3, which showed the Photomerge dialog. I clicked OK to proceed photomerging in Auto mode.

NOTE

It is hard to say if this is a bug or not, but the "Merge to" and "Open as Layers" commands are only available as menu items provided you are in the Library Grid view mode. However, if you are in the Library Loupe view or the Develop module, you can access these commands via the Filmstrip contextual menu.

3. Depending on the number of images and original file size, it may take a while to process the panorama. But once completed you should see a merged panorama like the one shown here with the component layers all masked.

Opening photos as Smart Objects in Photoshop

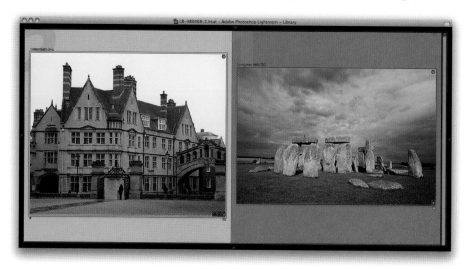

1. We start here with two photos in the Library module, where I wanted to merge them into a single composite image, yet retain the ability to edit the Lightroom Develop settings in Photoshop.

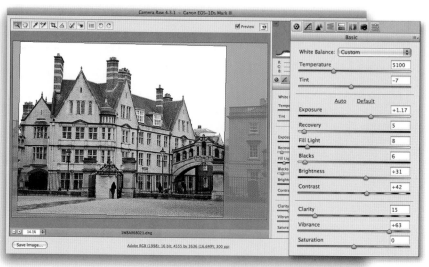

2. I began by selecting the photograph of the building and chose Photo ⇨ Edit in Photoshop ⇨ Open as Smart Object in Photoshop. This created the Smart Object layer shown here, with a Smart Object icon (⬛), where I expanded the canvas size and applied a layer mask to hide the sky area. I was also able to double-click the layer to edit the Develop settings via Camera Raw.

3. I opened the second image as a Smart Object in Photoshop and dragged this over to the first, to add it as a new layer below the Smart Object layer of the building. I was again able to open the Smart Object layer and revise the Develop settings via Camera Raw.

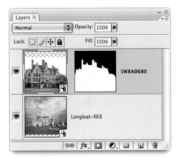

4. Here is the finished composite, where the two layers are preserved in their raw state and remain fully editable via Camera Raw.

Figure 9.7 *You can right-click to access the contextual menu and manage the export user presets.*

Figure 9.8 *The Existing Files menu.*

Exporting from Lightroom

The Export function lets you export single or multiple photos from Lightroom as finished files, allowing you to export copies of the master images as DNGs, TIFFs, PSDs, or JPEGs. But that's not all. You have full control over the exported file settings, such as where the files get saved to. You can also specify whether to incorporate a post-processing action and save the export settings as custom presets, making it easy for you to create and use different export routines. To export files from Lightroom, make a selection and choose File ⇨ Export or press ⌘ ⇧ Shift E (Mac) or Ctrl ⇧ Shift E (PC) to open the Export dialog.

Export presets

The Export dialog has a Preset section that already contains a few preset export options to help you get started. For instance, The For E-mail setting puts the exported JPEGs in a folder called *To* E-mail on the Desktop. Other presets include Export to DNG and Burn Full-Sized JPEGs. You can also use this section to create and save your own custom export preset settings, which can be managed using the contextual menu (see **Figure 9.7**). For example, you can use the contextual menu to update any of the user preset settings.

Export Location

The Export Location options allow you to export to the same source folder or to a specific folder. When the latter is selected, the folder location is remembered between exports, so you can regularly send your exports to locations such as the My Pictures folder. In our next example, I have the For E-mail preset selected and this automatically sends the exported photos to a folder called To E-Mail on the Desktop. You can also check the Add to This Catalog option if you want to automatically reimport the exported photos back into the Lightroom catalog. The Existing Files menu (see **Figure 9.8**) gives you several options. You can leave it set to "Ask what to do" when an existing file is encountered as an exported image is reimported back to the catalog, or choose from one of the following policies. If you select "Choose a new name for the exported file," this gives you the opportunity to rename the reimported image and create a new master image. You can also choose Overwrite WITHOUT WARNING, where the "all caps" hints that this is potentially a risky policy to choose, or you can choose Skip, where Lightroom exports the existing files still, but skips reimporting them. **Figure 9.9** shows the Export dialog using the To E-mail preset.

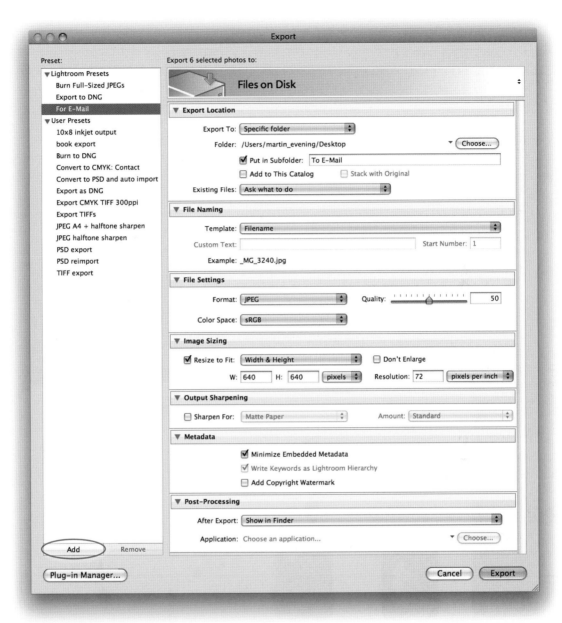

Figure 9.9 *The File ⇨ Export dialog is shown here using the To E-mail preset. You can configure your own custom export dialog settings and click the Add button (circled) to add these as new user presets.*

Exporting to the same folder

If you select the "Same folder as original photo" in the Export To box (**Figure 9.10**), this allows you to export a derivative version of a catalog photo such as a full-sized TIFF version of a raw original, export the photo to the same source folder as the original, and add it to the catalog. When this combination of settings is selected, you also have the option to stack the exported image with the original. The Export dialog therefore provides you with a simple one-step solution to create derivative versions of the raw masters and simultaneously add them to the catalog.

Figure 9.10 *This shows the Export Location options to create derivative versions of the master files and reimport them back into the catalog, stacked with the master.*

1. In this first screen shot you can see that I had filtered the photos in the catalog to select just the master raw, four-star images only.

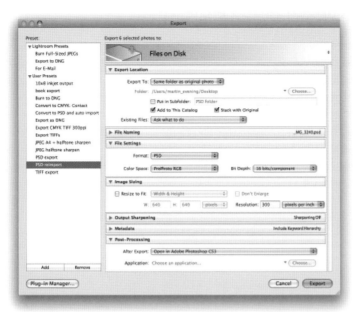

2. I used the Export command ($\mathbb{H}$ $\Uparrow$ Shift $\boxed{E}$ [Mac], $\boxed{Ctrl}$ $\Uparrow$ Shift $\boxed{E}$ [PC]) to export the visible photos with a custom PSD Reimport preset that used the same settings as shown in Figure 9.10.

3. When the Export process was complete, I could see the exported photos added to the catalog and stacked with the raw masters.

File Naming and File Settings

You can leave the File Naming section set to *Filename* if you want to retain the current naming, or you can add a text string such as *_email* or *_foliocopy* if you wish to somehow differentiate the export processed images from the original masters. In the File Settings section, images can be exported using the JPEG, PSD, TIFF, or DNG formats. The file format options will adjust according to the file format you have selected. In Figure 9.9 you can see the JPEG quality slider for JPEG exports. If you select DNG as the output format you will see the DNG options shown in **Figure 9.11**.

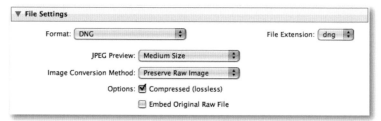

Figure 9.11   *When DNG is selected in the Format box, you will see the DNG options shown here. These are the same options that you will find in the Camera Raw and DNG Converter Save options.*

Saving non-raw files as DNG

Yes, it is possible to save non-raw files as DNGs just as you can convert any supported proprietary raw file to DNG. One advantage of doing this is that the DNG file format can combine the XMP data with the pixel image information in a single file document. But the downside is that if you save JPEG images in this way you will lose all the benefits of JPEG file compression; it's a bit like saving a JPEG image out as a TIFF or PSD—you will increase the file size to almost that of a normal uncompressed image file (DNG applies just a moderate amount of file compression). It is also important to point out that converting a JPEG to a DNG does *not* allow you to return a JPEG image to its raw state. This is a misunderstanding that has cropped up before on some email forums, and it must be stressed that once you convert a raw image to a TIFF or JPEG, there is no way of returning it to its raw state again.

Image Settings

Up to this point, all the catalog files will have been edited using the Lightroom internal RGB space, but you can now select an output color space for the exported files by choosing from sRGB, Adobe RGB (1998), or ProPhoto RGB. If you are exporting the photos for photo editing, your choice will boil down to Adobe RGB or ProPhoto RGB. Adobe RGB is a safer general choice, because it more closely preserves the appearance of the pictures as you have been used to seeing them on the screen and is a widely adopted space for general photo editing work in a program such as Photoshop. ProPhoto RGB is in many ways a better choice than Adobe RGB because the color gamut of ProPhoto RGB is a lot larger than Adobe RGB and more or less identical to the gamut of the native Lightroom RGB space. With ProPhoto RGB you can guarantee inclusion of all the colors that were captured in the original raw file, whether your display is able to show them or not. For this reason it is a favorite photo editing space for high-end print work where you want to maximize the color gamut to achieve the best print results. The downside of using ProPhoto RGB is that you must view the files in a color-managed application in order to see the colors displayed correctly. If you view a ProPhoto RGB image in a program that does not recognize profiles (such as most Web browsers) or where the color management is switched off, the colors will look terrible. Adobe RGB files won't look so hot either if you don't color-manage them, but ProPhoto RGB images will look even worse when they are not color-managed! If you are familiar with the basic concepts of color management and are using Photoshop color management switched on, it will be safe for you to export using Adobe RGB or ProPhoto RGB. If any of the preceding information scares or confuses you, you should perhaps stick to using sRGB, and I would definitely advise choosing sRGB if you are exporting images as JPEGs for Web use, or for client approval (especially if you are unsure of how well the client's systems are color-managed), or are preparing pictures to email friends. For the time being at least, sRGB is going to remain the most suitable lowest common denominator space for Web work and general use.

The Bit Depth can be set to 16-bit or 8-bit. One of the reasons so many professionals advocate working in 16-bit is because you can make full use of all the capture levels in an image when applying your basic tonal edits, rather than throw these away by converting to 8-bit and then making the edit adjustments. In Lightroom (and this is true for any raw processor) you are making all your basic edits in 16-bit regardless of how you export them. So at this stage you will already have taken

NOTE

You can never tell what the future may hold. There was a time when nobody could foresee any real need for deep-bit images. These days film and video editors regularly rely on 16-bit or higher bit depths for special effects work. And new screen technologies are emerging that can show deep-bit images on a wide dynamic range display.

full advantage of all the deep-bit levels data in the original capture. Therefore, choosing 8-bit at this stage is not necessarily such a damaging option to choose. If you think 16-bits will help you preserve more levels as you perform any subsequent editing work or you feel the extra levels are worth preserving, then choose 16-bit.

Image sizing

In the Image Sizing section (**Figure 9.12**) you have the opportunity to resize the exported photos except where the DNG file format or Original image is selected in the File Format settings. There are various options here. If you check the Resize to Fit box you can choose Width & Height to make the photos resize to fit within the values entered in the boxes. If you select Dimensions you can force the exported images to fit precisely within set dimensions (which may well change the aspect ratio of the exported images), and you can set the export to resize the photos along the Long Edge or the Short Edge only. If you have a selection of photos where some are landscape and others are portrait, you can specify a long edge or short edge dimension limit and all photos will resize to the same edge dimension constraints. The Resolution box allows you to set the number of pixels per inch or pixels per centimeter for the resolution.

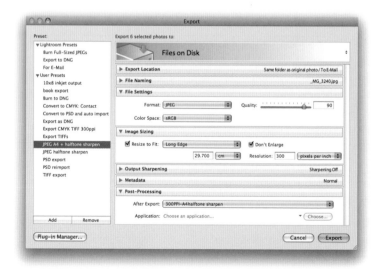

Figure 9.12 *Here is a view of the Export dialog in which you can see the Image Settings options. Note how when the other panels in the Export dialog are collapsed, the settings are summarized in the panel bar for quick and easy viewing.*

When to interpolate?

In Photoshop you have a choice of interpolation methods to select when resampling the image size. For example, it's recommended you choose a Bicubic (smoother) when making an image bigger for smoother results, or Bicubic (sharper) when reducing the image size. There are no interpolation options available in Lightroom. Instead, a single "Lanczos kernel" method of interpolation is used in both Lightroom and Camera Raw. However, this still leaves the issue of when you should interpolate an image up in size. There are a lot of digital photographers out there using cameras that produce files which sometimes need to be made bigger in order to meet the client requirements for blowup images. One of the questions that has arisen relates to capture sharpening. Is it OK to use the capture sharpening in Lightroom and interpolate the image up later when you need to create a bigger pixel sized image? Or, should you switch off the capture sharpening in Lightroom, export at the bigger pixel size, and capture sharpen afterwards? You could do this by either reimporting the interpolated TIFF or PSD file back into Lightroom and applying the capture sharpening to the file then, or by exporting the image and capture sharpening in Photoshop using a third-party plug-in such as Photokit Sharpener™. As you can see in **Figure 9.13**, there is a noticeable difference in output between using these two approaches. Interpolating up an image that has first been pre-sharpened in Lightroom may magnify the sharpening artifacts to an extent where they become obvious. If you interpolate up and then sharpen, you can get smoother results.

NOTE

Previously, there have been some concerns over the suitability of Lightroom's interpolation method when reducing an image in size. Some people were reporting halo edge artifacts when making big reductions in file size. In Lightroom 2, the interpolation has been improved slightly to help prevent this.

Figure 9.13 *The left half of this image was capture-sharpened in Lightroom and interpolated up at the export stage to twice the original file size. The right half was initially unsharpened and the exported version was interpolated to twice the original size and then reimported and sharpened in Lightroom using identical settings to the left half version. The pictures are printed here at the 100% output size.*

NOTE

It is worth bearing in mind that you don't always need a high pixel resolution to get good results in print. Clients are often fond of quoting a 300 ppi resolution as the solution for everything from a small newspaper photo up to billboard size posters! The truth is that 200–250 ppi is quite often all that you need for magazine reproduction. More pixels doesn't always necessarily equate to better quality.

NOTE

Photoshop author and digital imaging guru Bruce Fraser worked on the Pixel Genius Photokit Sharpener™ plug-in for Photoshop alongside Mike Skurski and Jeff Schewe. The code used for the inkjet and screen image sharpening has been licensed to Adobe for use in Lightroom in the Print module and also in the Export dialog as shown here.

This is a tricky one to advise on because the print result at 100% does show a difference between these two approaches. It is worth pointing out in the Figure 9.13 example that the image in question was initially a 5,000-pixel-wide image from a 16 megapixel camera and magnified to 10,000 pixels. This would be big enough to print at 50 inches wide at 200 pixels per inch. So the question is, how typical would such an extreme magnification be? Most of the time I find myself interpolating down at the export process, so such issues don't really concern me. But if the camera you are using has a small sensor and you find yourself needing to make significant enlargements in pixel size at the export stage, you may want to conduct your own tests here.

Output sharpening

Print output sharpening is new to Lightroom 2, and the Output Sharpening section in the Export dialog (**Figure 9.14**) provides the same sharpening controls as found in the Print module Print Job panel options. It should be stressed that the output controls here are designed to apply inkjet print sharpening routines to the exported images. What this means is that instead of using the sharpening controls in the print module to sharpen for print, you can use the Export dialog settings to sharpen a file for inkjet print output. For example, let's say you wanted to take photos from Lightroom and prepare them for printing in Photoshop or via a dedicated RIP. If you apply output sharpening at the Export stage in Lightroom, your files will be all nicely sharpened and ready to print!

In the Sharpen For section you can choose between Screen output (such as for a Web page or external slideshow presentation) and a matte paper or glossy paper inkjet output. These sharpening options are for screen presentation and inkjet printing output only and don't include halftone output yet. For CMYK output, you will still need to sharpen in Photoshop. The Amount settings include Low, Standard, and High. The original sharpening routines that Bruce Fraser devised (see sidebar note) were originally coded with the Standard setting. The Low and High settings simply allow you to make the sharpening effect strength slightly weaker or stronger.

Figure 9.14 *The Output Sharpening options.*

Metadata

The Minimize Embedded Metadata option allows you to export images without including custom informational metadata such as keywords. This option can be useful if you want to keep the metadata information to a minimum or hide the keyword metadata. Below this is the Write Keywords as Lightroom Hierarchy option. This is checked by default and ensures that keywords are always written to a file's XMP space so that the keyword hierarchy is preserved when the keyword metadata is previewed on another computer running Lightroom, where perhaps the keywords used are unknown or do not share the same hierarchy.

For example, let's say you have two computers that share the same controlled vocabulary, that is, they both share the same keyword hierarchy structure. If you were to export a photo from one computer and import it into the other, then the Write Keywords as Lightroom Hierarchy option won't make any difference because the keyword hierarchy for the individual keywords is recognized anyway (please note that I am talking about a normal export and import here and not about the Export/Import catalog command). But if this option is unchecked and the second computer does not share the same information, the keywords will otherwise be output as a flat View list without a Lightroom-recognized hierarchy.

If you happen to use a keyword hierarchy that uses *California > USA > Places*, that hierarchy will be preserved as long as either the computer you are importing the photo to already knows this hierarchy relationship or the Write Keywords as Lightroom Hierarchy option is checked. If it is not checked, the keywords will be exported as a flat list: *California, USA, Places*.

Post-Processing

The Post-Processing section is a powerful feature in the Export dialog. It lets you perform tasks such as showing the images in the Finder at the end of an export and opening the photos in Photoshop after exporting. You can even set everything up to directly burn the exported files to a disc. These are the default options you have in the Post-Processing section, but if you read further on the following pages, you can find out how to create Photoshop droplets (which are self-contained Photoshop action routines) and have these run at the post-processing stage of an export.

NOTE

When the Add Copyright Watermark option is checked in the Metadata section, this adds a small copyright notice to one of the bottom corners of the exported images (this is not available when exporting as DNG).

Adding Export Actions in Lightroom

TIP

You can also use drag and drop to copy images out of Lightroom to a new location (or to a Photoshop droplet). But be warned, Develop adjustments and other settings will not necessarily be transferred with the file if you drag and drop a file out of Lightroom in this way.

The post-processing options in the Lightroom Export module allow you to integrate Photoshop processing routines with Lightroom by adding them to the end of a Lightroom export. All you have to do is record an action of the Photoshop processing steps that you would like to see carried out at the end of an export. In the following few steps I show an example of how to create a Photoshop action for converting an RGB image to CMYK that includes the necessary pre-sharpening and profile conversion steps. This is just one example of a Photoshop routine that you might like to apply on a regular basis to photos that have been exported out of Lightroom. By following the steps shown here, you can adapt this to almost any type of Photoshop processing sequence.

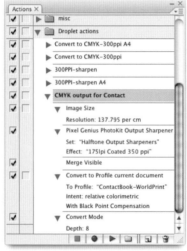

1. Here I want to show you the steps you would follow to create a Photoshop droplet that could be placed in the Lightroom Export Actions folder so that it appears as a selectable item in the Post-Processing section of the Export dialog. I started by opening an image in Photoshop and recorded some steps as an action. In this example I adjusted the open image to the correct ppi resolution, applied an automated sharpening routine for the above resolution, flattened the image, converted it to a specific CMYK profile, and lastly, converted to 8-bit.

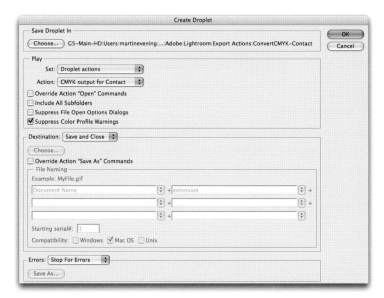

ConvertCMYK–Contact

2. Having recorded the action, I was now ready to save the action as a droplet. In Photoshop I went to the File menu, selected Automate ⇨ Create Droplet, and applied the settings shown here. The droplet was saved directly to the Lightroom Export Actions folder (see Step 3). In the Destination section, I chose Save and Close since I would be using the Export dialog to determine where the exported files would be saved to, so there was no need to establish an output folder here.

3. As I mentioned in the previous step, the Photoshop droplet needed to be saved to the Lightroom Export Actions folder. On a Mac, go to the Users/Library/Application support/Adobe/Lightroom folder and save the droplet to the Export Actions folder. On a PC, you will need to go to the Local Disk (C:)\Username\Application Data\ Adobe\Lightroom folder and save to the Export Actions folder.

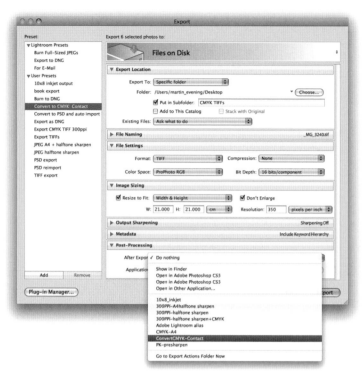

4. We are now ready to use the droplet action. In Lightroom, I selected the photos I wanted process, and then chose Export from the File menu to open the Export dialog shown here. In the Export Location section I instructed Lightroom to create a new export folder called CMYK TIFFs. In the File Settings section I selected the TIFF file format with the Compression set to None. In the Image Settings it did not really matter which RGB space was selected here because the output files would eventually be converted to CMYK. So I set the output color space to ProPhoto RGB since it is pretty similar to the native Lightroom RGB space. And lastly in the Post-Processing section, I clicked the menu to select the droplet that I had previously saved to the Export Actions folder. Once I had done that, it was time to save the customized settings as a new preset. In the example shown here, I saved the Export settings as Convert to CMYK: Contact, because this was the export routine I would use for resizing and converting photos ready for print in this particular book publication.

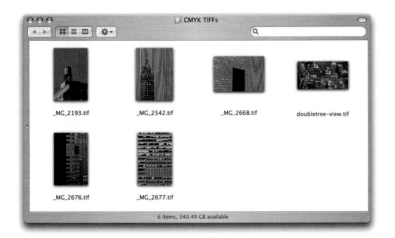

TIP

You can adapt the CMYK conversion action routine shown here for any publication. My recommendation would be to create separate droplet actions for different publications using the correct profile or CMYK setting for each. You can then build up a set of user presets for output to each different client.

5. All I needed to do now was click Export and Lightroom exported the images that had been selected in Lightroom as TIFFs and output them to the designated folder on the desktop that I had named CMYK TIFFs, and it did so using the following sequence of steps.

    As the files were processed out of Lightroom they were resized to fit dimensions of 21 cm x 21 cm at a resolution of 350 pixels per inch with the metadata information and keyword hierarchy preserved. Once the initial export was complete, the post-processing kicked in. The Lightroom exported TIFF files were then opened up in Photoshop, and the action step instructions contained in the droplet were applied to each image in turn and saved back to the CMYK TIFFs folder.

    That pretty much sums up the order in which a typical Lightroom export that has a droplet action included in the post-processing stage would process a series of images that are exported out of Lightroom. The folder here shows the final six photos after they had successfully been exported from Lightroom as CMYK TIFFs, ready for placement in a page layout.

Export plug-ins

The Lightroom Export dialog allows the use of Export plug-ins, which can now be downloaded from various third-party providers. To install a plug-in, click the Plug-in Manager button at the bottom of the Export dialog (**Figure 9.15**), which opens the Plug-in manager shown in **Figure 9.16**.

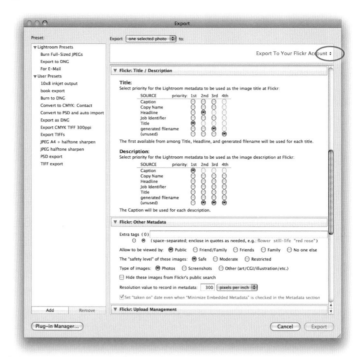

Figure 9.15 *An example of a Flickr Export Plug-in for the Export dialog.*

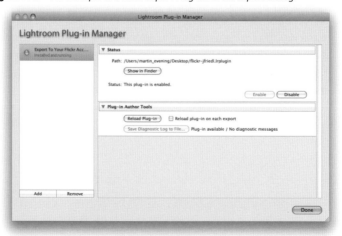

Figure 9.16 *The Lightroom Plug-in Manager.*

Exporting catalog images to a CD or DVD

If you want to export images to a CD or DVD, you can do so via the Export dialog. In our next example, in the Export dialog I used a custom export setting: Burn as DNG. I created this setting using the Files on CD/DVD Export plug-in, which I configured to convert all selected photos to DNG and burn them to a CD or DVD.

With this setting, the photos are first converted to DNG and placed in a folder called DNG on the Desktop. Lightroom then automatically launches the operating system disc burning utility (such as the one shown in **Figure 9.17**) and alerts you that Lightroom is ready to start copying the files to a blank recordable CD or DVD. If you have more than one CD/DVD burning device available, you can select which unit you want to use to burn the disc. Once you have done this, click Burn and you will then see the Burn Summary dialog, where you can enter a name for the archive disc you are about to create (**Figure 9.18**). **Figure 9.19** shows the Export dialog using the Files on CD/DVD Export plug-in.

If there is not enough room to burn all the data on a single disc, Lightroom informs you of this and enables a multidisc burn session. In the example shown here, I wanted to archive a total of just over 8 GB of data to disc. But because a single recordable DVD disc can only hold a maximum of 4.3 GB of data, Lightroom in these circumstances automatically divides the library export into batches of equal size (based on the space available on the first disc you inserted to record with) and proceeds to burn the data (and verify) to successive discs, appending each disc burn session with successive numbers.

Figure 9.17 *When you choose the "Burn the exported images to disc" option, you can select the device unit that should be used to burn the disc and click Burn.*

Figure 9.18 *In this Burn Summary dialog you can enter the name of the disc to be burned. If there is more data than can fit on a single disc, Lightroom automatically alerts you and sets up the burn to be made to a sequence of discs.*

Figure 9.19 *The Export dialog using the Files on CD/DVD Export plug-in.*

10 | Printing

*How to get perfect prints and work efficiently in
the Print module*

Digital printing has come a long way from the early days of
Photoshop when few photographers were convinced that you
could really produce a digital print from a computer to rival the
quality of a photographic print. Graham Nash and Mac Holbert
of Nash Editions were early pioneers of digital printing and the
first to demonstrate how inkjet technology could be used to
produce print output from the computer onto high-quality
art paper.

In the intervening years photographers have seen amazing
breakthroughs in technology and pricing. These days you can
buy a photographic quality printer for just a few hundred dol-
lars. But alas, many people still get beaten by the complexities
of the operating system Print dialogs and the inability to make
print color management work for them. Fortunately, the Print
module in Lightroom can make your life easier. To start with,
you are able to see previews of how the photographs will be
laid out on the page. In the Lightroom Print module, you can set
up batches of images in a print queue to produce high-quality
prints or work in fast print mode to generate quick sets of contact sheets. Best of all, once you master how to configure your
print settings, you can save those settings as part of a template
for more reliable and consistent printing results.

Preparing for print

The Print module

The Print module (**Figure 10.1**) provides you with complete control
over the print page layout and provides proper-sized previews of the
images that have been selected for printing. Starting from the top,
the Layout Engine panel offers a choice of print layouts: either the
previous Contact Sheet/Grid layout, or the new Picture Package layout.
The Image Settings panel can be used to apply basic rules such as
how a selected image or images fill the cell areas, whether to rotate
the images for the best fit, or zoom and crop the photos to fit a cell,
or add a stroke border. The Layout panel can then be used to define
the margins, grid layout, and cell size for the images. To help you get
started, several templates are included for you to choose from in the
Template Browser panel, and you can preview the layout format as you
hover over the items in the Template Browser list on the left.

The Guides panel lets you select the visibility of various guides items,
and the Overlays panel lets you add information to the print. Here, you
can place your Identity Plate as a logo or as custom text and add things
like page numbers. If you are using the Print module to print contact
sheets, you can also include additional file information below the print
cells. The Print Job panel lets you decide how the page or pages should
be printed (there is no need for an Image Resize dialog in the Print
module, because the Page Setup options and Print Resolution in the
Print Job panel are all you need to size an image correctly for print).
The Draft Mode Printing option is great for speedy print jobs, because
it makes full use of the large JPEG previews (that Lightroom has already
rendered). Providing the previews have all been built, the print processing is virtually instantaneous. When Draft Mode Printing is disabled,
Lightroom processes the image data from the original master file, and
you can then decide which level of output sharpening to apply. For easy
printing you can use the Managed by Printer setting, or you can select
a custom print profile and rendering intent.

You can click the Page Setup button at the bottom to specify the page
setup size and paper orientation, and then click the Print Settings button to specify the print output settings such as the paper media type
and print quality. Both the Page Setup and Print Settings configurations
can be saved as part of a print template, which helps reduce the
number of opportunities for a print error at the operating system level.
Lastly, click either of the Print buttons on the right to make a print.

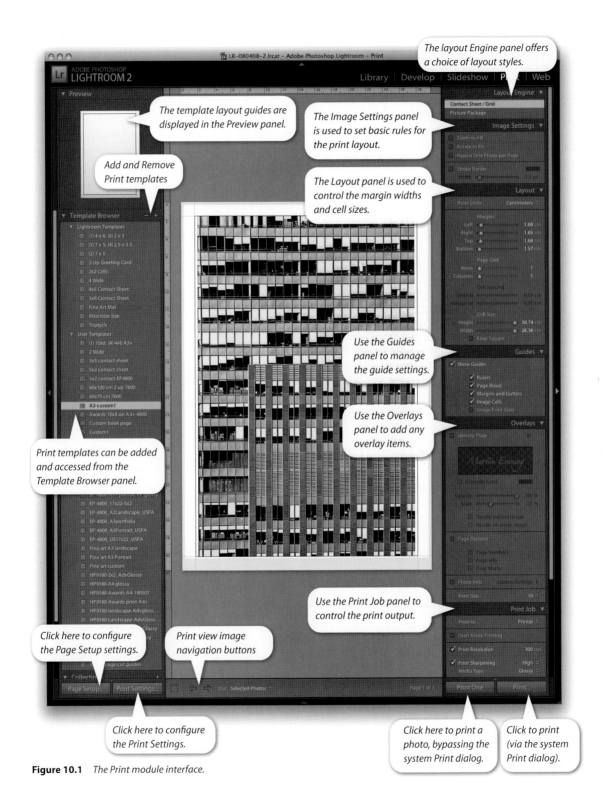

The layout Engine panel offers a choice of layout styles.

The template layout guides are displayed in the Preview panel.

The Image Settings panel is used to set basic rules for the print layout.

Add and Remove Print templates

The Layout panel is used to control the margin widths and cell sizes.

Print templates can be added and accessed from the Template Browser panel.

Use the Guides panel to manage the guide settings.

Use the Overlays panel to add any overlay items.

Use the Print Job panel to control the print output.

Click here to configure the Page Setup settings.

Print view image navigation buttons

Click here to configure the Print Settings.

Click here to print a photo, bypassing the system Print dialog.

Click to print (via the system Print dialog).

Figure 10.1   *The Print module interface.*

TIP

With version 2, a stroke border is added to outer cell area only. At lower print resolutions the width of a stroke border may have to be adjusted to suit the print output, because a narrow border may print unevenly.

Image Settings panel

The Image Settings provide some elementary control over how the selected image or images fill the print cell areas (**Figure 10.2**). If the Zoom to Fill Frame option is selected, the whole cell area is filled with the selected image so that the narrowest dimension fits within the widest grid cell dimension and the image is cropped accordingly. As you can see in the following steps, images that have been cropped in this way can be scrolled within the cells in the print layout. The Auto-Rotate to Fit option automatically rotates the images to fit the orientation of the print cells. For example, this option can be useful when printing a contact sheet of landscape and portrait images where you want each image on the contact sheet to print to the same size (see Step 4). The Repeat One Photo per Page option is applicable if the layout you are using contains more than one cell, and you want the image repeated many times on the same page. Step 5 shows an example of a 2x2 cells template with this option selected.

1. The images in this layout were selected from the Filmstrip and previewed in the Print module using a 2x2 cells template. No Image Settings have been selected yet.

2. In this example, a 2 Wide template was used and the Zoom to Fill Frame option was selected. The two images now fill the entire area of each print cell.

3. Even with the Zoom to Fill Frame option selected, there is still room to change image placement. If you click and hold on a print cell preview, you can scroll the image to obtain a better-looking crop.

4. The Auto-Rotate to Fit option ensures that all images are rotated to best fit the cells. In this example, two portrait-oriented images are rotated to best fit the landscape-oriented cells in the 2 Wide print template.

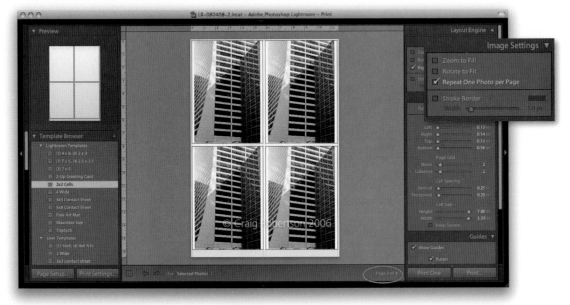

5. In this figure, I selected the Repeat One Photo per Page option, which makes each image in the current selection populate all the cells per page layout. Shown here is page 3 of 4 pages.

Layout panel in Contact Sheet / Grid mode

There are two Layout Engine options, but to start with, we'll concentrate on the Layout panel options that are accessible when you are in the Contact Sheet / Grid mode. This lets you decide how an image (or multiple images) are positioned in a page layout, and scrolling through the print templates gives you a quick feel for how the layout controls work. Notice how the Layout panel settings in **Figure 10.3** relate to the page layout diagram shown in **Figure 10.4**. Also note how the Margins settings take precedence over the Cell Spacing and Cell Size settings. Once the margins have been set, the Cell Spacing and Cell Size adjustments will adapt to fit within the margins.

Figure 10.3 *The Layout and Layout Engine panels.*

Figure 10.4 *The page layout divisions highlighted here can be controlled via the Page Layout panel.*

TIP

A quick way to adjust the margins or indeed any of these guides is to click on the guidelines in the Content area and drag them manually. Note when you make layout adjustments using this method (or casually adjust the sliders in the Layout panel), the images will often autoadjust in size as you make refinements. If it is essential that the images be a specific size on the page, it is best to use the Layout panel method because this allows you the most complete control over the image and layout measurements.

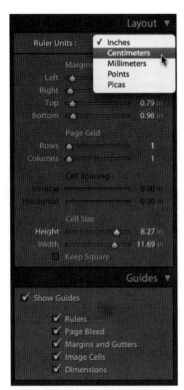

Figure 10.5 *You can set the Ruler Units measurements via the Page Layout panel.*

Layout panel and Guides panel options

The rulers can be made visible by checking the Rulers item in the Guides panel (or press ⌘R [Mac] or Ctrl R [PC] to toggle ruler visibility). Ruler Unit measurements can be altered by clicking on the measurement units in the Layout panel (**Figure 10.5**) to set the measurement units to inches, centimeters, millimeters, points, or picas.

Page grid and cells

To place an image precisely on the page, the first step is to set the widths of the margins. If you want to center the photograph, make sure that the margins are set evenly, and most important, to a measurement that places the image within the widest page bleed edge. Inside the margins is the Page Grid area, which when set to a 1x1 cell, prints a single image on the page. If you want to print multiple images on each page, as shown in some of the previous examples, you simply adjust the number of rows and columns. The Cell Size sliders determine the size of the print cell area. If the Cell Size sliders are dragged all the way to the right, the cell sizes expand to the maximum size allowed. But by making these smaller, you can restrict the printable area within each cell. However, note that the cell size adjustment is always centered within the Page Grid area set by the margins and the margin adjustments take precedence over the Page Grid area. Any readjustments made to the margins will therefore have a knock-on effect with the cell size area. The Cell Spacing sliders are only active if the page grid is set to use two or more cells. If you refer back to Figure 10.4, you can see how I was able to apply a 0.64 cm Vertical and Horizontal spacing to the 2x2 image layout. The other Guides panel items help you plan a page layout. The Page Bleed displays a light gray shading to represent the nonprintable areas, while the Margins and Gutters and Image Cells check boxes allow you to independently show or hide these items, and the master Show Guides check box displays or hides all of the previously mentioned Layout panel guides. The following examples illustrate how these adjustments work.

1. In the page layout at the top of the facing page, the margins (which I shaded red) constrain the printable area by 2.5 cm left, right, and bottom, and by 2 cm on the top. The cell height size is set to the maximum allowed, which is 25.2 cm. But since the image width is constrained by the 33 cm cell width setting, the image does not fill the full height of the cell.

2. In the example below, the margins remained the same, but the cell height and width sizes were reduced to an A4 metric size of 21 cm x 29.7 cm. Because Dimensions is checked in the Guides panel, the actual image print dimensions are displayed in the top-left corner.

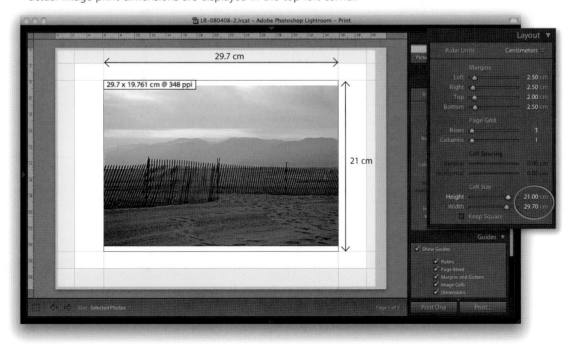

As you adjust the Page Setup settings to select different paper sizes, the Page Bleed area will vary and often be asymmetrical. This is because some printers require a wider page bleed gap along the trailing edge of the paper as it comes out of the printer. With some applications, centering the print centers the image without allowing for the offset page bleed area; therefore, prints may still print off-center. With Lightroom, turning on the Page Bleed view lets you take into account the page bleed and adjust the margin widths accordingly to ensure that your prints are always properly centered.

Instead of printing a contact sheet from the Print module, you can always output it as a PDF document via the Print dialog (see page 480). Printing a PDF can be useful for several reasons. For example, with some printers if you run out of ink during a print job of more than one page, the printer starts reprinting again from page 1 on. Instead of clicking Print you can generate a PDF and print the PDF via a program like Acrobat, which provides a means for you to select individual pages for printing. The other advantage of saving the print data as a PDF is that you can send a print document such as a contact sheet via email for others to open in Adobe Acrobat on their computer or for them to print remotely.

Multiple cell printing

When the page grid is set up to print with multiple cells, the Cell Spacing options become active and let you set the gap spacing between each cell. The Cell Size and Cell Spacing settings are interdependent, so any adjustment you make to one always affects the other. In **Figure 10.6**, I created a custom 3x3 contact sheet template in which the Cell Spacing was set to 0.5 cm for the Vertical and the Horizontal spacing. The Cell Spacing adjustments affected the Cell Size settings accordingly. So remember, if you adjust one setting, the other will compensate.

Notice that the Keep Square option was left unchecked. For some contact sheet template designs it can be useful to check this item because it ensures that both landscape and portrait images are all printed at the same size on the page and are always printed upright without having to rotate the images for the best fit within the cells.

A multiple cell printing template is ideal for generating contact sheet prints from a large selection of images. And when more images are selected than can be printed on a single page, the extra images will autoflow to fill more pages using the same template design. It is possible to generate as many contact sheet prints as necessary, even from a big shoot, but be warned that the Print Job settings will have a major impact on how long it takes to render the pages. For fast contact sheet printing, I suggest you always choose the Draft Mode Printing option in the Print Job panel. When this option selected, Lightroom renders the contact sheet images based on the high-quality preview images that should already have been generated. I say "should have" because this is something you may have to check before you click Print. Whenever a new batch of images are imported, Lightroom automatically generates the thumbnails followed by Standard previews and then the high-quality 1:1 preview images. If you have just imported a large number of photographs into Lightroom, it may take a little while to generate all the Standard previews, and until Lightroom has done so, Draft Mode Printing may result in some images appearing pixelated (because they will have been rendered from the thumbnails only). It is therefore a good idea when you are in the Print module to run a quick preview check of all the pages that are about to be printed and check if the image previews look like they have all been fully processed. If you see the ellipsis warning indicator in the top-right corner, it means Lightroom is still busy rendering a preview (see the callout in Figure 10.6).

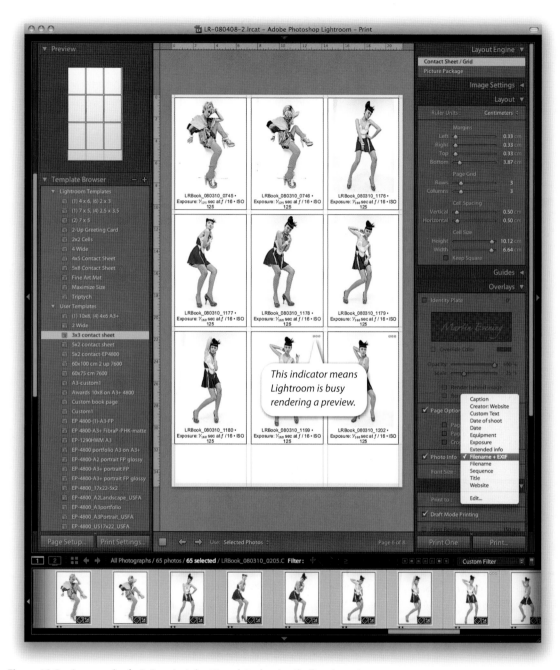

Figure 10.6 *An example of a 3x3 contact sheet template showing the Page Layout tools and Overlays panel settings.*

Figure 10.7 *When the Picture Package Layout Engine is selected, you will see the panel options shown here.*

Layout Engine panel

This panel determines whether the Contact Sheet / Grid or Picture Package option is selected, which will have a bearing on the other panels displayed in the Print module (**Figure 10.7**). So far we have looked at the Contact Sheet / Grid panel options, but we now also have a Picture Package engine mode that has its own set of configuration panels as well as a few custom templates that can be accessed from the Template Browser panel. These can be readily identified by the bracketed numbers such as the *(1) 4x6, (6) 2x3* template that is shown selected in **Figure 10.8**. The purpose of the Picture Package templates is that it enables you to produce multiple-sized photographs on a single page layout. For example, commercial portrait photographers may use this feature to produce multiple print variations on a single sheet of paper that can then be ready to trim to size, rather than be forced to print out two or more different sets of prints per image.

Image Settings panel

Here you have the Photo Border options as before in the Contact Sheet / Grid engine Image Settings panel. But in this instance there is a Photo Border slider that can be used to set the border width inside each cell and an Inner Stroke slider that can be used to set the stroke border width.

Rulers, Grid & Guides Panel

The Ruler check box and Units options are identical to the other Guides panel, while the Grid check box allows you to switch the Grid display (the colored graph pattern) on or off. Next to this are the Snap options, where basically, you can customize the Picture Package layouts by dragging and dropping the individual cells. This means that you can choose to snap to the gridlines or snap to other cells when adjusting the placement of the cells (or switch the snap option off if you prefer).

Cells panel

To create a new Picture Package layout, select the Picture Package Layout Engine and click the Clear Layout button in the Cells panel. You can now add new cells to a blank Picture Package layout by clicking the Cell size buttons. These range in size from 2 x 2.5 inches to 8 x 10 inches (or 5 x 7.5 cm to 13 x 18 cm, if using centimeter units).

Figure 10.8 *This shows an example of a Picture Package layout using the (1) 4x6, (6) 2x3 template.*

You can use these default sizes or click the button options and select Edit to add a new custom cell size, based on the current measurement units (see **Figure 10.9**). This process adds new cells to the page as can best fit the Page Setup page dimensions (**Figure 10.10**). To arrange the cells better on the page you could also try clicking the Auto Layout button. This rearranges the cells to find what would be the best fit for the page layout. Lightroom does so with a view to what would be the most efficient use of space, yet still allows you to trim your photos easily with a paper guillotine. As you try to squeeze in more cells, there will come a point where Lightroom may allow you to place one more cell, but this won't necessarily allow you to trim the pictures so easily. Even so, the Auto Layout option can otherwise be a useful paper-saving option. The other option is to click on a cell and drag it manually to a desired location on the page. This is where the Snap option comes in handy; it can help you align your cell images successfully. After this you can then use the Zoom to Fill, Rotate to Fit, and Photo Border options in the Image Settings panel to decide how a photo will fill the cell frames as well as refining the layout.

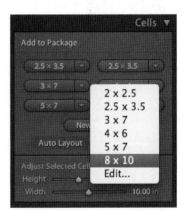

Figure 10.9 *You can create new cell size settings by clicking a cell size arrow and selecting Edit (the cell sizes shown here are using inches units).*

Figure 10.10 *This shows a new Picture Package layout being created, where a new cell has been added to the current layout. You can then click and drag to reposition the cell anywhere on the page layout.*

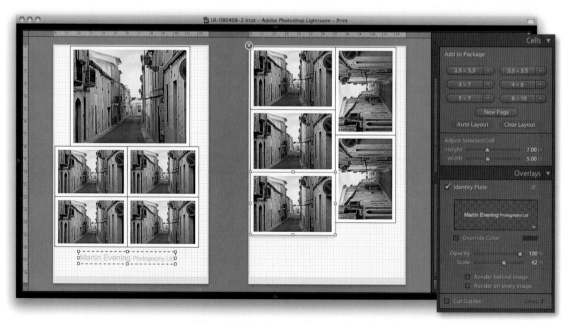

Figure 10.11 *As more cells are added, they will overflow onto new pages. Or, you can click the New Page button to add new pages to a Picture Package layout.*

As you add more cells and there is not enough room on the page, new pages are added automatically (as shown in **Figure 10.11**). Alternatively, you can click the New Page button to add a new page manually and adjust the arrangement of the cells layout across two or more pages. If you want to delete a page, click the red cross in the top-left corner.

Overlays panel

The Overlays panel allows you to add a custom identity plate to a Picture Package layout (as shown in Figure 10.11). I'll be explaining more about working with Print module overlays over the next few pages. One unique thing that this panel features is a Cut Guides option. Although you won't see any guides added in the Content area preview, when this item is checked, it will add cut guides to the finished print that can be in the form of crop marks at the edges or crop lines that intersect on the page. Now although this is a feature for Picture packaged images, it also happens to be useful for single-image print layouts such as the one shown in **Figure 10.12**, because this can makes it easier to trim prints to an exact size in cases where it is not easy to see where the print edge should be, such as a photograph like the one shown here where the background is all white.

TIP

It would be nice if the Contact Sheet / Grid engine had a Cut Guides option. But since it doesn't, you can use a workaround instead. First, figure out what the cell print area should be and add this as a new custom cell size. Add one cell to the page, check the Cut Guides option, and you can then use, say, the printed lines guides to align the image on the guillotine whenever you need to trim a photo to the exact border edge to produce a perfectly trimmed borderless print.

Figure 10.12   *This shows an example of where the Cut Guides option can be useful for adding crop guides to photos that are tricky to trim.*

Overlays panel

The Overlays panel options determine which extra items are printed (**Figure 10.13**). When the Identity Plate option is selected, you can click in the Identity Plate preview to reveal the list of Identity Plate presets, and choose Edit to open the Identity Plate Editor dialog. Here, you can choose between adding a styled text name plate or a graphical logo. Then use the controls in this upper section to set the Opacity and Scale. In the following steps I used the Scale slider to set the size of the Identity Plate to 40%, but you can just as easily do this by clicking and dragging on the corner or side handles of the box. You can also rotate the Identity Plate logo by clicking the Rotate button. If you want to repeat your logo in a multiple grid cell layout, use the "Render on every image" option. And there is also an option called "Print behind image," which can be used providing the graphical image used has a sufficient number of pixels to print well when blown up in size. For example, if you read through the following section on adding a photographic border to a print image, you will get the general idea of how large images can be added as a graphical Identity Plate.

1. When the Identity Plate option is enabled, the current Identity Plate can be added as an overlay in the print layout.

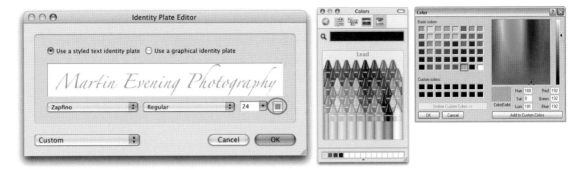

2. If you want to change the Identity Plate settings, click the Identity Plate preview (Figure 10.13) and choose Edit. The Identity Plate Editor dialog opens and lets you choose an alternative font and font size. To change the font color, click on the font color swatch and edit the color using the color picker that comes with the operating system.

3. Back to the Print module. In this example, I clicked on the Identity Plate box and dragged to move it downward, keeping it centered with the photograph, and then readjusted the scale to make the Identity Plate size smaller.

TIP

You can apply a print watermark by overlaying the image with a text styled Identity Plate set to a low opacity setting.

How to add a photographic border to a print

It's not immediately obvious that you can add an image of any size as a graphical Identity Plate, since the preview area in the Identity Plate editor (see the preview space in Step 2) is so small. Plus there is a warning message that tells you not to exceed 57 pixels in height! Well, this only applies to placing graphical logos that are intended as replacement Identity Plates in the top panel display. For print work and other Identity Plate uses, there is absolutely no reason why you should be limited by this constraint. For example, with larger graphical Identity Plates you can add graphical logos such as a scanned signature or a company logo to a print image and not worry about it appearing pixelated in print. Early last year, thanks to my buddy Sean McCormack, I was shown the following technique for adding a photographic border to Lightroom print images via the Overlays panel. In the example shown here I used a scanned border image, but you could easily substitute other types of borders, or even use the paint tools in Photoshop to create your own!

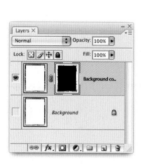

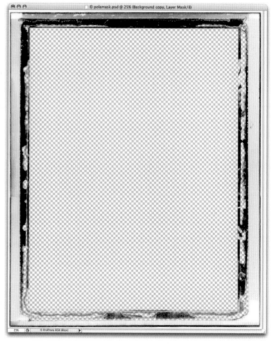

1. In this first step I edited a photograph of a border in Photoshop. This picture is a scan of a Polaroid™ film border, where I created a mask of the center and the semitransparent border edges and hid them with a layer mask. I saved this master image as a PSD, but also saved a flattened copy as a PNG file.

2. In Lightroom I clicked in the Identity Plate preview area and selected Edit. This opened the Identity Plate Editor window where I switched to the "Use a graphical identity plate" option, clicked the Locate File button to choose the recently saved PNG border file, and saved it as a new Identity Plate.

3. With the new Identity Plate selected, I enabled it in the Print module Overlays panel and adjusted the scale to fit the photo.

NOTE

The Sharpening info only displays the sharpening method (Standard, High, or Low) and doesn't tell you if the setting used was for Glossy or Matte.

Page Options

The Page Options allow you to add useful extras. I find the Crop Marks are handy for when I need to trim down a print in size after output (although the Cut Guides described on page 465 makes this even easier). The Page Info item prints all the information relating to the print output method, which can be useful if you are running tests to evaluate the effectiveness of various profiles and print settings with the printer, profile, and sharpening method printed along the bottom. The Page Numbers option allows you to label a collection of print outputs using a specific page order.

In **Figure 10.14**, I was about to print a high key photograph, so I added a thin black border (via the Image Settings panel) because it would frame the picture better. You can choose a border width setting between 1 and 20 points, but if you are using the narrowest border width, make sure you set the print output resolution to at least a 300 pixels per inch output.

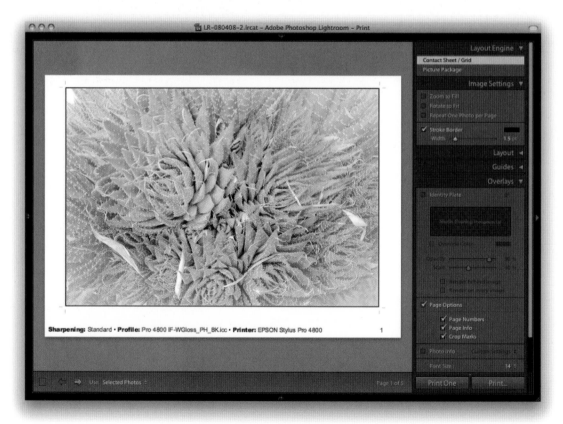

Figure 10.14   *The Overlays panel Page Options.*

Figure 10.15 *Photo Information can be added below each frame. In this example I clicked the Photo Info menu in the Overlays panel to select a custom template that was created using the setup shown in Figure 10.16.*

Photo Info

The Photo Info section lets you add photographic information below each frame (**Figure 10.15**). Click the menu to choose from a list of basic, commonly required items such as Filename and Date, but for more extensive naming, you should choose Edit, which opens the Text Template Editor (**Figure 10.16**). This dialog lets you select tokens from the pop-up menus. Click Insert to add these tokens to the Photo Info template design. You can also add typed text and save the template as a custom Photo Info preset. You can then simply select this preset from the Photo Info menu and choose a font size for the Photo Info text.

This feature has many practical uses, especially since there are many choices of photo information items that can be printed out below each picture. For example, if you are cataloging a collection of images, you may want to print out contact sheets with all the technical data included. Or, if you are sending contact sheets to a client, you may want to include just the filename, caption, and copyright information.

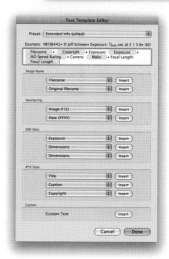

Figure 10.16 *The Text Template Editor can be used to create custom Photo Info templates. If you click to select a token and then click one of the Insert options, the selected token is changed. Otherwise, clicking Insert will add a new token.*

Page Setup

Before making an actual print, you first need to click the Page Setup button at the bottom of the left panel section. This takes you to the Page Setup system dialogs for the Mac or PC operating systems, shown in **Figure 10.17** and **Figure 10.18** respectively. The main aim here is to establish which printer you intend printing with and enter the paper size you are about to print to, followed by the paper orientation: either portrait or landscape. The Paper Size options will most likely vary depending on which printer model you have selected, and the subsequent options will be restricted to the various known standard paper sizes that are compatible with that particular printer. However, if the size you want to use is not listed, it is usually quite easy to create a new custom page size.

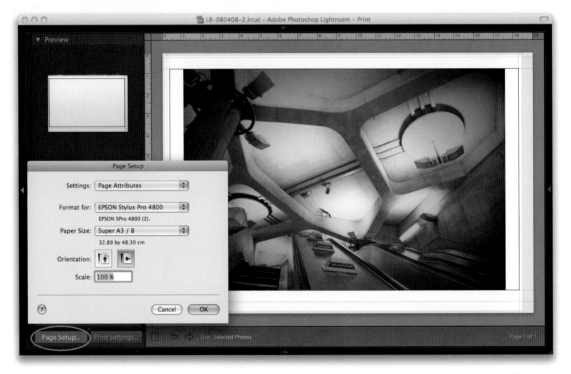

Figure 10.17 *When you click the Page Setup button in the Mac version of Lightroom, you see the Page Setup dialog shown here. You can then configure the printer to format for the paper size and page orientation (portrait or landscape). The Scale box allows you to scale the size of the print output, but I advise you to leave the Scale set to 100% and instead use the Layout panel in the Develop module to scale the output size for the printed image.*

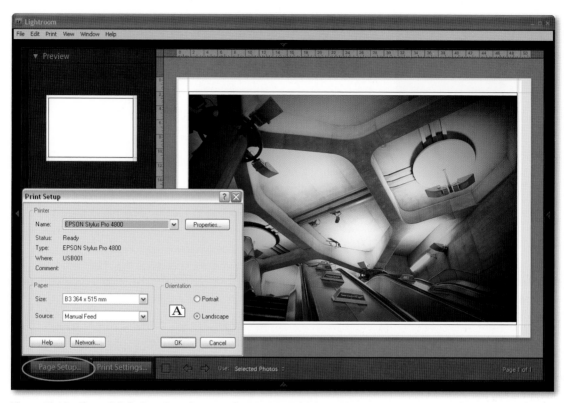

Figure 10.18 *If you click the Page Setup button in the PC version of Lightroom, you see the Print Setup dialog shown here, where you can choose a printer and set the paper size and orientation (either portrait or landscape). When you have done this, click OK to close the Print Setup dialog.*

The main difference between the PC Print Setup dialog and the Mac dialog is that the PC dialog allows you to click the Properties button and go straight to the Print Settings section of the system Print dialog, bypassing the need to configure these settings via the Print Settings button.

Print resolution

In Lightroom there is no need for you to resize the image for printing. After you have configured the Page Setup settings, you can decide which print resolution to use by setting the resolution in the Print Job panel. Depending on the resolution you select, Lightroom either samples the image down or up in size to produce a print image with the right number of pixels to match the image dimension size that was set in the Layout panel section.

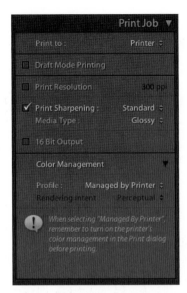

Figure 10.19 *The Print Job settings panel.*

Print Job panel

Print job color management

The Color Management settings provide you with simple and advanced printing options. For the simple printing method, leave the Profile set to Managed by Printer (**Figure 10.19**) and click the Print Settings button to open the Print dialogs shown on the following pages. Basically, you need to check that the right printer is selected (the same one selected in Page Setup) and then choose the appropriate print settings, such as the paper media type you are going to print on and the print quality. But most important of all, if you are using the Managed by Printer option, the ColorSync option must be checked in the Color Management section (Mac), or if you are using the PC version of Lightroom, the ICM button must be checked in the Advanced Print Properties panel. After you have configured the relevant print settings, click Save to save these print settings changes.

The Lightroom printing procedure

Regardless of which print method is used, the printing procedure is basically the same. You must first configure the Page Setup on the toolbar to tell Lightroom which printer you are printing to and the size of the paper you are using. Next, you configure the print settings to tell the printer how the print data should be interpreted. Then you can click the Print button (which takes you to the final Print dialog). Or better still, use the Print One button that bypasses the system dialog completely. The following steps show the settings that you would use for printing to an Epson R1900 printer. The print driver dialogs will vary from printer to printer; some offer different driver interface designs and in some cases more options. It is unfortunate that there is no easier, universal way to describe the printing steps that should be used here. But the print drivers are designed by the printer manufacturers, which in turn have to work within the limits imposed by the computer operating systems. Not even Microsoft or Apple can agree on a common architecture for the print driver settings. It may be helpful to know that once you have configured the page and print settings, you can save them permanently as a print template. Because you are able to save the page and print settings, you can lock the correct print settings to a template and avoid having to configure the print driver every time you make a print.

Managed by printer print settings (Mac)

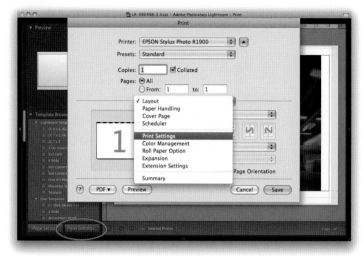

1. First, I clicked the Print Settings button in the Print module to open the Print dialog, which is shown here with the full list of options for the Epson Stylus Photo R1900 printer. Remember, you need to select the printer make here as well as in the previous Page Setup dialog.

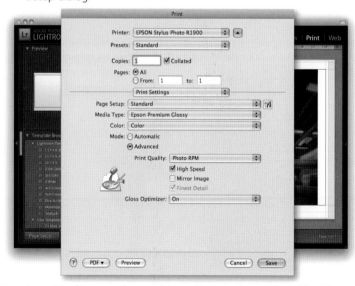

2. I want to focus on the most important sections only. In the Print Settings section, I selected the media type that matched the paper I was about to print with, chose the Color inks option, and set the print mode to Advanced, where I could select a high-quality print output setting.

As you configure the Page Setup and Print settings, they are saved as part of the current print layout setup. If you proceed to save a print template, the Print settings will be saved along with all the other Layout settings. Later in this chapter I show how to update an existing print template with any modified Print settings.

When you use the printer color management shown here, the important thing is to select the ColorSync or ICM color control option. There will sometimes be a further choice of Color Settings options. You definitely don't want to select Vivid, Charts and Graphics, or "No color adjustment." If offered the choice, select sRGB or better still, Adobe RGB.

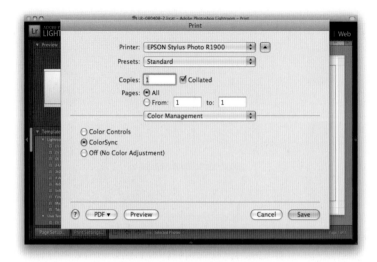

3. Although there is sometimes a panel called ColorSync, don't confuse this with the Color Management section shown here. With this driver, I needed to click the ColorSync button to enable the ColorSync color management. I then clicked the Save button to return to the Lightroom Print module.

Managed by printer print settings (PC)

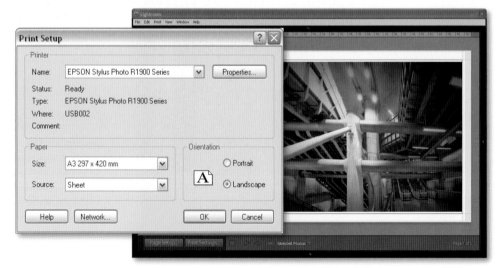

1. Here, I clicked the Print Settings button in the Print module. Note that the Print Setup dialog is the same as the one you saw when I clicked the Page Setup button. Basically, on a PC system you can click either Page Setup or Print Settings to get started here.

Custom profile printing

The simple print method allows you to make quick Draft Mode prints or normal quality prints with added sharpening. If you are printing with a modern inkjet printer, you can expect to get reasonable results when using the Managed by Printer option with the ColorSync or ICM option selected in the print driver settings. But if you want to make really good-quality prints, you will be better off getting Lightroom to handle the printer color management. To do this deselect the Managed by Printer option and select a printer profile from the Profile menu. You should choose a canned profile or a custom profile that was specially made for your printer. **Figures 10.24** and **10.25** show how I changed the Color Management Profile setting so that instead of using Managed by Printer I could choose from a list of individual printer profiles. This in turn offered me a choice of rendering intents for the print job (see page 484).

However, if you choose Lightroom to handle the printer color management, you must configure the print settings differently. For example, if you select a standard printer-supplied profile, the Media Type selected in the print settings must match the selected profile. If you select a custom print profile, you must also ensure that the ensuing print settings match those used to generate the original print target. Most importantly, the ColorSync/ICM settings should be set to No Color Management, because you will want to avoid double-color managing the print image data.

Figure 10.24 *When you click the Profile menu in the Print Job panel, you can choose a custom profile from the pop-up menu. This menu can be configured to display just the profiles that you want to see. To edit the profile list, select Other and use the menu shown in Figure 10.25 to check the profiles you want to see listed.*

Figure 10.25. *This shows the Profile list menu that you'll see when you click the Other option in the Print Job panel Profile menu.*

Managed by Lightroom print settings (Mac)

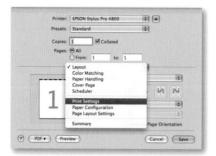

1. The steps outlined here are more or less the same as those for the "Managed by Printer" procedure. Start by clicking the Print Settings button to open the Print dialog, which is shown here with the full list of settings options for the Epson 4800 printer.

2. Once again, Print Settings and Color Management are the most critical sections. Let's say I had selected an Epson 4800 Premium Glossy profile in the Print Job settings panel, using the standard print profile supplied by Epson. I would need to ensure that the selected Media Type matched the profile that was chosen in Lightroom and that I had the correct (matching) paper loaded in the printer, since the subsequent Print Quality settings are governed by the choice of Media Type. I selected the desired print resolution and print speed quality and set the Color Settings to Off (No Color Adjustment), which ensured that the printer color management was disabled. If you are using a custom profile generated from a print test target, always make sure you enter the exact same print settings as you used to print the target. You can then click Save to save these print settings.

Managed by Lightroom print settings (PC)

1. When you click Print Settings in the PC Lightroom Print module, the main Print Setup dialog opens. Click the Properties button to open the Printer Properties dialogs shown in the next step.

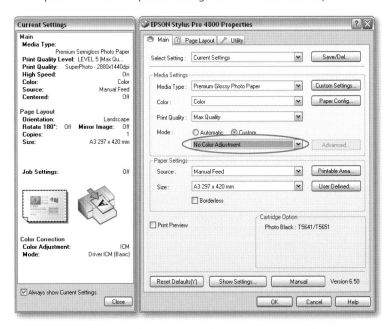

2. In the Properties dialog you can select the correct media type, set the Print Quality, and choose the No Color Adjustment option in the Mode section. Click OK to go back to the Print Setup dialog and click OK to save the new print settings and return to the Lightroom Print module. You can then click the main Lightroom Print One button to make a single print, bypassing the system print dialog.

NOTE

To make a custom paper profile for your printer, you need to print out a print target image from your computer without color managing the test image file and save the settings used to make the print (as described on these pages). When using the custom profile, make sure that the exact same settings are applied as you used to generate the test target.

If you want to have custom profiles made for your printer, your best bet is to contact a color management consultant who will supply appropriate test targets and direct you on how to print out a target from your printer.

But please note that you cannot use Lightroom to print out a test target image. Target images are always unprofiled, and in the absence of an embedded profile, Lightroom automatically assumes an sRGB profile for the imported image and then converts the data from this assumed space to the native Lightroom RGB space as it is processed through the (non–Draft Mode) Lightroom pipeline.

All you really need to know is that printer targets must be printed via Photoshop (where you can open a test target image file without color managing it). But the system Print dialog will be the same as the one used by Lightroom. Remember to save the print settings so that the saved preset settings can be recalled when establishing the print settings for Lightroom to use.

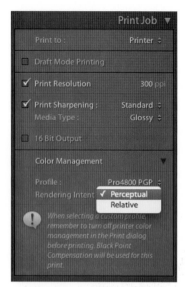

Figure 10.26 *When you click Rendering Intent, you can choose between Perceptual or Relative for the print output.*

Rendering intent

Whenever you deselect the Managed by Printer option and select a custom print profile in Lightroom, you have two choices of Rendering Intent: Perceptual or Relative (**Figure 10.26**). Unfortunately, there is no way in Lightroom to preview what the outcome will be onscreen when either of these rendering intents are selected, so you have to decide on your own which one to use.

The Relative (also referred to as Relative Colorimetric) rendering intent maps all the colors in the source image to the nearest equivalent in-gamut color in the selected print profile print space, but at the same time clips those colors that fall outside the gamut of the print space. The Perceptual rendering intent maps all the colors in the source image to fit smoothly within the destination print profile space. When Perceptual is used, all color differentiations are preserved. So, the brightest colors in the source image maps to the brightest printable colors in the print space and all the other colors will be evenly mapped within the gamut of the print space. The difference between these two rendering methods is most obvious when comparing an image that contains bright, saturated color detail, such as a photograph of a flower. With Relative rendering, the brighter colors may get clipped. But with a Perceptual rendering the bright color detail will be preserved better in the print.

Some people may point out that the downside of Perceptual rendering is that it has a tendency to unnecessarily desaturate the colors in an image where there were no out-of-gamut colors in the first place. In these situations, a Relative rendering produces a better result. Others argue that if the print does not look good when printed using a Perceptual rendering intent, it may be because you haven't fully optimized the image in the Develop module. Personally, I find both rendering intents to be useful. If the image is fairly standard without large areas of bright color detail, I often use Relative, especially if I am printing to glossy media with the wide gamut inks found in the latest inkjet printers. However, some printers have a more limited gamut; this is especially true when printing to matte art papers using photo matte black inks. For instance, I have an older Epson 1290 printer that has a limited color gamut in the shadows compared to more recent printers such as the Epson 4800. With a Relative rendering intent, I may well see noticeable gamut clipping in the shadow areas, so I find I get smoother tonal renditions in the shadows if I use the Perceptual rendering intent when printing images with a lot of dark colors.

Saving a custom template

After you have set up the page layout design and configured the Page Setup and Print Setup settings, you can save the print setup (including all the print settings) as a custom template. In the Template Browser panel (**Figure 10.27**), click the plus button at the top of the panel header to add the current print setup as a template and give it a name. To delete a template, select the template name in the Template Browser and click the minus button.

As you update the layout or print settings relating to a particular template, you can easily update the settings by right-clicking on the template name and choosing Update with Current Settings.

Figure 10.27 *To save a print layout as a custom template, click the Add button just below the Template Browser and give it a name. You can update existing settings by holding down the Control key (for the Mac) or right-clicking (PC) to reveal the contextual menu and Select Update with Current Settings.*

11 | Presenting your work

Making use of the Slideshow and Web modules

Despite the popularity of print, it is interesting to pause for a moment and speculate just how few of the photographs we shoot actually do end up being printed. There was a time when people would take their film to the local photo lab to be processed where every picture was printed. These days, a lot of people shoot with digital cameras, and instead of being shown set of prints, you are more likely to see people's holiday photos displayed to you on their computer, sent as email attachments or shown on a Web site.

This final chapter is therefore all about how to present your photographs so that they look their best when viewed on the screen. Lightroom's Web module helps you create an instant Web site of your pictures. After you have configured the settings the first time, you upload a Web gallery to the Internet, and can then create and upload more galleries with relative ease. But first let's take a look at how to create smart-looking slideshow presentations that can be displayed on the computer or exported as self-contained presentations for business or personal use.

The Slideshow module

The Slideshow module (**Figure 11.1**) lets you create onscreen presentations of your library collections in two ways: either as a Lightroom slideshow or as a PDF or JPEG export. You can play slideshows directly from the Slideshow module, but you can also initiate an impromptu slideshow while in the Library, Develop, or Print modules by pressing ⇧Shift Enter. Any time you want to exit a slideshow, just press Esc.

The Slideshow Options panel controls how the images are presented in the individual slide frames and offers the ability to edit the Stroke Border styles and Cast Shadow options. The Layout panel is similar to the page layout tools in the Print module and can be used to set up the margin widths for the slide frames. The Overlays panel is also similar to the one in the Print module, where you can add elements to a slideshow template design, such as a custom Identity Plate and rating stars information. When you enable the Text Overlays option, you can add custom text objects with full text editing control and optional drop shadows. The Backdrop panel lets you set a backdrop color and color wash effect, or you can choose to add an image from the Filmstrip as the backdrop. The new Titles panel lets you add slides at the beginning and end of a slideshow during playback, with the option to use the Identity Plate Editor to add text captions or graphics. The Playback panel provides playback duration, image fade, and randomize options, as well as the ability to select a music sound track for the slideshow.

As with most of the other modules, the Slideshow settings can be saved as a custom template setting via the Template Browser. Notice that as you hover over the listed presets the Preview panel generates a quick preview using the current, most selected image in the Filmstrip selection as a guide to the slideshow template's appearance. The playback controls in the toolbar area can be used to switch to the Preview mode, in which you can preview how the slideshow will look in the Content area before clicking the main Play button.

As I explained in Chapter 4, you can choose Create Slideshow from the Collections panel to add a new Slideshow collection. You can easily select a Slideshow collection from the other modules, such as Library, Print, and Web. Slideshows can also be exported as self-contained PDF documents or as individual JPEG slide images. Just go to the Slideshow module Slideshow menu and choose Export Slideshow. Or you can press ⌘ J (Mac) or Ctrl J (PC) to export a PDF Slideshow, or use ⌘ ⇧Shift J (Mac) or Ctrl ⇧Shift J (PC) to export JPEG slides.

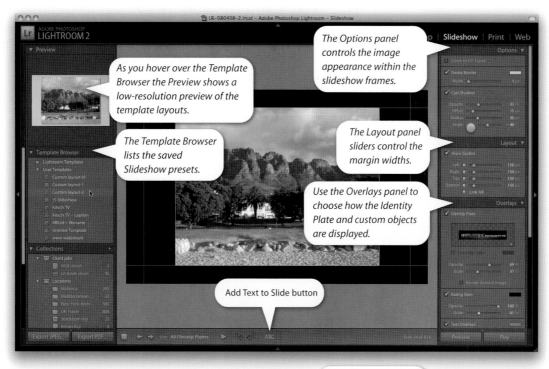

As you hover over the Template Browser the Preview shows a low-resolution preview of the template layouts.

The Template Browser lists the saved Slideshow presets.

The Options panel controls the image appearance within the slideshow frames.

The Layout panel sliders control the margin widths.

Use the Overlays panel to choose how the Identity Plate and custom objects are displayed.

Add Text to Slide button

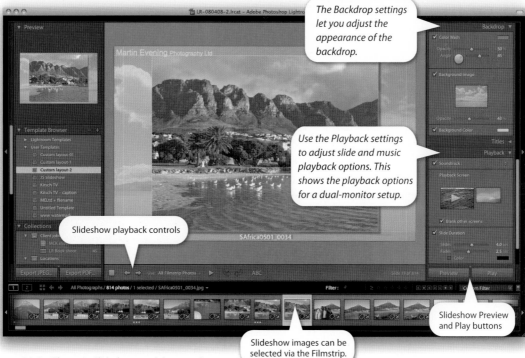

The Backdrop settings let you adjust the appearance of the backdrop.

Use the Playback settings to adjust slide and music playback options. This shows the playback options for a dual-monitor setup.

Slideshow playback controls

Slideshow Preview and Play buttons

Slideshow images can be selected via the Filmstrip.

Figure 11.1 *The main Slideshow module controls.*

NOTE

The toolbar offers options for choosing which photos are displayed in a slideshow. You can choose from All Filmstrip Photos, Selected Photos, or Flagged Photos.

The Slide Editor view in the Content area

The most selected image will appear in the Content area, which is used to display a Slide Editor view of the slideshow layout. You can change the image view by using the left and right arrow keys to navigate through the selected images in the Filmstrip (**Figure 11.2**).

As adjustments are made to the Slideshow settings in the panels on the right, these changes are reflected in the Slide Editor view. As with the other Lightroom modules, you can toggle between showing and hiding the toolbar using the T keyboard shortcut.

Figure 11.2 *The Slideshow module showing a view of the slideshow layout in the Content area and the Filmstrip below.*

Layout panel

The Layout panel lets you edit the slide layout by specifying the margins for the image content. **Figure 11.3** shows the layout guides highlighted in red. You can adjust the margins by dragging on the slider controls. Or simply double-click the fields in the panel, enter a pixel value, and fine-tune this value using the up and down arrow keys. A single arrow click increases or decreases the pixel dimensions by one unit, and a ⟨⇧Shift⟩–click increases or decreases the pixel dimensions 10 units at a time. If you just hover the mouse over one of the field boxes, a scrubby slider will become active, and you can then drag the mouse right or left to increase or decrease a value. Note that the unit dimensions have linking check boxes next to them, which means that when two or more boxes are checked, as you adjust one value, the other field values are linked to it. For example, in Figure 11.3 I checked the boxes for just the left and right margins, so that only they were linked as I adjusted the margin width on either side of the frame area. You can hide the slide layout guides at any time by unchecking the Show Guides box in the Layout panel or by pressing ⌘⇧Shift H (Mac) or Ctrl⇧Shift H (PC).

NOTE

The proportions of the Slideshow view are always relative to and dictated by the proportions of the monitor display you are working on. This can have ramifications for how you export a slideshow. I will discuss how to address this in "Exporting a Slideshow," later in the chapter.

Figure 11.3   *The slide Layout controls. Note that as I rolled the mouse over the pixel size field, the scrubby slider became active, allowing me to drag left or right to adjust the pixel size widths of the margins.*

Options panel

Now let's look at how the individual photographs are displayed in the slide frames. At the top of the Options panel is the Zoom to Fill Frame check box. In our next example, this option is deselected, and as you can see in the Slide Editor view, the slideshow photographs fit centered within the margins (as specified in the Layout panel). If the Zoom to Fill Frame option is checked, the slideshow photographs resize and expand to fill the available space. You should be aware that when you select this option, the Zoom to Fill Frame setting automatically centers each image in the slideshow as it applies the necessary cropping to the picture. The cropped view is aligned to the bottom edge of the frame. This is because I clicked on the slide preview image and dragged it upward to preserve the bottom edge of the photograph. This tweaking overrides the automatic cropping and is applied on a per-image basis. In other words, you can pre-edit a selection of pictures that will be included in a slideshow and customize the cropping in each picture. Be aware that these adjustments will be lost as soon as you make a new selection of images; it only makes sense to spend time making custom tweaks to a slideshow presentation in this way if your goal is to export the slideshow as a PDF presentation or as JPEG slide images. In our examples, I checked the Stroke Border option to add a light gray stroke to the slideshow frame images (the stroke border is always 1 pixel thick). If you want to change the stroke color, then double-click the color swatch to open the color picker dialog shown in **Figure 11.4**. Our examples are shown in **Figures 11.5** and **11.6**.

Figure 11.4 *The Lightroom color picker dialog.*

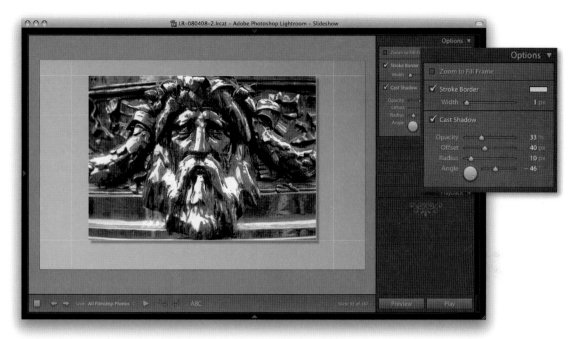

Figure 11.5 *The Options panel is shown here with the guides visible but all other objects hidden. I left the Stroke Border option checked and created a custom Cast Shadow setting.*

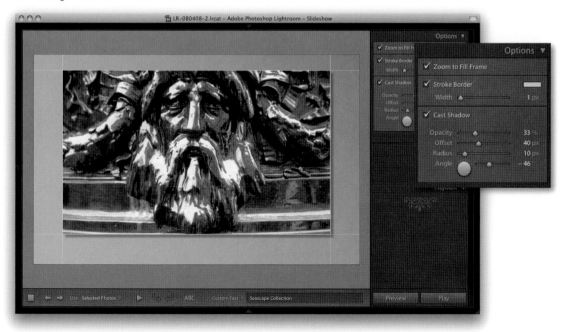

Figure 11.6 *In this next example, I checked the Zoom to Fill Frame option. Note how the same image expands to fill the area within the frame margins.*

Overlays panel

Having established the layout margins and image placement, you can begin adding extra content to the slide frames. If you enable the Identity Plate option, you can select a custom preset template by clicking on the Identity Plate preview, or choose Edit to create a new one. The Opacity and Scale properties let you customize the Identity Plate appearance and decide whether you want the Identity Plate to be on top or placed behind each slide photograph. Once enabled, the Identity Plate can be repositioned by simply clicking and dragging it anywhere inside the slide frame area, and in this respect, the Identity Plate is just like any other custom object. The Rating Stars options let you display the current image star rating as well as set the color and scale size. As with all custom objects, you can scale each object by dragging on a corner or side handle. The Text Overlays check box toggles displaying all other objects apart from the Identity Plate and ratings. For example, in **Figure 11.7** this option is checked, which allows us to see a filename text object that I had placed centered below the image. The Shadow check box lets you apply a drop shadow effect to each overlay object and apply independent shadow settings to each. I will discuss working with text overlays shortly, but let's take a quick look at the Identity Plate options first (**Figures 11.8** and **11.9**).

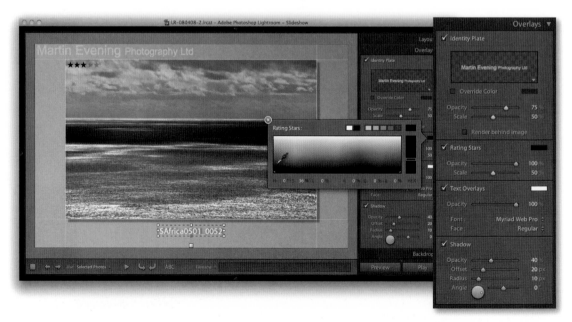

Figure 11.7   *The Overlays panel can be used to add an Identity Plate, rating stars, and custom text objects with or without drop shadows.*

Creating a custom Identity Plate

Figure 11.8 *To open the Identity Plate Editor, click on the Identity Plate preview in the Overlays panel and choose a pre-saved Identity Plate setting or select Edit. In this step I chose the "Use a styled text identity plate" option, modified the typeface, and saved it as a new Identity Plate preset.*

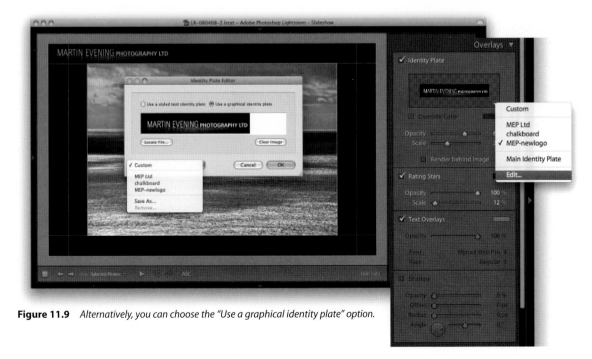

Figure 11.9 *Alternatively, you can choose the "Use a graphical identity plate" option.*

Adding custom text overlays

To add a custom text overlay, click the Add Text to Slide button (**Figure 11.10**), which opens the Text box next to it in the toolbar. You can at this stage start typing in some text. After you press Enter, the text will appear as a new text overlay in the Slide Editor view. You can also click Custom Text, or click and hold down the mouse to open the menu and select an item from the list such as *Date* or *Filename*. Or, you can choose Edit, which opens the Text Template Editor shown in **Figure 11.11** and **Figure 11.12** (or press ⌘T [Mac] or Ctrl T [PC]). This allows you to add various metadata items as tokens. Click an Insert button to add a new token to a template design and combine them with custom text to create your own custom text overlay presets. For example, in Figure 11.11 I show how you could create a text overlay that includes text such as *Date of Shoot,* followed by a "Date (Month, DD, YYYY)" token. You can add as many text overlays as you like and reedit them. If you click to select a text object in the Slide Editor view, you can edit the content by typing in new text, or by selecting a new item from the menu in the toolbar. You can also use the Rotate buttons on the toolbar to rotate text overlays by 90°. To remove a text overlay, just click to highlight it and click Delete.

Figure 11.10   *In this screen shot, I added a basic custom text object. You can use the various anchor points (I have shown all of them here) to help align a text overlay.*

Figure 11. 11 *To add other types of text overlays, you can click on the menu and select a text object preset, or click the Edit menu item to open the Text Template Editor and create a template design of your own.*

Figure 11.12 *Here are some example views of the Text Template Editor. The Date token options (left) can be used to apply different date and time formats. The token options (middle) include items relating to the camera capture data. The IPTC Data token options (right) include items relating to the IPTC metadata (see Chapter 4).*

Working with the anchor points

The anchor points serve as useful guides for the placement of text overlays within the Slide Editor view. You can use these points to help align a text overlay to the center or corner edges of the image, or to the entire Slide Editor frame. The anchor points of a text overlay will normally link and snap to whichever Slide Editor anchor point is in closest proximity. As you click and drag a text overlay around the screen, the linking points jump to whichever two points are nearest. If you click on the current Slide Editor anchor point, it becomes highlighted in yellow and locked to the text overlay. You can then move the overlay around the screen with it locked to this anchor point (although the anchor points on the text overlay itself will jump to whichever point is closest to the locked, Slide Editor anchor point). As you click and drag a text overlay, notice how the object tends to remain snapped to the current alignment. Alternatively, you can use the keyboard arrow keys to nudge an overlay, and use the [Shift] key to magnify the shift amount.

1. To add a custom text overlay, I clicked the Add Text to Slide button, which revealed the Custom Text options shown here, where I selected the Website token.

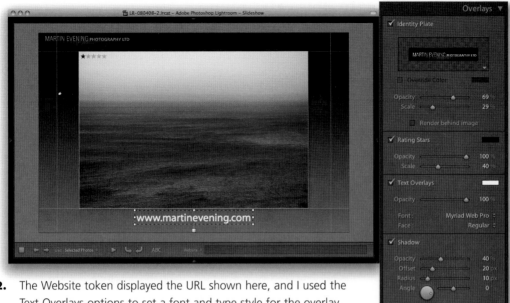

2. The Website token displayed the URL shown here, and I used the Text Overlays options to set a font and type style for the overlay.

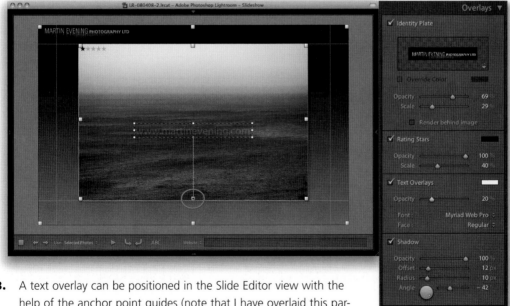

3. A text overlay can be positioned in the Slide Editor view with the help of the anchor point guides (note that I have overlaid this particular screen shot with a map of all the available anchor points). You can adjust the placement of a frame anchor point by clicking to select it and dragging it to a new position. Here, I placed the text in the middle of the frame. Lastly, I adjusted the Shadow settings and set the text opacity to 20% to create a watermark effect.

Backdrop panel

The backdrop appearance can be modified via the Backdrop panel. The Color Wash controls are a nice touch, because you can set up different color scheme combinations using the Color Wash and Background Color swatches and then adjust the Opacity and Angle sliders to fine-tune the effect; you can also place an image as a backdrop. The first time you check the Background Image option you won't see anything happen, because you have to select a photograph from the Filmstrip first and drag it into the backdrop area (or Background image preview) for the background image to register. After that you can use the check box to toggle the backdrop image on or off. Notice how the Color Wash colors can also be combined with the applied backdrop image and used to mute the backdrop image contrast. Whenever an image is applied to the backdrop, you still retain full control over the Color Wash Color, Background Color, and Color Wash settings, and can mix them any way you like to achieve the desired look for the backdrop. Remember also that all the settings, including those in the Backdrop panel, can be saved as a template. So you can create Backdrop panel designs that use different background images and save them to the Template Browser panel. The following steps show some examples of how to create different background effects.

1. The default backdrop color for this template design was black, but when I checked the Background Color option, I could click the color swatch to choose an alternative backdrop color.

2. When the Color Wash option was checked, I was able to introduce a secondary color to apply a gradient wash across the backdrop.

3. Lastly, I was able to add an image to the backdrop by dragging a photo from the Filmstrip into the slide Background Image preview area and adjusting the Background Image opacity.

How to create a novelty slideshow template

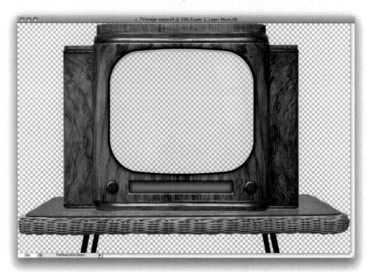

1. I devised this series of steps to show you some of the potential Lightroom has for creating customized slideshow layouts. First of all I used my Photoshop skills to create a cutout image of an old-fashioned television set on top of a table. I won't go into all the details about how I created this object, but I'd like to draw your attention to the screen area in the middle, which although you can't see too well against the checkered transparency pattern, contains soft highlight reflections. The insert image shows this more clearly against a black background.

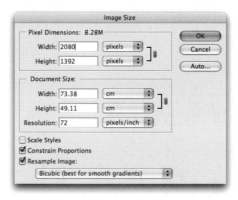

2. I went to the Image menu in Photoshop and used the Image Size dialog to resize the master image to the size shown here, which would be the maximum needed for a slideshow presentation on a 30-inch display.

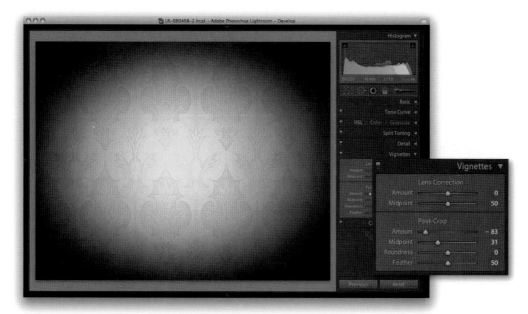

3. Meanwhile, I selected a suitable backdrop photo in Lightroom, which in this case was a photograph taken of a wallpaper design. I used the Post-Crop Amount and Midpoint sliders in the Develop module Vignettes panel to burn in the corners of this photograph.

4. In the Slideshow module I dragged the wallpaper photo from the Filmstrip to place it as a background image in the Backdrop panel.

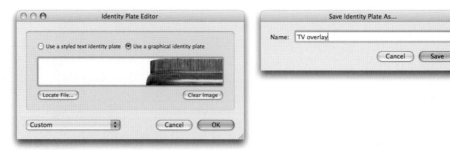

5. To load the foreground image that I had worked on in Photoshop, I clicked on the triangle in the Overlays panel Identity Plate preview (circled in Step 6) and chose Edit. This opened the Identity Plate Editor shown here. I checked the "Use a graphical identity plate" option, clicked the Locate File button, and chose the image I had worked in Photoshop. Don't worry about the warning in the Preview window about images being no more than 57 pixels tall. Just click OK and save this as a new Identity Plate setting.

6. The Identity Plate image appears as a new overlay where the photo selected in the Filmstrip appears sandwiched between the backdrop image and the Identity Plate overlay. The first stage here was to place and scale the Identity Plate image so that it almost filled the whole of the screen and was centered in the frame.

7. I then adjusted the Layout panel guides to position the photo frame so that the height of a landscape photograph would just fit within the top and bottom of the TV screen area. I also set the left and right guides so that any extra narrow landscape photos would still fit the frame height.

8. Here is a slide from the finished slideshow in which selected photos were played back via this television screen slideshow template.

Titles panel

The Titles panel allows you to add intro and ending screens to a slideshow presentation. You can add these screens using the Identity Plate Editor, as shown next. All you have to do is check the Add Identity Plate options to add a screen at the beginning and/or at the end of a slideshow. The Titles panel offers a few extra controls so that you can scale the Identity Plate and override the color of the Identity Plate content as well as set a background color.

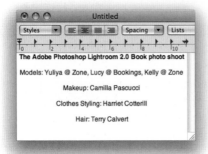
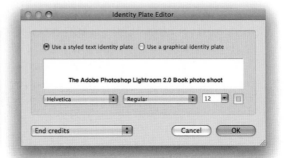

1. To create an end credit screen, I used a basic text editor program to write the credits, where I made the first line bold, added carriage returns, and centered the text. I copied and pasted this into the Identity Plate Editor dialog and saved as a new Identity Plate.

2. I was then able to select a standard Identity Plate company logo for the intro screen and select the credit list as the ending screen. This screen shot shows a preview where the last image in the slideshow sequence fades to the end screen credits.

Playback panel

When all the slide settings are configured, you will be almost ready to start playing a slideshow. But before doing so you need to visit the Playback panel and set the duration of the slides and the length of time for the fades between each slide (**Figure 11.13**). If you want the slideshow to run at a fast speed, you can try selecting shorter slide and transition duration times. But bear in mind that the ability to play back at a faster speed is governed by the size of the master library image files and whether they have all been fully cached yet, not to mention the performance power of your computer. Should you be so inclined, you can check the Random Order option at the bottom to shuffle the play order or click Repeat to have the slideshow run in a loop.

If the Soundtrack option is checked, Lightroom looks to see if you have any software capable of playing MP3 tracks, such as Apple's iTunes, and displays the music library and any collection lists via a drop-down menu (**Figure 11.14**). On the computer setup in my office, I maintain my complete MP3 music library and have created several customized music lists (**Figure 11.15**). I can choose a specific music track to accompany an image slideshow. When I click Play, the selected music track starts playing in the background, commencing with the first track in the selected list. When you have a list of favorite tracks, you need to drag them to rearrange the order of the music tracks to match the desired mood for your slideshow. I recommend making selections of a small number of tracks that blend well together, and then in iTunes choose File ⇨ New Playlist from Selection and name it as a new playlist selection. You will then need to choose the Refresh Playlist from iTunes option in the Playback panel to make the new playlist visible, and select it when choosing a playback track.

Figure 11.13   *The Playback panel (this shows dual-monitor options for selecting either screen).*

Figure 11.14   *As you add new playlists in iTunes, you need to choose the Refresh Playlist from iTunes item in the Playback panel to make the new playlist visible.*

NOTE

Apple iTunes is a free MP3 player program available for Mac and PC. To download the latest version, go to www.apple.com/itunes/.

Figure 11.15   *The iTunes program interface showing a playlist selection titled "Slideshow selections."*

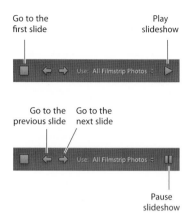

Go to the first slide   Play slideshow

Go to the previous slide   Go to the next slide

Pause slideshow

Figure 11.16 *The Slideshow Preview mode playback controls, showing the slideshow controls in both Play and Pause mode.*

Preview and Play

You are now ready to play the slideshow (see **Figure 11.16**). Choose Slideshow ⇨ Run Slideshow, click the Play button in the bottom-right corner, or press (Enter) to launch a full-screen slideshow using the currently selected slideshow template settings. When you switch to full Play mode, the screen fades out to black and then fades up to display the slides in sequence. To stop a slideshow, just press the (Esc) key.

If you just want to see a quick preview of a slideshow, click Preview next to the Play button ((Alt)(Enter)). This allows you to see the slide-show play within the Content area. **Figure 11.17** shows a slideshow being previewed, where the background is dimmed to black in the Content area. The main advantage of running a slideshow in Preview mode is that slideshows will typically start running a lot sooner (depending on the size of your slideshow images). While you are in Preview mode you can interact with the slideshow using the navigation keys located on the toolbar (see **Figure 11.18** for descriptions of the toolbar buttons). But you can also manually override a slideshow sequence by using the left and right arrow keys to go backward or forward through the sequence. You can press the (Spacebar) to pause a slideshow and press the (Spacebar) again to resume playing.

Figure 11.17 *If you want to check how your slideshow is looking without playing the full-screen version, click the Preview button (circled). You can pause a slideshow by clicking the Pause button or by hitting the* (Spacebar).

Navigating slideshow photos

As well as using the menu commands and toolbar buttons, you can use the ⌘ key (Mac) or Ctrl key (PC) plus the left or right arrow keys to progress through the slides. Of course, you can use the arrow keys on their own to navigate the photos in the Filmstrip. But by using the ⌘/Ctrl key plus the arrow keys, you can preserve any image selections that are currently active.

Slideshows and selections

There are Slideshow module options in the toolbar (Figure 11.18) as well as via the Play menu (**Figure 11.19**) that determine which images are accessed from the Filmstrip when playing a slideshow (providing there is more than one image selected). If Use All Filmstrip Photos is selected, the slideshow will play all the photos in the current Filmstrip starting from whichever is the most selected or target image on. If Use Selected Photos is selected, the Slideshow module plays only the selected images. If Use Flagged Photos is selected, only those photos that have been rated as "Flagged, Pick images" will be played.

Figure 11.18   *The Slideshow module toolbar showing the content options.*

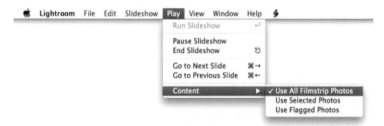

Figure 11.19   *The Slideshow module Play menu showing the content options.*

NOTE

If you want to run an impromptu slideshow in any of Lightroom's modules, press ⌘ Enter (Mac) or Ctrl Enter (PC).

Figure 11.20 *The Template Browser plus template preview. Note: If you save a slideshow setting that includes a backdrop image, the backdrop image must be present in the library in order for the template to work.*

Template Browser panel

When you have completed work on a slideshow layout design, you can select Slideshow ⇨ Save Slideshow Settings or use ⌘S (Mac), Ctrl S (PC) to quickly save the current slideshow settings (but without saving them as a template just yet). As you select other presaved templates and compare the look of different layouts, you can always go to the Slideshow menu and choose Revert Slideshow Settings, which will instantly return you to the last saved temporary slideshow layout.

However, after going to all the trouble of designing a slideshow layout with measured margins, Identity Plate, customized text objects, and backdrop image, it makes sense to save it as a template that can be used again later. To do this, click the plus button in the Template Browser panel header and give the template a descriptive name. **Figure 11.20** shows a template that I created in some of the earlier pages of this chapter that was saved as *Custom layout-2*. As you roll over the other template presets in the list, you will see a preview based on whichever is the most selected image in the Slide Editor view. As with the other Lightroom modules, you can remove a template by highlighting it and clicking the Remove button in the Template Browser panel. You can also update the settings for a particular template by right-clicking (also available as Ctrl –click on a Mac) and choosing Update with Current Settings. There is no nesting capability built into the Template Browser panel. To be honest, it is not something that you are likely to need because there should be enough room to accommodate all the slideshow templates you might use. Don't forget that, as with the Print module, you can save Slideshow settings and the associated image selections as Slideshow Collections. These settings can then be accessed when working in the Library, Print, or Web module.

You can also see how social and wedding photographers might find it useful to take a standard layout design and save variations of this template with alternative music playback settings to suit the music tastes of different clients, and how art photographers might like to create custom slideshows for exhibition displays on a large screen.

Exporting a slideshow

As well as displaying slideshows in Lightroom, you can export slideshows. For example, you can export a self-contained slideshow in the Adobe PDF format, which can be played via the freely available Adobe Acrobat Reader program or any other program capable of reading

PDF files (such as Apple Preview). Or you can export individual JPEG slides that can be placed as pages in presentation programs such as Microsoft Powerpoint or Apple Keynote.

To export a PDF slideshow, choose Slideshow ➪ Export PDF Slideshow, or press ⌘ J (Mac) or Ctrl J (PC). This opens the Export Slideshow to PDF dialog shown in **Figure 11.21**, where you can choose a destination to save the exported PDF to. Below this you have the PDF export options, such as the Quality slider (which sets the amount of compression used), and the Width and Height sections (which let you determine how large you want the slideshow document to be). You need to take into account the likely screen size of the computer the exported slideshow will be played on, although the format of the slideshow slides will have already been influenced by the computer display you are working with. For example, most Macintosh computers are hooked up to a display that uses a wide-screen format ratio of something like 16:9. If you want to scale down the slide size but preserve the full slide area, the size dimensions must match the ratio of the current pixel width and pixel height of your display. However, to make life easier for you, the Common Sizes menu will be set to the current monitor display resolution. If you click on this menu you can easily select a common monitor resolution size for other typical computer screens. The "Automatically show full screen" option determines whether the slideshow will start playing in full-screen mode when the person who receives the slideshow opens the exported slideshow PDF document on their computer.

To export a JPEG Slideshow, choose Slideshow ➪ Export JPEG Slideshow, or press ⌘ Shift J (Mac) or Ctrl Shift J (PC). This opens the Export Slideshow to PDF dialog shown in Figure 11.21, where again, you can select the desired compression and screen size settings.

NOTE

Adobe Acrobat Reader is a free PDF player program for Mac or PC. To download the latest version, go to www.adobe.com/products/acrobat/ and look for a link to download the Acrobat Reader program. Only the latest versions of Adobe Acrobat Reader are able to play a slideshow with transition dissolves, and even then they will be of a fixed speed.

TIP

When you play back a PDF slideshow in Adobe Acrobat using the full-screen mode, the default view fills the entire screen. This is fine if you make the slideshow match the full-screen pixel resolution. However, if you want to play the slideshow at the actual pixels resolution, press ⌘ 1 (Mac) or Ctrl 1 (PC) in Adobe Acrobat Reader.

The compression settings should be adjusted according to how you intend to use a slideshow. If a PDF slideshow is to be distributed by CD or DVD, use full-screen size and best quality compression setting. If you are sending a slideshow by email, keep the pixel size and compression settings low enough so you don't send attachments that are too large.

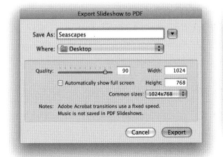
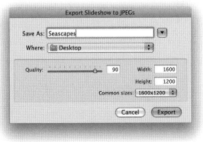

Figure 11.21 *The Export Slideshow to PDF and JPEG dialogs.*

NOTE

Photoshop has long had the ability to let you create Web photo gallery Web sites of your work. Yet it has often surprised me just how few photographers were using this feature, or even knew that it existed. Web galleries are incredibly useful if you need to quickly publish a collection of images on a Web site. You can use them to show photographs from a shoot you are working on to get feedback and approval from a client. Or you can use Web galleries for fun, to share pictures with your friends and family.

TIP

Quite a few templates are provided in the Lightroom Web module to help get you started. With a little patience and practice you can easily adapt these basic templates and customize them to create your own Web gallery design layouts.

NOTE

Lightroom 2 is now 64-bit enabled for Mac and PC. Unfortunately, the Web components of the Web module, such as Flash, are not updated yet for 64-bit, which means that for the early life of Lightroom 2, the Web module may not work as expected. Because of this I have used Lightroom 2 in 32-bit mode to show the full workings of this module. Depending on the current 64-bit status, you may or may not be able to use all the features described here while the program is in 64-bit mode. If this causes a problem, I suggest you restart in 32-bit mode (Mac), or run the 32-bit version program (PC).

The Web module

The Web module in Lightroom helps you to publish photo collections as Web sites with as little fuss as possible (**Figure 11.22**). The main difference between the Web module and the Slideshow module is that although you only have a small amount of control over the Web gallery designs, there is more emphasis on being able to customize the content information. The Web module works by taking the catalog previews and builds a Web site on the fly as you adjust the Web module settings. What you see in the Content area is not just a preview but the Web gallery as it might look when viewed via a Web browser. And as you adjust the Web module panel settings, the changes you make are constantly updated. As with the Slideshow module, a Web gallery can be generated from a selection of images such as a collection, a filtered catalog selection, or a subselection of images made via the Filmstrip.

In the Engine panel you can choose between a Flash Gallery, an HTML style, or one of the new Airtight gallery layouts. Depending on which basic gallery style you select, it in turn affects the options that are subsequently made available in the other remaining panels. In the Site Info panel you can enter custom information such as the site name and your contact details. With the Color Palette panel you can edit the color scheme for all the Web gallery design elements. In the Appearance panel, you can customize the appearance of the layout design for the HTML or Flash Gallery styles, decide how many rows and columns will be used in a thumbnail grid, and set the thumbnail and preview image sizes. The Image Info panel lets you customize the content that appears beneath (or alongside) the individual gallery images and provides an opportunity to add multiple items of relevant data information. The Output Settings panel is used to set the image quality, and output sharpening, and you can choose to add a copyright watermark to the Web gallery images.

At this stage you can either click the Export button to save the Web gallery to a named output folder or click the Upload button to upload the Web gallery using a preconfigured server setting. There is also a Preview in Browser button that lets you preview the Web gallery site in the default Web browser program first. Before clicking the Upload button, though, you will need to use the Upload Settings panel to configure and save the FTP server settings for uploading the gallery directly to a specific server. Lastly, custom web gallery configurations can be saved to the Template Browser panel.

As you roll over the Template Browser panel, the Preview panel shows a preview of the template layout.

The Engine panel is used to select a Gallery style.

Use the Site Info panel to enter specific Web gallery information.

The Template Browser lists all saved gallery template presets.

The Color palette is used to customize the gallery color scheme.

Enter the Title and Caption settings.

Choose the Output quality settings for the main preview images.

Configure the FTP settings for uploading a Web gallery.

Preview the current layout in a Web browser.

Navigation buttons: Go to home page, select previous/next photo

The Export and Upload buttons

Figure 11.22   *The Web module panels and controls.*

Figure 11.23 *The Gallery panel.*

Figure 11.24 *Adobe Flash Player Update warning dialog.*

NOTE

When the Gallery panel is compacted, you will see the name of the selected gallery style in the panel header.

NOTE

When Photoshop first introduced the Web Photo Gallery feature, the site title would always default to "Adobe Web Photo Gallery" unless you entered a name for the banner. Try doing a Web search using the above term (inside quotation marks) and watch as you get half a million or more results revealing the private photo galleries of Photoshop users who forgot to give their Web gallery a name!

Engine panel

The Engine panel is located in right-hand panel section and offers several choices of gallery styles, which are shown listed in **Figure 11.23**.

The Lightroom HTML and Flash galleries

The Lightroom HTML Gallery style is based on a classic HTML-coded template design that can be used to produce a simple Web gallery that has two viewing levels. Thumbnail images are displayed in a grid on the main index page. When you click one of the thumbnail cells, this takes you to a larger, single-image page view with room to include Title and Caption information above and below the photo. From there you can click on the image to return to the index page thumbnail view again. Because the Lightroom HTML Gallery uses classic HTML code, it is probably the most compatible gallery style that you can choose, as any visitor viewing a gallery created with an HTML gallery style will be able to access these pages. The custom options let you make some basic modifications, such as the size of the large image view, the metadata display options, and color scheme, but it is otherwise a fairly rigid gallery style.

The Lightroom Flash Gallery style builds a gallery that uses Adobe Flash (formerly Macromedia) code, which can render smooth, animated slide transitions between images. Flash-based Web sites are all the rage these days. They look cool and are a great way to present your images, but visitors to a site built using the Lightroom Flash Gallery style must have the latest Flash player installed in order to view the gallery. In fact, when you select a Flash Gallery style, you may see the warning dialog indicating that you need to install the latest Adobe Flash player (**Figure 11.24**). However, the Flash Gallery style does offer more options for customizing the gallery layout. For example, when a Flash Gallery style is selected, you have a choice of different layout modes, such as the Scrolling layout, where a large image is displayed in the main index page with the thumbnails below. Other options include a Paginated layout view where the main image is shown on the right with paginated thumbnails on the left; a left scrolling view where the thumbnails run down the side; and a slideshow layout where single images are displayed large in the window and you can view them as a continuous slideshow. The main differences between the HTML and Flash gallery styles can be seen over the next two pages.

HTML gallery

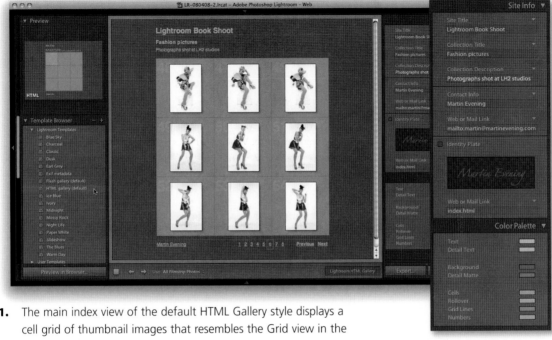

1. The main index view of the default HTML Gallery style displays a cell grid of thumbnail images that resembles the Grid view in the Library module.

2. You can click on a thumbnail to go to the main image view and click on the image to go back to the index view.

NOTE

Flash Galleries have four types of
Web page layout: the Scrolling type
layout (shown here), Paginated, Left
scrolling, and Slideshow Only view
modes. Examples of these other
layout designs are shown in Figures
11.43 through 11.47.

Flash gallery

1. The default Flash Gallery style displays a large image view with
scrolling thumbnails at the bottom. You can click a thumbnail to
select a new image, or click the Slideshow icon (circled) to go to
the Slideshow View mode.

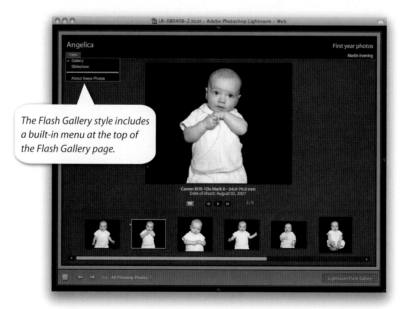

*The Flash Gallery style includes
a built-in menu at the top of
the Flash Gallery page.*

2. You can run the images in a slideshow autoplay mode or use the
left/right arrow keys to navigate the gallery collection.

AutoViewer gallery

Now that third parties have started to construct their own galleries for Lightroom, it is possible to load additional gallery styles. For example, the Airtight gallery styles have been incorporated fully into the Lightroom Web module. It is possible to install other gallery styles as well, such as the Turning Gate styles mentioned on page 520. As with the HTML and Flash Gallery styles, when you select one of these other galleries, the Web module panel options will look different and reveal custom options associated with each particular style (**Figure 11.25**).

The AutoViewer gallery creates a self-running slideshow Web gallery, for which you can adjust things like the frame size, padding and slide duration, and background and color of the frames. In the Output Settings panel you can adjust the size and JPEG quality for the gallery images. However, unlike with some of the other gallery styles, you won't be able to fully appreciate how the gallery style works until you hit the Preview in Browser button. **Figure 11.26** shows a screen shot of how a finished gallery page will look when viewed in a Web browser program.

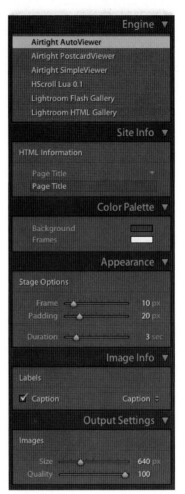

Figure 11.25   *The Airtight AutoViewer Gallery panel options.*

Figure 11.26   *A Web browser view of the Airtight AutoViewer Gallery style in action.*

Figure 11.27 *The PostcardViewer panel options.*

PostcardViewer gallery

This gallery features a rather interesting use of Flash to create the postcard layout you see shown here in the sample Web browser page. As you can see in **Figure 11.27**, the panel options allow you to set the number of columns to use plus the zoom factors for the small thumbnails and larger view images. The **Figure 11.28** screen shots show a Web browser view of the gallery in use. Once viewed via a browser you can try out some navigation shortcuts: use the Spacebar to toggle between the thumbnail and large image view, and use the keyboard arrow keys to navigate from one postcard image to the next.

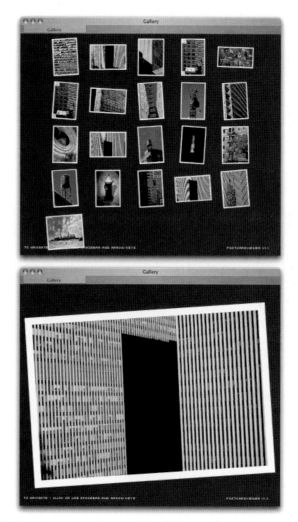

Figure 11.28 *Here are two views of a PostcardViewer gallery style.*

SimpleViewer gallery

The SimpleViewer gallery is fairly similar to the standard Lightroom
Flash gallery "paginated" layout, but it also offers a few nice touches,
such as the ability to precisely control the thumbnails layout, where
you can set the number of rows and columns in the Appearance panel
and customize the image size and quality as well as the frame size and
padding in the Output Settings. **Figure 11.29** shows an example of
how this gallery style looks when previewed in a Web browser. The
large arrows make this gallery style both functional and stylish. **Figure
11.30** shows the SimpleViewer gallery panel options.

Figure 11.29 *Here is a browser view screen shot of the SimpleViewer gallery. The
arrow in the image view allows you to move from the current image to the next, while
clicking on the arrow below the paginated grid jumps to the next batch of thumbnails.*

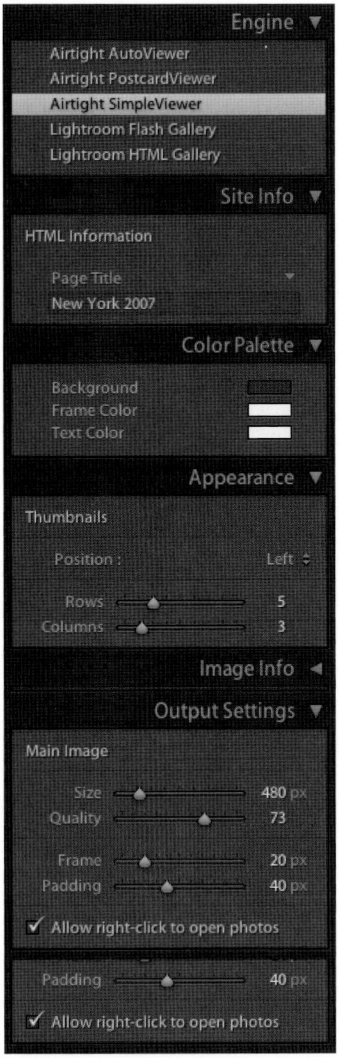

Figure 11.30 *The SimpleViewer
gallery panel options.*

Third-party gallery styles

Adobe have made it easy for third-party companies to create their
own gallery styles. Well, I guess it's only "easy" if you know how to
code such things! This has led to a number of third-party companies
and individuals creating their own brands of gallery styles, which when
loaded take over the right-hand panels in Lightroom and allow you
to customize these gallery styles just as you would when adjusting
the other gallery styles that I have mentioned. In fact, you may have

NOTE

To access the gallery styles shown here, go to www.theturninggate.net.

NOTE

Don't confuse Web gallery styles with Web gallery templates. To install a Web gallery template like theTurningGate.net styles shown here, place the downloaded gallery style in the following location: Username/Library/Application Support/Adobe/Lightroom/Web Galleries folder (Mac), Users\ Username\AppData\Roaming\ Adobe\Lightroom\Web Galleries folder (Vista PC), Documents and Settings\username\Application Data\ Adobe\Lightroom\Web Galleries\ (Windows XP).

On a PC you will need to make sure that hidden files and folders are visible and remember to quit and restart Lightroom after you have installed a new gallery style. Once you have done so, the newly added galleries will appear listed in the Gallery panel.

noticed the "TTG" gallery styles that appear in some of my Lightroom interface screen shots. These are gallery styles that I downloaded from TheTurningGate.net Web site. **Figure 11.31** shows a Lightroom Web module preview of a *TTG Polaroid™ Gallery* and **Figure 11.32** a preview of the *TTG Selection Gallery* style.

Figure 11.31 *The TurningGate.net Polaroid™ Type I 1.2 gallery style. With this Web gallery the photos are cropped to a square format and placed in a Polaroid™ style print border. The photos can then be dragged about however you like, and you can click on an individual picture to see a larger view.*

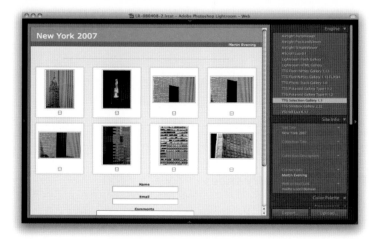

Figure 11.32 *The TTG Selection Gallery has a lot of practical uses. A Web gallery created with this style will allow visitors to the site to check the photos that they like, enter their name and email address, and automatically send an email with any added comments to the email address configured in the Site Info panel (see page 521).*

Site Info panel

The Lightroom gallery styles provide the core Web gallery structure. The gallery style you select will affect the range of options available in the panels that appear below the Engine panel. These additional panels allow you to customize the Web gallery content, so let's start by looking at the Site Info panel (**Figure 11.33**). Here you can complete the various fields that are used to either describe or provide information about the Web gallery images.

The arrangement and purpose of the Site Info items is as follows. The Site Title is used as the main heading in the template design. When an HTML Gallery style is chosen, the Site Title also appears in the Web browser title bar. The Collection Title is like a subheading to the main title. For example, if you were preparing Web galleries of a wedding, the main title would probably be a general description such as "Jones wedding." You might then prepare several galleries with different collection titles: one gallery might be for the ceremony, another for the family groups, and another for the reception. In the Collection Description you can write a slightly longer summary description of the Web gallery contents. When an HTML Gallery style is selected, this information appears just below the Collection Title header. If a Flash Gallery style is used, this information can only be viewed when visitors select View ⇨ About these Photos, as was shown in Step 2 on page 516. Note that this same built-in menu also allows visitors to switch from the Gallery to the Slideshow gallery mode, although they can probably do this more easily by clicking the icon next to the slideshow controls (⬛).

You can enter your own name into the Contact Info box, and then use the Web or Mail Link box to enter a link that you want to associate with the contact info. If you wish to add an email link here, it must be entered using the standard HTML code *mailto:* followed immediately by your email address (there should be no space between *mail* and *to*). When you do this, the contact info appears at the bottom of the page (HTML) or in the top-right corner (Flash). When a visitor clicks on this link, it automatically launches their email program and prepares a new email that is ready to send with your email address placed in the *To:* header. Alternatively, you can insert a Web URL that takes visitors to your Web site. Just remember that the full URL must be entered, including the *http://* at the beginning of the Web site address.

Figure 11.33 *You can use the Site Info panel to add information relating to the gallery page. Note that if you click on the down-facing triangles, you can access the most recent list of data entries.*

NOTE

The Identity Plate options show up in the Appearance panel when a Flash gallery style is selected. Please refer to page 528 for more about the Identity Plate options.

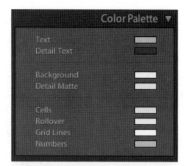

Figure 11.34 *The Color Palette panel for a Lightroom HTML Gallery.*

Figure 11.35 *The Color Palette panel for a Lightroom Flash Gallery.*

Figure 11.36 *When choosing a color scheme for a Web gallery layout, you may want to set the color picker to display the HEX (Web Safe Colors) palette.*

Color Palette panel

The Color Palette panel can be used to customize the gallery interface. The items in the Color Palette panel will be different, depending on whether the Lightroom Flash Gallery or Lightroom HTML Gallery is selected. **Figure 11.34** shows a Color Palette panel in HTML Gallery mode, which shows the color scheme used in the Ice Blue HTML template design. In this particular example, the Text and Detail Text color is dark blue, offset against a light blue background with pastel colors of blue/lilac used for the thumbnail cells, cell frame rollover colors, cell frame numbers, and gridlines (note that you need to switch to a detail page view to see what you are doing when editing the Detail Matte color).

Figure 11.35 shows an example of the Color Palette appearance when a Lightroom Flash Gallery style is selected. Here, I have shown the settings used for the *Mossy Rock* Lightroom Flash Gallery. In this example, the Text, Header Text, and Menu Text colors are all a light gray, and the Header, Menu, Background, and Border use different shades of green. The Header is the top bar that contains the site title and collection title, and the Menu is the bar that runs just beneath it. The Background is everything else in the background of the gallery layout, and the Border is the edging that defines both the main image and thumbnail list sections. The Controls colors are the colors used for the Flash Gallery playback controls at the bottom.

Choosing a color theme

With so many color choices, which should you use? There is a definite art to picking colors that work well together. The safest thing to do would be to select one of the gallery templates listed in the Template Browser—such as a Web-safe color palette—or stick to designing a layout that uses a neutral range of colors (**Figure 11.36**). Many photographers prefer to keep the color accent neutral since the presence of colors can be a distraction when evaluating color photographs. But you may also want to check out a new technology from Adobe called *Kuler*, which at the time of this writing is a Web-hosted application that enables you to explore, access, and share color harmonies. It is currently available as a free evaluation service and can be downloaded at http://kuler.adobe.com. This address may possibly change at some later date, but do check it out; it is a very cool service! **Figures 11.37** and **11.38** show some of the Color Palette themes available from the Template Browser.

Figure 11.37   *The Lightroom "Dusk" HTML Gallery template.*

Figure 11.38   *The Lightroom "Warm Day" Flash Gallery template.*

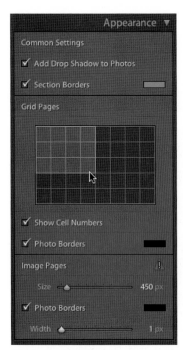

Figure 11.39 *The HTML Gallery Appearance panel.*

Appearance panel

The Appearance panel offers some additional control over the layout appearance of the different gallery styles (**Figure 11.39**).

Appearance settings for the HTML gallery

The grid layout must have a minimum of three columns and three rows. You can customize the design layout by clicking anywhere in the grid to set the grid cell range (**Figure 11.40**). When you create a gallery with more images than can fit the grid layout, these will overflow into successive, numbered index pages. If you have a saved collection of pictures and are creating a Web gallery of the entire collection, it can be useful to check the Show Cell Numbers option, because this may make it easier for people to identify a particular image by using the cell index number rather than the filename. Also included here are check boxes for customizing the look of the HTML grid, such as adding drop shadows and borders. At the bottom you have the Image Pages view options, where you can adjust the image size and color and width of the photo borders. The exclamation mark you see in Figure 11.39 indicates that these adjustments can only be seen if you click on a grid image to make a single page visible in the Content area preview.

Figure 11.40 *In this example, the Appearance panel was set to use a 3x4 grid in a Lightroom HTML Gallery style layout.*

Appearance panel settings for the Flash gallery

The Appearance panel for the Flash Gallery has four different layout options (**Figure 11.41**). The default Flash Gallery layout uses a Left scrolling thumbnail layout, in which the main image is displayed with a strip of thumbnails running down the left side of the layout with a scroll bar to navigate through the thumbnails. Individual images can be selected by clicking on a thumbnail or by using the right/down arrow keys to navigate forward through the pictures, or the left/up arrow keys to navigate backward one at a time. You can also use the slideshow navigation buttons to progress through the images in the gallery (**Figure 11.42**). **Figure 11.43** shows a Left scrolling thumbnail layout. In the Scrolling layout, the thumbnails are displayed in a horizontal row in the lower section with the scroll bar at the bottom (**Figure 11.44**). The Paginated layout presents the index page in two halves with the main image displayed in the right section. The thumbnails are shown on the left inside a paginated grid (**Figure 11.45**). The layout of the grid will adapt to the overall size of the Content area. This is how the final Flash Gallery will behave as well. Whenever you create a Paginated Flash Gallery, the cell layout automatically adapts as you resize the window of the Web browser. **Figure 11.46** shows the Left scrolling thumbnail layout. Slideshow Only view displays the images without the thumbnails (**Figure 11.47**).

Figure 11.41 *The Flash Gallery Appearance panel.*

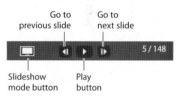

Figure 11.42 *The Flash Gallery slideshow navigation controls.*

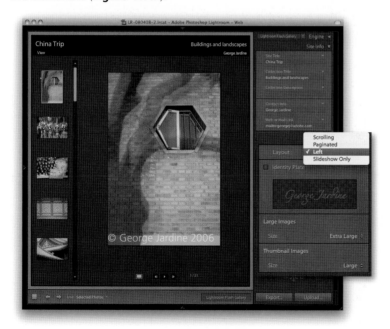

Figure 11.43 *A Flash Gallery using a Left scrolling style.*

Figure 11.44   *A Flash Gallery style using the Scrolling layout.*

Figure 11.45   *A Flash Gallery style using the Paginated layout.*

Figure 11.46 *A Flash Gallery style using the Left scrolling layout.*

Figure 11.47 *A Flash Gallery style using the Slideshow Only layout.*

Appearance panel settings for the Airtight galleries

The Appearance panel options for the other gallery styles are mostly self-explanatory. In **Figure 11.48**, I have shown the Appearance panel options for the Airtight Postcard Viewer gallery style.

Figure 11.48 *The Appearance palette options for the Airtight PostcardViewer gallery style allow you to set the zoom scale for the thumbnails and full-sized images.*

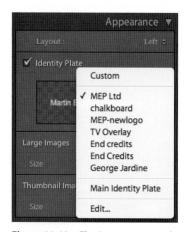

Figure 11.49 *The Appearance panel showing the Identity Plate options.*

Identity Plate

If you are editing a Flash gallery, the Identity Plate options show up in the Appearance panel (**Figure 11.49**). However, if you are editing an HTML gallery, they will show up in the Site Info panel. If you refer back to "Creating a Custom Identity Plate" on page 495, you can remind yourself of the steps required to design and edit an Identity Plate and save it as a new setting. When working with the Web module, the only real options you have are to enable or disable an Identity Plate from appearing at the top of the Web gallery interface (in place of the Site Title). Unlike the Slideshow module, there are no further options that allow you to alter the position of the Identity Plate in the site layout, or add a drop shadow.

Image Info panel

Adding titles and captions

The Image Info panel has a Title and Caption section where you can add image-related information to the main image views. In an HTML Gallery style, the Title appears above the main image in the main image view and the Caption is placed just below the picture. In a Flash Gallery layout, the Title is displayed beneath the main image view using a bold typeface and the Caption appears in a lighter typeface just beneath the Title.

To create a custom setting, the simplest way is to click the triangle to the right of the current setting and select an item from the pop-up menu. For example, in **Figure 11.50**, I chose *Custom Text* for the Title and *Equipment* from the Caption menu. **Figure 11.51** shows in detail the Title and Caption list menu options.

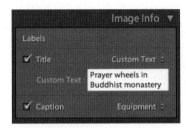

Figure 11.50 *Here is a view of the Image Info panel where the Custom Text item was selected for the Title, and I entered the custom text shown here.*

Figure 11.51 *Here is a view of the Image Info panel where I clicked on the Caption menu and selected Equipment from the list.*

It can sometimes take a few seconds
or more to see changes update in
the Content area. For this reason,
I sometimes recommend that you
have only one or maybe just a few
images selected while editing the
Image Settings to create a new Title
or Caption setting. You can choose
the Reload command in the Web
menu or press ⌘R (Mac) or Ctrl R
(PC) to force a refresh in the Content
area, but since Lightroom automatically updates the Content area all the
time anyway, you shouldn't really
need to use this command.

Customizing the title and caption information

When deciding what to add to the Title and Caption menus, you can choose from a limited number of items. But if you choose Edit from the Image Settings panel, the Text Template Editor opens (**Figure 11.52**). This dialog is identical to the one shown earlier in the Slideshow mod-ule section and allows you to insert metadata tokens from the pop-up menus and combine them with custom text.

Using the Image Info panel settings shown in Figure 11.50 and Figure 11.51, **Figure 11.53** shows a typical layout for an HTML Gallery that was customized. You can see that the custom text I entered for the Title appears in the matte frame just above the image, while the cap-tion is placed beneath the image and shows the name of the camera and lens used. In **Figure 11.54** you can see how the Title and Caption information in a Flash Gallery layout are displayed together just below the main image in this slideshow view. In **Figure 11.55**, I show how you can use the Text Template Editor to create a new custom preset that can be added to the Image Info panel menu list.

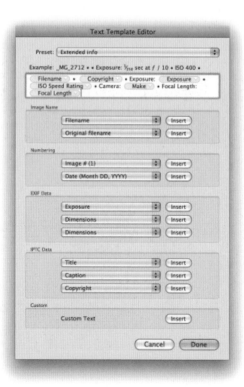

Figure 11.52   *The Text Template Editor.*

Figure 11.53 *This shows how the Title and Caption information is displayed in an HTML Gallery style view using the Image Info panel settings shown in Figure 11.50 and Figure 11.51. I have highlighted the Title (top) and Caption (just below the image).*

Figure 11.54 *This shows how the Title and Caption information are displayed in a Flash Gallery style page view using the text template settings shown in Figure 11.52. I have highlighted the Image Info items that are displayed directly below the image.*

Figure 11.55 shows a progression of screen shots in which the Text Template Editor was used to configure a new Image Info panel Title/Caption preset that can be seen in use in **Figure 11.56**. If you select a preexisting preset and choose Edit to make changes to the layout via the Text Template Editor, the preset name is marked as an edited version. If you want to update the preset settings, don't forget to choose Update Preset from the Preset menu in the Template Editor.

The presets you create cannot be formatted in any particular way; the information is always displayed as a continuous flow of text in the Title or Caption field. However, if you choose the EXIF Metadata template from the Lightroom Templates list, it includes a unique, built-in custom setting where some of the camera EXIF metadata information is presented in a formatted way in the Caption section (**Figure 11.57**). You can't actually edit this setting, and the only way to access it is by selecting the Lightroom EXIF Metadata gallery template.

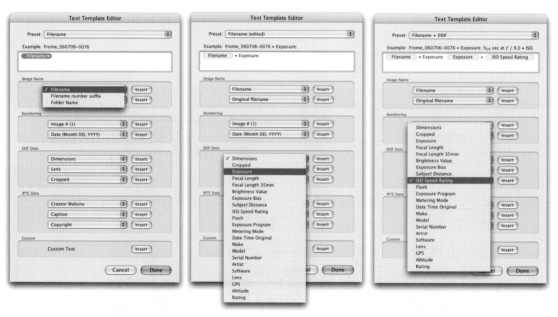

Figure 11.55 *This shows a sequence of screen shots where the Text Template Editor was used to create a new Title/Caption preset. I started by clicking on one of the Image Name pop-up menus and selected a Filename token. This action added a Filename token to the editor window above. I typed "Exposure:" and clicked one of the EXIF Data menus to add an Exposure token. I went to the EXIF Data section again and added an ISO Speed Rating token. Then from the Preset menu I chose Save as New Preset. I named the preset "Filename + EXIF" and clicked Done. The new preset was added to the Image Info panel menus.*

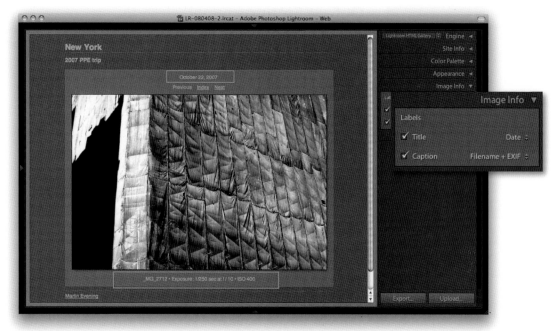

Figure 11.56 *Here is how the Caption information appears on an HTML detail page when using the custom "Filename + EXIF" preset I created in Figure 11.55.*

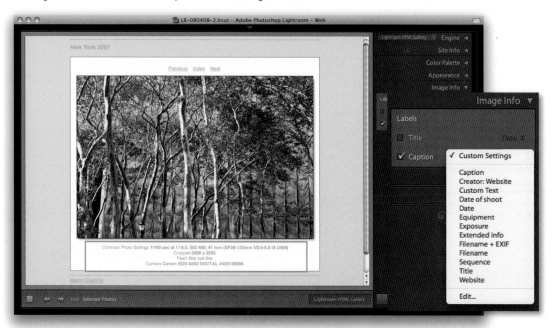

Figure 11.57 *This gallery uses the EXIF Metadata template from the Lightroom Templates Presets list. This features a unique custom setting that allows you to display the EXIF metadata information in a formatted layout (as highlighted above).*

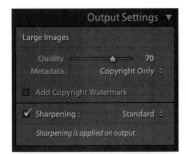

Figure 11.58 *The Output Settings panel.*

Output Settings panel

The Output Settings panel (see **Figure 11.58**) can be used to establish the image output settings. The Quality slider is used to set the amount of compression that is applied. The Web gallery images that you are previewing on the screen are all JPEG versions of the master images, and the JPEG file format uses a lossy method of compression to reduce the physical file size so that the JPEG images are small enough to download quickly. The choice boils down to high quality with minimal compression or lower quality with greater compression. Note that as you adjust the Quality slider, you should give Lightroom a chance to refresh the images so that you can accurately preview the effect of the compression setting used.

The Metadata section allows you to choose between embedding All Metadata or Copyright Only. Embedding the metadata is useful if you want to ensure that your photographs are output with all the essential metadata, such as the EXIF information and IPTC captions, and that they are preserved in the file header. The downside of doing this is that your JPEG Web images will become bigger in file size. So if your main concern is to keep the file size down and have your Web sites load quickly, then choose the Copyright Only option. You can also check the box below to add a copyright watermark to the bottom-left corner of each gallery image.

The Sharpening section makes use of the new sharpening routines that have been added to Lightroom 2. Adobe worked closely with Pixel Genius to bring Photokit Sharpener™ routines to Lightroom 2. When the Sharpening box is checked, Lightroom automatically calculates the correct amount of sharpening to apply to each image, based on the final output pixel dimensions. The sharpening that is applied here is not the same as that applied for print in the Print module, but is instead based on sharpening routines that have been devised specifically for computer screen output. You won't see any changes to the images that are previewed in the Web module until you choose Preview in Browser or "Export the Web gallery" and it is only at this stage that the photos are fully processed and sharpened. This will increase the time it takes to export the Web gallery, but if you test how the gallery images look with and without sharpening, you'll find it is definitely worth applying.

Previewing Web galleries

One of the benefits of working with the Web module is that the Content area gives you an almost exact preview of how a Web gallery will look (apart from the output sharpening), since it is effectively showing you a Web browser view. Even so, this might not be exactly how everyone will see your Web site after it has been uploaded. There are always a number of unknown factors, such as the variability of the monitors used to view images your Web site (see "Image Appearance in Slideshow and Web Modules"). However, in addition to previewing the gallery pages in the Content area, you can check how a site will look on your computer in an external Web browser application by clicking the Preview in Browser button (**Figure 11.59**) that appears below the panels on the left. When you click this button Lightroom creates a temporary export of the gallery and previews the result in whichever Web browser program is set as the default browser on your computer system.

Figure 11.59   *The Preview in Browser button can be used to preview how a Web site will look in an external Web browser program.*

NOTE

The default Web browser is the one set as the default by your operating system (there is no Lightroom preference for selecting this).

NOTE

Non-raw (rendered) files such as TIFF, JPEG, or PSD use their native RGB space to generate the previews. if the preview quality in the Catalog Settings File Handling section is set to Low or Medium, the Raw file previews are in Adobe RGB. If set to High, they will be in ProPhoto RGB.

Image appearance in Slideshow and Web modules

Slideshow module colors

Lightroom uses a large, wide-gamut RGB space to carry out its image processing calculations, but for screen presentation work, the color space needs to be tamed to something more universally recognizable. When you create a slideshow, Lightroom utilizes the JPEG previews that it has already generated to preview the library images onscreen. These preview images are typically created in the Adobe RGB space, and for slideshow work, the onscreen previews are always preserved in this space. Adobe RGB is optimal for making screen presentations because it prevents any unexpected shifts in the colors or contrast.

Web module colors

When you output images for the Web, you are usually heading into unknown territory. This is because once images have been published on the Web, you have absolutely no way of knowing how other people will be viewing these photographs. It is fair to assume that most people will be viewing them with monitors that are uncalibrated. Some Web browser programs such as Apple's Safari are able to color-manage images that have an embedded profile, but most will not. For these reasons, the Web module converts the image previews on the fly to the universal sRGB, which is an ideal choice for all Web output images.

Exporting a Web gallery

If you want a more permanent form of output from the Web module, you can export or upload a gallery as a complete Web site. The Export option is applicable if you wish to save a complete version of the Web site to a folder on the computer. This will then allow you to preview a Web gallery in different Web browser programs (not just the system default browser) and upload the Web content manually using a separate FTP program.

To export a gallery to the computer, click the Export button (**Figure 11.60**), or press ⌘J (Mac) or Ctrl J (PC). This opens a system navigational dialog where you can choose a location to save the exported gallery to (such as the Desktop), type in a name for the exported gallery folder, and click Save to start the export. If you are familiar with FTP software, you can manually upload the saved site folder to your server space.

Figure 11.60 *The Export and Upload buttons are located in the bottom right of the Web module interface.*

1. To save a Web site, click the Export button. Then choose a destination folder and save the Web site to it.

2. A self-contained folder holding all the Web site elements is created. You can preview the site offline by opening the Index.html file within any Web browser program. You can also upload the folder site contents manually using a program like Fetch for Mac OS X. The URL path used to access the site depends on where you upload the site to and how your server site space is configured.

Uploading a Web gallery

You normally choose the Export option for those times where you need to manually edit a site before uploading it, or you want to back up and store a gallery site offline. But for all other circumstances, you can configure Lightroom so that it uploads the files directly for you when you click the Upload button.

1. In the Upload Settings panel, click on the FTP Server preset menu and select Edit.

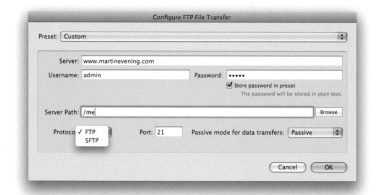

2. To create a new custom preset, enter all the information that is required to access your server space (if in doubt, check with your Internet service provider). The Server address is usually the first part of the Web URL, and the Username and Password can sometimes be the same as those used for your email account. The Server Path is used to set the folder location to place the Web folder you are about to upload. Again, talk to your provider, because there may well be a root-level name that has to be entered to access the server space allocated to you; otherwise, the connection won't work. In this example, I entered /me as the root-level directory. Note that it is important to always place a forward slash at the beginning of the server path.

NOTE

There are various File Transfer Protocol (FTP) programs that you can choose from. Fetch from www. fetchworks.com is a popular program for the Mac. If you are working on a PC, I recommend using WS_FTP Pro (www.ipswitch.com) or FlashFXP (www.flashfxp.com).

Whichever platform you use, the same steps will be used to establish an FTP connection. For the host, you will need to enter the server URL, the user ID, and the password. Your Internet service provider will be able to supply you with all this information (assuming your Internet account includes some server space).

NOTE

SFTP stands for Secure File Transfer Protocol and is a network protocol that provides both file transfer and manipulation across a reliable network connection.

NOTE

When you point a Web browser program at a Web link, it automatically searches for a Web page with the name index.htm or index.html. If you want to specify a subdirectory link, you must place a forward slash (/) before the directory folder name and another forward slash at the end to tell the Web browser to search for an index.htm or index.html page.

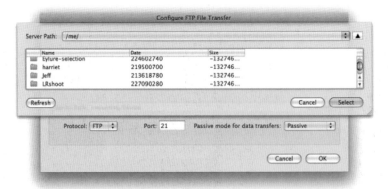

3. You don't necessarily have to memorize the structure of your server directory or type in the server path. Just click the Browse button in the Configure FTP File Transfer dialog and Lightroom will scan the server to reveal a folder view of the server directory. Here, I clicked the LRshoot folder and clicked Select to make this the Server Path.

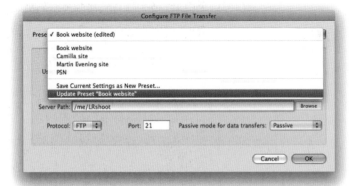

4. In the Configure FTP File Transfer dialog you can see that the server path directory has been automatically updated to point to the LRshoot folder. You can use the Browse feature in this way to access different folders or subfolders on the server and save them as different upload presets. If you experience problems getting a connection when you click the Browse button (or later when you try to upload), it could be because of the firewall software on your computer system or router. If this is the case, try selecting the "Passive mode for data transfers" option. Also, if you change any of the settings applied here, you need to go to the Preset menu and choose Update Preset. Once you are done, click OK.

TIP

If you are uploading Web gallery files to an existing Web server space that already contains your Web site, be careful that the subdirectory you choose does not conflict with existing folders. For example, it is not a good idea to upload new Web galleries to a folder called "images," because it is highly probable that your Web site already uses a folder of that name. Try using more unique and descriptive names for the folder locations, such as "client-review" or "snaps."

5. This takes you back to the Upload Settings panel where the Put in Subfolder field must be completed. The folder name you enter here completes the server path directory. The reason this section is left blank is because you *must* apply a unique name to the Web site folder you are about to create. Since the currently selected FTP Preset pointed to /me/LRshoot, all I needed to do here was type in a name for this particular Web gallery. In this example, I typed in *LRBook* as the next part of the server directory. Note that there is no need to add a forward slash at the beginning of this section of the path or after. Lightroom adds the slash automatically, because the complete path I have created is in fact */me/LRshoot/LRBook/*. Click the Upload button and Lightroom automatically uploads the gallery files to this location on the server.

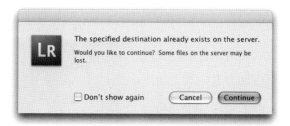

6. One of the reasons you are always required to enter a new server output path in the Upload Settings panel is to avoid uploading and overwriting a previous Web folder upload. If you enter a folder name destination that already exists, Lightroom warns you before letting you continue with the new upload. If you are reediting an existing gallery, you will see this warning each time you refresh the gallery contents on the server, so in these circumstances, it is safe to click Continue.

7. You will now want to let people know how to access the Web site. The best way to do this is to send them a link via email. But to make things even easier, I suggest you create a template email that contains a brief message and the first part of the server link, and save it as a signature (note that in this example the *me* section of the path is hidden and must therefore be omitted from the final link). In the email message shown here, I selected a presaved signature with a readily composed email and simply added the person's name and name of the output folder (both highlighted in red).

8. When recipients of the email click the link, it automatically launches their Web browser and takes them straight to the uploaded Web site on your server.

Template Browser panel

You can easily end up putting a lot of time and effort into designing a customized Web gallery template, so it makes sense to save any template designs that you work on via the Template Browser panel in the Web module (**Figure 11.61**). To add a new preset, click the Add button, or press ⌘N (Mac) or Ctrl N (PC), and enter a new name for the template. To delete a preset, highlight the name in the Template Browser and click the Remove button. Most likely you will continue to refine the design of your templates, so don't forget that as you select a preset, you can right-click (Control–click on older Macs) to access the contextual menu and select "Update with current settings." When you hover over the presets in the list, the Preview panel shows previews of the gallery page layout presets. The previews display the gallery showing the layout and colors used and also indicate if the gallery preset is a Flash or HTML layout design. You can also select Web ⇨ Save Web Settings, or press ⌘S (Mac) or Ctrl S (PC), to quickly save the current Web settings without saving them as a specific template. As you select other presaved templates to compare the look of different layouts, you can always go to the Web menu again and choose Revert Web Settings to instantly return to the current, temporary Web layout.

Lightroom provides you with a simple way to upload Web sites, but the downside is that there is no way to remove them so easily! Bear in mind that server space costs money and there may be a capped limit on how much space you have available, or there may be a surcharge if you exceed your limit. You will therefore still need access to FTP software in order to carry out general housekeeping maintenance of the server space and delete Web galleries that no longer need to be hosted.

Figure 11.61 *The Web Module Template Browser panel lists all saved gallery templates and shows previews of the layouts in the Preview panel above.*

Appendix A
Lightroom Preferences

I reserved the appendix as a special section of the book that would allow me to go into more detail about certain aspects of Lightroom, including how you can customize the program to suit specific ways of working. This appendix provides a more detailed summary of the Lightroom Preferences. The preference options described in this section can be accessed by choosing Lightroom ⇨ Preferences (Mac), Edit ⇨ Preferences (PC) (or use the ⌘, (Mac) Ctrl, (PC) keyboard shortcut). Where relevant, I have included references to earlier sections in the book.

Figure A.1 *The Lightroom startup splash screen.*

Figure A.2 *The alternative, Silvertone beta splash screen.*

General preferences

Let's begin with the General preferences and the startup options. If you deselect "Show splash screen during startup," you can avoid the Lightroom screen in **Figure A.1.** This is just a cosmetic thing and it depends on whether you want to see the splash screen or not as the program loads. Incidentally, there is a splash screen Easter egg in Lightroom. If you go to the Lightroom menu and choose About Adobe Photoshop Lightroom you will see the usual startup splash screen, but if you then hit the R key you'll see the alternate splash screen shown in **Figure A.2**. When you first installed Lightroom you would have had the option to choose whether to be notified automatically of any updates to the program. In case you missed checking this, you can check the "Automatically check for updates" option.

Catalog selection

In the Default Catalog section you can select which catalog should be used each time you launch Lightroom, such as "Load most recent catalog" (you can read on page 202 about how to create new catalogs in Lightroom). You can jump directly to the Catalog Settings by clicking the Go to Catalog Settings button at the bottom of the General preferences dialog (**Figure A.3**). From there you can use the backup section

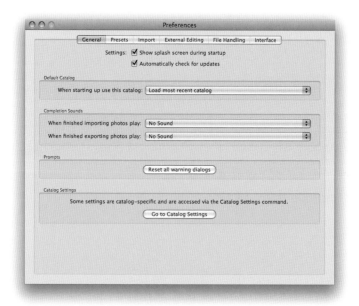

Figure A.3 *The Lightroom General preferences.*

to decide at which times you wish to back up the Lightroom catalog. For more information about these settings and working with catalogs in Lightroom, please refer to Chapter 5.

Completion sounds and prompts

Next are the Completion Sound options, where you can select to have an alert play after completing an import or export from Lightroom. You will often see warning dialogs with a "Don't show again" check box at the bottom. If you click the "Reset all warning dialogs" button, you restore all the default warning alerts.

Presets preferences

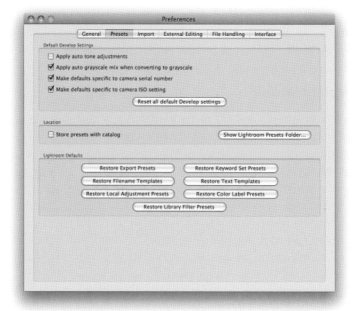

Figure A.4 *The Lightroom Presets preferences.*

Default Develop settings

If you are familiar with the controls found in Develop and Quick Develop, you know that you can click the Auto Tone button to automatically adjust the exposure, blacks, brightness, and contrast to produce what Lightroom thinks would be the best combination. Checking "Apply auto tone adjustments" (**Figure A.4**) will turn this feature on as a default setting.

Figure A.5 *The Keywording panel, showing the Keyword Set section.*

After this we have "Apply auto grayscale mix when converting to grayscale." You can leave this on because Lightroom automatic grayscale conversions usually offer a good starting point. Automatic grayscale is linked to the Temp and Tint slider settings in the Basic panel White Balance section. If you adjust those settings and then click the Grayscale button, you will see how the Grayscale settings adjust automatically.

Camera-linked settings

The next two items in the Default Develop Settings section are linked to a feature found in the Develop module Develop menu called Set Default Settings, discussed on pages 368–369. Basically, if you check "Make defaults specific to cameras serial number" and "Make defaults specific to camera ISO setting," you can use these preference check boxes to determine whether certain default settings can be made camera-specific and/or ISO-specific. The "Reset all default Develop settings" button allows you to revert all the Develop settings to their original defaults.

Location section

Now that we have the ability to export photos as a catalog, you can check the "Store presets with catalog" option if you would like Lightroom to save the custom presets you have created within the main catalog file. This is useful if you are migrating library images from one computer to another because it saves you having to transfer your custom settings separately (such as your Develop settings), should you wish to share your custom settings with other users. But then again, maybe you would prefer not to give away your own custom presets. This preference item gives you that choice. We also have the Show Lightroom Presets folder button, which conveniently highlights the Lightroom folder in the Finder (Mac), or Explorer (PC), so that you can quickly access the folders containing your Lightroom presets.

Lightroom defaults section

The other buttons in this section are all reset buttons that can be used to restore various Lightroom settings. "Restore Export presets" restores the preset list used in the File ⇨ Export dialog (see page 434).

Over in the Library module Keywording panel (see **Figure A.5**), you will notice that Lightroom provides a few Keyword Set templates that can be used for keywording photos. The default sets include Outdoor Photography, Portrait Photography, and Wedding Photography (**Figure A.6**). Each set contains nine custom keywords. If you click on the Keyword Set menu in the Keywording panel (or choose Metadata ⇨ Keyword Set ⇨ Edit) you can customize these default keyword sets. In the Lightroom Presets preferences, click Restore Keyword Set Presets to restore the original keyword sets.

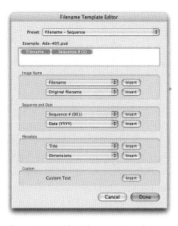

Figure A.7   *The Filename Template Editor.*

Figure A.6   *The Edit Keyword Set dialog.*

The Restore Filename Templates button reverts the default file rename templates used in the Filename Template Editor (**Figure A.7**). This does not affect any of the custom templates you have added here; it merely resets the settings for the default templates that you have edited. The same thing applies to the Restore Text Templates button that restores the default settings in the Text Template Editor (**Figure A.8**), as used in the Slideshow and Web modules.

Restore Local Adjustment Presets resets the pop-up menu settings and all the default tool presets for the Adjustment brush and Graduated filter tools.

On pages 187–189 I mentioned the potential confusion that can be caused through using color label text descriptions that don't match the text descriptions used in Bridge, or by another Lightroom user who sends you images labeled using another label description system. The Restore Color Label Presets button resets the label text descriptions to the default setting: Red, Yellow, Green, Blue, Purple.

In Lightroom 2 you can save Filter presets that not only include things like "Filter by one star or higher," but also things like the column layouts in the Metadata Filter bar (see page 165). The Restore Library Filter Presets button can reset the Filter Presets in case you inadvertently update the default settings with a new (incorrect) setting.

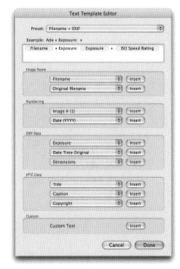

Figure A.8   *The Text Template Editor.*

Import preferences

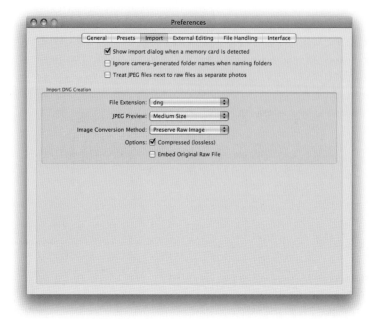

Figure A.9 *The Lightroom Import preferences.*

The Import preferences are shown in **Figure A.9**. When the "Show Import dialog when a memory card is detected" item is checked, this forces the Import dialog to appear automatically whenever you insert a camera card into the computer. The "Ignore camera-generated folder names when naming folders" option can help shorten the import process if you wish to import everything directly from a camera card into a single Lightroom folder. For example, maybe you have a camera card with photos that were shot using more than one camera and they have ended up in several different folders. When this option is checked, the card folder contents are all grouped into one folder.

Some photographers like using their camera's ability to capture and store JPEG file versions alongside the raw capture files. However, prior to the Lightroom 1.1 update, Lightroom would treat the JPEG captured versions as if they were sidecar files. But if the "Treat JPEG files next to raw files as separate photos" option is left checked, Lightroom treats them as separate files that must be imported into the Lightroom catalog along with the raw versions. In addition, Lightroom does not treat as sidecar files any non-JPEG files that can be imported.

DNG options

There are several places where you will come across the DNG save options. You will find them in the Export module as well as in the Library ⇨ Convert Photo to DNG dialog (see **Figure A.10**). However, the DNG options in the Import preferences (Figure A.9) refer only to the DNG settings that are used when you import photos as DNGs.

Figure A.10   *The Convert Photo to DNG dialog shares the same settings options as those listed in the Import preferences, except you have options to "Only convert Raw files" and "Delete originals after successful conversion."*

First off we have the File Extension options, which can use lowercase dng or uppercase DNG, whichever you prefer. Next is the JPEG Preview option, which can be set to None, Medium Size, or Full Size. If you want to trim the file size down, you could choose not to embed a preview, knowing that new previews are always generated again when DNG files are managed elsewhere. Therefore, you might select this option if you figure there is no value in including the current preview. A medium-sized preview economizes on the file size and would be suitable for standard library browsing. After all, most of the photos in your catalog probably only have medium-sized JPEG previews. But if you want the embedded previews (and remember, these are the previews embedded in the file and not the Lightroom catalog previews) to always be accessible at full resolution and you don't consider the resulting increased file size to be a burden, then choose the Full Size preview option. This has the added benefit that should you want to view these DNGs in other applications such as Microsoft Expression™, you can preview the DNGs at full resolution using a preview that was generated by Lightroom. This means that photos processed in Lightroom as DNGs should then preview exactly the same when they are viewed in other applications.

TIP

Personally I have no trouble converting everything I shoot to DNG and
never bother to embed the original
raw data with my DNGs. I do, however, sometimes keep backup copies
of the original raw files as an extra
insurance policy. But in practice I
have never had cause to use these.
Or at least not yet!

DNG image conversion options

For the Image Conversion Method setting, you have two options. You
can choose Preserve Raw Image to preserve the raw capture data in
its original "mosaic" format, or you can choose "Convert to Linear
image," which carries out a raw conversion to demosaic (convert) the
original raw data to a linear image (which is what Lightroom is doing
anyway when converting the raw image data to its internal RGB space).
However, if you do this as part of a DNG conversion you will end
up with huge DNG file sizes, and it's also a one-way process. If you
convert a raw file to a linear image DNG, you won't be able to take the
raw data back to its original mosaic state again and won't be able to
reconvert the raw data a second time. So why bother? In nearly every
case you will want to preserve the raw image. But there are a few
known instances where DNG-compatible programs are unable to read
anything but a linear DNG file from certain cameras. Even so, I would
be wary of converting to linear for the reasons I have just mentioned.

The "Compressed (lossless)" option is checked by default. This is
because the compression method the DNG file format uses can compress the file size without incurring any data loss. And by this I mean
there will be no loss of image data, and no loss of metadata or any
other secret source data embedded in the original proprietary raw file.
DNG compression may result in a file that is slightly smaller than the
original, but this is because the DNG compression method is often better than that used by the camera manufacturers. You can also reverse
the process quite easily (again without incurring any loss) by resaving
a DNG file with this compressed option turned off.

Embed Original Raw File embeds a copy of the original proprietary
raw file inside the DNG file. This option allows you to preserve the
original raw file data within the DNG file format but with the ability
to reverse the process in order to access the original raw file format.
The penalty for doing this is increased file sizes, and I do mean a *big*
increase, since you will be storing two versions of the raw file data in
a single file. One argument in favor of doing this is that by preserving
the raw file in its original form, you can still access the original raw file
and process it in the proprietary raw processing program. For example,
the proprietary CR2 raw files produced by the newer Canon cameras
allow the storing of dust-spotting data that can only be written or read
using Canon's own software. If you choose not to embed the original
raw file, you lose the means to process your photos using the camera
manufacturer's software.

External Editing preferences

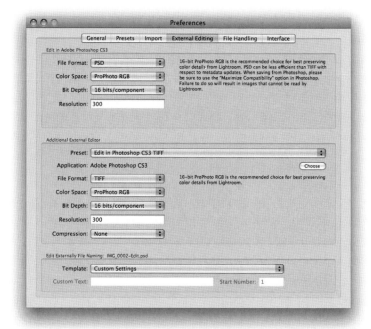

Figure A.11 *The Lightroom External Editing preferences.*

The Lightroom External Editing preferences (**Figure A.11**) let you customize the pixel image editing settings for Photoshop as well as one additional external, pixel editing program, such as Adobe Photoshop Elements, Corel Paint Shop Pro, or even the same version of Photoshop.

The Edit settings allow you to establish the File Format, Color Space, Bit Depth, and where applicable, Compression settings that are used whenever you ask Lightroom to open a catalog image in an external pixel editing program. As was explained in Chapter 9, the Open in Photoshop command (⌘ E [Mac], Ctrl E [PC]) opens photos from the Lightroom catalog directly into whatever is the most current version of Photoshop, without adding an edit copy version of the master to the catalog. The same also applies when you choose one of the extended editing options such as Merge to HDR. It is important to note here that the External Editing preferences are the only place where you can establish the file format settings for opening images in this way. So with this in mind, you must use the Edit in Photoshop section to establish what the default file editing settings should be. In Figure A.11, ProPhoto RGB was selected as the color space, using a bit depth of 16-bits per channel and saving to the PSD file format.

NOTE

When you open an image using the Edit in Photoshop command, the image will open using the color space, bit depth, and resolution settings applied in the External Editing preferences. However, the file format choice only comes into play when you choose to save the image out of Photoshop. The default behavior is to save the file to the same folder as the original master, using the file format specified in the preferences (but it won't be added to the catalog).

TIP

In Figure A.11 you will notice that you can save the Additional External Editor settings as preset settings. Saved presets will then appear as menu options when you open the "Edit in" submenu from the Photo menu. For example, you might find it useful to have saved export settings for both TIFF and PSD formats and for different pixel editing programs.

Figure A.12 *When you choose the External Editor command (⌘ Alt E [Mac], Ctrl Alt E [PC]), you have the option to override the file format and other settings in the External Editor preferences.*

Below this you can specify the default settings to use when editing photos in an Additional External Editing application. The difference between this and Edit in Photoshop is that when you choose the External Editor command (⌘ Alt E [Mac], Ctrl Alt E [PC]), an edit copy of the master is always added to the Lightroom catalog. For example, you might want to use the settings shown in Figure A.11 to create new edit versions that are saved as TIFF files in 16-bits per channel using the ProPhoto RGB color space. However, when you choose the Edit in External Editor command you do have the opportunity to override the file format and other settings (**Figure A.12**).

At the bottom we have the Edit Externally File Naming section. Previously, Lightroom would always append *–Edit* to each externally edited image filename, and as you created further edit copies, Lightroom would increment the numbering: *–Edit1, –Edit2,* and so on. In Lightroom you can now customize the file naming. For example, you could create a custom template that adds a date stamp after the original filename (**Figure A.13**) and apply this renaming scheme whenever an edit copy version of a master file is created.

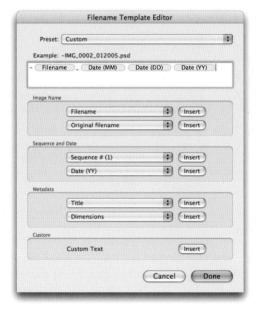

Figure A.13 *The Filename Template Editor.*

File Handling preferences

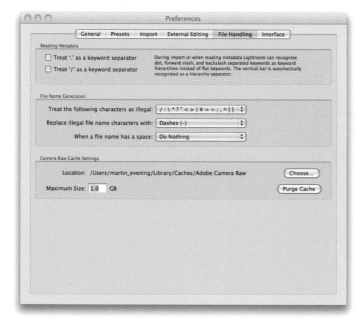

Figure A.14 *The Lightroom File Handling preferences.*

If only there could be agreement on common standards for the way metadata information is handled between different programs. Adobe's open source XMP specification has certainly gone a long way toward providing the industry with a versatile standard format for storing metadata information. But there are still a few gotchas that can prevent the smooth integration of informational data from one program to another. The Reading Metadata section in the File Handling preferences (see **Figure A.14**) is there to help solve such inconsistencies. If you check "Treat '.' as a keyword separator" and "Treat '/' as a keyword separator," this enables Lightroom to better interpret the keyword hierarchy conventions used in other programs.

Filenames that contain illegal characters can also cause hiccups when you import such files into Lightroom. The "Treat the following characters as illegal characters" item can be set to recognize "/:" as an illegal character, or alternatively, you can select the extended list of characters to encompass more potential bad characters that would need to be replaced. In the "Replace illegal file name characters with" section you can then choose a suitable replacement character to use, such as a hyphen (-), an underscore (_), or similar characters.

TIP

Some database and FTP systems may prefer spaces to be removed from filenames. For example, when I upload files to my publisher, the FTP server they use will not allow such files to be uploaded. This is where the "When a file name has a space" item can come in useful, because you can choose to replace a space with a hyphen (-) or an underscore (_) character.

NOTE

The Camera Raw cache is used to store the image preview cache data. If you increase the cache size, you can allow more preview data to be held in the Adobe Camera Raw cache. This in turn means that Lightroom keeps more of the recently visited catalog photo preview data in the cache folder location, which can result in swifter preview generation when you revisit these photos.

Interface preferences

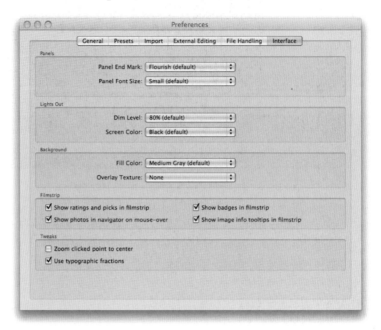

Figure A.15 *You can use the contextual menu to quickly access the full range of panel end mark options.*

Figure A.16 *The Lightroom Interface preferences.*

Panel end marks

The panel end mark is the squiggly flourish that appears at the bottom of the panel list in the Lightroom modules. You can access Panel End Mark menu options via the contextual Panel End Mark menu shown in **Figure A.15**. Just right-click on the end of the panels list, navigate to the Panel End Mark submenu, and select the desired panel end mark from there. You can also access these options in the Panels section of the Interface preferences (**Figure A.16**). You can choose None if you don't want to see any kind of panel mark appearing in the Lightroom modules. **Figure A.17** offers a visual reference of all the different panel marks you can choose from.

Custom panel end marks

Do you prefer creating your own panel end mark design? Well, it's quite easy to do. Take a screen shot of one of the current panel end marks to get an idea of the scale of the design and how it will look against the panel background color. Create a new custom design in Photoshop scaled to the correct size and on a transparent layer. Save this graphic using the PNG file format (which supports transparency). Now go to the Panel End Mark menu and select Go to Panel End Marks Folder (see Figure A.15). This reveals the folder in the Finder/Explorer location where all the panel end mark image files are stored. Place the PNG file you have just created in there and reopen the Lightroom preferences. You will now see your custom design listed in the Panel End Mark menu!

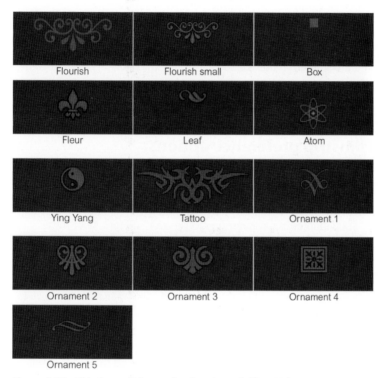

Figure A.17   *This shows all the panel end marks available in Lightroom.*

Figure A.18   *This shows a comparison between the default Small panel font size setting (top) and the Large panel font size setting (bottom). Note how the Large panel font setting will make the panels slightly bigger in size.*

Panel font size

There are two font size options: Small (which is the default setting) or Large. If you refer to **Figure A.18**, you can see how the difference between these two settings is actually quite subtle. But by choosing the Large setting, you can make the panel fonts more legible when viewing on a large screen at a distance. However, this change will not take effect until after you have relaunched Lightroom.

NOTE

You can see an example of the Lights Out mode in use on page 34 and an example of working with different Background settings on page 16.

Lights Out

The Lightroom Interface preferences let you customize the appearance of the interface when using the Lights Out and Lights Dim mode. Bear in mind that these preference settings also allow you to create a "Lights up" setting. So instead of using black as the Lights Out color, you could try setting it to light gray or even white.

Background

The Background section lets you customize the background appearance in the Lightroom modules. You can set the fill color to several diferent shades of gray as well as white or black. In the Overlay texture section you can choose to add a pinstripes pattern.

Filmstrip preference options

In the Filmstrip section you have the "Show ratings and picks in filmstrip," "Show badges in filmstrip," and "Show tooltips in filmstrip" options. Examples of these are shown in **Figure A.19**. There is also a "Show photos in navigator on mouse-over" option. All of these combine to make information about the catalog and catalog navigation more flexible. With these items checked you have fuller access to Library module functions while working in other modules. For example, let's say you are working in the Develop module. You can use the Filmstrip to see at a glance all the current filtered images, with their labels, ratings, and pick status. You can use the mouse to hover over individual images to see a slightly larger preview in the Navigator panel, and the tooltip floating window can be used to quickly reveal the filename, time of capture, and pixel dimensions. The badge icons indicate whether keyword metadata has been added or the Develop settings have been edited. Clicking on a Metadata badge immediately takes you to the Keywording panel in the Library module, highlighting the keywords so they are ready to edit. Clicking on the Develop edit badge takes you back to the Develop module again where you can resume editing the Develop settings. These Filmstrip options extend the usefulness of the Filmstrip as a way to manage the Lightroom catalog photos.

Figure A.19 *The Lightroom Filmstrip extra view options.*

Interface tweaks

When "Zoom clicked point to center" is checked, the Loupe view uses the click point as the center for its magnified view. To understand how this works, try clicking on the corner of a photo in the standard Loupe view. If "Zoom clicked point to center" is checked, the corner zooms in to become centered on the screen. When this option is unchecked, the photo zooms in with the corner point positioned beneath the mouse cursor. Personally, I find that deselecting this option offers a more logical and useful zoom behavior. The "Use typographic fractions" option affects the way the fractions are presented in the Metadata panel in the Library module. When checked, Lightroom uses proper fraction characters or superscript and subscript characters. For example, **Figure A.20** shows how a shutter speed is displayed when this option is checked and unchecked.

Figure A.20 *The panel view of the Metadata panel (left) shows the shutter speed displayed when "Use typographic fractions" is switched off. The panel view (right) shows the shutter speed displayed when "Use typographic fractions" is switched on.*

Appendix B
Lightroom settings

This appendix provides information and details on the Lightroom settings, such as the template settings files, catalog folder, and Lightroom RGB space. I decided to keep these topics separate, mainly because I did not want to clutter the earlier chapters with information that might have been too distracting. This is an unashamedly technical section aimed at advanced users, although I have tried to keep the explanations as clear and simple as possible.

The contents of this appendix are placed in no particular order. Some of the information and tips mentioned here are likely to go out of date as later updates of the program are released, so please bear this in mind as you read through the following pages. But if you are keen to find out more detailed information about specific areas of Lightroom or want to explore some of the customization options, read on.

Lightroom settings and templates

The Lightroom preference file

The Lightroom preference file keeps a record of all your custom program settings. On a PC, the Lightroom 2 preferences.agprefs file is located in the Local Disk (C:)\Documents and Settings\Username\Application Data\ Adobe\Lightroom\Preferences (**Figure B.1**). On a Mac, the Lightroom preference file is named com.adobe.Lightroom.plist and is located in the Username/Library/Preferences folder (**Figure B.2**). If the Lightroom program is behaving strangely and you have reason to believe that the preferences might be corrupted, delete this file and Lightroom will generate a new preference file the next time you launch the program.

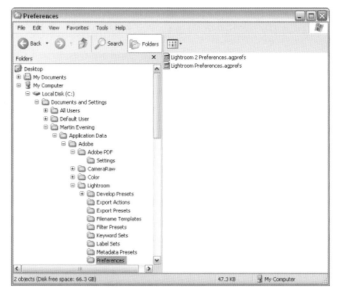

Figure B.1   *The Adobe Lightroom preference file for a PC is located in the Local Disk (C:)\Documents and Settings\username\Application Data\Adobe\Lightroom\ Preferences folder.*

Figure B.2   *The Adobe Lightroom preferences file for Mac OS X is located in the Username/Library/Preferences folder.*

Accessing saved template settings

When you save a setting in any of the Lightroom modules, the saved template settings are normally stored in the Local Disk (C:)\Documents and Settings\Username\Application Data\Adobe\Lightroom folder (PC) (**Figure B.3**) and the Username/Application Support/Adobe/Lightroom folder (Mac) (**Figure B.4**). Inside these folders you will see a set of subfolders that contain all the saved settings (and default settings) for the various Lightroom modules. For example, in Figure B.3 I highlighted the Develop Presets\User Presets folder, which contains a list of all the user-added Develop preset settings. You can then make copies of these files and distribute them as preset settings for other Lightroom users to install on their computers, which they can do by dragging and dropping presets into the folder directories shown here.

TIP

Richard Earney hosts a Web site called Inside Lightroom that lists various Develop module presets: http://inside-lightroom.com/index.php.

NOTE

If the "Store presets with catalog" option described on page 546 is checked, this will copy the Lightroom settings folder from the locations shown here and place a copy folder of the Lightroom settings inside the Lightroom catalog folder, which is shown in Figures B.5 and B.6.

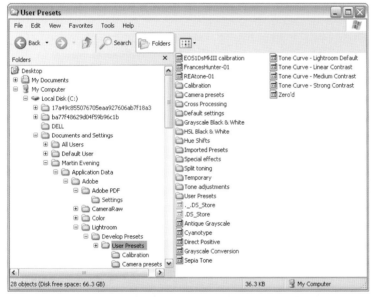

Figure B.3 *The Adobe Lightroom template settings folder (PC).*

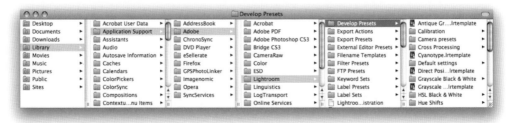

Figure B.4 *The Adobe Lightroom template settings folder (Mac OS X).*

The Lightroom catalog folder

The first time you launch Lightroom, a catalog folder titled *Lightroom* is automatically placed in the username/Pictures folder (Mac OS X) or the My Documents\My Pictures folder (PC). This folder will have a Lightroom catalogname.lrcat database file and a Lightroom Previews.lrdata file that contains all the thumbnail previews and library image metadata information. The Backups folder that is seen in **Figures B.5** and **B.6** will only show up after you have carried out your first catalog backup. The Backups folder is used for storing the backup Library database files. But let's first take a look at the two catalog files.

The catalog database file

The Lightroom catalogname.lrcat file is written using the SQLite3 database format, which is a robust database format that keeps all the library data in a single file and is easily transferable for cross-platform use. This file is used to store a database of information relating to all the images in the Lightroom catalog, such as the metadata and Develop settings for each image, and which folder and/or collection the file belongs to. Depending on the overall size of your image library, the Lightroom catalogname.lrcat file can grow to be quite large in size.

Figure B.5   *The Lightroom catalog folder contents in Mac OS X.*

Figure B.6   *The Lightroom catalog folder contents in Windows XP.*

If you perform a new install of Lightroom or upgrade the program, a new catalog database file (containing all the current data about the library) will be generated and the old one saved to the Backups folder. So, if you have the General Lightroom preferences configured to automatically create backup copies of the Lightroom database, the backup will normally be saved to the Backups folder, but you can choose an alternative location if you wish (**Figure B.7**). If you choose to run an integrity test of the catalog during the backup procedure, you'll see the dialog shown in **Figure B.8**.

Figure B.8 *In the Backup Catalog dialog is an option to test the integrity of the current database file. Depending on the size of your catalog, running an integrity check may take a few minutes to complete. If you do come across any errors, replace the current catalog database file with the most recently saved file from the Backups folder.*

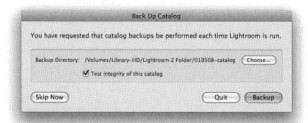

Figure B.7 *In the General preferences you can schedule how often Lightroom makes a backup copy of the Lightroom catalog database file. Then, when Lightroom is due for a catalog backup, you will see this dialog at launch time. This gives you the option to skip the backup for now, quit launching Lightroom, or proceed with the backup.*

Figure B.9 shows how a couple of older catalog database files have been saved automatically as backup copies. If for some reason you encounter a problem with the current catalog database when you launch Lightroom (or after running an integrity test), you can replace the main Lightroom catalogname.lrcat file with the most recent backup version. The catalog database file is therefore a precious component of the Lightroom folder, and you need to safeguard it as you would a financial account file or other important data document. Treat the catalog database file with care, and remember to perform regularly scheduled backups to a secondary storage system.

Figure B.9 *The Lightroom folder showing an expanded view of the Backups folder contents.*

If you want to select a new catalog file or need to check that the correct catalog database file is selected, you can do so by holding down the [Alt] key (Mac) or [Ctrl] key (PC) while restarting Lightroom (**Figure B.10**). When you do this, the Select Catalog dialog appears and allows you to navigate to the correct Lightroom catalogname.lrcat file. Or, you can click the Create New Catalog button to create a new Lightroom catalog in a new folder location. It is possible to have any number of separate Lightroom catalogs. For example, when several people are sharing the Lightroom program such as in a college environment, each student can maintain his or her own separate catalog.

Figure B.10   *If you hold down the [Alt] key (Mac) or [Ctrl] key (PC) as you launch Lightroom, the Select Catalog navigation dialog appears onscreen, allowing you to select a new Lightroom catalog file.*

Journal file

The Lightroom catalogname.lrcat-journal file is a temporary file that you may see while Lightroom is processing library information. This is an important, internal work file that appears briefly and then disappears again. If your computer crashes, do not delete the journal file because it may contain important data that can help Lightroom recover recently modified data information.

Lightroom previews data

The Lightroom Previews.lrdata file is a self-contained file that holds all the previews and thumbnail data. In **Figure B.11**, I used the contextual menu to show the package contents of the Lightroom Previews.lrdata file. This particular package is just over 3.62 GB in size, and contains lots of .preview.noindex files. These are the thumbnail and preview cache files that are used by Lightroom. The size of the thumbnail cache depends partly on how you set the File Handling preferences in the Catalog Settings (**Figure B.12**) as well as the Camera Raw cache limit size that is set in the Lightroom File Handling preferences (see page 553). If you want to keep the Lightroom Previews.lrdata size to a minimum, select Automatically Discard 1:1 Previews and then choose the After One Day or One Week option. If you don't mind it growing in size, select After 30 Days or Never. The choice is yours, but as long as you have plenty of hard disk space, I suggest you choose the After 30 Days option. Otherwise, Lightroom will have to constantly rerender the 1:1 previews for the most commonly visited folders.

Figure B.11   *A package contents view of all the .lr-preview.noindex files that are contained in the Lightroom Previews. lrdata file.*

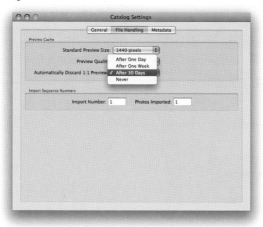

Figure B.12   *The File Handling section in the Catalog Settings.*

Thumbnail processing routines

When photos are first imported into Lightroom, the Import dialog offers a choice of options for the initial previews (**Figure B.13**). The Minimal option is quickest because highest priority is given to importing the photos into Lightroom. Where there are previews, Lightroom assumes everything to be in sRGB and the previews are only updated once all the images have been imported. This is a good choice for importing pictures quickly from the camera. Such previews are usually fine as a rough visual of how the image looks, but they don't always offer much in the way of detail, since they are normally the small-sized JPEG previews that were embedded in the camera file at the time of capture. These types of preview will appear pixelated. In addition, the color appearance is always likely to change after Lightroom has had a chance to build a proper preview from the image data. After the initial import, Lightroom makes a second pass in which it processes the raw data using its internal color engine to build the standard-sized previews. These previews let you see a greater level of detail when displaying large thumbnails in the Content area or at a fit-to-view Loupe magnification. Lightroom then makes a third pass where high-quality, 1:1 resolution previews are generated (**Figure B.14**). If Embedded & Sidecar is selected, Lightroom uses whatever previews are available as it imports all the images, utilizing either the embedded JPEG previews or sidecar file previews to quickly build the thumbnails. This is useful if you are importing photographs that have already been edited in Lightroom (or some other program), as it can make full use of the larger previews that are already associated with the files.

Figure B.13   *The Import Photos dialog offers a choice of Initial Preview options.*

With Standard previews, Lightroom avoids using the embedded previews altogether and renders the standard previews directly. It reads the full image data and builds the thumbnails and initial previews to a standard size only, based on the default Lightroom Develop settings, but without applying Detail panel adjustments (this helps speed up the preview generation). However, if the 1:1 Initial Preview option is selected, Lightroom reads the full image data, builds thumbnails, creates standard- and full-sized 1:1 previews, and applies all the Develop settings (including the Detail panel settings). The advantage of the Standard or 1:1 Initial Preview option is that you won't get confused by seeing low-resolution previews that show one color interpretation (the embedded preview version), only for them to be replaced shortly by a new color interpretation (the Lightroom processed standard-sized preview version).

TIP

The Embedded & Sidecar initial preview option is a particularly useful choice for importing DNG files as there is a good chance that the preview is already using Lightroom Develop settings of one form or another. In such circumstances the previews will not actually change in appearance when they are rerendered in Lightroom.

NOTE

Whenever you launch Lightroom, it initially loads all the low-resolution thumbnails, and within 30 seconds or so, starts running checks on the current library contents, checking the thumbnails in order of quality. Lightroom will look to see if any of the standard resolution thumbnails need to be rebuilt first before going on to build the high-resolution, 1:1 previews for these images. At the same time it checks the existing thumbnail previews against their modification dates. If any file has been modified since the last time a preview was built, Lightroom rebuilds a new set of previews, starting with a standard preview, followed by a high-quality 1:1 preview.

Embedded low-res thumbnails

Standard-sized preview

High-quality 1:1 preview

Figure B.14 *Lightroom builds progressive quality thumbnails and previews. If Minimal or Embedded & Sidecar are selected (see Figure B.13), it starts by utilizing the embedded thumbnail already contained in the image or sidecar file, followed by a standard-sized preview that is suitable for large thumbnail or standard Loupe mode viewing, and finally, a high-resolution 1:1 preview.*

You can set the Standard Previews size in the Catalog settings (**Figure B.15**). As was explained in Chapter 3, if you have a 30-inch screen, you should choose the 2048 pixels option, but if you are working from a laptop computer, the 1024 pixels setting will probably be more appropriate.

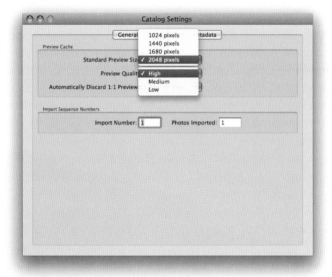

Figure B.15 *You can control the size of the standard previews and image quality via the File Handling section in the Catalog settings.*

Customizing the Lightroom contents

The Adobe Lightroom application is made up of modular components: the Library, Develop, Slideshow, Print, and Web modules. If you want to peek inside the Lightroom Application folder, follow the instructions shown in **Figure B.16** and **Figure B.17**. After you have revealed the package contents, you can see the various folders and files that make up Lightroom. In both screen shots I have expanded the program folders to reveal the individual module components. Now that you know where the modules are kept, you can customize Lightroom by temporarily removing specific modules from the program contents. For example, if you remove the SlideshowModule file from the folder shown in Figure B.16, Lightroom will open with the Slideshow module missing. Similarly, if you choose Show Package Contents on the Mac, open the Plug-ins folder, remove the Slideshow.agmodule folder, and relaunch, Lightroom will open without the Slideshow module. The Mac package contents even let you access the graphic files (these are located inside the various Resources folders). This gives you the opportunity to sneakily customize the interface. Obviously you want to be careful when playing around with the program components, because it is quite easy to damage or remove files that shouldn't really be messed with. If you are not careful, you can create problems that can only be addressed by carrying out a fresh reinstall of the program!

NOTE

Note that the Scripts folder in the Mac OS X Lightroom package contents is a Lightroom-only Scripts folder. Should you want to add custom scripts, place them in the Username/Library/Application Support/Adobe/Lightroom folder. Alternatively, go to the Scripts menu next to the Help menu and choose the Open User Scripts folder.

Figure B.16   *On a PC, go to Local Disk (C:)\Program files\Adobe\ to locate the Adobe Lightroom folder. There you will find the Lightroom application program along with the program files and modules.*

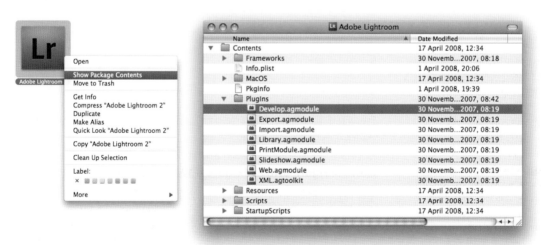

Figure B.17   *On the Mac OS X system you can reveal the package contents by right-clicking or* Ctrl *-clicking the Adobe Lightroom icon and selecting Show Package Contents from the fly-out menu. This opens a separate folder and allows you to access the program files and modules.*

NOTE

I tend to call the Lightroom edit space Lightroom RGB, although it isn't officially named as such. Mark Hamburg has suggested it might be more appropriate to call it "bastardized RGB" since the space is using ProPhoto RGB chromaticities, but with a gamma of 1.0 instead of 1.8. Meanwhile, the Lightroom viewing space uses the same ProPhoto RGB chromaticities but with an sRGB tone response curve. Melissa Gaul, who is the QE manager for Lightroom, suggested this space should be called Melissa RGB since all RGB spaces to date have been named after men!

NOTE

All image processing in Lightroom is carried out using the Lightroom RGB space. This means that grayscale images imported into Lightroom are in fact edited in RGB, and Grayscale mixer conversions keep the data in RGB. The same goes for Lab mode images—the Lab mode data is converted to RGB when processed in Lightroom (although the master file does remain in Lab mode). There is currently no planned support for CMYK files.

The Lightroom RGB space

As you have probably gathered by now, there are no RGB workspace color settings options in Lightroom as there are in Photoshop. This is because the ICC-based color management system was introduced in Photoshop at a time when color management was not that well understood and it was therefore necessary to incorporate the new, ICC color management system in a way that could satisfactorily allow Photoshop users to accommodate their existing non-ICC color managed workflows. In addition, the RGB spaces that were recommended for use as RGB workspaces in Photoshop were mostly quite conservative.

Lightroom has largely been freed from these constraints and it is therefore safer these days to assume that most photographers are now working with RGB files that have embedded profiles. Since Lightroom is mainly intended as a tool for editing digital capture images, these photos will mostly be imported into Lightroom either as profiled JPEGs or as raw files (in which case the Adobe Camera Raw color engine will know how to interpret the colors, based on the embedded white balance information). If an imported RGB image happens to be missing a profile, Lightroom assumes the profile to be sRGB and assigns it when performing the image processing calculations.

Lightroom carries out the image processing calculations in its own RGB space, which uses the ProPhoto RGB coordinates but has a gamma of 1.0 instead of 1.8. The 1.0 gamma was chosen with raw image processing in mind, because raw files all have a gamma of 1.0 and Lightroom can therefore process the raw images in their native gamma without needing to convert them to a gamma of say, 1.8 or 2.2. Keeping Lightroom's image processing in the native gamma of the raw capture files is a better way to work because Lightroom processes the raw data directly without applying a gamma conversion to the raw data. Also, Lightroom can provide smoother blending when you perform certain types of image processing adjustments.

The ProPhoto RGB coordinates describe a massively large color space (so big it includes colors that are invisible to the human eye). So the gamut of ProPhoto RGB is certainly large enough to include every possible color that a digital camera can capture, which means that the RGB space used by Lightroom never clips any important colors when carrying out its calculations. Also, bear in mind that the image processing is carried out mostly in 16-bits per channel (some specific processing is even done in 32-bits) and because Lightroom uses a 16-bit RGB edit space, it is able to preserve all of the levels that a digital camera can capture. For example, a typical digital SLR captures up to 12-bits of levels data per channel. When a raw file from one of these cameras is edited in Lightroom, the 16-bit edit space is able to process the raw image data without losing any of the levels information. The deep-bit editing space should also allay any concerns about the risks of banding that might be caused by gaps in a color value representation between one level's data point and the next. I have to say that even with an 8-bit edit space, these initial concerns have been overstated and I do accept now that it is safe to work with ProPhoto RGB, even if the final destination space will be an 8-bits per channel image. But obviously, if you are able to make all the principal image edits using all the captured levels data in a wide gamut RGB space (as you are when you work in Lightroom), then so much the better.

But let's now take a look at why raw images are in a linear gamma space to start with. All digital images, whether they are scans or captures from a digital camera, contain data that is a linear representation of the light hitting the sensor. As the light intensity doubles, a sensor records a brightness value that is two times higher. This all sounds logical enough, but when you actually view an image that has been recorded in this way, you begin to realize that human vision perceives things quite differently to the way a sensor sees and records light. This is because, unlike a scanner or camera sensor, our eyes compensate for increasing levels of brightness in a nonlinear fashion, which is why we are able to distinguish shades of tone over a wide dynamic range from the darkest shadows to the brightest highlights. When the light levels double, our eyeballs do not literally record the light levels hitting our retinas as being twice the brightness. Our human vision system is able to adapt to widely changing light levels by constantly compensating for such extremes in the light levels. So if we compare the way a sensor records light and represents the captured image data, we see an image that looks very dark, even though it may in fact be perfectly exposed and contain a full range of usable tones from the shadows to the highlights. To get a normal digital capture to look right to *our eyes*, the linear data must be gamma corrected (effectively lightened at the midpoint). Once a gamma curve has been applied to the linear capture data, the captured image will look more representative of the scene we perceived at the time the photograph was taken.

NOTE

Non-raw images are processed via the same Lightroom RGB space as the raw files. As long as the image you are editing has a profile attached, Lightroom will recognize this, preserve the master file in its original RGB space, and use this space to calculate the histogram and display the image previews in Lightroom (except the Develop module). But Lightroom will carry out all its calculations in the linear gamma Lightroom RGB space. If an image is missing a profile, Lightroom assumes the image should be in sRGB whenever it carries out an on-the-fly conversion to the Lightroom RGB space for the Lightroom image processing. Note: Lightroom does not actually assign a profile to an unprofiled master.

TIP

For a more detailed explanation of working in linear gamma, download the "Raw Capture, Linear Gamma, and Exposure" white paper written by Bruce Fraser (www.adobe. com/digitalimag/ps_pro.html).

RGB previews

As I explained on page 568, the previews you see in the Library module are either Adobe RGB or ProPhoto RGB JPEG previews, which are stored in the cache and used to provide the Grid and Loupe view previews. However, the Develop module preview space uses the same ProPhoto RGB coordinates as the Lightroom RGB space, but with an sRGB tone response curve. Therefore, the Develop module previews will always show you a reliable color view of the image you are editing since the Develop module preview space shares the same chromaticities as the Lightroom RGB edit space. You may see some slight color shifts between the Develop and Library modules if the Library module is using Adobe RGB previews or if an image is exported from Lightroom using Adobe RGB. You may also see some clipping if you export using sRGB, because sRGB has an even smaller color gamut.

Tone curve response

There are clear advantages to working on raw data in a native, linear gamma edit space, but a linear gamma space is not so good when it comes to making direct image edit adjustments. When you edit an RGB image in Lightroom, there are two things going on. First, the Develop controls used to carry out the image processing do so filtered through the preview RGB space with its sRGB response curve. As a result, the data points in the underlying Lightroom RGB edit space are distributed more evenly so that the Basic and Tone Curve adjustments applied in Lightroom correspond to a more balanced tone scale (the sRGB response curve is also used to generate the histogram display and color readout values seen in the Develop module). What you see in the histogram is effectively the Lightroom ProPhoto RGB space in linear 1.0 gamma with an sRGB response curve applied to it. **Figure B.18** shows a plot of the sRGB curve (in black), which matches closely to the 2.2 gamma curve (shown in pink). I had to show this graph quite big so you could see the subtle difference between these two curves. But note that the sRGB curve rises steeply from 0,0 and away from clipping the blacks just a little sooner than a pure 2.2 gamma curve—although the 2.2 curve hugs the y axis high enough that several potential values very close to black (in the linear space) are crushed to black. The sRGB curve then leans away from the y axis much sooner, and you maintain at least a tiny bit of differentiation between those very dark values. So in the transformation from the linear space to the sRGB space, the sRGB curve is just a bit less draconian in where it leaves values in the very dark shadows.

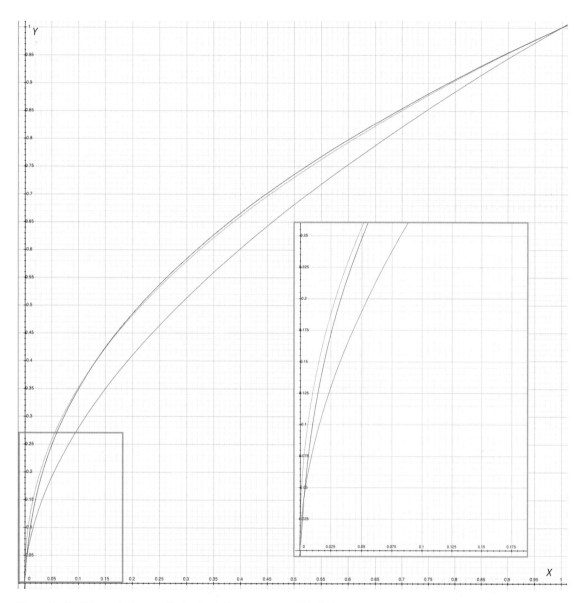

Figure B.18 *This graph shows a plot for the sRGB response curve (black) for the Lightroom preview RGB space (also known as Melissa RGB), plotted against a standard 2.2 gamma curve (pink) and a 1.8 gamma curve (blue). Note the description in the main body text, which explains the subtle difference between the sRGB and 2.2 gamma curve shapes. The inset box shows a close-up view of the bottom end of the gamma curves.*

Balancing the tone curve

Figures B.19 and **B.20** explain why it is necessary for the Lightroom preview RGB space to use an sRGB response curve before the linear RGB data reaches the Develop controls. Remember, you are in fact always editing 1.0 gamma data, and the sRGB response curve is only applied to make the Develop adjustments easier and more logical to control. Even so, you will still notice an element of asymmetric response when adjusting the Blacks slider. For example, have you noticed how small incremental adjustments to the Blacks have a far more pronounced effect than adjustments made with the Exposure slider?

Figure B.19 *The problem with trying to edit the linear 1.0 gamma directly is that the midtones are all condensed in the left portion of the tone curve (shown here as a continuous gradient). If you were forced to directly edit an image with a 1.0 gamma, any attempt to make small adjustments in the shadow to midtone region would be very much amplified in the midtone to highlight regions. As shown here, it would be a bit like trying to balance a seesaw with an offset fulcrum point.*

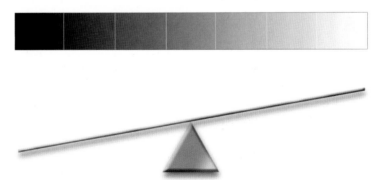

Figure B.20 *When an sRGB tone response curve is applied to the underlying linear gamma data, the tones on the tone curve are more evenly distributed. This provides an image editing environment in which you are able to edit linear 1.0 gamma image data in a more balanced (and more natural) nonlinear fashion.*

Lightroom vs. Photoshop curves

On the face of it, the Tone Curve panel in Lightroom appears to work the same way as the Curves adjustment in Photoshop. If you use the Tone Curve controls in Lightroom to edit a color image, a steep curve will increase the tonal contrast but will also boost the saturation as well. The same thing happens when you use Photoshop curves to increase the contrast of a color image. Now in Photoshop you can use the Luminosity blend mode to fade a curves adjustment (or if using an adjustment layer, set the layer blend mode to Luminosity). This, it is argued, will apply the curve adjustment to the image luminance only, without affecting the color information. It is a useful technique to be aware of and can often be used in Photoshop when you wish to apply a contrast correction without affecting the color. Although the Luminosity curve method might seem to be the "correct" way to go about applying curves, your photographs will tend to look unnaturally dull if you use the Luminosity curve approach when carrying out global adjustments. According to Thomas Knoll, it would be easy enough to program curves to not affect the color, but they chose not to because the mild saturation boost produces more pleasing, film-like results.

However, Lightroom/Camera Raw curves do work slightly differently from Photoshop curves. This is because Lightroom curves have a hue lock, which means that when Lightroom maps the RGB values from a before state to the Tone Curve state, it will map the minimum and maximum RGB values (in the linear Lightroom RGB workspace) allowing the hue to vary. But when mapping the middle RGB value, the hue is always preserved. Photoshop curves have no hue lock; when you apply a strong curve adjustment in Photoshop, the hue values can shift quite a bit from the original before values. This in turn can lead to some noticeable color shifts in the processed image. Lightroom/ACR curves produce hue shifts as well, but these are more tightly controlled so that what hue shifts there are, are usually within plus or minus 3°. As I said, tone curves in Lightroom that increase the contrast will boost the saturation, but from the conclusions I draw on page 580, Lightroom/ACR tone curves are *on average* about 1–2% less saturated than the curves that are applied via Photoshop in the Normal blend mode. In practice this means that Lightroom tone curve adjustments will have smaller hue shifts and the colors are represented better. So how can you test this? The following steps show the method I used to create a Photoshop curve that matched a tone curve adjustment that had been applied in the Lightroom Develop module.

NOTE

For further reading on this subject, I recommend a PDF article written by Mark Segal that was published on the Luminous Landscape Web site: www.luminous-landscape.com/essays/Curves.shtml.

Mark has carried out some very thorough research here. He does reach a slightly different conclusion about the saturation differences between Lightroom and Photoshop curves. I have discovered that most of the time, Lightroom curves are less saturated than Photoshop curves. But they can sometimes produce stronger saturation values, so this does not necessarily disprove Mark's observations.

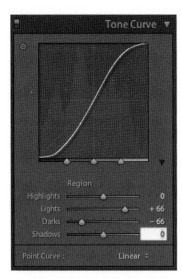

Figure B.21 *This shows a close-up view of the curve applied in Step 2, left.*

1. To replicate a Lightroom tone curve in Photoshop, I made a virtual copy of a color image and converted it to grayscale in Lightroom. In this example I applied a high-contrast tone curve (see **Figure B.21**) and exported two versions: one with a neutral linear point curve and one using a high-contrast curve setting (as shown here).

 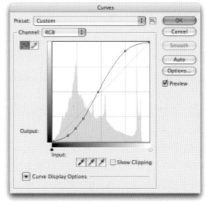

2. In Photoshop I placed the Linear Tone Curve image as a layer above the High Contrast Tone Curve layer, inside a new layer group. I then added a curves adjustment layer above the Linear Tone Curve layer and set the layer group blend mode to Difference. The objective now was to open the Curves adjustment layer and create a curve shape that matched the Lightroom tone curve shown at Step 1. Because the layer group had been set to Difference, the image would appear solid black when the curves adjustment applied to the Linear Tone Curve layer made it match the appearance of the High Contrast Tone Curve layer.

High contrast.acv

3. Once I had made a perfect matching curve, I saved it as a new preset and named it High contrast.acv.

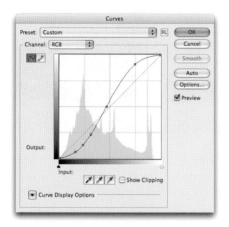

NOTE

These steps for creating matching Photoshop curves will be specific to the RGB space you export the files to. In the following example I exported the images from Lightroom to the ProPhoto RGB space.

4. I was now able to test the difference in the hue and saturation response of a Lightroom tone curve compared to a curve that had been applied to an image in Photoshop. I repeated Steps 1 and 2, but this time I processed the image in full color. I then used the Eyedropper tool to measure and compare the colors in the image and compile a table of measurements.

About the curve comparison creation method

For the first step, I deliberately processed the image in Grayscale mode because at this stage I only wanted to compare the tone curve luminosity. Once I had discovered the Photoshop curve setting that matched exactly the Lightroom grayscale tone curve adjusted image, I had a Photoshop curve that when applied to any Grayscale mode image would match Lightroom exactly. Note that it did not matter which image I used to test with at stages 1 and 2, just as long as it was an image that had been edited in the Lightroom Grayscale mode.

When I started putting the curve to use and tested the difference between the Lightroom and Photoshop curves using color images, I was able to confirm that the brightness values did indeed always match wherever I sampled in the image area. This therefore allowed me to test for just the variations in hue and saturation between the Lightroom and Photoshop curve methods.

Labels on image: Lightroom Tone Curve, A, Photoshop Luminosity Mode Curve, D, Photoshop Normal Mode Curve, C, B

Figure B.22 *In this sectioned image you can see a comparison view of a Lightroom high-contrast curves adjustment (top), a Photoshop high-contrast curve blended using Luminosity (middle), and a Photoshop high-contrast curve blended using Normal mode (bottom).*

Comparison results

The Photoshop HSB values at points A, B, C, and D in **Figure B.22**, using the HSB readouts from the Photoshop Info panel (**Figure B.23**), are recorded in **Figure B.24**. These numbers allowed me to analyze the differences between the three curve methods used here and help understand why they each produce slightly different results. The Hue value is expressed in degrees (°) on a scale of 0–360, while the Saturation and Brightness values are expressed as percentages.

Compare the Lightroom adjusted Hue values with the original image and you will notice that there is only a small difference. Now compare them with the Photoshop Normal blend mode values and you will see a much wider variance in the Hue values. However, when the Luminosity blend mode is applied to the curve in Photoshop the Hue values will be preserved exactly.

If you now look at the Saturation values, you will note that the Saturation is almost the same with both the Lightroom and Photoshop curves. In the testing I've done, however, the Lightroom curve saturation is on average always slightly less than a Normal mode Photoshop curve (by about 1–2%). Sometimes it is higher, but mostly it's less. But what is interesting about the Photoshop luminosity curve is its tendency to suck some of the saturation out of an image; the figures in the Luminosity curve Saturation column back this up. Compare these values with the Saturation values for the Lightroom and Photoshop normal blend curves.

The Brightness columns confirm that the luminance values are identical for both the Lightroom and Photoshop Normal blend mode curves, but the Luminosity mode curve values do end up being different.

Figure B.23 *The HSB values shown in Figure B.22 were noted in the Info palette in Photoshop. I went to the Info palette preferences (via the fly-out menu) and altered the coordinate second color readouts to show HSB values.*

	Original image			Lightroom Tone Curve			Photoshop Curve (Normal blend mode)			Photoshop Curve (Luminosity blend mode)		
	H	S	B	H	S	B	H	S	B	H	S	B
Point A (green)	80°	39%	37%	78°	61%	32%	83°	62%	32%	80°	46%	31%
Point B (blue)	232°	54%	45%	230°	77%	47%	235°	78%	47%	232°	67%	36%
Point C (yellow 1)	43°	88%	50%	44°	98%	57%	35°	97%	57%	43°	89%	50%
Point D (yellow 2)	46°	56%	93%	47°	59%	99%	56°	59%	99%	46°	38%	99%

Figure B.24 *This table shows a comparison between the Photoshop HSB values for points A, B, C, and D in Figure B.20. These figures show the differences between the original values and those for the image after it has been processed in Lightroom and in Photoshop using a normal blend and a Luminosity blend mode curve.*

Figure B.25 *If you want to achieve the Luminosity curve desaturated effect, it is easy enough just to turn down the Vibrance and Saturation in Lightroom. In this example, the left half shows the image treated with a –25 Vibrance and –15 Saturation. The right half shows a version created using a Photoshop Luminosity curve. The Hue and Saturation values can be made to almost match, but the tone luminance characteristics will always be slightly different. In this example the Lightroom adjusted tone curve retains more tonal contrast in the highlights than the Luminosity curve version.*

Conclusions

It is all very well running involved tests like the one described here to calculate the numeric differences between Lightroom and Photoshop curves, but at the end of the day, the only way to judge anything is to let your eyes compare the results visually. The differences between the two curve methods can be quite subtle, but where it is noticeable, I would say the Lightroom/Camera Raw curve result always looks more pleasing. The testing data kind of backs this up, because as I mentioned earlier, the figures show that there is a much finer tolerance in the amount of hue shift you get with a Lightroom curve. This is why the colors tend to be preserved better.

It is interesting to examine what happens when you apply a Luminosity blend mode to a Photoshop curve. The accepted wisdom here is that a Luminosity curve will only affect the luminance values of the image and the color values are preserved. At least that is what I have written in the past! If you compare a contrast-increasing Luminosity curve with a Normal mode curve, the Luminosity curve will look flatter in color, which you might assume is because the curve has been filtered to target the luminance only. While a Luminosity curve may always preserve the hue, it can still have a marked effect on the saturation values. And whereas the luminance values will always match between a Lightroom curve and a Photoshop curve in Normal mode (using the test method described here), the Luminosity mode curve brightness values can actually deviate a lot from these two other curve methods. The conclusion I draw here is that Photoshop Luminosity curves are useful for preventing unwanted hue shifts and taming any saturation boost, but you should be aware that the saturation values can shift up or down, and there will not be an exact tonal match between the effect of a Luminosity and a Normal mode curve. This last point should not necessarily represent a problem. It should not matter whether the curve outcome is different because you can always manipulate a curve in Photoshop to get the luminance balance you do like. For Photoshop users it could be argued that what is needed is a slider control in the Curves dialog going from a Normal mode to a Luminosity mode curve adjustment. That way, you could tweak the way the curve was applied to the image from within the Curves dialog. That might work, but if we go back to the subject of tone curves in Lightroom there is already an easy method for taming the saturation boost: the Vibrance and Saturation sliders. You can easily take the Vibrance or Saturation down if you find that the Lightroom tone curve has made a photo look too colorful (see **Figure B.25**).

The ideal computer setup for Lightroom

The ideal computer setup for Lightroom depends on the size of the files you intend working with. The raw file captures you can work with in Lightroom may vary from 5 to 22 megapixels, and the larger files will place more demands on your computer resources. So when looking for an ideal computer to run Lightroom, you will definitely need to take the image file size into account. The most important factors affecting Lightroom performance will be the processor speed and the amount of RAM memory that is available for Lightroom to use. This is followed by the speed and size of the hard disk, and then the type of graphics card. At a minimum, you need a Macintosh G4 with a 1 GHz processor and 1 GB of RAM, running Mac OS X 10.4.3 or later. And on the PC side, you need an Intel Pentium 4 with a 1 GHz processor and 1 GB of RAM, running Windows XP Pro or Home Edition with Service Pack 2. Lightroom is optimized to run on the latest Intel computer processors, and from the testing I have done so far, it does seem to run very fast on the latest high-end Core 2 Duo, Intel-based Macs and PCs.

RAM memory

You will benefit from having as much RAM as possible and should take into account that the operating system and any other open applications will also consume some of the RAM. For example, if you happen to have just 1 GB of RAM installed in your computer, the operating system may use about 256 MB, and another 50 MB might be used up by various utilities. And that is before taking into account any other, more memory-intensive applications that may be running in the background. So if you double the amount of memory installed on the computer to 2 GB, you could easily triple the amount of RAM that is effectively made available to Lightroom. Keep in mind that you are limited to installing 3 GB of RAM in most laptops. But if you have a desktop machine, you can probably install a lot more. Judging by the reports from various power users, you will see significant benefits in performance if you install 4 GB of RAM or more on a fast desktop computer—especially now that Lightroom is able to run in 64-bit and can therefore access more RAM memory than the previous 4 GB limit.

Graphics card

The graphics card does not play such a vital role in Lightroom's overall performance. You simply need a graphics card that is capable of running the screen display at its native resolution, but unless you intend to use your computer for editing movies or playing games, you don't really need an ultrafast graphics card. For example, all the latest Apple Mini and MacBook computers, with the Core 2 Duo processor, use 64 MB of the system RAM to run the graphics display. As long as you have a substantial amount of memory installed, the amount of memory the graphics card uses should not limit the speed with which you can work in Lightroom.

Hard drives

A default Lightroom installation chooses the main computer hard drive to store the Lightroom catalog files. On both the Mac and the PC, the Lightroom catalog is stored inside the users' Pictures folder and the Lightroom catalog files contain all the Lightroom metadata information along with standard and 1:1 previews. The catalog files will increase in size as your catalog grows bigger, although there are options in the preferences to limit the growth of how many 1:1 previews exist at a time by automatically deleting them after a certain number of days.

The main considerations when selecting a hard drive are the interface type, hard drive configuration, speed, and buffer memory. All these factors affect the overall speed. Let's start with the interface connection. Internal drives usually offer a fast ATA interface connection, so one option would be to add more internal drives. I have learned from experience to be wary of relying too much on working files being kept on an internal hard drive. Twice I have had an internal power unit die and had to physically remove the drives and place them in a temporary drive housing in order to access the data. For this reason you could choose to store all the Lightroom library image folders on fast, external drives. This would allow you to free the main computer hard drive from an accumulating library of image folders. This approach has the added benefit of keeping the library portable so you can, if necessary, switch computers and use Lightroom on another machine to access the same image catalog. However, with some of the newer computers it is actually easy to swap out the internal drives and move them from one machine to another. So I am now more inclined to use internal drive units because of their faster internal interface connection speeds.

Several external connection types are available. A USB 1 connection limits the data transfer rate and should be avoided. Instead, choose a USB 2 or a FireWire 400/800 connection. You can now also buy Serial ATA (SATA) drives that promise very fast rates of data transfer, but you might need a PCI card to provide a SATA connection from your computer.

The hard drive spindle speed determines how fast data can be written to and retrieved from the disk drive unit. Most 3.5-inch desktop drives have a spindle speed of 7200 RPM, whereas the smaller 2.5-inch drives found in laptops and portable bus-powered drives mostly run at a speed of 4200–5400 RPM. You can get 7200 RPM 2.5-inch drives, but they are more expensive and are usually only offered as a custom option when buying a laptop. Extra disk buffer memory helps take the pressure off the disk drive activity and also leads to improved drive performance.

Drive configurations

It is tempting to look for a solution whereby all your data can be stored in a single location, such as a RAID system capable of storing a large amount of data on a single volume drive. A simple way to explain RAID is that it allows you to treat multiple drives as a single drive volume to provide increased data integrity, capacity, transfer rates, or fault-tolerance compared to a single volume. How it does this depends on the RAID level you choose. You need a minimum of two disks to configure a RAID system, and most off-the-shelf RAID solutions are sold as a bay dock that can accommodate two or more drives with a built-in RAID controller. With RAID it is possible to store several terabytes of data on a single volume with built-in mirroring backup, but such systems do come at a very high price. Not only that, but they can also be quite noisy and are not particularly energy efficient. For some businesses, RAID is the perfect solution; for small photography businesses it can be overkill. But let's look at some of the more popular RAID configurations and how they might suit a digital photography computer setup.

Striped RAID

With a striped RAID 0 setup, two or more drives can work together to create a single, large-volume drive. RAID 0 is useful when you require fast hard-drive access speeds, because the drive access speed increases

NOTE

These days it is worth purchasing a computer that has plenty of free internal space that allows you to install additional internal drives. For example, the latest Intel Mac computers have enough room to fit three extra drives. You can therefore equip a modern Intel Mac with either an internal mirrored RAID 1 or a striped RAID 0 setup. These will have to be controlled by software on the Mac via the Disk Utilities program. In the past, software-created RAIDs were a lot slower than a dedicated system with a hardware controller. The read/write speeds from a software RAID will still be slower than a true dedicated RAID system since a software RAID will steal some of your computer processor cycles. But these days the speed loss is not as bad as it used to be. A software-driven, internal striped RAID 0 can increase disk access speed by about 45 percent, but comes with the inherent risk of losing all data in the event of a single disk failure. A software-driven, internal mirrored RAID 1 reduces speed by about 25 percent, but improves reliability.

proportionally to the number of drives that are added. So if you have four 200 GB drives as a RAID 0 system, you will end up with a single 800 GB volume, and the hard drive access speed will be four times that of a single 200 GB drive. This setup might seem like a good idea for improving the data access speeds, but the disadvantage of such a setup is that if a single drive should fail, the entire RAID system will fail and all data will be lost. A RAID 0 setup is therefore ideal for use as a Photoshop scratch disk.

Mirrored RAID

A mirrored RAID 1 system stores an exact duplicate of all the data on a backup drive. So as data is written to one drive, a copy of the data is also written to the other drive. The main advantage of a RAID 1 system is that should any single drive within the system fail, you can swap it with a new one and the data stored on the mirrored drive automatically rebuilds a copy of the data on the replacement drive. RAID 1 therefore offers you the most secure method for storing important data such as an image archive. The downside is that you need double the disk size to store all your data. For example, a mirrored 2-terabyte RAID 1 drive setup only allows you to store up to 1 terabyte of data.

RAID 5 has gained in popularity recently. A RAID 5 setup requires a minimum of at least three drives and allows you to store data more securely and more economically through "parity striping." In practice, a RAID 5 configuration allows you to use the full drive storage capacity, less the capacity of one of the single drive units, and provides complete data backup should any single drive fail. So a 2-terabyte RAID 5 using four 500 GB drives is able to store up to 1.5 terabytes of data. RAID 5 offers the most economical form of storage that can withstand a single drive failure, but the write speeds are necessarily slow.

A mirror of stripes

Another alternative is a RAID 0+1 setup, which requires four disks. The first two disks are configured using RAID 0, creating a single volume but with twice the disk access speed of a single disk. The other two disks are configured to create an overall RAID 1 setup, in which the data on the RAID 0 volume is safely mirrored across the two backup disks. This RAID system is both fast and secure. Mirroring can provide security against immediate drive failure, but it does not offer a complete backup protection solution. Mirrored drives are necessary for businesses that must have absolute access to the data 24 hours a day,

7 days a week. But mirrored systems don't necessarily provide the full data security you would expect, because if the directory becomes corrupted, the continuous mirroring copies the corruption to the mirrored drive. This could happen before you even were aware of the problem, which could lead to loss of data. For absolute protection, scheduled backups need to be carried out to a secondary storage system, which should be kept off-site.

Just a bunch of disks

There are varied opinions about which is the best way to manage a photography archive storage system. In my view, RAID storage is ideal but is not always the best solution for all photographers. A perfect solution would be to have a high-capacity RAID drive system that is capable of storing all your images securely on a single RAID unit. I have seen photographers work with such setups, but even so, it is quite costly to have a multidrive unit that holds all your data running continuously and consumes lots of power just so that once or twice a year you can dig up a file you shot six years ago. If you analyze your storage requirements, most likely you will find that the vast majority of the files you access are no more than 12 months old. When you think about it, the files you need to work with on a regular basis can probably be accommodated on a standard single-drive unit. This leads to a simpler solution known as "just a bunch of disks," or JBOD for short. With a JBOD setup you can have a file storage system that is scalable to meet your expanding storage needs, and that is economical to maintain as well as being reliable, providing that you maintain a proper backup strategy. In my office, I use three internal 750 GB drives to store all the current catalog files and back these up to three external 750 GB drives. I also have eight other 250 GB drives that are used to store all of my older raw and master file images that date back over the last 14 years, plus another eight drives that are for backing up to. Most of the time I only need to have the internal drives running and I back up regularly to the main three 750 GB drives. Whenever I need to access older images, I can switch on the necessary hard drive, as directed by Lightroom. JBOD can never be as foolproof as a RAID system, but it may be more appropriate for those photographers who think this would be an acceptable solution for their storage needs.

TIP

When assessing your overall storage requirements, don't try to build a system to last you the next five years. Buy the storage system you need today, but make it expandable for the future.

NOTE

When you select a scheduled library backup option, the "Back up library" dialog appears each time you are due to carry out a scheduled backup. You can select a location where the backup library file should be stored as well as select an option that runs a test to see if there are any corruptions in the database. If so, you will have the opportunity to replace the current (corrupt) database with the previously backed-up database copy file.

NOTE

It is also a good idea to go to the File Management preferences and switch on the "Automatically write changes into XMP" option. This causes Lightroom to push the metadata information such as the Develop settings and other metadata information into the file (or sidecar file). This means that the files contain a backup of the information that is also stored in the central Lightroom library file.

Backup strategies

Earlier I made the distinction that a mirrored RAID system was essential in a mission-critical environment to ensure continuity of data access. But this does not amount to the same thing as having a fail-safe backup strategy. For that you need to perform scheduled backups to a secondary set of drives, which should be stored in a safe location such as a fire-proof safe or somewhere off-site. In a simple office setup, you could use one external drive to hold the main Lightroom image library and a duplicate drive of similar capacity to keep a regularly backed-up copy of the data. The important feature of this kind of setup is that backups can be scheduled manually. If a problem were to occur on the master disk, such as an accidental file deletion or a directory corruption, you have the opportunity to rectify the problem by copying data over from the backup drive. And because you are keeping the data on a separate drive, it can be stored in a separate location away from the main computer. Running scheduled drive backups in the manner described reduces the chances of losing data. But as long as the files are stored on read/write disk media, they will always be vulnerable to accidental erasure or a virus attack that could infiltrate from the masters to the backup drives. To reduce the risk further, make DVD copies of your files and keep them in an appropriate storage location. Of course, it would be a pain to have to reload all the data from DVDs again, but writing data to DVD ensures that the data is free from virus attack or human error. A DVD is the most economical removable media storage offered at present. But keep an eye out for newer media systems such as Blu-ray that are bound to become more affordable and practical for storing larger amounts of data on single disks.

Also, in the General section of the Catalog Settings there is an option to create an automatic scheduled backup of the master Lightroom catalog file at a frequency of your choosing. I would strongly advise you to select one of these options because it provides an extra level of built-in backup security that may well prevent you from losing valuable library data information (**Figure B.26**).

Figure B.26   *The Back Up Catalog dialog.*

Backup software

You can use various programs to carry out data backups. On the Macintosh platform, I like to use ChronoSync from Econ Technologies (www.econtechnologies.com) because it is simple to use and very effective at synchronizing all the files on a backup disk with the master disk (**Figure B.27**). I usually configure backup settings for my main work data drives such as the primary hard disk, plus the two other main drives that are used to store most of the raw file data and working files. Whenever I want to back up any data, I switch on a backup drive and run the backup process. I have the settings configured so that ChronoSync first compares all the data on the left target disk (the drive I want to back up) with the right target disk (the drive I want to store the backup data on) and then copies all the newly added files. I also have the Sync Deletions option checked, so that file deletions on the master disk are applied to the data on the backup disk. At the end of a synchronization I empty the Trash (or Recycle Bin in a PC backup program), and the backup is complete. Setting up backup drives and copying all the data takes a long time the first time around, but thereafter, if you carry out regular backups, like once a day or every few days, the backup procedure should only take a few minutes. If you are in the habit of leaving your drives switched on overnight, you can schedule the backups to happen in the early hours of the morning.

TIP

I have provided just a simple overview of how to devise a suitable backup strategy. If you would like to find out more about how to manage your image collection, check out *The DAM Book: Digital Asset Management for Photographers* (O'Reilly Digital Studio, 2005) by Peter Krogh.

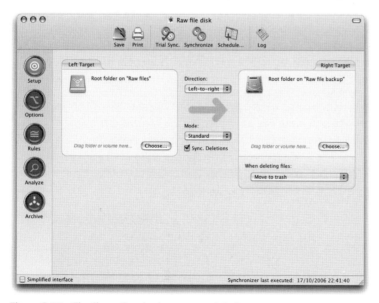

Figure B.27   *The ChronoSync backup program interface.*

Index

NUMBERS

1:1 previews, 87, 403, 416, 567
16-bit editing, 226, 570–571
    export processing, 439–440
16-bit printing, 480
32-bit processing, 475, 512
64-bit processing, 10, 475, 512

A

ACR Calibrator script, 310–311
actions, export, 444–447
Add Copyright Watermark option,
    443
Adjustment brush, 330–341
    Auto Mask option, 334–335
    clarity adjustments, 276
    Clarity effect, 340
    Color effect, 338–339
    editing brush strokes, 332
    example of using, 333
    initial settings, 331–332
    previewing stroke areas, 336
    saving effect settings, 332
    Sharpness effect, 340–341
    Soften Skin effect, 336–337
Adobe Acrobat Reader, 511
Adobe Bridge. See Bridge program
Adobe Camera Raw. See Camera
    Raw
Adobe color engine (ACE), 482
Adobe Photoshop. See Photoshop
Adobe Photoshop Lightroom. See
    Lightroom
Adobe RGB color space, 255, 420,
    439, 535, 572
Airtight galleries, 517, 528
All Edges correction, 303–305

Amount slider
    Sharpening controls, 404–405
    Vignettes panel, 306, 503
anchor points, 498–499
Aperture program, 330
Appearance panel (Web module),
    524–528
    Flash gallery settings, 525–527
    HTML gallery settings, 524
Application Data folder, 560
Armes, Timothy, 448
artist name metadata, 133, 164
aspect ratios, 246–249
attribute filter searches, 161
audio
    sidecar file playback, 190
    slideshow options, 507
Auto Dismiss option, 259
Auto Import Settings dialog, 23, 66
Auto Layout button, 463
Auto Mask option, 334–335
Auto Show mode, 254
Auto Sync mode, 325, 352
Auto Tone setting, 235, 265, 361
Auto White Balance setting, 261
Auto-Align Layers dialog, 430
Auto-blend command, 430
Auto-Rotate to Fit option, 454, 456
Auto-Stack by Capture Time dialog,
    114, 115
AutoViewer galleries, 517

B

Back Up Catalog dialog, 563, 586
Backdrop panel (Slideshow module),
    500–501
Background Color swatches, 500
Background Image option, 500, 501

backgrounds
    module preferences, 556
    slideshow options, 500, 501
backups, 586–587
    catalog, 563
    imported photo, 46, 47
    scheduled, 586
    software for, 587
Barroso, Clicio, 336
Basic panel (Develop module),
    256–281
    Auto Tone setting, 265
    Blacks slider, 264, 267, 270,
        280–281
    Brightness slider, 265, 281, 291
    Clarity slider, 274–277
    Contrast slider, 265, 281, 291
    Exposure slider, 256, 264, 269,
        278–281, 290
    Fill Light slider, 264, 291
    Grayscale button, 372
    Histogram panel and, 264–270
    image adjustment procedure, 258
    overview of controls in, 256
    Recovery slider, 264, 269,
        278–279, 290
    Saturation slider, 271–273
    Temperature slider, 262, 376,
        377, 380
    Tint slider, 262, 376, 377, 385,
        387
    Tone Curve panel and, 265,
        288–295
    Vibrance slider, 271–273, 393
    White Balance tool, 259–263,
        268, 289
beauty retouching
    Sharpness effect, 340–341
    Soften Skin effect, 336–337

Before/After viewing modes,
314–319
Copy settings buttons, 316
keyboard shortcuts, 315, 316
managing previews in, 316–319
Better Finder Attributes application,
131
Bibble Pro software, 63
bit depth, 311, 420, 439
black and white conversions,
372–395
desaturating color for, 392–395
fine-tuning B&W images,
388–395
Grayscale panel sliders for, 375
infrared effect and, 384–387
manual adjustments for, 382–383
RGB channels and, 374
Saturation slider for, 372
Split Toning panel for, 381, 387,
388–391
Temperature slider for, 376, 377,
380
Tint slider for, 376, 377, 385, 387
Blacks adjustment
Basic panel, 264, 267, 270,
280–281
Quick Develop panel, 236
Blacks slider, 264, 267, 270, 280–281
border options, 462, 468–469
Bridge program, 58–61
adding watched folders in, 60
color labels used in, 105
importing folders via, 61
navigating to Lightroom from,
58–59
previewing photos in, 61
Brightness adjustment
Basic panel, 265, 281, 291
Quick Develop panel, 236
burning CDs/DVDs, 449

C

calibrating the display, 228–233
devices used for, 229
steps in process of, 230–233

white point and gamma,
229–230
Camera Calibration panel (Develop
module), 310–313
Camera Raw, 4
ACR Profile versions for, 310
Adobe programs and, 5
cache folder for, 553
Lightroom integration with, 227,
354–357
Photoshop curves comparison,
575
processing images in, 4, 227
See also raw files
cameras
calibration settings for, 310–313
connecting to computers, 62–63
default settings for, 546
Develop presets for, 368–369
exposure settings for, 257
importing photos from, 62
memory cards for, 44–47
metadata info about, 133, 164
tethered shooting with, 62–67
Candidate images, 90
Canon EOS Utility, 62, 63, 67, 133
captions
viewing in Metadata panel, 126
Web gallery, 529–533
capture sharpening, 398
capture time editing, 132
Cast Shadow option, 492, 493
Catalog panel (Library module), 74
Catalog Settings dialog, 12, 85, 86,
176, 218
catalogs, 199–223
copying between computers,
207–211
creating new, 202
database file, 562–564
explanatory overview, 200
exporting, 203–205, 207, 208,
210, 449
filtering photos in, 106–113
folders and, 219–223
importing, 205–206, 207, 211
journal file, 564

merging, 212–217
opening existing, 202, 209
previews data file, 565
removing photos from, 117
settings for, 218
storing presets with, 546
troubleshooting, 200
using multiple, 201
Causa, Ettore, 336
CDs
exporting images to, 449
See also DVDs
cells
Contact Sheet/Grid options,
457–461
Picture Package layout options,
462–465
printing with multiple, 460–461
Cells panel (Print module), 462–465
Chromatic Aberration adjustments,
300–305
All Edges correction, 303–305
Highlight Edges correction, 302
lens aberration correction,
300–301
Chromoholics Web site, 311
ChronoSync backup program, 587
Clarity adjustment
Adjustment brush, 340
Basic panel, 274–277
negative, 276–277, 336–337
Quick Develop panel, 236
Clarity slider, 274–277
clipping
highlight, 255, 266, 269
shadow, 267
clipping warnings, 255, 266
Clone mode, Spot Removal tool, 322
Close-up Loupe view, 79, 83
CMYK files, 48
collections, 35
module-specific, 172–173
print, 452
Quick Collections saved as, 170
renaming, 173
sets of, 174
slideshow, 173

collections *(continued)*
    Smart Collections, 35, 174
    Web gallery, 521
    See also Quick Collections
Collections panel (Library module),
    172–174
color adjustments
    Adjustment brush, 338–339
    desaturated color, 392–395
    HSL/Color/Grayscale panel,
        296–299, 392–395
    noise reduction, 416–417
    Quick Develop panel, 234–235
    Split Toning panel, 390–391
Color effect
    Adjustment brush, 338–339
    Graduated Filter tool, 344
color labels
    assigning to photos, 104–105,
        166–167
    Bridge label compatibility, 105
    choosing colors for, 104
    filtering photos with, 110–111,
        163
    sort functions and, 187–189
Color Management settings, 474,
    482
Color Palette panel (Web module),
    522–523
color picker, 338, 522
Color sliders
    Detail panel, 314, 416, 417
    HSL panel, 392
color spaces, 228, 255, 420, 439
color themes, 522, 523
Color Wash controls, 500, 501
ColorChecker chart, 261, 311
colorimeter, 229
ColorSync option, 476, 481
Compact Cells view, 76, 77
Compare view, 90–93
    display options, 91
    steps for using, 92–93
Completion Sound options, 545
compression settings, 511
computers
    connecting cameras to, 62–63

ideal setup for Lightroom,
    581–587
system requirements for, 9, 581
See also Macintosh computers;
    Windows computers
Configure FTP File Transfer dialog,
    38, 537, 538
Constrain Aspect Ratio button, 246
Contact Info box, 521
Contact Sheet/Grid mode, 457
contact sheets, 32
Content area, 19
contextual menu
    for panels, 72, 73
    for photos, 223
contiguous selections, 78, 162, 163
Contrast adjustment
    Basic panel, 265, 281, 291
    Quick Develop panel, 236
Contrast slider, 265, 281
controlled vocabulary, 149, 150
Convert to DNG feature, 54, 550
copy names, 128, 130
Copy Photos as DNG option, 45, 47
Copy Settings buttons, 316
Copy Settings dialog, 358
copying
    catalogs between computers,
        207–211
    Develop module settings,
        358–359
    importing photos by, 50
copyright information, 143, 443
corrupted files, 47
Create Collection dialog, 172
Create Droplet dialog, 445
Create Folder dialog, 222
Create Folder with New Catalog
    dialog, 213
Create New Catalog button, 564
Crop Frame tool, 248
Crop Guide overlays, 251–252
Crop Lock button, 250
crop marks, 470
Crop Overlay mode, 246
Crop Ratio menu, 240
Crop tool panel, 246, 247

cropping photos, 246–253
    aspect ratios for, 246–249
    cancelling crops, 253
    guide overlays for, 251–253
    metadata info on, 131
    post-crop vignettes, 308–309
    Quick Develop options, 240
    repositioning crops, 250
    rotating and, 246
CRT displays, 228, 229
curves comparison, 575–580
custom filters, 165–169
custom keyword sets, 152
custom metadata, 134–139
custom profile printing, 481–484
Cut Guides option, 465

D

*DAM Book: Digital Asset Management
    for Photographers, The* (Krogh),
    105, 587
Darks slider, 284, 287, 292, 297
date/time information
    capture time editing, 132
    displayed in Metadata panel, 131
    filtering data by, 162
    format for entering, 137
Default Catalog options, 544–545
Default Develop settings, 545–546
defringe controls, 302–305
    All Edges correction, 303–305
    Highlight Edges correction, 302
deleting
    files from memory cards, 47
    history list, 346
    metadata presets, 136
    photos, 117
    templates, 485
    See also removing
Density slider, 331
desaturated color adjustments,
    392–395
Detail panel (Develop module),
    300–305, 398, 403–417
    Chromatic Aberration controls,
        300–301

Noise Reduction controls, 416–417

Sharpening controls, 398, 403–415

Detail slider, 408–410

Develop module, 5, 29, 225, 244–369

Adjustment brush, 330–341

applying settings from, 359

Auto Tone setting, 265, 361

Basic panel controls, 256–281, 288–295

Before/After viewing modes, 314–319

Brightness adjustments, 265, 281, 291

Camera Calibration panel, 310–313

Camera Raw compatibility, 227

camera-specific presets, 368–369

Chromatic Aberration adjustments, 300–305

Clarity adjustments, 274–277

color adjustments, 296–299

Contrast adjustments, 265, 281, 291

copying settings from, 358

cropping procedures, 246–253

default settings, 545–546

Detail panel, 300–305, 398, 403–417

Exposure adjustments, 256, 264, 269, 278–283, 290

Fill Light adjustments, 264, 291

Graduated Filter tool, 342–344

Grayscale controls, 372–395

guide overlays, 251–253

highlight recovery, 264, 278–279, 286

Histogram panel, 255, 264–270

History panel, 345–346

HSL/Color/Grayscale panel, 296–299

image processing engine, 226–227

interface overview, 244–245

localized adjustments, 330–341

Match Total Exposures command, 282–283

non-destructive editing, 227

presets used in, 360–369, 399

Recovery adjustments, 264, 269, 278–279, 290

Red Eye Correction tool, 326–330

retouching tools, 320–349

Saturation adjustments, 271–273

shadow adjustments, 267, 280–281, 288, 293

Snapshots panel, 346–349

Spot Removal tool, 320–325

synchronizing settings, 30, 239, 241, 352–353

Tone Curve panel, 284–295

Tool Overlay menus, 254

Vibrance adjustments, 271–273

Vignettes panel, 306–309

White Balance tool, 259–263, 268, 289

Develop Settings menu, 55

Diagonal crop guide overlay, 251, 252

Discard Photos warning dialog, 85, 87

display screen

calibrating, 228–233

dual-monitor setup, 96–99, 429

tips on choosing, 228

DNG files, 9, 54

converting raw files to, 54, 550

copying photos as, 47

exporting images as, 449

import preferences for, 549

previews of, 549, 567

saving non-raw files as, 438

updating, 54

Draft Mode Printing option, 32, 460, 475, 479

drag-and-drop import method, 57

drop shadows, 492

droplets, Photoshop, 444–447

dual-monitor setup, 96–99, 429

DVDs

backing up to, 586

exporting images to, 449

E

Earney, Richard, 361, 561

Edit a Copy with Lightroom Adjustments option, 37, 421

Edit Capture Time dialog, 132

Edit in Additional External Editor command, 422–423, 424

Edit in External Editor dialog, 422

Edit in Photoshop command, 422, 551

Edit Keyword Set dialog, 152, 547

Edit menu, 116

Edit Metadata Preset dialog, 135

Edit Original option, 421

editing

brush strokes, 332

capture time, 132

external editor options, 422–425

images in Photoshop, 37, 420–422

metadata presets, 136

non-destructive, 227

email

exporting photos to, 434, 435

links to Web sites in, 540

metadata links to, 142

preconfigured signature for, 540

Web gallery links to, 521

Embedded & Sidecar preview option, 566, 567

empty field searches, 165

Engine panel (Web module), 514–520

Eraser mode, 332

EXIF metadata, 126, 133, 532

Expanded Cells view, 76, 77

Export as Catalog dialog, 203, 208, 210

Export dialog, 40, 434, 435, 440, 446, 448, 449

Export Slideshow to JPEG dialog, 511

Export Slideshow to PDF dialog, 511

exporting, 40, 434–449

actions for, 444–447

bit depth options for, 439–440

catalogs, 203–205, 207, 208, 210, 449

exporting *(continued)*
    to CDs or DVDs, 449
    color space options for, 439
    file formats for, 438
    keywords, 149
    location options for, 434
    minimizing metadata for, 443
    naming files for, 438
    output sharpening for, 442
    plug-ins for, 448
    post-processing options for, 443
    presets for, 434, 435
    to same folder, 436–437
    sizing images for, 440–442
    slideshows, 510–511
    Web galleries, 536
exposure
    Basic panel adjustments, 264, 269, 278–283, 290
    camera settings for optimum, 257
    highlight clipping and, 256, 278–279
    Match Total Exposures command, 282–283
    overexposed image correction, 278–279
    Quick Develop panel adjustments, 235–236
    underexposed image correction, 280–281
Exposure slider, 256, 264, 269, 279, 290
external editing options, 422–425
    explanation of, 422–423
    setting preferences for, 420, 422, 551–552
    steps for using, 424–425
External Editing preferences, 420, 422, 551–552
Eye-Film technology, 63
Eye-One Photo calibration, 229, 230

F

Feather slider, 331
Fetch software, 537
file extensions, 560

File Format options, 13, 438
File Handling preferences, 553
File Transfer Protocol. *See* FTP
Filename Template Editor, 53, 547
files
    corrupted, 47
    metadata saved to, 175, 176–177
    moving to new drive, 219
    naming/renaming, 128, 438, 553
    organizing, 51–53
    sidecar, 128, 190, 548
Files on CD/DVD Export plug-in, 449
Fill Light adjustment
    Basic panel, 264, 291
    Quick Develop panel, 236
Fill Light slider, 264, 291
Fill view, 88
Filmstrip, 21
    applying Develop settings via, 359
    filtering photos via, 108, 109
    navigating photos via, 94–95
    setting preferences for, 556–557
Filter bar, 19, 75, 107, 157–169
    advanced searches, 168–169
    Attribute section, 161
    component layout, 158
    custom settings, 165–167
    Metadata section, 161–164
    searching with, 122–125, 158–160, 165, 168–169
    shortcut for toggling, 157, 162
    Text section, 158–160
filtering photos, 35, 106–113, 157–169
    attribute searches, 161
    catalog options for, 107
    collections based on, 35, 174
    color labels for, 104, 105, 110–111
    custom settings for, 165–169
    Edit menu options for, 116
    filmstrip options for, 108, 109
    flags used for, 100, 101, 109
    master copy filtering, 112
    metadata searches, 161–164
    refined selections for, 109

    rules defined for, 159–160, 165–167
    star ratings for, 102, 103
    subfolder filtering, 113
    text searches, 158–160
    virtual copy filtering, 112
FireWire connections, 583
Fit view, 88
flagged photos, 77
    deleting rejects, 117
    filtering picks/rejects, 109
    rating picks/rejects, 100, 101
Flash galleries, 514, 516
    Appearance panel settings, 525–527
    Color Palette panel settings, 522
    Identity Plate options, 528
    Site Info panel settings, 521
    Title/Caption information, 529, 531
FlashFXP software, 537
Flickr Export plug-in, 448
Flow slider, 331
Folder Action button, 220
folders
    catalogs and, 219–223
    creating new, 222
    exporting to same, 436–437
    importing photos from, 48–49, 56, 61
    locating for photos, 221
    moving to new drive, 219
    organizing photos in, 51
    renaming, 222
    synchronizing, 68, 184–185
    system, 219, 223
    template settings, 561
    watched, 60
Folders panel (Library module), 68, 69, 75, 184, 222
Fors, Thomas, 310
Fraser, Bruce, 398, 411, 442
Friedl, Jeffrey, 128, 448
FTP (File Transfer Protocol)
    programs for using, 537
    settings configuration, 38, 537
full-screen mode, 27

G

galleries. *See* Web galleries
gamma, 229–230
    Macintosh 1.8, 230
    use of linear, 570–574
Gaul, Melissa, 570
General Catalog Settings interface, 218
General preferences, 544–545
Google Maps, 193
Gorman, Greg, 267, 378
GPS metadata, 191–197
    embedding into photos, 194–197
    Google Maps and, 193
    recording, 194
GPSPhotoLinker software, 195
GPX log file, 194–197
Graduated Filter tool, 342–344
    adjustment modes, 342
    steps for using, 342–344
graphics card, 582
Grayscale button, 372, 376, 379, 386
grayscale images
    converting color images to, 372–387
    fine-tuning, 388–395
    See also black and white conversions
Grayscale mode (Develop module), 48, 372, 375
    Auto button, 379
    manual adjustments, 382–383
    slider controls, 375, 383, 386
grayscale previews, 411
Gretag Macbeth ColorChecker chart, 261, 311
Grid crop guide overlay, 251
Grid view, 24, 76–78, 80
    develop adjustments, 80
    navigation, 78, 79
    options, 76–77
grouping photos, 114–115
guides and rulers, 458–459
Guides panel (Print module), 458–459

H

halo suppression, 408
Hamburg, Mark, 2, 282, 296, 570
hard drives, 582–583
Heal mode, Spot Removal tool, 322, 323, 325
Help menu, 17
hiding panels, 26, 72
hierarchy, keyword, 148–149, 443
High Pass filter, 411
Highlight Edges correction, 302
highlights
    clipping warning, 255, 266, 269
    detail recovery, 278–279, 292
    reflective vs. nonreflective, 256, 266
    Tone Curve zones and, 286
Highlights slider, 286, 292
Histogram panel (Develop module), 255, 264–270
History panel (Develop module), 30, 345–346
Holbert, Mac, 274, 451
HSL/Color/Grayscale panel (Develop module), 296–299
    desaturated color adjustments, 392–395
    example of using, 297
    Grayscale button, 372, 376, 379, 386
    overview of controls in, 296
    selective color darkening, 298–299
HTML galleries, 514, 515
    Appearance panel settings, 524
    Color Palette panel settings, 522
    Identity Plate options, 528
    Site Info panel settings, 521
    Title/Caption information, 529, 531
Hue sliders
    HSL/Color/Grayscale panel, 296, 298, 393
    Split Toning panel, 388

I

ICM Color Management, 477, 481
Identity Plate, 14–15, 466–467
    photo border options, 468–469
    slideshow options, 495, 504, 506
    steps for creating, 466–467
    Web gallery options, 528
Identity Plate Editor, 495, 504, 506
Image Info panel (Web module), 529–533
Image Settings panel (Print module), 454–456, 462
Image Size dialog, 502
images. *See* photos
implied keywords, 150
Import from Catalog dialog, 206, 211, 214
Import Photos dialog, 23, 45, 49, 50, 56, 566
importing photos, 23, 43–69
    backing up and, 46, 47
    camera connection for, 62
    catalog imports, 205–206, 207, 211
    copy options, 50
    DNG conversion options, 54, 550
    drag-and-drop method for, 57
    folder imports, 48–49, 56, 61
    keyword imports, 149–150
    memory card connection for, 44–47
    metadata info and, 55, 68, 136, 144, 145
    organizing and, 51–53, 56, 68–69
    preferences for, 548–550
    renaming options, 45, 52–53
    tethered shooting and, 62–67
impromptu slideshows, 509
information
    camera, 164
    caption, 529–533
    copyright, 143, 443
    date/time, 131–132, 137, 162
    overlays, 471, 496, 497
    title, 529–533
    See also metadata

infrared effect, 384–387
inkjet printers, 451, 475
Inside Lightroom Web site, 361, 561
installing Lightroom, 10, 207
interface
    component overview, 18–21
    modes for hiding, 34
    setting preferences for, 554–557
    simplifying, 26–27
Interface preferences, 554–557
    Filmstrip settings, 556–557
    Lights Out mode, 556
    module backgrounds, 556
    panel settings, 554–555
interpolation methods, 441–442
IPTC metadata, 55, 126, 136–138, 164
ISO settings
    metadata information on, 164
    noise reduction and, 417

J

Jackson, Jonathan, 378
Jardine, George, 22
JBOD systems, 585
Jonsson, Michael, 4
JPEG files
    advantages of, 242
    print files saved as, 478, 480
    raw files vs., 242–243
    saving metadata to, 175, 179–182
    slideshows exported as, 511
    Web gallery images as, 534

K

keyboard shortcuts, 41, 244
Keyword List panel (Library module), 144–148, 150, 154
Keywording panel (Library module), 144, 145, 146, 148, 150–152
keywords, 144–156
    adding to photos, 144–145
    applying existing, 146, 147

auto-completion of, 55, 146
exporting, 149
hierarchy of, 148–149, 443
implied, 150
importing, 149–150
Painter tool and, 154–156
removing, 148
sets of, 151–152, 547
suggested, 153
See also metadata
Knoll, John, 4, 310
Knoll, Thomas, 4, 274, 296, 310
Krogh, Peter, 105, 587

L

Lab mode, 48
labeling photos
    Bridge settings, 105
    color labels, 104–105, 166–167
    sort functions, 187–189
landscape sharpening, 401
Layout Engine panel (Print module), 457–465
    Contact Sheet/Grid mode, 457–461
    Picture Package mode, 462–465
Layout panel
    Print module, 457–459
    Slideshow module, 491, 505
LCD displays, 228, 229
lenses
    chromatic aberration from, 300–305
    digital vs. film camera, 300
    metadata information on, 164
    vignetting problems, 306–307
Library module, 71–117
    Catalog panel, 74
    Collections panel, 172–174
    color labels, 104–105
    Compare view, 90–93
    dual-monitor setup, 96–99
    Filmstrip, 94–95, 108–109
    filters, 75, 106–113, 157–169
    Folders panel, 68, 69, 75, 184, 222

    Grid view, 24, 76–78, 80
    Keyword List panel, 144–148, 150, 154
    Keywording panel, 144, 145, 146, 148, 150–152
    Loupe view, 25, 79, 80, 82–83
    Metadata panel, 126–143
    Navigator panel, 74
    numbered star ratings, 102–103
    Painter tool, 154–156
    panel controls, 72, 73
    pasting Develop settings in, 358–359
    picks and rejects, 100–101
    previews, 84–87, 234
    Quick Collections, 35, 170–171
    Quick Develop panel, 234–241
    Sort menu, 186–189
    stacks, 114–115
    Survey view, 33, 88–89
    toolbar, 74
    View options, 24–25, 76
Library.lrcat file, 200, 201, 202
Lightroom
    appearance options, 16
    Bridge integration, 58–61
    Camera Raw integration, 227, 354–357
    catalog folder, 562–568
    computer setup, 581–587
    curves comparison, 575–580
    customizing contents of, 568–569
    Export function, 434–449
    Help menu, 17
    Identity Plate, 14–15
    image processing engine, 226–227
    installation, 10, 207
    interface, 18–21
    modular design, 2–3
    performance, 4–5
    Photoshop integration, 8, 420–433
    preferences, 11–13, 543–557, 560
    previews data file, 565
    quickstart guide, 22–40

simplicity, 2
speed issues, 218
system requirements, 9, 581
thumbnail processing, 566–568
workflow, 6–8
Lightroom RGB color space, 255, 570–574
Lightroom-News.com Web site, 402
Lights Dim mode, 34, 556
Lights Out mode, 34, 556
linear gamma space, 571
links
to email addresses, 142, 521
restoring to source images, 68
to Web sites, 142, 521, 540
LoadMyTracks program, 194
localized adjustments, 36, 330–344
Adjustment brush, 330–341
Graduated Filter tool, 342–344
lock files, 562
Loupe view, 25, 79, 80, 82–83
develop adjustments, 81
keyboard shortcuts, 88
navigation, 79, 83
options, 82
zoom views, 83, 88
Luminance sliders
Detail panel, 416, 417
HSL/Color/Grayscale panel, 296, 298, 393, 395
luminance targeted sharpening, 403
Lyons, Ian, 190, 191, 197, 430

M

Macintosh 1.8 gamma, 230
Macintosh computers
Canon EOS Utility and, 67
Lightroom Preferences on, 11–13, 44
Page Setup dialog, 472
printer settings on, 475–476, 482
switching between modules on, 3
system requirements for, 9
Managed by Lightroom print settings, 481–483
Macintosh computer, 482

Windows computer, 483
Managed by Printer option, 481
Masking slider, 411–413
master images
filtering for, 112
virtual copies and, 350
Match Total Exposures command, 282–283
McCormack, Sean, 468
megapixels, 581
Melissa RGB, 570, 573
memory cards
deleting files from, 47
importing photos from, 44–47
menu bar, 18
Merge to HDR method, 430
merging catalogs, 212–217
metadata, 120–156, 175–185
copyright status, 143
custom information, 134–139
definition of, 120
displayed in Metadata panel, 126, 128–133
editing for multiple images, 140
entering in Lightroom, 139
file organization and, 51, 68
filter searches using, 161–164
GPS coordinates as, 191–197
imported photos and, 55, 136, 144, 145
keywords and, 144–156
mail and Web links, 142
presets, 135–138
saving to files, 175, 176–177
searching with, 122–125
status information, 130, 178, 355, 357
synchronizing, 183
target photos and, 140–141
tracking changes to, 177–178, 183
types of, 121
virtual copies and, 350
Web gallery images, 534
XMP space and, 175–182
Metadata Browser, 55

Metadata panel (Library module), 126–143
action buttons, 142, 143
All view mode, 128, 129
customizing data in, 134–139
editing data in, 140–141
information displayed in, 126, 128–133
Metadata Status item, 130, 178
view modes in, 126–127
metadata presets, 135–138
editing/deleting, 136
IPTC metadata, 136–138
Microsoft Expression Media, 200
Midpoint slider, 306, 503
Minimize Embedded Metadata option, 443
Mirror Image mode, 82
mirrored RAID system, 584
modules
Lightroom design using, 2–3
menu for selecting, 18
removing from Lightroom, 568–569
shortcuts for, 3, 41, 244
See also specific modules
Mogrify plug-in, 448
monitors
calibrating, 228–233
dual-monitor setup, 96–99, 429
tips on choosing, 228
music for slideshows, 507

N

Nack, John, 191
naming/renaming
collections, 173
exported photos, 438
folders, 222
illegal characters for, 553
imported photos, 45, 52–53
photo files, 128, 553
Nash, Graham, 451
navigation
Filmstrip, 94–95
Grid view, 78, 79

navigation *(continued)*
    Loupe view, 79, 83
Navigator panel (Library module),
    28, 74
negative Clarity adjustment, 276–277
negatives
    exporting catalogs with/without,
        203–204
    importing catalogs without, 206
Never Show mode, 254
New Catalog dialog, 202
New Develop Preset dialog, 360, 362
newscodes.org Web site, 137
Nikon Capture, 63
no content searches, 166–167
noise reduction, 416–417
    shadow noise, 402
    tips on using, 417
non-destructive editing, 227
nonreflective highlights, 256, 266
novelty layouts, 502–505
numbered star ratings, 102–103
numbering sequence, 52

O

Open as Layers option, 430
Open Catalog relaunch dialog, 205,
    209
Options panel (Slideshow module),
    492–493
organizing files, 51–53, 56, 68–69
Output Settings panel (Web
    module), 534
output sharpening, 399, 442
overexposed image correction,
    278–279
Overlay blend mode, 411
overlays, 466–471, 494–499
    crop marks, 470
    Identity Plate, 466–467, 495
    information, 471, 496, 497
    photographic border, 468–469
    text, 471, 496–499
Overlays panel
    Print module, 465, 466–471
    Slideshow module, 494–499

P

Page Bleed view, 458, 460
Page Grid area, 458
page layouts
    Contact Sheet/Grid mode,
        457–461
    Picture Package mode, 462
Page Setup dialog, 472
Painter tool, 154–156
panels
    contextual menu options, 72, 73
    end mark options, 554–555
    font size options, 555
    hiding and revealing, 26, 72
    left panel controls, 20
    opening and closing, 21, 25
    right panel controls, 21
    "solo" mode for, 244
    top panel controls, 18
    See also specific panels
panoramas
    creating via Photoshop, 430–431
    processing via Lightroom, 430
paper
    print profiles, 475, 477, 483, 484
    size settings, 472
pasting
    settings from Develop module,
        358
    See also copying
PCs. *See* Windows computers
PDF documents
    print files saved as, 460, 478
    slideshows exported as, 511
Perceptual rendering intent, 484
Photo Border options
    Image Settings panel, 462
    Overlays panel, 468–469
photo galleries. *See* Web galleries
Photo Info presets, 471
Photokit Sharpener, 441, 442, 479,
    534
Photomerge dialog, 431
photos
    deleting, 117
    exporting, 40
photos

filtering, 35, 106–113
importing, 23, 43–69
labeling, 104–105
presharpening, 397
rating, 31, 100–103
restoring links to, 69
retouching, 36, 320–349
rotating, 76
searching for, 122–125
selecting, 116
sorting, 186–189
stacking, 114–115
viewing, 24–25
Photoshop, 7–8, 419, 420–433
    camera calibration, 310–311
    curves comparison, 575–580
    droplet creation, 444–447
    editing images in, 37, 420–422
    extended editing in, 430–431
    Lightroom integration with, 8,
        420–433
    opening photos as Smart Objects
        in, 432–433
    setting editing preferences for,
        551–552
    steps for working in, 426–429
picks and rejects, 77
    deleting rejected photos, 117
    filtering photos flagged as, 109
    flagging photos as, 100–101
Picture Package mode, 462
pixel limits, 48
Playback panel (Slideshow module),
    507
Plug-in Manager, 448
plug-ins, export, 448
PNG file format, 555
Point Curve menu, 285
portrait sharpening, 400
PostcardViewer galleries, 518
Post-Crop vignettes, 308–309
post-processing options, 443
preferences, 11–13, 543–557
    accessing, 11, 44, 543
    External Editing, 551–552
    file for storing, 560
    File Handling, 553

General, 544–545
Import, 548–550
Interface, 554–557
Presets, 545–547
preferences file, 560
presentations, 487–541
    slideshow, 488–511
    Web gallery, 512–541
presets
    Auto Tone, 361
    camera-specific, 368–369
    Develop module, 360–369
    export, 434, 435
    how they work, 363
    keyword set, 151, 547
    metadata, 135–136
    Photo Info, 471
    preferences, 545–546
    resetting, 367
    sharpening, 399–401
    steps for using, 364–367
Presets folder, 360
Presets panel (Develop module),
    360–362, 373, 399
presharpening images, 397
previews, 84–87
    Adjustment brush, 336
    Adobe Bridge, 61
    Before/After, 314–319
    camera vs. Lightroom, 566
    data file for, 565
    Detail slider, 411
    Develop settings, 84–85
    DNG file, 549, 567
    exporting catalogs with, 204–205
    generating 1:1, 87, 567
    Identity Plate, 467, 469, 504
    Library module, 84–87, 234
    Masking slider, 412
    Photoshop edit, 429
    processing routines, 566–567
    quality settings, 85–87, 568
    Radius slider, 411
    RGB color, 572–574
    size settings, 85–87, 568
    slideshow, 508
    Web gallery, 535

Previews.lrdata file, 200, 205
Print button, 478
print collections, 452
Print dialog, 475, 482
print drivers, 474, 477
Print Job panel (Print module), 39,
    474–484
    Color Management settings, 474
    Draft Mode Printing option, 479
    Lightroom printing procedure,
        474–478
    Print Sharpening option, 479
    Print to JPEG File option, 480
    Profile menu, 481
    Rendering Intent options, 484
Print module, 452–485
    Cells panel, 462–465
    Contact Sheet/Grid mode,
        457–461
    Guides panel, 458–459
    Image Settings panel, 454–456,
        462
    interface overview, 452–453
    Layout Engine options, 457–465
    Overlays panel, 465, 466–471
    Page Setup dialog, 472
    Picture Package mode, 462–465
    Print Job panel, 474–484
    Rulers, Grid & Guides panel, 462
    Template Browser panel, 485
Print One button, 478
print profiles, 475, 477, 481–484
Print Resolution option, 479
Print Setup dialog, 473, 476, 483
Print Sharpening option, 399, 479
Print to JPEG File option, 478, 480
Printer Properties dialog, 483
printing, 451–485
    16-bit, 480
    contact sheets, 32
    custom profiles for, 481–484
    draft mode for, 32, 460, 475, 479
    high-quality prints, 39
    image resolution and, 442, 458,
        473, 479
    to JPEG file, 478, 480

Lightroom procedure for,
    474–478
margin adjustments for, 457
mode settings for, 479
paper size options for, 472
to PDF file, 460, 478
rendering intent for, 484
saving settings for, 39
sharpening images for, 399, 442,
    479
templates for, 452, 476, 485
processor speed, 581
ProPhoto RGB color space, 255, 420,
    439, 535, 570, 572
PSD files, 49
    edit copy options and, 420
    saving metadata to, 175,
        179–182
Pupil Size slider, 328

Q

Quality slider, 511, 534
Quick Collections, 35, 170–171
    saving as permanent collections,
        170
    searching for photos using,
        124–125
Quick Develop panel (Library
    module), 234–241
    color controls, 234–235
    cropping options, 240
    synchronizing settings, 241
    tone controls, 235–236
    typical workflow, 237–239
quickstart guide, 22–40

R

Radius slider, 406–407
RAID systems, 583–585
RAM memory, 581
rating photos, 31, 100–103
    numbered star ratings, 102–103
    picks and rejects, 100–101
    slideshow options, 494

raw files
    advantages of, 242
    converting to DNG, 54, 550
    Detail panel adjustments, 399
    editing in Photoshop, 421–422
    JPEG files vs., 242–243
    previews of, 566
    See also Camera Raw
Real World Image Sharpening with Adobe Photoshop CS2 (Fraser), 411
Recovery slider, 264, 269, 278–279, 290
Recycle bin, 117
Red Eye Correction tool, 326–330
    cursor size adjustment, 326
    steps for using, 327–330
Redo command, 346
reflective highlights, 256, 266
rejects and picks. *See* picks and rejects
Relative rendering intent, 484
Relaunch and Optimize button, 218
removing
    keywords from the Keyword List, 148
    photos from the catalog, 117
    spots from photos, 320–325
    See also deleting
Rename Photos dialog, 53
renaming. *See* naming/renaming
Rendering Intent options, 484
Repeat One Photo per Page option, 454, 456
Reset All button, 236
resetting presets, 367
Resize to Fit options, 440
resizing. *See* sizing/resizing
Resnick, Seth, 400
resolution
    image size and, 440, 479
    print reproduction and, 442, 458, 473, 479
Restore Filename Templates button, 547
retouching photos, 36, 320–349
    Adjustment brush for, 330–341

Graduated Filter tool for, 342–344
History panel and, 345–346
localized adjustments, 36, 330–344
Red Eye Correction tool for, 326–330
Snapshots panel and, 346–349
Spot Removal tool for, 320–325
Revert Web Settings option, 541
RGB channels, 374, 375
RGB workspace, 226, 228, 570
Riecks, David, 150
rotating photos, 76
    cropping and, 246
    printing and, 454, 456
rulers and guides, 458–459
Rulers, Grid & Guides panel (Print module), 462

S

SATA drives, 583
Saturation adjustment
    Basic panel, 271–273
    Grayscale panel, 393
    Quick Develop panel, 236
Saturation sliders
    Basic panel, 271–273
    HSL/Color/Grayscale panel, 296, 298, 392
    Split Toning panel, 388
saving
    Adjustment Brush settings, 332
    Develop settings as presets, 360–367
    metadata to photo files, 175, 176–177
    non-raw files as DNGs, 438
    print templates, 485
    Quick Collections as Collections, 170
    slideshow templates, 510
    variations as snapshots, 346–347
    Web gallery templates, 541
Schewe, Jeff, 442

Screen output option, 442
Scripts folder, 569
searching
    attribute filter for, 161
    example of advanced, 168–169
    metadata used for, 122–125, 161–164
    rules defined for, 159–160, 165–167
    text filter for, 158–160
Secure File Transfer Protocol (SFTP), 537
Segal, Mark, 575
selections, 79
    contiguous vs. noncontiguous, 78, 162, 163
    Edit menu options for, 116
    Slideshow module, 509
sequence numbers, 52
sets
    collection, 174
    keyword, 151–152
SFTP (Secure File Transfer Protocol), 537
shadows
    clipping, 264, 267
shadows
    darkening, 267, 293
    drop, 492
    lightening, 280–281, 288
    noise in, 402
Shadows slider, 288, 293
sharpening, 398–415
    capture, 398
    effects sliders, 403–407
    evaluating at 1:1 view, 403
    grayscale previews of, 411
    interpolation and, 441
    luminance targeted, 403
    output, 399, 442
    presets for, 399–401
    print, 399, 442, 479
    sample image for, 402
    steps for using, 414–415
    suppression controls, 408–413
    Web gallery images, 534

Sharpening controls
    Adjustment brush, 340–341
    Amount slider, 404–405
    Detail panel, 398, 403–415
    Detail slider, 408–410
    Masking slider, 411–413
    Quick Develop panel, 236
    Radius slider, 406–407
shortcuts, 41, 244
shutter speed information, 164
sidecar files, 128, 190, 548
SimpleViewer galleries, 519
Site Info panel (Web module), 521
Size slider
    Adjustment brush, 331
    Spot Removal tool, 320, 322
sizing/resizing
    images for exporting, 440–442
    interpolation and, 441–442
    previews, 85–86
    print output, 479
Skurski, Mike, 442
Slide Editor view, 490, 498–499
Slideshow module, 488–511
    Backdrop panel, 500–501
    interface overview, 488–489
    Layout panel, 491, 505
    Options panel, 492–493
    Overlays panel, 494–499
    Playback panel, 507
    Preview mode, 508
    Slide Editor view, 490
    Template Browser panel, 510
    Titles panel, 506
slideshows, 488–511
    backdrops, 500–501
    collections for, 173
    color processing for, 535
    exporting, 510–511
    Identity Plates, 495, 504, 506
    impromptu, 509
    navigating, 509
    novelty layouts, 502–505
    PDF or JPEG, 511
    playing, 508
    previewing, 508
    selections for, 509
    soundtracks, 507

speed/duration options, 507
templates, 488, 510
text overlays, 496–499
titles for, 506
Smart Collections, 35, 174
Smart Objects, 432–433
Smugmug plug-in, 448
Snapshots panel (Develop module),
    30, 346–349
    history state management, 348
    saving variations using, 346–347
    Sync Snapshots feature, 346, 349
Soften Skin effect, 336–337
sorting photos, 186–189
    color labels and, 187–189
    overview of options for, 186
    tethered shooting and, 67
    text labels and, 189
sounds
    task completion, 545
    See also audio
soundtracks, slideshow, 507
specular highlights, 256, 266
Split Toning panel (Develop module)
    black and white conversions, 381,
    387, 388–391
    color image adjustments,
    390–391
Spot Removal tool, 320–325
    instructions for using, 320–323
    synchronized spotting with,
    324–325
sRGB color space, 420, 439, 535,
    572
Stacking menu, 114, 115
stacks
    collapsing/expanding, 115
    grouping photos into, 114–115
Standard Loupe view, 79
star ratings, 102–103
startup splash screen, 544
Stern, Zalman, 4
Straighten tool, 249
striped RAID system, 583–584
subfolders, filtering, 113
Suggested Keywords option, 153
Survey view, 33, 88–89

Sync Snapshots feature, 346, 349
Synchronize Folder command, 355
Synchronize Metadata dialog, 183
Synchronize Settings dialog, 239,
    241, 324, 352, 353
Synchronize With Snapshots dialog,
    349
synchronizing
    Auto Sync mode for, 325, 352
    Develop settings, 30, 239, 241,
    352–353
    folders, 68, 184–185, 355
    Lightroom with Camera Raw,
    355–357
    metadata settings, 183
    Photoshop edits, 427–428
    snapshots, 346, 349
    spot removal settings, 324–325
system folders, 219, 223
system requirements, 9, 581

T

Target Adjustment tool, 284, 286,
    296, 298, 393
target images, 140–141, 483
Temperature slider
    Grayscale conversions, 376, 377,
    380
    White Balance adjustments, 262
Template Browser panel, 32
    Print module, 485
    Slideshow module, 510
    Web module, 541
templates
    print, 452, 476, 485
    saving custom, 485
    settings folder, 561
    slideshow, 488, 510
    updating, 485
    Web gallery, 520, 541
tethered shooting, 23, 62–67
    cable connection, 65
    camera capture software, 63–67
    connecting cameras for, 62–63,
    65
    speed considerations, 67

text
    filter searches, 158–160
    overlays, 471, 496–499
Text Template Editor, 547
    Print module, 471
    Slideshow module, 496, 497
    Web module, 530, 532
TheTurningGate.net Web site, 520
third-party gallery styles, 519–520
thumbnails
    Flash gallery size settings, 525
    processing routines for, 566–568
    restoring links from, 69
TIFF files
    edit copy options and, 420
    saving metadata to, 175,
        179–182
time/date information. *See* date/time
    information
Tint slider
    Grayscale conversions, 376, 377,
        385, 387
    White Balance adjustments, 262
titles
    slideshow, 506
    Web gallery, 521, 529–533
Titles panel (Slideshow module), 506
tone controls
    Quick Develop panel, 235–236
    Tone Curve panel, 284–295
Tone Curve panel (Develop module),
    284–295
    Basic panel and, 265, 285,
        288–295
    Darks slider, 284, 287, 292
    Highlights slider, 286, 292
    overview of controls in, 284–285
    Photoshop curves comparison,
        575
    Point Curve menu, 285
    Shadows slider, 288, 293
    Tone Curve zones, 286–288
    Tone Range Split Points, 285,
        294–295
Tone Curve Target Adjustment tool,
    383
Tool Overlay menus, 254, 323

Toolbar, 20
Trash bin, 117
Triangle crop guide overlay, 251, 252

U

underexposed image correction,
    280–281
Undo command, 346, 500
Unsharp Mask filter, 398
updating templates, 485
Upload Settings panel (Web mod-
    ule), 537–540
uploading Web galleries, 537–540
    creating custom presets, 537
    naming gallery subfolders, 539
USB connections, 583

V

Vibrance adjustment
    Basic panel, 271–273
    Grayscale panel, 393
    Quick Develop panel, 236
Vibrance slider, 271–273, 393
view modes
    Develop panel, 314–319
    Metadata panel, 126–127
View Options (Library module)
    Compare view, 91
    Grid view, 24, 76–78
    Loupe view, 25, 82
    Survey view, 88–89
Vignettes panel (Develop module),
    306–309
    Lens Correction sliders, 306–307
    Post-Crop sliders, 308–309, 503
vignetting
    applying to photos, 308–309
    correcting problems with,
        306–307
virtual copies
    copy names for, 128, 130
    creating for photos, 350–351
    external editing with, 427–428
    filtering for, 112
    snapshots vs., 350

W

warning alerts, 545
watched folders, 60
watermarks
    copyright, 443
    print, 467
Web browsers, 535, 536
Web galleries, 38, 512–541
    Airtight, 517
    AutoViewer, 517
    captions for, 529–533
    color processing for, 535
    color themes for, 522–523
    exporting, 536
    Flash, 514, 516
    HTML, 514, 515
    Identity Plate options, 528
    layout appearance, 524–528
    metadata information, 534
    PostcardViewer, 518
    previewing, 535
    quality settings, 534
    sharpening images in, 534
    SimpleViewer, 519
    styles for, 514–520
    templates for, 520, 541
    third-party, 519–520
    titles for, 529–533
    uploading, 537–540
Web module, 38, 512–541
    Appearance panel, 524–528
    Color Palette panel, 522–523
    Engine panel, 514–520
    Export and Upload buttons, 536
    Image Info panel, 529–533
    interface overview, 512–513
    Output Settings panel, 534
    Preview in Browser button, 535
    Site Info panel, 521
    Template Browser panel, 541
    Upload Settings panel, 537–540
Web sites
    email links to, 540
    metadata links to, 142
    Web gallery links to, 521
Web-safe color palette, 522

white balance
    Basic panel adjustments,
        259–263, 268, 289
    Grayscale conversions, 376, 377,
        378–381
    monitor calibration, 230
    Quick Develop panel adjust-
        ments, 235
White Balance tool, 259–263, 268,
    289
white point, 229, 262
Windows computers
    Canon EOS Utility and, 67
    Lightroom Preferences on, 11–13,
        44
    Print Setup dialog, 473
    printer settings on, 476–477
    switching between modules on, 3
    system requirements for, 9
wireless shooting, 63
Write Keywords as Lightroom
        Hierarchy option, 443
WS_FTP Pro software, 537

X

XMP space
    explanation of, 179
    read/write options, 179–182
    saving metadata to, 175, 176–177
X-Rite Eye-One Photo, 229, 230
X-Rite Gretag Macbeth ColorChecker
        chart, 261, 311

Z

Zenfolio plug-in, 448
Zoom to Fill Frame option
    Print module, 454, 455
    Slideshow module, 492, 493
Zoom view slider, 83
zooming in/out, 28, 83, 88